# The Cambridge Introduction to
# Modern British Fiction, 1950–2000

DOMINIC HEAD

**CAMBRIDGE**
UNIVERSITY PRESS

PUBLISHED BY THE PRESS SYNDICATE OF THE UNIVERSITY OF CAMBRIDGE
The Pitt Building, Trumpington Street, Cambridge, United Kingdom

CAMBRIDGE UNIVERSITY PRESS
The Edinburgh Building, Cambridge CB2 2RU, UK
40 West 20th Street, New York, NY 10011-4211, USA
477 Williamstown Road, Port Melbourne, VIC 3207, Australia
Ruiz de Alarcón 13, 28014 Madrid, Spain
Dock House, The Waterfront, Cape Town 8001, South Africa

http://www.cambridge.org

First published 2002
Reprinted 2003

Printed in the United Kingdom at the University Press, Cambridge

*Typeface* Bembo 11/12.5 pt.     *System* LATEX 2$_\varepsilon$   [TB]

*A catalogue record for this book is available from the British Library*

*Library of Congress Cataloguing in Publication data*
Head, Dominic.
The Cambridge Introduction to Modern British Fiction, 1950–2000 / Dominic Head.
    p.   cm.
Includes bibliographical references (p. ) and index.
ISBN 0 521 66014 9 (hardback) – ISBN 0 521 66966 9 (paperback)
1. English fiction – 20th century – History and criticism.   I. Title.
PR881 .H43   2002
823′.91409 – dc21   2001043261

ISBN 0 521 66014 9 hardback
ISBN 0 521 66966 9 paperback

*The Cambridge Introduction to*
## Modern British Fiction, 1950–2000

In this introduction to post-war fiction in Britain, Dominic Head shows how the novel yields a special insight into the important areas of social and cultural history in the second half of the twentieth century. Head's study is the most exhaustive survey of post-war British fiction available. It includes chapters on the state and the novel, class and social change, gender and sexual identity, national identity, and multiculturalism. Throughout Head places novels in their social and historical context. He highlights the emergence and prominence of particular genres and links these developments to the wider cultural context. He also provides provocative readings of important individual novelists, particularly those who remain staple reference points in the study of the subject. In a concluding chapter Head speculates on the topics that might preoccupy novelists, critics, and students in the future. Accessible, wide-ranging, and designed specifically for use on courses, this is the most current introduction to the subject available. It will be an invaluable resource for students and teachers alike.

Dominic Head is Professor of English at Brunel University and was formerly Reader in Contemporary Literature and Head of the School of English at the University of Central England. He is the author of *The Modernist Short Story* (Cambridge, 1992), *Nadine Gordimer* (Cambridge, 1994), and *J. M. Coetzee* (Cambridge, 1997).

# Contents

## Acknowledgements

A number of colleagues and friends have brought favoured novels and authors to my attention in the course of writing this survey. I can remember particular recommendations from the following: Michael Bell, Terry Gifford, Eamon Grant, Tricia Head, Victor Head, Howard Jackson, Richard Kerridge, Tim Middleton, Jo Rawlinson, Ray Ryan, Martin Ryle, and Niall Whitehead. One of the pleasures of researching this book has been making 'discoveries', and I am grateful for every recommendation, even if each one hasn't surfaced in the final draft.

A special thank you is due to Josie Dixon who, while at Cambridge University Press, originally encouraged me to expand my work on the post-war novel in Britain, and to write an inclusive survey of this kind. Josie's energy and enthusiasm initiated things, and Ray Ryan's sure editorial hand helped realize the finished article. I have also benefited from Rachel De Wachter's sagacious editorial advice, and from Sue Dickinson's professional and diligent work on the manuscript.

I am grateful to the Faculty of Computing, Information and English at the University of Central England for awarding me a Readership, and for allocating funds to cover study leave in the second semester, 1999–2000: both awards have materially helped the completion of this survey, and special thanks are due to Judith Elkin and Howard Jackson for facilitating my role in the Faculty's research culture in my final three years at the University of Central England.

Some of the material appeared in different forms in the journals *Key Words: A Journal of Cultural Materialism* and *Green Letters*, and in the collection *Expanding Suburbia: Reviewing Suburban Narratives*, ed. Roger Webster (Oxford: Berghahn, 2000). Thanks and due acknowledgements go to the editors and publishers. I am particularly grateful to the ILL staff at Kenrick Library, the University of Central England, and to Sarah Rudge for her assistance while working as English subject librarian.

My greatest debt is to Tricia and Felicity for putting up with a house swamped by papers and files, and for tolerating all the lost evenings and weekends.

January 2001

# Introduction

This is a book that is devoted to the discussion of fiction – reference is made to more than a hundred novelists, and to some two hundred fictional works. I am concerned chiefly with novels, but I also discuss significant works of shorter fiction. My aim has been to produce a history of post-war fiction in Britain that places the literary texts centre stage, and that allows them, rather than a predetermined critical agenda, to reveal the significant patterns and themes in the literary culture. Inevitably, one's own critical perspective is fashioned by a particular intellectual climate, but the withholding, or (at least) the judicious deployment, of favoured critical frameworks is often a necessary part of uncovering the significance of a novel. One needs to bear in mind that the theoretical preoccupations that have become dominant in the academy since 1980 – and that may be overtly alluded to in the work of a Carter, a Rushdie or a Winterson – had no relevance to the novelists of the 1950s and earlier 1960s, whose work unfolded against a very different cultural and intellectual background.

At the beginning of such a project, however, some kind of general framework for reading is required, most especially to explain what is unique to the novel as a form of knowledge, and to help justify the claim, which underpins this work, that the novel in Britain from 1950–2000 yields a special insight into the most important areas of social and cultural history. The survey as a whole stands as a full justification of this claim; but to sketch a short explanation I can do no better than turn to a novel for a suggestion about the effects of narrative fiction.

In John Fowles's *Daniel Martin* (1977) there is an important symbolic scene at an abandoned site of Amer-Indian habitation in New Mexico. Daniel Martin, on a quest for personal authenticity, and the means by which this quest might be advanced in the form of a novel, sees the ancient site of Tsankawi as hugely significant to his goals. He begins to long for a particular kind of medium, 'something dense, interweaving, treating time as horizontal, like a skyline; not cramped, linear and progressive'. The longing is inspired by the ancient inhabitants of Tsankawi, and 'their inability to think of time except in the present, of the past and future except in terms of the present-not-here'. This approach to temporality creates 'a kind of equivalency of memories and feelings, a totality of consciousness that fragmented modern man has completely lost' (p. 371).

What Fowles does here is identify the key element of the novel in a secular, individualistic age; for this is a medium that follows a notional present in the life of one or more characters, but traces necessary connections with the 'past' and 'future' experiences in this imagined life, in the course of narrative exposition. Since this temporal interplay is compressed in a (relatively) short narrative span, the structure of the novel is one that demonstrates the horizontality of time, and can deliver the complete temporal consciousness that is sometimes felt to be missing in contemporary life, governed by short-term goals and ephemeral cultural forms. This component of the modern novel is, perhaps, that which most clearly accounts for its ability to strike the desired balance between imagination and reality (p. 310). In Daniel Martin's moment of creative epiphany at Tsankawi, the novel's credentials as a vehicle of knowledge are underscored: the novel, through its ability to fictionalize and reimagine, affords a reinvigorating perspective on the real. And, through its fluid yet cohesive treatment of time, the novel fashions a mode of temporal understanding that is unavailable in other forms of writing, and that assists our comprehension of the individual's ongoing role in social history.

In making this kind of special claim for the post-war novel, I am (partially) supporting Steven Connor's proposition to view the novel since 1950 'not just as passively marked with the imprint of history, but also as one of the ways in which history is made and remade'.[1] I am also working in the spirit of Andrzej Gąsiorek's important demonstration of the ways in which realism has been extended in this period.[2] In their different ways, Connor and Gąsiorek discover creative impulses that reinvigorate the immediate social function of the post-war novel. In seeking to illustrate that function, however, this book asserts several principles that would seem to be currently unfashionable. First, I am implicitly suggesting that a large sample of novels is a necessity in the attempt to establish a tentative literary history. My selection of two hundred novels, and more than a hundred authors, is, of course, a selective representation of the literary activity between 1950 and 2000; there are inevitable practical constraints – on the number of years one critic can devote to a single project, and on the word-limit for a publishable book – and these have prevented me from ranging still further. But the sample is significantly larger than has been attempted hitherto in comparable surveys, and the representativeness I can claim for this book is bestowed by its attempt at coverage.

I have, however, operated a stringent understanding of the 'social novel', and this brings me to my second principle: the concentration on those works that treat of contemporary history and society, even though such an emphasis may seem to be out of kilter with recent literary fashion. Indeed, a turn towards the historical novel has been frequently observed in the 1990s, in marked contrast to the gritty working-class realism of the 1950s and 1960s. The career of Beryl Bainbridge would seem to illustrate this development; yet this survey privileges the close observation of social mores in the Bainbridge of *The Bottle Factory Outing* (1974) and *A Quiet Life* (1976) over the later Bainbridge who turned to the broad canvas of public history in works like *Every Man for Himself* (1996), inspired by the Titanic disaster, and *Master Georgie* (1998), set in the time of the Crimean War. I am not disputing that the turn to history can still tell us something very interesting about a writer's own time; but I am suggesting that the claim for the novel's participation in the *making* of cultural history is more justifiable in relation to those works that strike a chord in the public consciousness by virtue of their engagement with the present. *Lucky Jim* (1954) by Kingsley Amis, *Poor Cow* (1967) by Nell Dunn, *The History Man* (1975) by Malcom Bradbury, *Money* (1984) by Martin Amis, and Helen Fielding's *Bridget Jones's Diary* (1996) are all novels – one from each of the five decades, 1950–2000 – that have struck such a chord.

The most unfashionable emphasis (or de-emphasis) in this survey follows from this second principle, and this is the demotion of fantasy and magic realism from its position of pre-eminence in much critical discussion. Again, I am not oblivious to the special access to the contemporary psyche that the initial departure from realism can afford. The huge popularity of J. R. R. Tolkien's *The Lord of the Rings* trilogy (1954–5) is not simply a reflection of a mass desire for escapism. Through the apparent escape, Tolkien's 'Shire' (for instance) can be seen to form an imaginative link with other social developments, such as the emergence of the early Green movement in Britain.[3] In a similar connection, I find (in Chapter One) a commentary on the nascent youth culture of the 1950s and 1960s fairly close to the surface of Anthony Burgess's future fable *A Clockwork Orange* (1962). Yet fable is a mode that can also operate in the reverse direction, obscuring particular contextual correspondences, and implying universal truths about human nature: it is a wilful reading which side-steps the revelation of timeless human evil in William Golding's *Lord of the Flies* (1954), for instance.

Two of the problems I have been outlining here – the use of a theoretical perspective to determine rather than facilitate a reading, and the distorting claims that can be made for the flight from realism – are illustrated in the critical interest in Angela Carter. Looking at the vast body of critical material on Carter and Bakhtinian carnival, say, one is struck by a *de facto* cultural misrepresentation, especially where carnival has been used to imply a utopian ideal unhooked from the British context. Bakhtin is a useful theorist of the novel, and Angela Carter is a significant writer; but she does not deserve the status of (by some margin) the most-written-about post-war British novelist.

If the number of academic theses devoted to an author were to be taken as a reliable measure of the author's relative importance, Carter would emerge as the single literary giant of the period. One may legitimately wonder whether or not Carter is being used to illuminate the theory, rather than vice versa.

I do not wish to deny the importance of some theoretical perspectives, or the intellectual impact these have had on writers, especially from the 1980s onwards. Rushdie's allusion to postmodernist critiques of the West in *The Satanic Verses* (1988) obliges an effort of theoretical explication, for instance, as does the apparent extended reference to Donna Haraway in Zadie Smith's *White Teeth* (2000). There is also a sense that some contemporary texts grow organically out of their intellectual milieu and have profound and sustained affinities with theoretical writing. Thus, Homi Bhabha's 'DissemiNation' is an obvious companion piece to *The Satanic Verses*.[4] This may be no more than to observe that serious literature responds imaginatively to its intellectual climate, but this does make the appropriate application of critical theory a variable, and context-dependent business.

As an example, it is worth remembering that to critics in the 1960s, the influence of existentialism loomed large. Thus James Gindin was prompted to suggest that the perceived iconoclasm of John Wain, Kingsley Amis, and Alan Sillitoe, directed against established religious and political structures, was an attribute of a particular existential *Angst*.[5] Existentialism certainly had some influence as a point of debate – most notably on the work of Iris Murdoch – but this now seems a less pressing concern. (Gindin's discussion of how a typically working-class defence contributes to a dual mood of simultaneous estrangement and assertion, in the early post-war novel, now seems more pertinent.[6])

It is necessary, then, to recognize the existence of different period epistemes over a dramatically changing half-century. Such an inclusive perspective resurrects (for example) the class-consciousness of David Storey, the liberal anxieties of Angus Wilson and Malcolm Bradbury, and the social conscience of Margaret Drabble to stand beside those postmodernists whose work has dominated recent critical discussion.

The novel has clearly been shaped by non-literary ideas that go beyond the frame of reference established by the more self-contained intellectual debates. Certainly one of the most dominant contextual factors, with a decisive impact on the novelistic imagination, was the Cold War. Until 1989 and the collapse of communism in Eastern Europe, the fear of nuclear conflict between the US and the Soviet Union was a constant presence in international relations. (Whether the dissipation of these immediate fears in the 1990s is fully justified is debatable, given that the weapons of mass destruction are still extant, often in a state of neglect.) Novelists were often obliged to think through their themes in terms of the blunt opposition of political systems. In *Daniel Martin*, for instance, John Fowles allows the conflict between East and West to stand as a backdrop to his exploration of individual free will, finally promoting a progressive liberal philosophy in which will and compassion might be seen to inform one another (p. 703). The anxious mood is evoked more explicitly in Angus Wilson's *The Old Men at the Zoo* (1961), where an apocalyptic theme – in this case the vision of a major European war – unsettles Wilson's social comedy, producing an unnerving hybrid style. The fear of apocalypse reaches a culmination in Martin Amis's *Einstein's Monsters* (1987), which begins with a polemical essay designed to prompt a visceral horror in the reader at the prospect of imminent nuclear devastation. It seems incredible that this polemical intent, which was compelling in 1987, could become apparently anachronistic in little over a decade.

This note of caution about historical variability and the importance of context is written with an eye to the propensity of the novel to engage with history. If a claim can legitimately be made for the novel's role in a broader social process of imaginative liberation, its limitations are equally clear. The novel may make a tangible impact on contemporary culture, on our memory of recent social history, and on our perceptions of self-identity; but the novel cannot be said to make identifiable and immediate interventions in given social problems. The 'liberation' in which it participates is a complex process, a combination of a variety of forces and influences within the social super-structure. Thus, one can argue that a sympathetic reading of Sam Selvon in the 1950s may have produced recognition or fresh understanding; but, of course, *The Lonely Londoners* (1956) could not in itself eradicate racism.

Perhaps the most liberating feature of the post-war novel is the democratic conception of art it has come to embody. An increasingly well-educated population makes incremental advances towards an egalitarian literary culture possible, and the mass-market paperback supplies the practical route for its transmission.[7] It is the form of the novel, however, that gives it the uniquely privileged position of a serious art form – the novel is the major literary mode at the end of the twentieth century – and yet one that is *ordinary*. Anyone literate can become a novelist; and anyone who is sufficiently well read could even become a good one. There are no arcane rules of expression, since the novel, by its very nature, is a form that continually evolves; and in the computer age, generating the text of a novel is a simple enough matter. At the end of the century, it seems that the Internet, and the ebook, bucking the trend towards publishing conglomerates, could put publishing back into the hands of authors.

More important than this, however, is the status of the social novel as a form of discourse that can reach into all other areas of social experience.

Here there is a direct bridge between the seriousness of novels that scrutinize the status quo, and less reflective expressions of popular culture. The post-war novel has done much to discredit a rigid distinction between 'high' and 'low' culture, and, indeed, the prominent protagonists, from Jim Dixon to Bridget Jones – characters that have been rightly seen to typify new social moods – have invariably had popular, or at least middlebrow tastes.

The novel, in short, has managed to cultivate a new intellectual space: it is the middlebrow art form *par excellence*, with unique and unrivalled access to every corner of social life, but a form that retains that 'literary', or serious quality, defined as the ability to deliberate, or to stimulate reflection on social and cultural questions. Reviewing British fiction of the 1980s, D. J. Taylor, a prominent and important critic, detected a widening gap between 'the novel of ideas and the (usually comic) novel of action', or, put more crudely, between 'drawing-room twitter and the banana skin'.[8] My sense is that this gap between the novel of ideas and the more popular (especially comic) novel has become less, rather than more, distinct in the post-war years, as a natural consequence of the gradual democratization of narrative fiction.

Successive critics of the novel in Britain, and especially England, have been less sanguine about its state of health, however. Arthur Marwick states the social historian's view that the novel in the immediate post-war period is 'fading', characterized by 'a national, even parochial quality' in the inward-looking manner of contemporary political thought; and throughout the period literary critics have found cause for concern about the novel's future.[9] There is, for example, a perceived moment of crisis in David Lodge's famous declaration from 1969 that the 'English novelist' then stood at a crossroads, faced with the alternative routes of fabulation and experimental metafiction. Lodge's advice was to go straight on, remaining on the road of realism and adhering to the liberal ideology it enshrines.[10]

More pessimistic was Bernard Bergonzi's assessment of 1970, that 'English literature in the fifties and sixties has been both backward- and inward-looking', indicating that 'in literary terms, as in political ones, Britain is not a very important part of the world today'. Preoccupied with parochial matters, and less innovative than the novel elsewhere (especially in America), English fiction offers little, Bergonzi argued, 'that can be instantly translated into universal statements about the human condition'.[11] He was only able to mount a partial challenge to this overview (as in the case of Lodge, this was based on a defence of English liberalism), so that his negative suggestions retain some of their force. One has to grant, further, that the picture he painted has remained partially true of the post-war novel, notably the preoccupation with parochial themes and topics, and the distrust of experimentation and formal innovation.[12] A focus on the particular, however, need not be taken to signify an inferior form of attention. As successive chapters in this survey seek to show, just such a focus might well produce a literature that is rich in its social relevance and historical density.

Bergonzi's appraisal set the tone for critical discussion throughout the 1970s, the decade that is generally held to embody the nadir of British fiction, since the gathering economic crisis had a deleterious effect on publishing, and on the range of fiction that found an outlet; but from the longer perspective of literary history (and we may just be able to glimpse this now) it is hard to see how even the 1970s will go down as a period of suppressed creativity. On the contrary, this was a decade which saw the publication of important novels by Iris Murdoch, John Fowles, J. G. Farrell, and David Storey, among others. It also witnessed the first books by Martin Amis and Ian McEwan.

Yet the sense of a literary malaise has persisted beyond the 1970s, with Taylor characterizing the literary scene of the 1980s as 'a sprawling landscape of underachievement', and reformulating Bergonzi's impression of the innate superiority of American fiction.[13] The critic who most clearly stands in opposition to the Jeremiahs of British fiction is Malcolm Bradbury, who sadly died as I was completing this book; in the course of my research, I have found myself agreeing more and more with his assessment of a vigorous postwar novel, which stands up well to international comparison.[14] The range and diversity I have continued to uncover seems to support this opinion.

An interesting novel in connection with the international reputation of fiction in Britain is Bradbury's own *Stepping Westward* (1965), in which the comparison with the American novel supplies the thematic core. James Walker, a provincial novelist from Nottingham, associated with the Angry Young Men, finds his liberal attitudes tested, and his literary amateurism exposed, when he takes up the post of resident writer at a university 'on the edge of the middle' West (pp. 113–14). Here, the professional approach to analysing and teaching creative writing forces Walker into the first explicit assessment of his own convictions. Bradbury, who subsequently was to pioneer an MA in Creative Writing at the University of East Anglia, a course which produced a number of distinguished novelists, including Ian McEwan and Kazuo Ishiguro, has Walker observe the absence of creative writing courses in English universities (p. 244);[15] but the relative professionalism of the American approach is also subject to scrutiny. The careerist and libertine Bernard Froelich, who has engineered Walker's invitation, seeks also to manipulate Walker's period of tenure as creative writing fellow at Benedict Arnold University. Froelich, who is planning a book on contemporary fiction, intends to write a chapter on Walker and the liberal's dilemma, but only after witnessing the personal dilemma of the English liberal at first hand. Walker walks out of his post when the full implications of Froelich's experiment become clear, and his return to his mundane life in England seems a repudiation of self-serving and unethical professionalism.

Froelich, however, also stands for Bradbury in the sense that the novel is composed to test the adequacy of the liberal English novelist. Here, too, there are ethical shortcomings. The 'Anger' with which he is associated seems a sham, whilst Walker's own behaviour is often pusillanimous. He embodies a confused, and self-divided code, the 'very English brand of liberalism' that Froelich considers 'a faith of unbelief' (p. 317). Yet the lessons he learns suggest the need for more rather than less hesitancy: 'I've learned that literature is a bit more precarious in the future than I expected, that the new world of technology is one I don't understand at all, that democracy is not what I thought it was, and that there's more than one way of being a writer' (p. 360). This is a position that is quite distinct from the one suggested by Walker's own three novels in which he has projected heroes moulded on himself, 'trapped by their remoteness from history', but inclined to condemn social corruption (pp. 32–3). Walker thus becomes a figure of literary renaissance, formerly the epitome of mannered provincialism, but now on the cusp of change, embracing the uncertainties of the post-war novel, and anticipating the catholic range of contemporary British fiction.[16]

The focus of this survey, on the novel that concerns itself with contemporary social life in Britain since 1950, necessarily excludes a distinguished body of Second World War fiction, including Olivia Manning's *Balkan Trilogy* (1960–5), Evelyn Waugh's *Sword of Honour Trilogy* (1952–61), and Lawrence Durrell's *The Alexandria Quartet* (1957–60). Also omitted is the growing and equally distinguished corpus of First World War fiction, of which Pat Barker's *Regeneration Trilogy* (1991–5) is the most prominent example. Malcolm Lowry's mystical and symbolic late modernist *tour de force*, *Under the Volcano* (1947), is deemed to belong to an earlier period, by temperament as well as date, while Graham Greene's fictional concerns have floated free of particular social issues, and towards an engagement with larger religious and philosophical dilemmas.

The established parameters throw into relief the distinctive impulses of a half-century of creativity; and the pertinent themes and topics that present themselves establish my chapter divisions. The first chapter demonstrates how the tradition of 'the state of the nation' novel has been reconfigured in the years since 1950: a sense of social atomization is reflected in the difficulty novelists have had in sustaining an authoritative 'whole picture' of society. The political novel of public life has been largely eclipsed by the novel that concentrates on isolated individual lives, and that registers the fractured and complex nature of post-war society. This shift is epitomized in Margaret Drabble's exploratory shift from 'nurture' to 'nature' in her treatments of society.

Chapter Two traces the tension between economic and ideological per-ceptions of class status, and the mood of confusion that results, a mood reflected most tellingly, perhaps, in the novels of David Storey. The gradual waning of class-consciousness generates anxiety in the treatment of both working- and middle-class experience, and a growing recognition that tradi-tional divisions no longer apply. The gritty working-class realism of the 1950s and 1960s looks, with hindsight, like the swansong of a dying genre. However, the rise of the underclass from the 1980s onwards denotes a new kind of social division that has attracted the disapprobation of novelists. (Livi Michael is a prominent writer in this connection.) More hopefully, this is also an era in which the self-conscious process of class formation supplants the older, given divisions, and this has a particular bearing on the role of the intellectual, as Raymond Williams has cogently shown.

The dramatic shift in post-war gender relations was given an unstoppable impetus by the war effort, which depended upon the toil of women, disrupt-ing, in the process, traditional perceptions of the home and the workplace. As Chapter Three explains, however, the precise articulation of feminist concerns – notably in the fiction of Fay Weldon – only became mani-fest in the fiction of the 1970s, though an incipient feminism is found in some important novels of the 1960s. The 1990s saw the emergence of post-feminism, and a re-evaluation of feminism's oppositional stance undertaken by several significant feminist commentators, including Weldon. The gene-ral drift was towards a more inclusive projection of 'human' rather than 'women's rights'. Gay fiction, in an arresting contrast, is shown to have established a self-defined tradition of its own, in reaction to a prejudiced and inhospitable culture.

The focus of Chapter Four is the fictional investigation of national iden-tity, which has repeatedly produced treatments suggestive of a kind of post-nationalism, a trend that reveals a vein of idealism in the novel that is not reflected in the prevailing popular mood. For Welsh and Scottish writers, and for Irish migrant writers in Britain, a reappraisal of traditional natio-nalist convictions and a relinquishment of old shibboleths, are the ine-vitable consequences of mongrelization – both cultural and genetic. The most noteworthy engagements with Englishness emphasize either the cons-tructed nature of the English persona, or the dissolution of the colonial self. The displacement of English identity, however, can be viewed as an opportunity, the space in which the multicultural novel might flourish, as the appropriate legacy of the imperial past.

The term 'British', of course, is fraught with difficulties. Used to iden-tify a geographical aggregation, it has a suitable looseness that acknowl-edges the separate development of four nations.[17] (The new subject area 'British Studies', in accordance with this non-prescriptive usage, has been conceived in such a way as to examine competing traditions and diverse cultural identities.[18]) As a modern political concept, however, Britishness has often been deployed in questionable ways. The articulation of the Empire as British enabled England to 'avow and disavow its empire' by making the colonial British subordinate to England, whilst also establishing their difference.[19] Britishness, in this conception, begins as a tool of subjection, but evolves into a slippery non-category that facilitates the evasion of responsibility. For similar reasons, Britishness, in the view of some Welsh nationalists, is simply another word for Englishness. Despite these connotations, however, British identity remains open to contestation, and is available for appropriation, as in 'Black British' or 'Jewish British': it is this more fluid and inclusive understanding that my title is intended to register.

Chapter Five considers the extent to which a genuine mode of multicultural expression has already established itself. The more extravagant hybridized novel – associated especially with Salman Rushdie at the end of the period – implies the eventual emergence of a productive cultural intermingling. More typically, however, the migrant identities that are represented in the novel are faced with hostility. Post-war multicultural writing is thus often restricted in its modes of expression by a society that is slow to embrace the human inheritance of Empire. The mood of post-nationalism exemplified by Zadie Smith, however, betrays the emergence of a 'planetary humanism' to enshrine the hopes of the new millennium.[20]

The area of experience that has proved most elusive to the post-war novelist has been geographical transformation. As Chapter Six shows, the rapid alteration of the countryside and the dramatic expansion of suburbia have made definitions of 'urban' and 'rural', and the relationship between them, intensely problematic. As a consequence, the period has witnessed the demise of a clearly differentiated 'Nature Novel', and the development of self-conscious re-evaluations of pastoral, in which ideas of rural life are seen to have an impact on urban experience. Often the spread of urbanization gives rise to a dystopian vision, though more positive – even partly celebratory – representations have come from both Jim Crace and Hanif Kureishi.

In the final chapter I seek to anticipate the topics that might preoccupy novelists and critics in the twenty-first century by charting the treatment of additional topics that remain current. Thus, a retrospective demonstration of the falsity of the realism/experimentalism dichotomy implies that new hybrids, and fresh extensions of realism, can be expected. Similarly, the general trend away from third-person narrative, and towards a first-person 'confessional' style, promotes the special capacity of narrative fiction to capture personal moods in an increasingly fragmented historical period. The predominantly sceptical treatment of science and technology projects a significant intellectual disharmony for the future, if the novel continues to find technological advances to be at odds with genuine human needs.

The book concludes with a consideration of Iris Murdoch's moral philosophy of fiction, a conception of the novel that is shown to have great affinity with the work of several significant post-war novelists. Murdoch's conviction about the novel also reinforces the larger claim I make, implicitly, throughout the survey: that narrative fiction plays a crucial role in assisting our comprehension of public life, our understanding of cultural forms, and our recognition of divers personal identities.

A further explanation of the social novel's special capacities, and an extension of John Fowles's awareness of the novel's unique treatment of time, is found in Paul Ricoeur's explanation of mimesis in narrative fiction, which emphasizes the reader's role in the process of generating meaning. I will conclude this introduction by breaking the rule that governs the following chapters – the principle of prioritizing the discussion of the novels – in order to include a theoretical digression that amplifies this crucial technical point about time and narrative.

In Ricoeur's account, mimesis is understood as 'representation' rather than 'imitation'. To account for the procedure more fully, Ricoeur separates mimesis into three stages. Mimesis$_1$ concerns routinely acquired human skills of perception and self-consciousness: the pre-understanding of action and the need for it to be mediated in articulation, and a pre-understanding of the human experience of time. Mimesis$_2$ is the configuration of action in the plotting and composition of the work itself. Of particular importance to this level is how the fictive present in a work of narrative fiction supplies a framework for conjoining recollection and anticipation: it is this capacity to treat time horizontally that emulates our authentic experience of Being in time. The process of reading then supplies a bridge to mimesis$_3$. This is the stage of 'refiguration' in Ricoeur's terms, the point of intersection between the world of the text and the world of the reader. In this model, narrative asserts its full meaning when it is restored to the time of action and suffering in mimesis$_3$; and an essential feature of this restoration is a quest for personal identity in the act of reading and interpretation – that is, in our assuming responsibility for a story.[21]

Ricoeur's three-stage mimesis, then, begins with our worldly experience of time and action; it then shows how these elements of pre-understanding are drawn on in the composition of a text; and, finally, it stresses a return to the world of the reader in the active process of reception and interpretation. It seems to me that this kind of understanding of the novel, and its *modus operandi*, is essential to explaining its social and historical role in an era of secular individualism. Ricoeur's model of mimesis indicates how the customary novelistic connecting thread between private and public realms is invigorated by the reader's experience: these are connections that we must articulate in that process of 'assuming responsibility'. The account of mimesis as representation rather than imitation also circumvents one of the greatest obstacles to understanding novels: the presumed divergence of 'realism' and 'experimentalism'. Ricoeur shows that the more self-conscious and artificial a novel is, the more effort is required in its interpretation, and so its potential impact at the level of mimesis₃ may be all the greater.

The apparently paradoxical claim that is being made is that the less a novelist attempts to *imitate* the real, the more s/he may enable the reader to return to it. By way of analogy one might think of wildlife field guides, where, very often, a stylized painting of a bird or butterfly – with key markings exaggerated – assists identification more swiftly than a photograph can: it is the stylization that produces the recognition.[22] The novelistic effect, one might say, is produced by a complex stylization that is the determining feature of a substantive mimesis. In the readings that follow, this kind of mimetic procedure can be taken as a given. It is an approach that justifies the conception of this book, in which the novel is held up as a form of discourse that grants unique insight into the key themes of post-war life in Britain.

Where historical and political accounts with pretensions to authority must necessarily deploy elements drawn from the rhetoric of the external overview, the novel, with its emphasis on the personal, and (increasingly) on the first-person confessional style, offers an imitation of lived social experience, and does so within a structure that emulates our own experience as social beings with a consciousness of a bounded temporal history. Where the mimetic effect of the great nineteenth-century realists like George Eliot is sometimes said to hinge on the ability to reproduce a society in microcosm, the mimesis of the post-war period is defined by the reverse impetus, but a similar objective. The cultivation of broader social identification and recognition is achieved by the stress on personal history. An era of individualism is acknowledged in the structure of a literary mode that, in its most significant instances, seeks to challenge the worst effects of the post-Christian secular world, with its tendency towards anomie. More than a consolation for social atomization, the novel establishes itself as a discursive opponent in the process of social definition, seeking to appropriate the self-awareness of the twentieth century, with the emphasis on human rights and privileges, as (in the view of Fowles's Daniel Martin), 'an essentially liberating new force in human society' (p. 555).

## Chapter 1

# The State and the Novel

The name that comes most readily to mind in a consideration of the state and the novel is George Orwell. His two most famous political fables, *Animal Farm: A Fairy Story* (1945) and *Nineteen Eighty-Four* (1949), have proved hugely significant in the post-war world, influencing many subsequent literary dystopias, and also supplementing our use of language. Terms like 'Big Brother', 'doublethink' and 'unperson' from *Nineteen Eighty-Four* have become part of the contemporary political lexicon. It is also possible to see the cautionary note of these novels as establishing a liberal world-view, based on a deep scepticism of political extremes that helps fashion 'a new lineage of liberal and socially attentive writing' that is dominant in British fiction in the 1950s and beyond.[1]

The mood of Orwell's fables, however, might now seem backward-rather than forward-looking in some respects. At the level of prophecy, it is true, the repudiation of the corrupt mechanics of the communist state implicit in both *Animal Farm* and *Nineteen Eighty-Four* chimes with the Cold War mood, which is dominant in Western society through into the 1980s. But in terms of gestation, both works have an eye to the past, and particularly to Orwell's disillusioning experiences fighting for the revolutionary POUM (Partido Obrero de Unificación Marxista) militia in the Spanish Civil War.[2] The immediate resonance of both books in Britain, moreover, was dependent upon the post-war experience of austerity, where shortages, rationing, and government control and bureaucracy made (in particular) the confinement of 'Airstrip One', Orwell's depiction of London in *Nineteen Eighty-Four*, seem a faintly plausible extension of reality. In the 1950s, however, with the end of rationing, and a developing consumer boom, a new public mood emerged. This survey takes 1950 as a dividing line that separates the war and its aftermath from the distinctive nature of post-war society, governed by new economic and social energies. If the work of Orwell helps define this historical divide, however, there is little sense that fiction writers subscribed to the general celebration of prosperity. Post-1950 novelists, in fact, were not easily persuaded that the work of social rebuilding was always benign or coherent.

The blueprint for post-war social policy was contained in Sir William Beveridge's review of social security, *Social Insurance and Allied Services* (1942), popularly known as 'The Beveridge Report'. Beveridge's plan was for a comprehensive welfare programme, premised on the expectation of full employment, and involving a universal national insurance scheme, and a national health service. It was a social vision that caught the public mood. Astonishing as it may now seem for a political document, the Beveridge Report became a bestseller, with more than 600,000 copies sold.[3] The enthusiasm for this political vision indicates a popular mandate for its implementation, and Beveridge's plan helped fashion the emergence of the welfare state after 1945. Clement Attlee's Labour government of 1945–51 put in place the central planks of the new society, redesigned to offer insurance for all citizens against the risks of unemployment, sickness, and disability. The National Health Service, instituted in 1948, was the most celebrated initiative of this phase of social restructuring, but the keynote feature of the new political scene was an economic policy designed to embrace common ownership and full employment. By the early 1950s, a consensus in British politics – in the sense of an approach to policy that was broadly shared by the Labour Party and the Conservatives – had emerged, embracing full employment, the welfare state, and state intervention in industry. In this period, 'the vocabulary . . . of modern capitalism and social democracy' was defined, a lexicon which signified a consensus (within government, at least) about domestic policy.[4] The historical judgement of this period is generally one that celebrates an achievement deemed to be considerable, given the impoverishment of Britain during the war, and the huge financial burden of fighting it.[5]

## The Post-War Wilderness

The mood of post-war optimism was built partly on hope, of course, and this hopeful projection is not reproduced in the novel. This should give little cause for surprise, since the task of serious fiction is not to collude with the prevailing popular view, but rather to offer an alternative perspective, to locate those areas that might generate a sense of concern about history and society. In 1950, serious writers were already finding fault with the celebratory mood associated with a new beginning. In *The World My Wilderness* (1950), for instance, Rose Macaulay establishes a critical view on the project of social reconstruction, choosing to place emphasis on a breakdown of the social order, suggesting that this is also a psychological problem. Resisting the popular patriotic mood of a nation victorious in war, and steeling itself to the task of rebuilding its infrastructure, Macaulay offers an independent external view at the beginning of her novel. This is the perspective of a French character Madame Michel, 'a good anglophobe', who feels the British, lacking 'literature, culture, language and manners', flatter themselves as the liberators of the French (it is the French and the Americans who did the liberating, she thinks). England, she believes, 'always came well out of every war, losing neither lives nor money' (pp. 9, 13).[6] The novel does not endorse this economic analysis, but seeks to identify the sense of crisis – cultural as well as material – that popular patriotism can easily conceal.

Macaulay focuses on the seventeen-year-old Barbary, whose divorced parents decide she will come to live in London in 1946, having spent the war years in occupied France, associating with the Maquis (the French Resistance). Haunted by her betrayal of her stepfather (a collaborator), she is unable to adjust to the peacetime goal of rebuilding a 'civilised' society, a concept that Macaulay, in any case, holds up for interrogation. Absconding from her studies at the Slade School of Art, the 'barbarian' Barbary finds her 'wilderness' in the bombsites of London, associating with spivs, deserters, and thieves. She feels she belongs to these ruins (p. 181), and Macaulay stresses that this visible collapse of civilization signifies also an inner dearth that is both spiritual and intellectual. The frequent quotation from T. S. Eliot's *The Waste Land* keeps this link in view, but the most arresting association is made by the appearance of a deranged clergyman, preaching about Hell in a bombed-out church, convinced he is burning in hell-fire for his sins, having been trapped in his own church when it was bombed in 1940 (pp. 166–8).

Macaulay is seriously posing the question that passes through the mind of Barbary's half-brother Richie: whether or not Western culture has 'had its day' (p. 152). The post-war cultural initiative becomes an object of satire when one character quips that the 'Third Programme' might be used in a prison punishment cell (p. 73). The 'punishment' is that of the state-sponsored attempt to inculcate an appreciation of High Art: the BBC began broadcasting its highbrow Third Programme in 1946, projecting it as an educative and civilizing force, though its small audience – it had a one per cent share of listeners in 1949 – indicates failure in this regard.[7] Macaulay's implication is that misdirected social rebuilding may fail to attract the necessary popular support. When Richie walks across the ruins that comprise Barbary's wilderness in the final chapter he witnesses an archaeological dig in progress, transforming the area from a delinquents' refuge to a site of historical interest: 'civilised intelligence was at work among the ruins', it is suggested (p. 252). But a sense of pointlessness overcomes Richie, who turns from 'the shells of churches' which 'gaped like lost myths' whilst 'the jungle pressed in on them, seeking to cover them up' (p. 245). The emptiness that Macaulay evokes embraces both existing social structures, such as conventional family life, and the obvious alternatives, particularly the Bohemian self-expression of Barbary's mother Helen. When it is revealed that Barbary's real father was a Spanish painter that Helen had met one summer (rather than her London barrister husband), the disconcerting theme of the uncertain origin – discomfiting to the very idea of national pride – becomes central. This effect is cogently reinforced by the sense of futility that mars the archaeological dig, where 'the wilderness' is imagined to be slipping away from trowels and measuring rods, seeking instead 'the primeval chaos' that precedes human habitation (p. 253).

A novel that is less apocalyptic in its style, though scarcely less negative in its implications, is William Cooper's *Scenes From Provincial Life* (1950). Fifty years after its publication, *Scenes From Provincial Life* seems a modest and unambitious work, in the manner of an unassuming autobiographical first novel (though in fact 'William Cooper' had previously published novels under his real name, H. S. Hoff). It was, however, very influential, 'a seminal influence' on novelists of his generation according to John Braine; Malcolm Bradbury, too, claimed to have found belief in himself as a writer through Cooper's example of a kind of ordinary reflectiveness.[8] Bradbury's celebration of Cooper's method of producing 'a book about how dense, substantial, and complex life is, taken on its ordinary terms' fits well with Cooper's avowed project:[9] he affiliated himself clearly with the realism lobby in the realism-versus-experimentalism debate that emerged in the 1950s.[10] The full effect of the novel, however, hinges on a particular brand of quiet self-consciousness that delivers a subtle, but ultimately depressing verdict on the possibilities of 'ordinary' life.

The setting is the key to this. The tribulations of the four main protagonists in love and career are set against the backdrop of the threat of Nazism, since the principal action occurs in 1939 before war has been declared. The central characters have a plan to flee to the US to escape the totalitarian state that may result from the continuing appeasement of Hitler. As a consequence, there is a mood of 'dissolution' in which private miseries seem to match the impending collapse of Europe (p. 87). Later, however, narrator Joe Lunn casts doubt on his tendency to equate private and public 'disintegration', claiming that the link rings false (p. 149). And, of course, it rings false for the reader, too, since this is a comic novel that catches a mood of qualified post-war optimism far more than it embraces the nihilistic abandonment of England that is proposed. Lunn's various rural idylls (he spends weekends at a country cottage with the girlfriend he refuses to marry) convey an attachment to place that belies his stated intention to emigrate. In this way Cooper manages to play two contexts off against each other: historical hindsight renders anodyne the pessimism of 1939.

This double-focus is an integral part of the novel's effect, and it serves to place attention on preoccupations more pressing for a post-war audience, such as the changing nature of social and sexual relations, and the apparent dullness of provincial existence. Joe Lunn's boredom with his life as a schoolmaster in an anonymous provincial town (based on Leicester) is offset only by his writing. He has published three novels at the outset, and has completed a fourth that he considers to be superior. The persona of the narrator is infused with a conviction of this vocation, but since this self-belief is sustained by the desire to escape, a fundamental paradox structures the work. If the book's originality lies in 'the particular kind of ordinary life, the particular culture' it evokes, then Cooper succeeds in embracing and celebrating the way of living that dissatisfies Lunn, but only through the device of Lunn's involvement with the object of his dissatisfaction.[11] It is a formal paradox that explains the novel's peculiar tension. In the final chapter, entitled 'Provincial Life-Histories', Lunn presents us with a list of the characters, all of which have married beyond the action of the novel. This dismissive gesture implies the essential predictability and conformity of provincial existence. At the same time, Lunn refuses to reveal his own life history, and, by virtue of this omission, he conjures up the escape he had wanted. But the omission is also a form of exile that leaves Lunn excluded from the propitious comic ending, and that makes the withdrawal of the author-figure seem artificial, even whilst it is necessary for the desired effect.

This kind of paradoxical gesture suggests an uncertainty about the solidity of the social world, and about the role of the novelist in commenting upon it. It is a hesitancy that strikes a dissonant chord in the context of national reconstruction (where the tasks ahead might seem self-evident); yet this anxiety about the role of the novel in the national narrative is expressed in a number of quarters – Pamela Hansford Johnson's novel *The Humbler Creation* (1959) is another example of this wariness. Superficially, *The Humbler Creation* may seem a distinctly old-fashioned novel to readers at the end of the twentieth century. The dilemma faced by the clergyman-protagonist Maurice Fisher, a dilemma of marital fidelity, and moral responsibility, arising principally from his Kensington parishioners' propensity to gossip, seems to belong to an entirely different social era. The stable third-person narrative style, untroubled by its omniscient reach, bespeaks a certainty about the contract between author and reader, and the shared assumption that a transparent narrator can mediate between world and text in a straightforward manner.

The stable realism this implies, however, is here being conscientiously asserted, as part of a broader reaction against the modernist legacy. Yet in its topical content, the novel demonstrates an uncertainty about the reach of realism – or, perhaps, an acknowledgement of its need to adapt – in the face of the incipient break-up of key elements of social consensus. The moral focus is the perceived need to be truthful; this is emphasized in the relatively trivial matter of a road traffic offence, an episode in which Hansford Johnson uses the realist contract to push her modest social code. A general loss of spiritual faith, and the perceived social irrelevance of the Christian church are governing concerns in *The Humbler Creation*; but the fact of a predominantly secular society is really a 'given' for novelists in the entire post-war period, so this 'crisis' seems anachronistic, even for 1959.

The novel is also forward-looking in a number of ways, however. The concern about delinquency, and about violent crime, specifically the crime of sexually assaulting children (committed by one of Fisher's young parishioners) – issues that remain prominent into the twenty-first century – demonstrates a continuity through the period that is not always recognized. Hansford Johnson also broaches tentatively some of the period's primary concerns. The issue of re-evaluating sexual identity, for instance, is broached by the gay couple Peter and Lou for whom Fisher acquires some sympathy (p. 141). The shadow of the atomic bomb, which becomes so prominent in the fiction of the 1980s, also obtrudes, making one character feel that her own problems are negligible (p. 231). There is even, in this Caucasian fictional world, a brief acknowledgement of multicultural London in the respectful description of a patient and dignified Indian woman, walking with a perambulator (p. 118).

It is the novel's title, however, that most aptly conveys its intriguing duality, simultaneously anachronistic and contemporary. The 'humbler creation' denotes, in the hymn from which the phrase is taken, humankind beneath the angels (p. 146), and it resurfaces in Maurice Fisher's final reflections, when he has resigned himself, for the sake of decorum, to a loveless marriage and to giving up the woman he loves. Comparing himself with a sixteenth-century martyr, burnt at the stake, Fisher realizes that he is 'so much more obviously of the humbler creation' than this martyr, who is reputed to have managed a heroic gesture at the moment of death (p. 315). Fisher recognizes his human frailty, and also the relative unimportance of the dilemma that has preoccupied him (and the novel). Hansford Johnson is tacitly announcing the irrelevance of her portentous Christian imagery, and promoting a new breed of protagonist, whose concerns may be trivial in comparison with the heroic gestures of earlier literature. In this conclusion she is actually embracing two of the elements that are sometimes seen as the bane of the post-war British novelist: the limited scope of the novel, and the uncertainty about character and motivation that accompanies it. But since that sense of limitation and uncertainty stems from the state of the nation the novel discovers, then these formal limits are also an integral aspect of this realist vision; and this formula is representative of a dominant strand in post-war writing.

## The Testing of Liberal Humanism

The post-Christian morality of *The Humbler Creation* suggests a philosophical perspective very much in tune with Peter Conradi's description of liberal humanism, glossed, in his account of Angus Wilson, as 'a disparate bundle of belief and unbelief'. This liberal humanism

> was momentarily forced into illusory coherence after the last war. The space it defended was anti-Marxist, post-Christian, anti-capitalist, socially progressive. It proposed a political alternative to cold war extremes, and, in the teeth of the experience of Hitler, tested belief in goodness and progress.[12]

For Hansford Johnson, of course, that testing of belief in goodness and progress is also a testing of the liberal philosophy itself. The same is true of the novels written by Angus Wilson in the 1950s in which the adequacy and integrity of liberal humanism is subjected to continuous critical scrutiny. Wilson ponders the nature of English society and culture, and tacitly asks whether or not liberalism will prove adequate as a moral centre for the new social formation.

*Hemlock and After* (1952) is set prior to the defeat, in 1951, of the Labour government that had instituted the Welfare State, and a debate implicitly provoked by Wilson is how far the 'modified socialism' (p. 83) of the post-war state might support the cultural life: at the outset esteemed novelist Bernard Sands has secured a government grant to help set up his centre for talented young writers at Vardon Hall. This project, however, becomes a test of Sands and his personal humanist vision, rather than a deliberation about policy. It is precisely the 'illusory coherence' of liberal humanism that Wilson sets out to expose, without quite relinquishing it as the preferred moral stance. This is the paradox that orders his writing, and the crucial question in an assessment of Wilson is whether or not the contradictions that embarrass his characters result in structural flaws in the novels themselves.

In the case of *Hemlock and After* it is important to distinguish between the novelist's project, and the career of his protagonist, so that the contradictory elements of Sands's humanism – an odd combination of moral wisdom and vindictiveness – need not be seen to issue from Wilson's narratorial point of view. To the extent that this perspective is *tainted* by the confusion, the qualification still applies: the significant point is that Wilson cultivates this sense of dissonance as part of his art. Admittedly, there is, apparently, a troubling association between Sands's homosexuality and his personal dissolution, a link that looks repressive (I discuss this more fully in my chapter on gender and sexual identity). But Wilson's concern transcends the question of sexual identity, and produces a controlled confrontation between a moral, or humanist, or realist emphasis on social solidity, and a less stable investigation of psychological indeterminacy. The ambiguous form that results is less flawed and more innovative than is sometimes acknowledged.

Wilson's ostensible purpose is to present a test of humanism, and the resolution lies in the business of making novels, for the work of Sands the novelist is shown to comprise a beneficent social contribution that overshadows the personal dissolution. This positive implication is not clear-cut, however. Indeed, Sands's humanism is destroyed by a new Dostoevskyan awareness of the doubleness of all human motivation, including his own, and he dies without recovering from this spiritual devastation. Neither is there hope in the continuation of his personal projects or convictions;[13] but the implications of Sands's work, it is suggested, may prove more enduring. Here the vocation of writing is central to a more constructive perception of 'testing'. Reviews of Sands's most recent novel celebrate 'a wider view of life' and a 'testimony to the endurance of the human spirit' (p. 14). The transcendence this suggests is precisely that which his sister Isobel condemns, finding in his later novels a 'quietism' with 'an almost unreal religious quality' (p. 72).

Sands's last act, however, is to write to Isobel affirming his convictions 'to be on the side of the oppressed, the weak and the misfits', even though 'we shall not see anything of what we wish come in our lifetime' (p. 220). Despite his disillusionment, he retains (like his creator) the broad humanist stance that his reviewers praise, and this persisting faith in a kind of 'long revolution' forms the positive term in his ambivalent identity. This sense of indeterminacy, which may not fully answer the charge of 'quietism', is reinforced by the parallel with Socrates implied in the title. Socrates was forced to drink hemlock for corrupting the youth of Athens; Sands's 'hemlock' is the self-knowledge that destroys him, his realization of his moral wavering. What comes 'after' is uncertain, but faith is placed in the continuity of Sands's social vision. If one evaluates the achievement of Wilson in a similar light – and clearly the self-doubt that inspires the creation of Sands invites us to do so – it may be significant that the testing of liberal humanism in *Hemlock and After* remains a pertinent ethical topic fifty years on.

The task that remains, however, is to ascertain the degree of purchase that a liberal philosophy can achieve in a world that is increasingly illiberal. This concern underpins Bernard Bergonzi's discussion of the 'moral preoccupations' of Angus Wilson's first three novels, in which Wilson emerges as 'a distinguished practitioner' in a tradition of English fiction, 'whose brightest luminary is George Eliot', and in which 'the novel is seen as the vehicle for a particular liberal ideology, where characters are secure in their freedom to refine on their motives, truly to understand each other and, above all, themselves.'[14] For Bergonzi, this tradition is 'beginning to look trivial' in the work of 'a mid-twentieth-century representative', given 'the larger context of the history of our times':

> It is in the centripetal nature of its preoccupations that English culture can look parochial and irrelevant to outsiders. For writers who have known, and often still live in, a world where torture and deportation, the arbitrary exercise of unlimited power and the familiarity of casual violence are part of daily experience, the dilemmas of the English liberal are likely to seem a little fine drawn.[15]

This objection raises a larger doubt about the moral justification of the novel *per se*, since the serious novel is a form of expression that always traces or invites a link between personal conviction and the broader public sphere. The real issue may be the (relatively) undramatic nature of social life in post-war England, which has not provoked the intense kinds of novelistic discourse that one associates with unstable or extreme political systems, such as have obtained in South America or South Africa.

In any case, if Wilson belongs to a peculiarly English novel-writing tradition of self-discovery, he also embodies the dismantling and transformation of this tradition, especially as it is found in the limited liberalism of E. M. Forster.[16] The trajectory of this development is discernible in Wilson's second novel, *Anglo-Saxon Attitudes* (1956), a work of transition, in which the predicament of its main character Gerald Middleton is revealed as being less important than the novel's structure initially suggests. Extending the model established in *Hemlock and After*, Wilson makes the dilemmas of another English liberal speak to the larger problems of nationhood.

Middleton, a history professor in his sixties, and a scholar of great but unfulfilled promise, faces a dual challenge: to confront his failures in both the professional and domestic spheres.[17] Gerald's great personal failure was to have continued an affair without ever making the break with his apparently progressive (but actually domineering) wife. A different pattern of deception haunts Gerald's professional life. This originates in an archaeological dig in 1912, where a phallic wooden fertility figure – a pagan idol – was planted in the grave of a seventh-century Christian bishop. The historical implications of the hoax (inspired by the Piltdown man scandal) are enormous, since it suggests that the accepted version of the Conversion of Britain to Christianity may be flawed. Middleton has had an intimation of the hoax, but has concealed the knowledge for forty years, partly to protect the reputation of his mentor Lionel Stokesay, father of the perpetrator of the hoax. As Middleton uncovers the truth of the scandal, so does his professional star rise until, at the end of the novel, he accepts the Chair of the History

Association. He has become equally clear-headed about his dealings with his family, accepting now the limits to his influence and to the affection he can hope for.

This apparent resolution of Middleton's dilemmas is significantly undercut, however. As he departs for a flight for Mexico, and a working holiday over the Christmas vacation, the popular novelist Clarissa Crane voices a dismissive summary of his underachieving life, concluding 'one could say that Gerald Middleton had taken life a bit too easily' (p. 336). This stands as a fair commentary on Middleton's limitations. Indeed, the significance of his new vitality is qualified in several ways. First, there is a sense that his personal problems, partly of his own making, are only significant to the site of unearned luxury that he inhabits. His evident wealth has come from the family firm, a steel-construction business which he has nothing to do with, and which is now in the charge of his eldest son. Before his recommitment, the depressed and unfulfilled Middleton expends most of his energy on his art collection, an effort of displacement matched by his inability to concentrate seriously on any interaction with women – for much of the novel his responses to women are determined by his assessment of their sexual attractiveness. These are curiously unlikeable characteristics, given the liberal tradition from which Wilson emerges, and in which 'characters are secure in their freedom to refine on their motives', as Bergonzi suggests. The nature of Gerald Middleton's 'freedom' is subject to critical scrutiny, making his sluggish moral responses all the more inadequate. We are presented with an anachronism: the man of independent means, not fully responsive to his context; but that seems to be Wilson's conscious purpose, indicating that the novel makes a partial break with the liberal tradition, presenting a central character who must reinvent himself, as best he can, whilst seeking a path through the muddle of English identity.

Wilson's early novels are largely confined to the middle-class and upper-middle-class echelons of society; but he is also interested in the dismantling of these categories of class (as the next chapter demonstrates). This is an integral part of his impetus to push at his own ideological boundaries. Wilson's liberal project, with its recognition of social change, seems particularly worth defending when it is compared with less socially responsive writing. Anthony Powell's twelve-novel sequence *A Dance to the Music of Time* (1951–75), for example, stands in marked contrast, and this is surprising on the face of it, since one might expect this project to deliver a substantial fictional treatment of the state of the nation. The sequence begins in 1921, though the entire enterprise embraces two world wars, and contains episodes that span the period 1914–71. By virtue of its historical coverage, and on account of the quarter-century of composition, Powell's cycle would seem a major contribution to the literature of English social life, tracing the implications of twentieth-century history through to the contemporary period. In fact, *A Dance to the Music of Time* fails in this regard, setting itself the more limited comic goal of delineating the quirks of human character. It is precisely in this projection of a comic mood that eludes social change that Powell's sequence now seems irredeemably anachronistic.

The governing motif of the dance is introduced in the first volume *A Question of Upbringing* (1951) through the reflections of narrator Nicholas Jenkins, concerning the Poussin painting that gives the sequence its name. Jenkins's recollection of the painting suggests that the dancers (the dancers are the seasons personified in Poussin's conception) are controlled by the dance, and he imagines them disappearing and reappearing as Time progresses (p. 6). Powell's narrative method, in which the paths of his various characters cross repeatedly, emulates this impression, but the 'dance' that governs them through the decades does not convincingly imitate a broad social fabric binding the characters together; rather, this governing motif underscores the restricted range of Powell's fictional world, confined to 'the English professional, upper-middle and upper classes' in which it appears 'everyone knows everyone else'.[18] In this sense, the sequence limits its range to a stratum of society that becomes increasingly insignificant, in demographic terms, through the period of composition and beyond.[19]

Powell thus recreates a social world of greater relevance to England in the 1920s or 1930s, and this renders his comic vision out of kilter with the prevailing social mood. This discrepancy is particularly marked in the portrayal of Kenneth Widmerpool, Powell's great comic creation, the egregiously ambitious *arriviste* whose successive advances in status (he is eventually made a Life Peer [*Temporary Kings* (1973), p. 43]) never guarantee his acceptance in the upper social echelons, where he remains the 'freak' or 'oddity' he had seemed at school (*A Question of Upbringing*, pp. 125–6). Thus, even if Widmerpool is successfully realized as 'the most stupendous cad in English literature',[20] his conception as a comic grotesque hinges on repudiating the kind of self-advancement, or questioning of fixed social categories that is usually a focus of egalitarian celebration in post-war society.

Widmerpool becomes the vehicle for some pointed satirical observations in the final volume, *Hearing Secret Harmonies* (1975). Here (in 1968) he is installed as the Chancellor of a 'newish' university (p. 48), and has made efforts to associate himself with the student movement and the counter-culture (p. 42). He joins forces with a cult, having retired to his mother's former house to run a centre for dissident youth, and finally dies in 1971, dispossessed, after a series of humiliating episodes (p. 245). In this novel Widmerpool's insatiable quest for power and status latches on to the new social movements of the 1960s, with the inevitable consequence that these are tainted by his lack of integrity. Powell's conservative comic mood, in alliance with the social status quo, is here revealed more directly than elsewhere in the sequence. The static conservative overview of Powell indicates that alternative fictional strategies were needed to register adequately the implications of the new social movements.

## The Sixties and Social Revolution

The decade in which post-war social change is felt to have been concentrated is the 1960s. This is certainly a simplification, but it does help pinpoint some of the more dramatic changes that may have been longer in the making. For example, one of the key social changes of the 1960s is the emergence of 'youth culture'. The sense of a newly empowered sector of society is conveyed principally by the new spending power of young people, and the emergence of mainstream youth-related cultural forms, especially pop music, that quickly become significant components of the economy. This sea change in age perception results in the emergence of important individuals – intellectuals as well as entertainers – who are fifteen or twenty years younger than they might have been hitherto.[21] This change even had an effect on the public perception of the novelist: the received wisdom that novelists produce their best work after the age of forty is challenged by the new trend of youthful achievers. Shena Mackay is perhaps the most obvious example of this, celebrated as a glamorous young novelist in the early 1960s when, she recalls, 'all books by young persons were treated in the papers as dispatches from front-line Swinging London'.[22]

The most memorable fictional treatment of youth culture in the 1960s, however, puts a very different construction on the changing balance of power. In *A Clockwork Orange* (1962) Anthony Burgess isolates the tribal, antisocial elements of youth culture in a dystopian fable of violence as leisure. Alex, fifteen at the outset, the gang-leader whose drug- and music-inspired 'ultra-violence' embraces murder and rape, narrates the novel. The teenage patois or 'nasdat talk' (p. 126) spoken by the gang members (the 'droogs') is a mannerism designed to exclude adults, a point underscored when the predatory Alex encounters two ten-year-old girls in a record store and discovers their idiom is different to his (p. 37). The 'nasdat' vocabulary combines influences to produce what Blake Morrison calls a 'Russo-Anglo-American patois', an international form that implies that the adolescent male impulse towards aggressive behaviour transcends national boundaries.[23]

Though problematic, *A Clockwork Orange* is, in fact, a highly moral work. The unreformed Alex, having spent two years in a conventional prison, is put through a two-week 'Reclamation Treatment' (p. 75), a programme of conditioning, enhanced by drugs, that makes the patient sick at the thought of violence. He is thus 'reformed', not through moral choice, but only insofar as his mind will not allow him to pursue his violent urges (p. 99). He becomes that unnatural thing, 'a clockwork orange' (p. 100) acting without volition. Alex becomes a pawn in the struggle between two political systems, and is subsequently de-programmed so that he can return to a life of gang violence. He is finally redeemed, not by state intervention, but by the arrival of maturity, which he glimpses, appropriately, in the twenty-first (and final) chapter, which anticipates his eventual adulthood. (At this point he is just eighteen [p. 146], though the structure of twenty-one chapters seems significant – in the early 1960s, of course, twenty-one was the age generally reckoned to mark the point of accession to mature adulthood.)[24] Showing signs of paternal feeling, and of material acquisitiveness, Alex has lost interest in the cult of violent excess.

The conclusion that the novel offers is that youthful excess is a necessary phase in the process of growing up, though this is an uncomfortable and reluctant conclusion given the novel's evocation of violence, and the clear warning about a society that produces a cult of youth.[25] Burgess's more pressing anxiety, however, has to do with the unpredictable function of art and the aesthetic response, and the concern that the responses of the young do not make for a considered set of cultural values. Alex is a devotee of classical music, for whom Beethoven inspires extreme expressions of violence. This moral crisis about art, illustrated by the Nazi appropriation of high culture, is investigated most fully through the role of the author in the novel. This is the writer F. Alexander, originally a victim of one of Alex's attacks (his wife, raped and beaten, eventually dies), who (a 'bleeding heart' liberal) later champions the cause of the brainwashed Alex, until he realizes his true identity. This author, who stands for Burgess in some ways, has written a book called *A Clockwork Orange*, which seems to be a plea for the organic development of humanity, and a rejection of the dehumanization of the machine world (p. 124). Burgess is, effectively, demonstrating the unsatisfactory nature of the moral position he feels obliged to take. If to permit the expression of humanity is to tolerate the antisocial expression of youth power, this might also be to allow the rapists into your own home, into the writer's own inner sanctum.[26]

Burgess asserts the novelist's prerogative to a long-term philosophical view of a social trend that is nevertheless extremely significant and irreversible. In Arthur Marwick's view, British youth subculture generated 'highly liberating patterns of behaviour and forms of self-presentation'. From this perspective, the new credibility of the young is a productive social change, an integral aspect of the 'cultural revolution' identified with the 'long sixties' from 1958–74. For Marwick, then, the new youth phenomenon had established its positive contribution only shortly after the publication of *A Clockwork*

*Orange*: this is the kind of social commentary that stands in direct contrast to the implications of Burgess's novel.[27]

The 1960s phenomenon that has fuelled the greatest controversy is hippy culture. The hippy dream of reintegrating society with nature, if naive, produced a positive long-term intellectual legacy, since it lies behind many subsequent reworkings of the relationship between humanity and the rest of nature. However, the hippy promotion of drugs to expand consciousness, and to expedite the achievement of social harmony, has attracted much disapprobation. Here social historians and novelists are commonly in agreement.[28] Hippy idealism, linked with drug experimentation and an unfocused dabbling in Eastern mysticism, is gently punctured in Esther Freud's *Hideous Kinky* (1992), where the child narrator's view generates an implicit criticism of her feckless mother's pursuit of adventure in Morocco. Freud employs an oblique method to show that the trappings of the West cannot easily be divested, as when the narrator and her elder sister are recalling the pleasures of Mars bars and mashed potato while their mother sleeps in with her African lover (p. 83).

Two assumptions about the 'long sixties' in particular have attracted the critical eye of the novelist: first, the notion that sexual permissiveness led to 'a new frankness, openness, and indeed honesty in personal relations and modes of expression'; and, second, the claim that 'the challenge to established authorities and hierarchies' has led to a fruitful process of subversion, supplanting (especially) 'the authority of the white, the upper and middle class, the husband, the father, and the male generally'.[29] Were either of these assumptions beyond question, the satirical thrust of Malcolm Bradbury's *The History Man* (1975) would have been entirely misdirected. As it is, *The History Man* is one of the most important satires of post-war manners.

There is also an element of reflective self-consciousness in Bradbury's novel, flagged up by a minor character, a university lecturer in English who, ten years previously, had written two novels filled 'with moral scruple'. Since that time he has been silent, as if 'there was no more moral scruple and concern, no new substance to be spun' (p. 204). Bradbury's response to this parlous state is to write a savage satire of university life (set in 1972), demonstrating how a particular constellation of social and historical forces produces an amoral society, cut adrift by the 'freedoms' of the 1960s, and misled by the dogmatic convictions which paradoxically follow.

Bradbury's great comic grotesque is Howard Kirk, the trendy sociology lecturer at a fashionable campus university, whose Marxist convictions about the plot of history run counter to his own egotistical, and libidinous desires. He has written a book about the myth of bourgeois individualism, impugning bourgeois capitalism for its false projection of a personal morality (p. 91).

The convictions of Kirk thus place him in opposition to the liberal moral tradition, associated especially with Angus Wilson in the post-war era, but a liberalism with which Bradbury also has an affinity. The amoral Kirk is a development of Bernard Froelich from Bradbury's earlier novel *Stepping Westward* (1965), a character who seeks to control and manipulate others. His intellectual hypocrisy is revealed most emphatically in the clash with George Carmody, a student he has persecuted for holding the 'wrong' ideas about sociology. Carmody's position (which is clearly also Bradbury's) is that 'the superstructure is a damned sight more important than the substructure' and that 'culture's a value, not an inert descriptive term'. Kirk's vulgar Marxism, in which the economic base determines all cultural phenomena, enables him to dismiss Carmody's thought as 'incompatible with sociological analysis' (p. 138). Bradbury's condemnation in Kirk of what, a generation later, came to be known as 'political correctness' is made telling by its echo of the 'one-system world' projected by Fascism. One character describes Fascism as another 'sociological construct' that is opposed to 'contingency or pluralism or liberalism' (p. 158).

Kirk is a vulgar Marxist, and it should be recognized that Western Marxism, as an intellectual tool for understanding capitalism, is a far more complex phenomenon. The role of culture in the superstructure, for example, is usually seen to be characterized by a degree of autonomy in Marxist criticism; economic determinism is invariably dismissed as a blunt tool.[30] Bradbury, then, presents Kirk as a convenient caricature, but he does so in order to align himself with the forces of contingency, pluralism, and liberalism in this debate, and in an attempt to exercise the creative autonomy of the novelist's art.

The picture that emerges of England in the 1970s, however, is less clearcut than the caricature suggests. Howard and Barbara Kirk, the swinging couple with the open marriage, are representative figures, having been transformed by the 'revolution of rising expectations' concerning sex, class, and work which the 1960s brought forth (p. 24). This promise of liberation has ossified into the hard Leftism that the novel vilifies, a world-view that is an early sign of the end of consensus politics. In a seminar discussion the unfortunate Carmody is taken to task, by one of Kirk's more compliant students, for his conception of 'a society as a consensus which bad people from outside set out to upset'. The novel is unable to endorse either position in this dispute: if an intransigent radicalism is satirized, its very existence marks the eclipse of the traditional consensus view to which it stands opposed (p. 133). If Howard Kirk epitomizes a pseudo-intellectualism that has 'substituted trends for morals and commitments' (p. 32), the representativeness of the Kirks suggests that the failure is a general one. Their shared 1950s background of 'vestigial Christianity and inherited social deference' represents a lost social world in which ethics was privileged over politics (p. 23). In Bradbury's conception of 1972, politics has displaced ethics, a reversal that calls the adequacy of the novelist's intervention into question. It is in tacit acknowledgement of this apparent impasse that Bradbury's reclusive and 'depressed-looking' lecturer, the erstwhile novelist of moral scruple, has been silent for a decade (p. 204).

Set a year later, Piers Paul Read's *A Married Man* (1979) raises similar doubts about the ethical efficacy of fiction in a story of political and social collapse that embraces the 1973–4 winter of strikes, and the ensuing February election. In an intriguing process of mapping the personal on to the political, Read's novel treats the mid-life crisis of forty-year-old barrister John Strickland as the litmus test for a more general social malaise, embracing the corrupting effects of the legal and political systems. The crisis for Strickland is brought on by the chance selection of Tolstoy's novella 'The Death of Ivan Ilych' as a holiday read. Reflecting on the public's lack of taste for fiction, since it no longer affects people's lives, Strickland very soon has his secure identity entirely shaken up by Tolstoy's tale. Crucially, Strickland's epiphanic encounter with fiction is rooted in his profound identification with 'his fellow-lawyer, Ivan Ilych', whose fear of death sparks in Strickland a comparable intimation of mortality, and the kind of professional and sexual re-evaluation commonly associated with the male menopause (pp. 18–22). The overt irony of Strickland's Tolstoy-induced crisis, in an age when fiction is not seen as a cultural form capable of direct intervention, is well managed. Read is also seeking to resurrect this function of the novel by flagging up its role in the cultivation of the empathic response, and, as a consequence of this, in the construction of ethical conduct.

There is no sense in this novel, however, of social revolution – of the overturning of traditional hierarchies, or of a more open and honest epoch in personal relationships. Pursuing a new career as a politician, with a resuscitated socialist vision, and chasing a mistress, too, Strickland is successful in these aims, the visible signs of his masculine ego asserting itself. He is elected as Labour member for Hackney and Harringay in the 1974 election, and conducts an affair with Paula Gerrard, daughter of a wealthy banker. His association with Paula, however, is severed when he realizes that she has planned the murder of his wife Clare. He decides, finally, to give priority to his family commitments, and resolves that he will not be standing in the autumn election (the second of 1974).

It is easy to detect in Read's novel the moral parable of a man who neglects his domestic duties, and who loses his life partner before coming to his senses. This dimension is complicated, however, by the political parallel, which serves to devalue Strickland's rediscovered political commitments as another attribute of his personal crisis. He comes to doubt his convictions, wondering if his wife had been right that his political ambitions were the product of vanity and not idealism (pp. 242, 254). Here the personal and the political begin to diverge. Strickland certainly raises a number of issues that are central to the uncertain identity of socialism in the early 1970s and beyond. He wishes to challenge social inequality, but in the spirit of (Tory) Disraeli's one nation (p. 121); he wants a pragmatic policy of partial nationalization (p. 187); and, in general, he promotes a distinctly modern form of socialism based on 'enlightened self-interest' (p. 94). These convictions are made compatible with his celebration of the achievements of welfare-state socialism in the post-war years (p. 51), and an increasing unease that the benefits of the State are being 'expropriated and exploited' by a 'new bourgeoisie' which, for example, finds ways of monopolizing the best comprehensive schools (p. 150). In all of this there is a calm, retrospective summation of the claims of socialism, set against the fears of Left extremism that were prominent throughout the 1970s.

The conflict that eventually emerges between the personal and the political is perhaps best described as a tension between the 'case-by-case' pragmatism that Strickland acquires from his legal training, and a contrary desire for general principles of ethical behaviour. Indeed, Strickland's crisis is set in motion, in one sense, by the professional failure of the opening scene, where, to save himself some time, he wrongly advises an innocent man to plead guilty. Rather than the anticipated suspended sentence, six months' imprisonment results. Having been drawn into a criminal lifestyle, this unfortunate character (in the pay of Paula Gerrard) is later to murder Strickland's wife. The element of parable is, again, striking: the man who neglects the needs of others will reap what he sows. What the novel is really pushing towards is a combination of such a general ethical principle – respect for the other's needs – with the kind of flexible, negotiated politics that might (for example) produce a case-by-case assessment in the policy of nationalization. Read's implicit message is that such a combination is necessary for the proper unification of private and public realms, even though it seems impossible in a secular world bereft of moral principle, but governed by simplistic political sloganeering. Only the novel, Read suggests, supplies a way of holding the contrary impulses together in a meaningful tension.

## The Post-Consensus Novel

A general loss of faith in post-war consensus politics became manifest in the 1970s, although this had been brewing for over a decade. During the period 1950–1970, despite the consumer boom, Britain lost its prosperous standing as a world power, and became one of Europe's less significant states. This is a relative matter since the British economy continued to grow, but not quickly enough to keep pace with its European competitors. Economic recession – for example in the midst of the oil crisis of 1973–4 – compounded matters, as did a worsening of industrial relations through the 1970s.[31] The agreement between political parties about the post-war style of government, with its commitment to state intervention, a managed economy, and a conciliatory approach to industrial relations, was ready to collapse.

The election of Margaret Thatcher as Prime Minister in 1979 signalled the definite end of the post-war consensus. The policies of Thatcherism attacked consensus politics on every front: her government stood for privatization and a free-market economy, and for the reform of trade union law. Backed by an authoritarian approach to resisting groups, and a monetarist squeeze on inflation, the Thatcher government 'redefined' British politics just as the point of impasse had been reached. It is, consequently, possible to overstate the importance of Thatcherism as a political philosophy, since the state of the nation, as well as developing global trends, facilitated its success. Nevertheless, the changes to British society and culture were dramatic, generating a spirit of either adventurous entrepreneurship or deplorable avarice, depending on your point of view. Novelists tended to take the latter view, lamenting the imminent collapse of the welfare state, and a new era of inequality and social division.

Martin Amis's *Money* (1984), set in 1981–2, is a transatlantic satire of the emerging Reagan–Thatcher era and its mood of acquisitiveness. The protagonist's name, John Self, proclaims the intention to make him representative of the period. He shuttles between London and New York in the process of making a movie, and leading a hedonistic lifestyle on apparently inexhaustible funds. Self is a gross figure, 'addicted to the twentieth century' (p. 91), and most particularly to alcohol, pornography, and his own misogynistic world-view. The defining aspect of the urban junk culture he inhabits is its vicious triumvirate of money–power–sex, the commodification of sexual relations along patriarchal lines, which also characterizes the culture more generally. This dehumanization is attached to the cities that fashion Self's high-octane lifestyle. London, which in summertime is 'unlovely', an 'old man with bad breath' (p. 85), is a place of population density and psychological confusion, where the ongoing division of houses into smaller dwellings is replicated in the inhabitants who 'are doubling also, dividing, splitting' (p. 63). American cities, meanwhile, are credited by one character with 'the worst, the biggest, the most desperate ratshit slums in the civilized world' (p. 115).

Self is an apolitical figure, yet he is perceptive enough to carry the satirical load in his realization (gleaned from the tabloids) that unemployment is producing 'social crack-up in the torched slums', that 'inner cities crackle with the money chaos' (p. 66). The satire is directed at the condition of England principally, and specifically at the context of the 1981 inner-city riots (p. 155), which began in Brixton, but soon spread to other cities;[32] but this political critique implies an alternative, that things need not be so, and signals the element of the book that takes it beyond an earnest satire, with a fixed anchor.

Insofar as *Money* is able to establish a moral position, this is achieved through the merging of Self and Amis, a process which involves the occasional projection of the writer's sensibility on to his vile creation, making him seem imprisoned and unable to realize the potential within: Self is an addict of the urban money culture from which he sometimes longs to escape (p. 123).

A very different fictional strategy, but no less inventive, is pursued by Margaret Drabble. At first glance the seriousness of *The Radiant Way* (1987), her most important political novel, can seem puzzlingly forced or artificial. In D. J. Taylor's reading, for example, Drabble's 'deliberate refraction of the national consciousness' can be read off from the list of topics that her characters discuss, producing 'an inventory rather than a piece of art'. Taylor is making a general complaint about the political fiction of the 1980s, based on his impression that it was newspaper headlines, rather than the observation of real life, that supplied the inspiration.[33]

Drabble, certainly, is intrigued by the media representation of political life; but this is a substantive theme in her fiction, and so something more than an indication of sterile research. But Taylor's real charge stems from the 'stylisation' which 'was endemic to nearly every area of 1980s analysis'; with the consequence that novelists, like everyone else, betrayed a tenuous 'grip on political reality'.[34] If there is something stilted in *The Radiant Way*, perhaps this can be explained, following Taylor, as a product of a broader cultural drift towards surface explanations. However, a more convincing reason for the constrained earnestness of Drabble's novel may be the tension between the drive towards a panoramic social inclusiveness and the narrower focus on the middle-class lives of the three central female characters. Often with the novel, this kind of structural tension is productive rather than debilitating; and this is particularly true of *The Radiant Way*.

Despite the situation of (relative) privilege that all three protagonists share, their experiences allow the novel to range from middle- to working-class concerns (and to register the weakening of this distinction), and to encompass North and South. The novel treats major themes – poverty, education, crime, and punishment – as well as more sharply focused topics: the break-up of the traditional nuclear family; the violence of modern society; the problem of psychological disorder; and the possible consequences of satellite broadcasting. This is a vision of post-war society in which hopes and aspirations are partially fulfilled, only to be deflated or devalued through the perceived social disintegration of the 1980s.

Liz Headleand, Alix Bowen, and Esther Breuer meet at Cambridge in the 1950s, forming an enduring bond of friendship. Their careers emerge in a new mood of national optimism, 'the brave new world of Welfare State and County Scholarships, of equality for women'. The fate of these characters, the narrator informs us, 'should ... be in some sense at least exemplary' (p. 88). Anticipating their university years the three articulate their aspirations:

> 'I would like,' said Liz, ... 'to make sense of things. To understand.' By things, she meant herself. Or she thought she meant herself. 'I would like,' said Alix, 'to change things.' By things, she did not mean herself. Or thought she did not mean herself. 'You reach too high,' said Esther. 'I wish to acquire interesting information. That is all.' (p. 85)

The narrator leaves Esther's more modest ambitions unmolested, but ironically undercuts the confused naivety of both Liz and Alix, in ways that prefigure their experiences. Liz, the successful psychotherapist with premises in Harley Street, has the most to lose at the outset, and indeed loses her husband, her stepchildren (technically), and her house. The circumstances of these losses provide an index of political change in a novel in which personal bonds and actions are inevitably conditioned by political affiliation and commitment. Her husband, Charles Headleand, is presented as a turncoat in all aspects of his life. Formerly a maker of 'punchy social-conscience documentaries', he has enjoyed a rise 'through managerial and executive posts', and is to abandon Liz, as the 1980s commence, for Lady Henrietta Latchett, who 'closely resembled the dead wood to which, as a younger man, he had taken the axe' (p. 118). Liz, the psychotherapist with the repressed history of childhood abuse, is shown to be ill-equipped to 'make sense of things', including herself.

For Alix Bowen, too, the 1980s bring disillusionment. Her work teaching English language and literature to female prisoners is undermined by her failure to change materially the lives of her pupils. Although poor, she and her husband Brian – the working man turned novelist and lecturer in Adult education (p. 105) – seem to represent a strong ideological pact. Alix, however, comes to feel that she has been fighting 'the wrong battle' (p. 337), that the socialist vision has been defeated, and this affirms the narrator's arch premonition that her desire to change the world may be made opaque by a change in herself.

Only Esther, pursuing 'interesting information' in her career as art historian, seems to fulfil her ambitions. There are disillusionments for her as well, but in her relatively modest aspirations to be a brilliant lecturer with no desire to publish, the novel might seem to advocate a kind of quietism. As is often the case in Angus Wilson's novels, however, the possibility of low impact living, and the social disengagement it implies, is exposed as a false option.[35] When Esther's upstairs neighbour is arrested as the Harrow Road murderer, media attention forces her to sell her flat. In retreat from the social connectivity the episode demonstrates, she then decides to move to Italy. The novel, in fact, is an enactment of Alix's perception of 'the social structure' as 'a vast web, a vast network' in which 'we are all but a part of a whole which has its own, its distinct, its other meaning' (pp. 72–3). *The Radiant Way* insists that this 'other meaning' has become inscrutable: Charles and Liz were both brought up on a reading primer called 'The Radiant Way', a title that Charles adopts ironically for the fêted documentary series, attacking privilege and divisiveness in British education, that makes his name (p. 174). The irony rebounds, of course, as Charles divests himself of all vestiges of that 'radiant' social vision. For Liz the memory of the reading primer helps unlock the memories of her abusive father, a decidedly double-edged illumination (p. 386).

The ironic associations of the title are caught in the studied closing image, when the three friends witness an arrested sunset, after a summer picnic that approaches a pastoral idyll:

> The sun is dull with a red radiance. It sinks. Esther, Liz and Alix are silent with attention. The sun hangs in the sky, burning. The earth deepens to a more profound red. The sun bleeds, the earth bleeds. The sun stands still. (p. 396)

The stasis of this conclusion embodies a curious ambivalence in which the progression from radiance to an image of blood and suffering is interrupted by the checked sunset. It is the narrator's artifice, in effect, that arrests the characters' attention, and that underscores the difficulty of weaving a cohesive social web or network in fiction. This challenging ending achieves in miniature that which the novel attempts as a whole. Despite the portrayal of a society that is losing its head through blood-letting of one kind or another (the activities of the Harrow Road murderer, decapitating his victims, symbolizes that which is happening to the body politic), there is a sense of *density* in this novel, by virtue of its thematic layering and complex plotting, that delivers a resistant form, defying the perceived social collapse through its own intricacies.

This kind of intricate formal 'resistance' is an artistic response to an era of political simplification, and the blunt policies it engendered. The authoritarianism of the Thatcher years was marked by intolerant and repressive responses to dissident groups, for instance. Dissidence, however, was broadly defined, so that responsible individuals, believing themselves to be acting according to their moral conscience, were hailed as part of Thatcher's 'enemy within'. The oddity of this is nowhere more apparent than in relation to the Green movement, which later came to be very much in tune with public concerns following the successive food health scares of the 1990s (the BSE crisis, the popular distrust of Genetically Modified foods, and so on). In the 1980s, however, to be Green was sometimes to be an enemy of the state, a subject for surveillance.

The suspicious death in 1984 of an elderly anti-nuclear campaigner, Hilda Murrell, brought this question of repressive surveillance into the open. The Labour MP Tam Dalyell suggested in parliament that Murrell, who had been writing a paper for the public inquiry into the building of a new nuclear reactor at Sizewell in Suffolk, was murdered by members of the British Intelligence Service.[36] The episode inspires Maggie Gee's novel *Grace* (1988), in which her eighty-five-year-old eponymous heroine seems doomed to experience the same kind of fate that Hilda Murrell may have suffered, targeted by a deranged private investigator, in the pay of a shady government official. Gee's ostensible purpose is to identify the insanity of a repressive state that might wish to kill a Hilda Murrell on account of what 'she thought, and wrote, and argued'. On this basis, thinks Grace's niece Paula, 'no one is safe any more in England' (p. 100). After the Chernobyl disaster in 1986, and the Great Storm, which buffeted Britain in 1987, Gee is able to put Murrell's concerns about the hazards of nuclear waste in a broader environmental perspective.

In an article lamenting the dominance of the historical novel, and arguing that historical fiction inhibits the fictive imagination through its appeal to factual authority, Gee suggests that in *Grace* she sought to keep fact and fiction quite separate. The story of Grace, she claims, is conceived as a parallel to the real life episode, a 'fictional metaphor' revitalized by fact.[37] Gee is also interested, however, in the kind of novel that combines fact and fiction, producing the hybrid sometimes described as 'faction'. Paula is a writer trying to write a novel about Hilda Murrell, though doubting that her story is substantial enough for the purpose (p. 69). Gee, by supplying the parallel with Grace, supplements the Murrell case and usefully bridges fact and fiction. Grace is imaginary, but her experiences imply that the alleged state killing of an elderly lady could occur in more than one scenario.

The important technical issue for Gee, however, and a question that the novel asks out loud, is what kind of political novel remains possible. Conscious that a form of direct angry commentary might destroy the novelist's art, in the way that Paula's plays about nuclear waste and related themes have been deemed 'untheatrical' (p. 5), Gee interweaves explicitly fictional devices and allusions with her political theme. The most obvious of these is the dynamic of the thriller, which leaves Grace's fate unclear until the final page. The other is an extended allusion to Virginia Woolf, in Grace's planned (and continually deferred) trip to the lighthouse in the seaside town in which she grew up. The storms of 1987 finally intervene, causing her to abandon all notion of the trip. Human destructiveness, this time in the form of the presumed effects of global warming, cuts Gee's fictional world off from the redeeming symbolism of Woolf. This is ominous, since the lighthouse, saviour of countless human lives, is almost as old as Grace (p. 172). The doom this seems to presage, however, is denied when Grace is pulled from the clutches of the murderous Bruno, the machismo lunatic who is a pawn in a bigger political game (p. 196).

Gee imposes the relief of the customary resolution to the cliffhanger, the heroine snatched from the jaws of death at the last possible moment. But the relief is artificial, superimposed; and in this respect Gee is suggesting something gloomy from the perspective of the political writer in the 1980s. The structure of the popular thriller, particularly in this kind of felicitous outcome, is shown to be at odds with the political logic of the chosen scenario. At the same time, the conventional devices of the novelist are either unavailable or inappropriate in a culture where the popularly recognized trappings of espionage – surveillance and extermination – have been overlaid on everyday experience, and so, normalized. Artificial forms, Gee's *Grace* implies, are required to engage with artificial forms of government.

Unquestionably the most significant novel about the effects of Thatcherism is Jonathan Coe's *What a Carve Up!* (1994), a work that, again, demonstrates the novelist's conviction that an elaborate fictional form is required to offer a meaningful commentary on a fragmented society. Coe's is an extraordinary literary achievement: a work of high moral outrage that avoids polemics; a work of great flair that ranges assuredly between the poles of comedy and tragedy; a book that alludes confidently to both 'highbrow' and popular culture; and that places its judgement of Thatcherism tellingly in a broader post-war perspective.

The present of the novel runs from September 1990 to January 1991, and encompasses the enforced resignation of Thatcher in November 1990; the political coverage of the novel is extended to embrace the escalation of the Gulf War and the commencement of the assault on Iraq in January 1991. The trends that the novel examines, however, are identified as Thatcherite trends. The novel holds up the following as the consequences of Thatcherite free-enterprise, privatization, and deregulation: the hypocrisy of the arms to Iraq affair; the undermining of the National Health Service; the intellectual impoverishment of the media; a sequence of stock-market scandals; the poisoning of the food chain in the pursuit of profit; and the displacement of aesthetic values in the art world. The chief villains are the younger Winshaws, siblings and cousins, and each of them pursues a self-serving career in one of these areas, fertile for exploitation. These characters are caricatures of a new unethical elite, and together they represent the full range of social devastation, which the novel lays at the door of the Thatcher era. Thatcher's contemptuous definition of consensus as 'the process of abandoning all beliefs, principles, values and policies', cited approvingly by one of the Winshaws (p. 135), is the kind of tenet that justifies brute competition, and, so Coe's novel suggests, elevates the demolition of collective organization to a principle of government.[38]

In all of this there is an implicit debate about what kind of state-of-the-nation novel it is still possible to write. Coe's elaborate and ingenious plot has at its heart the writer Michael Owen, who in some measure stands for Coe. (He has written two well-received novels, 'Accidents Will Happen' and 'The Loving Touch' [p. 284], with titles similar to Coe's first two novels, *The Accidental Woman* (1987) and *A Touch of Love* (1989).) Owen has undertaken to write the history of the Winshaw family, but his own life is gradually revealed to be inextricably bound up with their activities. Agribusiness, the running down of the NHS, the embezzlement of a pension fund – these are some of the nefarious endeavours that play a causal role in successive personal tragedies for Owen. Thus, the writing persona becomes the symbolic victim of an era in which the promise of the Beveridge Report – that blueprint for the post-war welfare state – is shown to have been finally extinguished. This is Coe's ingenious device for generating recognition in his readership in the post-consensus era: through an intricate plot of apparent chance and coincidence, Coe is really demonstrating the social interconnections that remain, and that, neglected, have become channels for exploitation and suffering.

The reinvigoration of social connection, then, depends on Owen's status as a kind of Everyman, shaken from his own withdrawn existence, and galvanized into an angry repudiation of the Winshaw dynasty. This reinvigoration also draws in the function of the novel. In a review of a novelist hailed as 'a socialist realist', Owen highlights the failure of the contemporary political novel to offer anything more radical than a few 'elementary tricks with narrative' (p. 276). The review continues to set out the difficult task for the post-consensus novel in re-establishing moral order:

> We stand badly in need of novels . . . which show an understanding of the ideological hijack which has taken place so recently in this country, which can see its consequences in human terms and show that the appropriate response lies not merely in sorrow and anger but in mad, incredulous laughter. (p. 277)

Of course, it is precisely such a novel that Coe sets out to write, a novel that veers dramatically from farce to pathos, realism to metafiction, in a unique satirical statement. The role of the author in this is an acknowledgement that all citizens, and all aspects of cultural life, have a role to play in fashioning an equitable kind of society. The condemnation of the public's indifference to politics – expressed as the madness of tolerating greed (p. 485) – places expectations on the writer, too; though it may be that the unique nature of *What a Carve Up!* indicates that Coe's gesture is unrepeatable.

For both Coe and Drabble, the need for inventive fictional forms betrays the urgent need to fashion some surrogate form of social network, and this can be seen as an elaborate creative reply to Margaret Thatcher's infamous conviction that society does not exist. Thatcherism, of course, promoted the efforts of competing individuals in the place of the welfare state, but this is rarely seen by the novelist as the stimulus for a revitalized economy. Rather, it is a strategy deemed to have introduced an ethos of competitive self-advantage into British life, thereby undermining the vestiges of social cohesion. In *The Child in Time* (1987) Ian McEwan speculated about how far the attack on society could be taken. He projects an unchecked Tory regime in the Thatcher mould, still in power in the mid-1990s for a fifth term of office, and now seeking to fashion from birth the citizen receptive to authoritarian government, through the publication of an illiberal HMSO Childcare Handbook.[39] The novelist, confronted with a political philosophy founded upon the competition between individuals, would invariably take the view of Sheila Rowbotham, that 'the end result was not a more stable country but a disintegratory sense that survival, success or cardboard city was a matter of chance.'[40]

Philip Hensher's *Kitchen Venom* (1996) provides an apt conclusion to this discussion of the Thatcher era, since this is a novel which seeks to dramatize the point of view of the principal figure: the conceit of Hensher's book is that its omniscient perspective is supplied by Margaret Thatcher herself. Her voice is heard at the outset, at the point of her 1990 downfall, reflecting on the loss of 'omnivolence' ('willing everything') (p. 2) even whilst her omniscient capacity remains intact, though she acknowledges that this, too, has gone at the novel's close (p. 259). The narrative over which she is then taken to preside, by virtue of two or three further moments of direct address, concerns the sterility of the Palace of Westminster, and the subtle corruption that infects the principal character John, Clerk of the Commons Journal. (This is the journal in which decisions are recorded; it is distinct from Hansard, the inclusive record of proceedings in the Commons.)

Hensher, who was himself a House of Commons Clerk, conveys a deadened human response in his depiction of the Clerks, whose lives are governed by the unchanging procedural principles of the House. The hump-backed and recently widowed John, a man with a passion for secrets, has taken to visiting a handsome Italian rent-boy (Giacomo) in the afternoons, and has even begun to wonder if he might like his homosexuality to be recognized, and to settle down with a man. However, when Giacomo expresses a similar desire to make things more permanent, John murders him in a shocking moment of apparently unmotivated violence (p. 176). It is the threat to secrecy that generates John's murderous terror, indicating that secrecy is the *modus operandi* at the heart of government. This reversal of the democratic principle, at its source, is neatly figured in the idea of 'kitchen venom' and the paradox of 'a place nourishment was produced, and a place from which poison could come' (p. 183).

Rather than a vague truism about how power corrupts, Hensher seems to imply something more specific in his reliance on the 'omniscient' Thatcher, ousted from power, yet still obsessed with it (p. 209). The idea of 'kitchen venom', the poison which emanates from the supposed source of nourishment, fits very well the public perception of Thatcher, the Iron Lady, who formerly had made her capacity to combine domestic competence with her career ambitions a focus of her political identity.[41]

## Intimations of Social Collapse

As an encompassing social vision has become increasingly difficult to sustain in the post-consensus era, there has been a shift of focus, a recalibration of the typical point of view in political fiction. The impressive technical efforts of Coe and Drabble to resurrect the collective also indicate that the alternative option, the focus on marginal and dispossessed figures, is more natural, because more representative of prevailing social changes. Indeed, the political novel since the 1980s has invariably had recourse to this approach, with its tacit acknowledgement of social fragmentation, or even the suggestion of social collapse.

A good example of the off-beat or quirky breed of political novel that can result from this shift of emphasis is Hilary Mantel's *Every Day is Mother's Day* (1985), which depicts a society in confusion and chaos, beyond the redemption of the welfare state. The novel is a savage black comedy, with its focus on a deranged woman and her handicapped daughter, that represents an oblique approach to questions that assume a social centrality as the novel unfolds. The novel is set in the mid-1970s, but is published a decade later; the mood it reflects, however – the loss of faith in welfare measures – is representative of the public mood throughout the 1980s and beyond.

Evelyn Axon, once a spiritualist medium, now tormented by the thought that she has allowed malign forces into her house (the novel cultivates some credulity in the supernatural), lives with her handicapped grown-up daughter Muriel, fending off the attentions of a long line of social workers.

Her resentment of 'the Welfare' (p. 19) has a more general significance, identifying a popular cynicism that assists the obstruction of progressive social measures, a frustration also felt by the Labour Party, according to one character (p. 106). The Axons are the focus of a social dysfunction that socialism is now failing to address. There are no direct references, but a Labour government is in power for most of the novel's action; and Mantel holds up the chattering classes as the principal object of satire.

There is a dinner-party scene, hosted by schoolteacher Frank O'Dwyer, which is governed by drunken mayhem and violence, and this, ironically, is the novel's most dysfunctional episode. This scene establishes the social irresponsibility of the aspiring professional set (O'Dwyer has become an educational advisor in the sequel, *Vacant Possession* (1986)), with its Bohemian affectations. In the course of conversation social workers are dismissed as 'interfering do-gooders', while the 'Caring Society' is contemptuously discounted (p. 159). The whiff of despair and social collapse is endemic: even the social worker assigned to the Axons is affected, as she has a drunken elderly father who finds sexual solace amongst the female down-and-outs he can pick up in the local launderette, or in Woolworth's café (p. 58).

The political context to which Mantel responds in *Every Day is Mother's Day* is one in which 'the personal social services became a prime candidate for economies', particularly from the mid-1970s onwards.[42] In the sequel, *Vacant Possession* (1986), it is the requirement for cutbacks and efficiency gains in healthcare through the 1980s, a period in which health authorities 'were instructed to abandon previously agreed norms for services', that supplies the political backdrop.[43] The loss of hospital places for psychiatric patients, released into the community as a consequence, is central to Mantel's theme of social chaos. Much of the plot, indeed, is generated by the release of Muriel Axon from her hospital ward, and her determination to settle old scores.

Mantel's concern, however, is not simply with government, and a particular climate of political policy, but more especially with the disappearance of traditional modes of social responsibility that make care in the home or the community so problematic. Muriel's fellow psychiatric patients are scheming to find a way back to their hospital ward soon after release (p. 159), whilst the care of the elderly Mrs Sidney (who imagines she is a member of the royal family) presents an intolerable burden to her son and daughter, even though they live next door to each other. The title *Vacant Possession* denotes an increasingly materialistic, but spiritually bankrupt society incapable of coping with the problems it generates. Emulating the black comedy of the earlier novel, the sequel employs an exaggerated plot of coincidence, and a generous hint of the supernatural to make the case that bad faith and deceit will rebound on the perpetrator. The Sidney family, who have suffered the manifestations of a possessed dwelling in the former Axon home, finally decide to move, but with the realization that 'it's us the flaws are built into' (p. 205). In the eerie conclusion, implying the tragic collapse of his family, Colin Sidney receives a phone call in his new modern home, apparently from the gloating dead spirits now in sole possession of the vacant Axon house (pp. 238–9).

The focus on marginalized and dispossessed figures presents a technical challenge, since without a modulating influence, such as Mantel's offbeat humour, it is an emphasis that can become mawkish. Handled carefully, however, the concentration on the personal plight can produce a telling impression of the state of the nation. In *Liza's England* (first published as *The Century's Daughter* [1986]) Pat Barker manages to combine a poignant individual portrait with a vivid evocation of changing social history. At one level the book is a depressing portrait of England in the 1980s, on the brink of social collapse; but Barker qualifies this impression by structuring her novel in such a way as to give a longer historical perspective.

Liza Jarrett is the century's daughter, born at the beginning of the twentieth century, and in her eighties in the novel's present. Living in a street earmarked for demolition, Liza witnesses the destruction of her community, transformed into a derelict wasteland populated by vandals, glue-sniffers, and muggers. Scenes from the 1980s are interspersed with episodes from different stages in Liza's hard working-class life, and this establishes a certain continuity in the portrayal of social inequality and dispossession. However, Barker stresses a crucial difference between the disappearing working-class community of Liza Jarrett and the new social wasteland of the 1980s. In a discussion with Stephen, the gay social and youth worker who befriends her, Liza presents political consciousness as a matter of maturity (she was a member of the Labour Party), but also as a logical extension of the community's social code: 'we had a way of life, a way of treating people', she avers (p. 218). Stephen seeks to locate an index of social change in the contrasting attitude of the disaffected and violent youths he works with, concluding that the link has gone that drove the community socialism of earlier decades. One of the group claims that the enthusiasm for Mrs Thatcher amongst 'the lads round here' is that she gave them the Falklands War, 'the only *real* thing that'd ever happened to them'. This one-dimensional view of politics, and the deluded idea of reality (these lads had watched the war on television) depicts a generation with an infantile understanding of politics, and with distorted, solipsistic expectations of self-fulfilment (p. 196).

Liza startles Stephen with her optimism for the future. In her view, poor social planning and provision merely suppresses positive impulses: 'shut people up in rabbit hutches and what are they supposed to do? But give them a chance and it's still there.' The transition from traditional terraced housing to high-rise estates is shown to be accompanied by a loss of 'spirit', a loss marked by possessiveness and lack of trust (p. 250). Stephen, more pessimistic than Liza, feels the change is permanent, that he is 'witnessing the creation of a people without hope' (p. 219). When Liza is attacked and robbed in her home (an assault from which she does not recover) Stephen's gloomier prognosis appears to be the more accurate: Liza's assailants are those disaffected youths whom, in her discussion with Stephen, she had not allowed to perturb her fundamental social optimism. In a country in which 'every fortnight somebody tries to burn an Asian family alive in its own home' (p. 263), the mugging of a sickly old lady in a virtually derelict street might be taken as just another depressing statistic. Barker's achievement, with the readjustment that fiction facilitates, is to make the death of Liza, and the destruction of Liza's England, a national tragedy, denoting that pervasive loss of spirit that seems inevitable in the absence of a shared social vision.

The shifting terrain of the modern political novel, from the scene of public life to urban dereliction, is exemplified in Carol Birch's *Life in the Palace* (1988), a novel apparently set in the late 1970s, but which also catches the perception of inner-city decay that persists into the 1980s. *Life in the Palace* is thus a political novel that is deliberately vague in its analysis. Its depiction of the disappointed individuals gathered together in a condemned tenement block in Waterloo thus implies a trend of social decay that is beyond the control of any one government.

The lack of specificity might seem to suggest a brand of existential despair, an acknowledgement that violence and squalor must simply be ignored in the battle for sanity and survival, that (in the internal reflections of one character) 'you had to become like all the other eyeless, earless, mouthless human beings' (p. 42). This dehumanized image obviously refutes the 'human', and this kind of contradiction pervades the struggle of Birch's characters to find meaning in their lives. Drug addiction, alcohol abuse, poverty – these are the factors that hamper the residents of the Kinnaird Buildings in their efforts to make something of their lives. Loretta, a shop assistant convicted of running a credit-card scam on her till, at one moment glances at a photograph of a bunch of chrysanthemums on the back of a magazine, but what she actually sees is 'a hydrogen bomb exploding all in purple' (p. 223). This misperception denotes the profound alienation that leads to Loretta's suicide. When she makes her resolve to kill herself, Loretta is overcome by a curious perception of her relationship to London, viewed from the roof of the tenement block:

> Looking down, she saw cars and cats and kids. Looking up . . . she saw
> St Paul's, Big Ben, skyscrapers, tower blocks, chimneys, advertisement

> hoardings, back streets, traffic, shops, the railway, and it was in her power
> to banish all London into the void.
>     Somewhere inside her was a Black Hole sucking it all in,
> everything... She'd be the last to go. (p. 232)

The negativity of Loretta's alienation is imagined by her as more powerful
than the city, with its infrastructure, its public buildings, the seat of power
itself. The idea of Big Ben being sucked into the Black Hole of the dispossessed signals the political dimension, but the most arresting feature, here,
is the inverse image of one insignificant suicide unleashing chaotic forces
on the city. This serves economically to make the point that without an
engaged citizenship the city is as nothing; but it also underscores the sense
of a social armageddon, a developing post-war psychological collapse in
which immediate personal fears lead on to the greater fears, 'war, illness,
loneliness, cruelty, death, the whole caboodle' (p. 193). This is a new kind
of 'political' novel, offering no precise satirical observations, but conveying
a sense of broader alarm at the ongoing trends of late capitalism.

The realignment of political fiction, particularly in the turning away from
overtly public themes in some novels, suggests a tacit admission that the
inclusive social novel is less viable. The new focus on psychology is a means
of passively registering the effects of political change where a comprehensive
grasp of the political scene is elusive. Drabble's *A Natural Curiosity* (1989) is
another significant example of this adjustment, especially in the manner in
which it 'reads back' to *The Radiant Way*. It is a self-consciously paradoxical
book, which represents a deliberate change of focus from that embodied
in the earlier novel. This, the second book in a loosely connected trilogy,
follows the principle of curiosity that Liz Headland admits to, the desire
'to know *what really happened*... when human nature began' (p. 75). In
this, Drabble makes a hugely significant shift of emphasis from nurture to
nature, and this lends some validity to the narrator's arch claim that this is
'not a political novel', but rather a 'pathological' or 'psychotic novel' (p. 194).
No clear answers are offered; indeed, curiosity seems here to be the single
ennobling impulse, but one that is not sufficient in itself.

Paul Whitmore, the Harrow Road murderer from *The Radiant Way*, is
shown to have been brought up by a psychotic mother (before she abandoned her family), and this is one area in which Drabble extends the inquiry
begun in the first novel. But the question of whether Whitmore's brutality
is genetic or acquired is left open. The scene which condemns the mother
contains a resonant image of evil: she runs a dog kennel, on the premises
of which a closed annexe is found containing a heap of dead or dying dogs
beneath a maggoty horse's head, which has been suspended just out of the
dogs' reach, their only source of food (p. 283). This unfathomable cruelty

resonates beyond the novel's frame of explication, and seems to reinforce the tendency to view human atrocity from a broad historical perspective.

The texture is thus inconclusive, free of the density of contextual reference that anchors the earlier book, and this gives rise to a lighter mood overall. It has been observed that although 'the world view is still bleaker' in *A Natural Curiosity* than in *The Radiant Way*, its humour is 'richer' than in any earlier novel by Drabble.[44] This paradox implies the therapy of humour as a way of countering inexplicable brutality, an essentially apolitical response that also limits the function and purpose of curiosity. This limit is most evident when a productive resolution begins to emerge for Liz Headland over the problem of her dead mother: Drabble's self-consciousness spawns what is almost a burlesque of novelistic closure, and a disappointment of the consoling ending. It emerges that Liz's uncommunicative and selfish mother had had a child out of wedlock, before Liz was born, a child she was obliged to give up for adoption (p. 268). This social explanation for some of the distortions and misunderstandings of her family life – left unresolved in the earlier novel – is undermined by the authorial narrator's dismissal of Liz's new 'sister *ex machina*', an acknowledged convenience for plot resolution (p. 291). Drabble here draws attention to the political novelist's new doubt about the relative importance of nature and nurture, and the artificial props that may be necessary to achieve a determinate view. In *The Peppered Moth* (2000), a novel much preoccupied with the question of genetic inheritance, Drabble strays still further from her social concerns of the 1980s.

A self-conscious exposition of the limits of the political novel can also impose additional limits, however. This pitfall is well illustrated in David Lodge's *Nice Work* (1988), a parody of the Victorian condition-of-England novel. In producing this comic, but also sketchy representation of the divisions between industry and academia, Lodge is also parodying the mechanistic binary oppositions of some structuralist literary criticism. However, the England he depicts seems riven by the same failure to think beyond the schematic level, so there may be a surface mimesis in Lodge's method; but this still reveals a significant lacuna, and a widening gap between the complex nature of modern society and the impact of straightforward narrative realism, written in the third person.

## After Thatcher

The erosion of the kind of collective representation associated with third-person narrative realism has a variety of causes – there are literary and technical reasons, as well as social and historical ones – and the process really begins in earnest with the emergence of modernism at the end of the nineteenth century. The focus here is narrower, concentrating on how that ongoing development ties in with particular social anxieties in post-war Britain. But because the literary-historical trend is longer-term, one has to tread with caution in drawing conclusions about the contemporary social and political novel.

The example of Irvine Welsh's *Trainspotting* (1993) is instructive, here, since this is a novel that is sometimes taken as the embodiment of a definitive break with a lingering bourgeois tradition. Welsh has become the voice of junkie culture, devising a mode of fiction that reproduces social fragmentation and alienation, and that seems profoundly nihilistic in its implications. The novel is narrated from a variety of perspectives, and comprises a collection of violent and desensitized episodes, written in a broad Edinburgh dialectal form, that seems designed to alienate (especially) the liberal English literary mainstream. In social terms, the challenge is well founded. Welsh's depiction of heroin addiction in Edinburgh, the city with the highest rate of HIV infection in the UK (p. 193), uncovers a new kind of social divide in the festival city.

The morality of high culture is in question, but then so is the very idea of morality. The novel's vitality, argues Ian Haywood, stems from its 'debunking of the western Enlightenment tradition'.[45] In the scene in which Renton retrieves his opium suppositories from a filthy toilet bowl, he smears a bluebottle on the toilet wall, transforming it 'intae a work of art' (p. 25). This scene, occurring pointedly on the first day of the Edinburgh Festival, implies an alternative kind of cultural expression, alien to the liberal sensibility. In one sense, the novel finds a way of registering underclass disaffection, and showing that 'the prospects appear to be living on your wits more or less outside the law, and suffering the illnesses that accompany drug dependency in a deprived environment'.[46] Yet the pursuit of that alternative kind of expression indicates that Welsh is striving for something more than the raw exposure of new manifestations of inequality.

Here there is a paradox, because the book is held together by a series of quasi-epiphanic moments that signal a submerged moral code. There are a number of these moments. For example: Spud's realization that hate is futile (p. 129); Spud's horror at Renton's intended cruelty to a squirrel (p. 159); the realization of what it means 'to become a human being' in the episode 'Bad Blood' (p. 262). Even the pathologically violent Begbie is shown to be emotionally vulnerable (although the vulnerability unleashes further violence) after the encounter with his wino-father in the episode which gives the book its title (p. 309). In all of this there is a suggestion of a human collective struggling to re-emerge, suppressed by deprivation and social dysfunction. This collective is rooted in the glowing embers of a simple kind of human warmth, glimpsed momentarily when Renton visits the dying Tommy in hospital, and senses that 'something flashes between us' (p. 317). The cement that binds the multi-voiced work, with its cast of isolated individuals, turns out to be a still-persisting humanism, which is akin to the kind said to be repudiated by Welsh in the more iconoclastic interpretations of *Trainspotting*. A more sober assessment suggests that the novel is a disguised lament for a simpler and more human world – the stereotypical home and hearth values of the pre-war working classes, perhaps – an environment of nurture that is regrettably unavailable.

*Trainspotting* is thus quite distinct from the earlier cult-novel by another Scottish writer, with which it is sometimes linked: *Cain's Book* (1963) by Alexander Trocchi. (*Cain's Book* is a nihilistic account of drug-addiction often compared with *The Naked Lunch* by William Burroughs.) The submerged community of *Trainspotting* also distinguishes it from Welsh's subsequent fiction, in which a recurring theme of misogynistic sexual violence has become manifest; and that submerged community also implies that the coherence of the novel form depends upon some kind of appeal to the collective view, however concealed this may be.

It is an apparent paradox that the Thatcher era, systematically vilified in much of the literature it provoked, seems with hindsight to have ushered in a period of renaissance in English fiction. This may represent a coda to Bergonzi's evaluation of insignificance, in global terms, of English fiction in the earlier post-war decades. Thatcherism, as an international political phenomenon, was a radical and divisive political strategy that stimulated outrage from the novelist, whose broadly liberal sensibilities were deeply offended by the attack on traditional collective values. The apparent paradox, then, is merely one that confirms that valuable literature often feeds on a sense of moral outrage. Yet it is true that by the end of Thatcher's lengthy period of government, some of her most articulate opponents had established themselves in such a way as to make them the beneficiaries of the very policies they had decried.

In *Amsterdam* (1998), Ian McEwan offers a satirical portrait of those who 'had flourished under a government they had despised for almost seventeen years' (p. 12). In a sense, this is a deliberation on compromise, on left-intellectual achievement in an (apparently) hostile political context. Despite the author's first-hand knowledge of this stratum of the intelligentsia, there is no sense of explicit self-analysis: the narrative tone is detached, befitting the clinical dissection of amorality in the two principals. These two, newspaper editor Vernon Halliday and composer Clive Lindley, both face an ethical dilemma that will expose a fatal lack of substance in their professional conduct. For Halliday, the key moment involves his decision to publish compromising photographs of the xenophobic foreign secretary Julian Garmony. His paper 'The Judge' (modelled on 'modernizing' broadsheets

like *The Guardian*, *The Observer*, and *The Times*) faces its own internal struggle over editorial policy, so for Halliday his scoop should boost circulation,
and help take 'The Judge' downmarket in accordance with his policy of
modernization. But when Halliday chooses to publish his photographs of
the cross-dressing Garmony – a decision in any case tainted by personal
motivation – he is out-manoeuvred, and the 'scoop' explodes in his face.
Halliday fills an entire front page with an image of Garmony, sporting a
three-quarter-length dress, false breasts, and make-up. The 'highest professional standards' discernible in this 'classic' front page are those of a professional elite operating without an ethical code (p. 116). Halliday – 'once an
apologist for the sexual revolution' – now cashes in on a reactionary moral
conservatism (p. 73).

For Linley, the key moment of decision is more clear-cut. Linley considers
himself to be 'Vaughan Williams' heir' (p. 21), and his conservative musical
style has secured him the commission to write 'The Millennium Symphony'
for the celebrations in 2000. Unable to find the decisive variation that
will conclude the symphony satisfactorily, Linley goes walking in the Lake
District for inspiration. Here he begins to discern the motif for his finale in
the call of a bird, only to be disturbed by a disputing couple. (It transpires
that the woman is actually in the clutches of a serial rapist.) Linley leaves
her to her fate in order to preserve his creative spark, and departs hastily
from the Lakes in a state of agitated self-justification, concentrating on his
new-found 'sublime sequence of notes' (p. 89). The symphony, it transpires,
is flawed by its final movement when completed. In fact, the performance
is cancelled: the work is pronounced 'a dud', containing 'a tune at the
end' derivative of Beethoven (176). McEwan, in the portraits of his two
principals, exposes the vacuity of an enclosed professionalism, unresponsive
to the contradictions and complexities of social life. Linley turns his back
on a woman in distress, refusing to interpret the scene before him, much
as Halliday allows his obsession with ends to uncover the crudeness of his
professional means.

McEwan's real target is the decontextualized Grand Gesture, powerfully
symbolized in Linley's ruined Millennium Symphony. (Hindsight inevitably
brings the ill-conceived Millennium Dome to mind.) This consummately
realized novella – a sonata rather than a symphony – concludes with an
elegantly counterpointed dispensing of just deserts. Linley and Halliday have
a pact, so that if either of them were to develop a condition such as rapid-
onset Alzheimer's disease, the other would arrange a trip to Amsterdam,
with its relaxed Euthanasia laws, to curtail the suffering and indignity.[47] In
a mutual vendetta inspired by their pact, and justified by their respective
moral failures, they prove each other's nemesis, poisoning one another at
a drinks party in Amsterdam. A short novel can bear the neatness of this

plot device, which in any case conceals the more substantial point that it may be in the nature of an unselfconscious professionalism to dispense with ethical foundations. Such a state, satirized in this portrait of the 'humane' achievers of McEwan's own generation, is presented as a kind of dementia, best expunged.

The state-of-the-nation novel, it seems, struggles to survive in its conventional guise. It now requires the rare ingenuity of a Jonathan Coe to breathe life into the corpse. There are, however, some writers still striving to depict a broad and representative social range. Tim Pears is one such writer, whose third novel, *A Revolution of the Sun* (2000), uncovers significant continuity in the era of New Labour with the political and social values established by the previous administration. Coe is beginning to emerge as the instigator of this still-persisting school of political fiction. *A Revolution of the Sun*, in fact, contains echoes of Coe's two principal works to date. In Pears's concern with the arms trade and with animal rights one is reminded of *What a Carve Up!*, whilst his treatment of laboratory experiments brings Coe's *The House of Sleep* (1997) to mind. (The use of narcolepsy, both as a plot device, and to suggest some broader social amnesia, looks like a particular borrowing from the latter novel.) Both Coe and Pears contribute to a broader millennial *Angst* in British fiction, directed against the corporate (and political) control of medical and agricultural science. In other respects, however, Pears diverges from Coe. He is more explicit in his treatment of a disenfranchised underclass and the failure of socialism, and this is one of several ways in which Pears's novel is specifically located in the political climate of Tony Blair's first year in office.

Pears uses the nineteenth-century convention of a year's span for his narrative, opening at a New Year party on the eve of 1997. This unashamed use of a traditional structure is matched by the straightforward use of a third-person narrator, in marked contrast to the technical juggling which has become common in the attempt to discover a new authenticity for the narrative voice. 'Sam Caine', an amnesiac bereft of his social identity, is the novel's martyr, kidnapped and killed for experimentation by 'The Laboratory'. This research institute, appropriated by financial and political players, is Pears's main satirical target. The institute's goal is to find a route to immortality through biological engineering, though the hubris of this is explicitly condemned in the allegorical strand involving Sam Caine (anagram of 'amnesiac'), the man without a history, whose death symbolizes the self-destructive impulse of profiteering medical science.

Before his death, however, the amnesiac has sired a child whose birth occurs at the end of the novel, with the dawning of a new year. Pears uses explicitly Christian imagery to evoke the second coming, and the emergence of a new era of hope. He even has angelic figures popping up at key moments to guide and reassure the protagonists who will preside over the birth. This curiously unembarrassed device is another aspect of Pears's reassertion of broader social 'faith'; but it also – and quite deliberately – stretches credulity, and in doing so tacitly acknowledges the difficulty of winning back a fictional mode suitable for a consensus vision at the end of the millennium.

Like Coe, Pears is deeply concerned about a society without historical dimension or collective responsibility, and that is preoccupied with immediate future gain. But the extravagant devices to which he has recourse to contest this trend seem to expose the limits of the fully fledged political novel at the dawn of the twenty-first century. This is not to suggest that the novel is unable to engage closely with history and society, but rather to indicate that a narrower focus has become necessary to make this engagement convincing, and to represent the particularity of individual voices in a society comprised of disparate groups. The subsequent chapters of this survey demonstrate some of the ways in which this has been achieved.

## Chapter 2

# Class and Social Change

It is often argued that the Second World War marked a watershed in British class relations. Obvious class distinctions were set aside in the face of a common crisis, and this pragmatism can be seen to have accelerated a process of change in the perception of class status.[1] This is not to deny the existence of inequality, or the persistence of class struggle in the post-war era. What the change in perception instigated is a popular demand for a wider share in the new prosperity that emerged in the 1950s, after the years of austerity. If the egalitarian social reconstruction proposed during the war did not materialize, it is still true that the post-war Labour government enacted policies that 'in general...favoured the working class'.[2] The broad trend since then has been towards greater prosperity for working people, a process that undermines the economic basis of class affiliation. Despite this, however, class in British culture was (and remains) fraught with contradiction and confusion, especially where persistent class loyalties are shaken, or even rendered irrelevant, by social and economic change, and yet are not relinquished.

The shape of British politics, however, helped to consolidate a more simplistic understanding of the class struggle. In David Cannadine's reading, perceptions of class for 'the Welfare State generation of 1945–79' were governed by a presumed instrumental link between economic change and social change, and by the assumption that class conflict governed the key economic and social debates. Lying behind this dominant mood of political and social conflict was the formation of the Labour Party, which in 1918, in the infamous Clause Four of its constitution, had made 'the common ownership of the means of production' a defining goal. A phase of class struggle, polarized along party-political lines and that was to dominate twentieth-century British politics, was thus ushered in, with the Labour Party advancing the interests of the workers in a direct clash with the Conservatives, the party of capitalism.[3]

Arthur Marwick has shown how conventional images of class have persisted in surveys of public opinion. Referring to data from 1945 through to 1984, he demonstrates that the distinction between the 'middle' and 'working' classes remained constant in the popular imagination, with the term 'upper class' remaining in view, but with a dwindling relevance. (In 1984 only 0.2 per cent of those surveyed placed themselves in an 'upper' class. In 1945 the figure had been 2 per cent.)[4] Of course, ingrained class loyalty is often based on social markers that resist brute economics, so that the tension between the ideological perception of class and its material under-pinnings becomes more and more pronounced. Even so, there is also a common perception that the codes and offices of a ruling class are being steadily dismantled, and this implies a dynamic of social levelling, and the expansion of a middlebrow culture. Narrative fiction has played its part in this changing perception, and the dominant schools of writing in the 1950s and 1960s were overtly populist.

## 'The Movement'

'The Movement' of the 1950s was first given this significant appellation – the definite article, the capital M – in 1954 by J. D. Scott, the literary editor of the Spectator, in an anonymous leading article. Two poets (Donald Davie and Thom Gunn) and three novelists (Kingsley Amis, Iris Murdoch – oddly, as it now seems – and John Wain) were named as leading figures in a developing tide of progressive robustness.[5] Scott's article was not the first to detect a new mood, especially in poetry, that was dismissive of modernist obfuscation; yet his piece did serve to consolidate this emerging critical view. Even so, discussion of the Movement is sometimes complicated by its overlap with the (only slightly later) School of Angry Young Men, including the playwright John Osborne, and novelists like John Braine and Alan Sillitoe. Kingsley Amis's *Lucky Jim* (1954) is sometimes seen to have heralded the impending arrival of the 'Angry' generation, associated with Osborne's play *Look Back in Anger* (1956). It may be more appropriate, however, to read *Lucky Jim* as embodying the sensibility of the Movement primarily, since its 'anger' is of a distinctly different hue to that of Osborne or Sillitoe.

Blake Morrison authoritatively defines the sensibility of the Movement, rooted in the qualities of rationalism, realism, and empiricism. (He also makes a convincing case for Amis's central role, despite the writer's own disavowals.)[6] Thus, despite the apparent 'invention' of the Movement in a piece of literary journalism, it did have a kind of coherence. The shared values of the central Movement writers, Amis, Davie, and Philip Larkin, were expressed as impatience with complexity, symbolism, and opacity. For Amis, it was retrograde to admire the modernists – Joyce, Woolf, and Proust all attracted his disapproval. Effective writing, he felt, should be direct, transparent.[7] Rather than an absolute rejection of formal values, however, Amis's 'manifesto', according to Richard Bradford, was in fact a populist 'technique of blending form and content' so that 'the intelligent reader will not require the professional critic' to explicate their interdependence.[8] Amis wanted to claw back whatever cultural power resides in literature on behalf of the ordinary intelligent reader, and it is this kind of challenge which identified the Movement with a spirit of social transition.[9] Movement writers thus appeared to ride a tide of class change, standing in opposition to the writing elite of previous generations. This was an impression instantly confirmed by those older writers, such as Stephen Spender, Edith Sitwell, Evelyn Waugh, and Somerset Maugham, who associated the Movement with declining social standards.[10]

The Movement's rebelliousness, however, was less substantial than it seemed. Indeed, it was riven by contradiction in its three main areas of assertion: the challenges to the class system, to cultural elitism, and to the metropolitan centre. *Lucky Jim*, which reveals contradictions in all three areas, thus supplies an excellent summation of the Movement's values and its limitations.

The inferiority of Jim Dixon, the 'shabby little provincial bore' as Margaret Peel calls him, in a moment of anger (p. 158), is conveyed in class terms, and in such a way apparently to reverse the assumed hierarchy: his escapades make him a kind of lower-middle-class Everyman exposing the sham gentility of people like the Welches. Even so, the object of his desire, Christine Callaghan, clearly occupies a higher social stratum and without the sham. Her uncle Gore-Urquhart, particularly, seems to be the epitome of upper-middle-class metropolitan values. There is, then, a distinct blurring of social status and sexual status in the novel's love plot, particularly in the portrayal of Christine Callaghan as the object of Dixon's social *and* sexual desire.

The novel's contradictions are systematically laid bare in the conclusion, where Dixon, the champion of ordinary provincialism, is rewarded by being stripped of his middlebrow credentials: his relationship with Christine, and his new job as private secretary to her aristocratic London-based uncle, a 'rich devotee of the arts' (p. 47), remove him from his class, cultural, and geographical bases. It would be ridiculous to suppose that Amis was unaware that his provincial fairy-tale undermined his own intellectual position. For Amis there appears to be a kind of inevitability about this, and this is the root of the quiet, but significant anger in *Lucky Jim*: it is a wry exasperation at the status quo and the compromises it seems to enforce. What the novel demonstrates historically, beyond its identification of a new cultural mood and the glimpse of social change, is a tacit acknowledgement of the gradual nature of these changes. It also dramatizes the Movement's impotence and incoherence, its inability to mount an effective challenge to existing institutions in the terms it set for itself. Jim Dixon's 'luck', the unmerited success that dislocates him so radically, reveals the absence at the heart of Amis's comic mode; but Amis identifies the source of this absence, and so offers a quiet warning about the essentially conservative nature of English society, and the obstacles that block the path to a genuine meritocracy.

A similar paradox is discernible in John Wain. Looking back on *Hurry on Down* (1953), nearly a quarter of a century later, John Wain suggested it originated in a young man's dissatisfaction with 'the shape of English society'. He claims to have been 'impatient' with 'class-distinctions' but only in the manner of a 'typical young person'.[11] Wain's hero Charles Lumley is burdened by middle-class expectations, but seeks to remain 'outside the class structure altogether' (p. 52). The series of jobs he takes on place him either in a lower-class bracket (window cleaner, hospital orderly, chauffeur), or outside the legitimate structures of society (drug-runner, bouncer in a seedy nightclub-cum-brothel). The limited challenge or rebellion he embodies tallies with Morrison's overview of the Movement writers, presented as less class-conscious or responsive to social change than their reputation suggests.

Writers like Amis and Wain identified with socialist agitation early in their careers (both Lumley and Dixon put forward socialist arguments), but never mounted a serious challenge to class distinction or privilege.[12] Indeed, the Movement writers have 'tried to discourage critics from thinking of their work as class-conscious and responsive to social change'; novels like *Lucky Jim* and *Hurry on Down* then appear to belong to 'a literature resourceful in managing to play down class differences whilst at the same time making class one of its central themes'.[13] George Orwell is sometimes revealed as the influence behind this partial rebellion, and as the justification for a later inclination towards the Right, in the name of anti-totalitarianism in the careers of writers like Amis and Wain.[14] There are certainly contradictions in *Hurry on Down* particularly with regard to its treatment of class, though it may be possible to ascribe these to the broader sense of social upheaval rather than simply to an inherited literary quietism.

## Anger and Working-Class Fiction

The contradictions that accompany class transformation are particularly marked in the working-class fiction of the 1950s and 1960s. This body of writing, often associated with 'Angry Young Men' John Braine and Alan Sillitoe, amounts to a school of gritty realism associated with the depiction of (especially) northern life. This apparent resuscitation of the working-class novel (which had previously been strong in the 1930s) might seem to reinforce class distinctions, or an 'us' and 'them' view of society.[15] A closer look at these novels, however, reveals that the identities on which such an opposition depends are now insecure.

The discordance between established class credentials and material self-advancement determines the mood of John Braine's *Room at the Top* (1957). This is probably the most famous post-war novel of class mobility, charting the material success of its working-class protagonist Joe Lampton, whose triumph flies in the face of more conventional power structures – Oxbridge, family connections, inherited wealth. The novel is narrated retrospectively by Lampton ten years on (p. 7), and this establishes a temporal framework of particular political significance. The novel's 'present' is established as 1946–7, so the time of narration a decade later is made to conform to the date of publication, with the wealthy Lampton reassessing his avaricious drive.[16] This dual temporal focus determines the reception: strictly speaking, Lampton's experiences belong to the immediate post-war years of rationing and austerity; yet the impetus towards re-evaluation by the older and wiser Joe connects the action with the later 1950s and the consumer boom.[17] In this way the novel invites its initial readership to make an anachronistic identification with Lampton's predicament, and so to think again about the preceding decade, which results in the material affluence of the later 1950s. The older wiser Lampton leaves us in no doubt what to think about his 'success': he acknowledges that his younger self 'was of a higher quality', more emotionally sensitive and responsive to others (p. 123). This is an explicitly cautionary tale, with Lampton, whose rise is 'the classic sell-out', appearing as 'a modern Faust'.[18]

It is immobility rather than mobility, however, that characterizes the predominant mood of the northern working-class novel of the period, indicating that ideological convictions do not keep pace with economic reality. In *This Sporting Life* (1960), David Storey produced an affecting work that is not easily explained. Usually taken as a piece of provincial documentary realism, the book draws on both the author's and his brother's experiences as professional rugby league players.[19] The success of Arthur Machin as a rugby league professional opens up an intriguing treatment of working-class ambitions.

Despite his status as a local celebrity with spending power, Machin is still caught in a familiar class trap, crystallized in the episode in which he takes his landlady Mrs Hammond and her children out for a meal in the restaurant of 'Howton Hall'. This converted old country house has separate eating areas: a café for the *hoi polloi*, and a more exclusive restaurant, which Machin favours. The waiter seeks by intimidation to make them feel that they have 'strayed over to the wrong side'. He points to the high prices on the menu with his pencil, and even underlines one or two prices for emphasis. Machin retaliates by ordering the most expensive items, by pedantically querying the bill, and by leaving a derisory tip. The 'sense of achievement' that Machin reports on their departure is belied by the sense of class stigma, and the failure of mobility that the episode underscores (pp. 82–4).

A sense of ossification pervades the novel, and the relationship between Machin and Mrs Hammond is doomed by the exploitative environment that has conditioned them. She lives in a state of perpetual shock after the death of her husband in an industrial accident (possibly suicide), and is by turns impassive and resistant in the face of Machin's aggressive (and confused) passion. It is not simply that she can no longer respond (p. 28); more significant is the fact that when she begins to tolerate Machin's interest, she knows he defines her, partly, as an acquisition (p. 145). She understands that his passion is of a piece with the exploitative system that has destroyed her husband and her happiness, and when Machin finally declares his love for her, she tries to spit in his face (p. 175).

Storey underscores the circular viciousness of a world of brute commodification. Machin works as a lathe operator at Weaver's, the same factory in which Mrs Hammond's husband had been killed. Weaver is also one of the two main backers of Primstone, the club for whom Machin signs, and for a handsome fee. This reward stands in pointed contrast to Weaver's refusal to admit liability for Eric Hammond's death. An iniquitous system of evaluation and human commodification links the worlds of sport and industry, and undermines the notion of escape through heroism and sporting prowess. Professional rugby, like manual labour, emerges as harsh, dangerous, and destructive: its element of alienated aggression has been falsely glamorized.

Alan Sillitoe's short story 'The Loneliness of the Long-Distance Runner' (1959) presents a similarly petrified class structure, but puts this observation into something that approximates an existentialist framework. The emphasis is on the ways in which individual free will is curtailed by pervasive systemic controls. The narrator of the story is the teenage Smith, sent to a borstal in Essex for stealing the takings of a bakery. Smith defines his social experiences in terms of an inescapable struggle between 'us' and 'them', that is social 'Out-laws' like him, in a perpetual contest with the 'In-laws', the forces of authority and conformity. In Smith's conception, this is essentially a struggle over wealth between those wage-earners in 'shops, offices, railway stations' (p. 10) who uphold bourgeois standards, and an underclass, epitomized by his own family.

The focus of the contest in the story is the battle of wills between Smith and the borstal governor, who wants him to train as a long-distance runner and win the All-England Borstal Cross Country Running Prize Cup (p. 39). Predictably, Smith throws the race on the big day, and is punished by the governor, motivated by petty vengeance (p. 53). Smith has an unshakeable conviction concerning the integrity and honesty of his refusal to conform, to become the governor's 'prize race horse' (p. 12), and the story's celebration of this 'honesty' goes beyond a confirmation of predetermined roles. The governor is not interested simply in the rehabilitation of Smith; rather, he wants the glory that winning the Prize Cup will bring (p. 39). It is this hypocrisy, this concealed use-function, that Smith resists. As when he is running, Smith experiences rootlessness and isolation – together with an ambivalent sense of liberation – in asserting himself against the pressure to conform.

More rooted in its context is Sillitoe's earlier *Saturday Night and Sunday Morning* (1958), a frank treatment of the short-term aspirations and satisfactions of a working-class Nottingham community. Arthur Seaton is a lathe operator in a bicycle factory who endures the hardships of factory life for the pleasures of Saturday night (despite the repentance that Sunday morning inevitably brings). He is a figure of ambivalent vitality. On the one hand, his distrust of authority enables him to avoid the exploitative pitfalls of piecework, and to earn (he feels) a reasonable wage (p. 32). Seaton is a distinctive example of the working-class protagonist in novels of this era since, unlike Joe Lampton or Vic Brown (in Stan Barstow's *A Kind of Loving* [1960]), he has no aspirations for material advancement or class mobility. Thus he betrays an element of class solidarity; but this political identity, an 'instinctive working-class anarchism' in Bradbury's phrase, is merely embryonic, unfocused.[20] And being 'instinctive', this anarchism is also ambivalent, since Seaton's energy leads him to excessive acts of hedonistic self-assertion, drinking, fighting, and pursuing married women. At one point he is conducting affairs with two married women (the sisters Brenda and Winnie) whilst also courting the girl he is to marry.

A pattern of personal development is implied after Brenda becomes pregnant by Seaton, and her sister Winnie's husband arranges a sound beating for him. He recuperates for several days, comforted by the loyal Doreen to whom he soon becomes engaged. The novel ends with Seaton self-consciously comparing himself to a caught fish, implying his willingness to be apparently 'trapped' in marriage, though he imagines his life will still be governed by the kind of 'trouble' that has characterized his youth (p. 219).

In Sid Chaplin's *The Day of the Sardine* (1961), Arthur Haggerston relates the story of his gradual acclimatization as a factory worker in the North-East, another story of adolescent rebellion defeated by the necessities of working-class life in an industrial city on the Tyne. The title conveys the sense of an inevitable destiny for sardine packers like Haggerston, compared to the sardines, caught in their masses to be tinned (p. 24). Haggerston's awareness that he's been 'caught' (like Arthur Seaton) only adds to the claustrophobia that this novel successfully evokes (p. 263). Chaplin does not, however, offer a properly articulated class struggle; indeed, the novel demonstrates that Haggerston does not have an effective alternative to his looming fate.

In the novel's one overt discussion of class, Haggerston's elder co-worker George Flack insists that there is no such thing as 'class', that society is governed by 'caste' instead. Arthur and his pals, advises Flack, 'could get together and make a caste' from which they would derive 'as much satisfaction as the nobs' (p. 110). Much of the novel serves to underscore the inadequacy of this analysis. Haggerston, in fact, becomes increasingly involved in gangland activities that culminate in a violent episode, after which his capitulation and conformity seem inevitable. This gang culture is unstable, vulnerable to the emergence of individual interests.[21]

The only consolation for Haggerston (as is typical of the working-class anti-hero of the 1960s) is an 'illicit' sexual liaison with a married woman, the eventual failure of which leaves him bereft (p. 263). An interesting aspect of many of these novels is how the narrative impetus often colludes with adolescent male desires for sexual gratification or initiation, and a self-advancement that is linked to sexual assertiveness. This is important because it sheds some light on the confused treatment of class issues I have been tracing, particularly where a sense of being contained or entrapped within the given social structure may coincide with the exhaustion of the youthful rebellion. Maturity may then be confused with the need for social passivity as a necessary adult state. This problem looms large in Keith Waterhouse's *Billy Liar* (1959), which is comparable to *Saturday Night and Sunday Morning* in that the rebellious energy of its protagonist is, to a great extent, a question of male adolescent dissatisfaction. The attendant class issues that are drawn into the vortex of rebellion are treated in a confused or contradictory fashion, though this seems less a part of the design than is the case in Sillitoe's novel.

Waterhouse's protagonist Billy Fisher is also a figure of transition, however, an office-worker with aspirations, whose father runs his own haulage business; and there is no evocation of class solidarity, since Fisher's concern is simply to improve his lot and escape from his oppressive existence as a clerk for a firm of undertakers in the Yorkshire town of Stradhoughton. By way of compensation, Fisher constructs various levels of fantasy thinking, and it is this characteristic that makes him a memorable protagonist, and which gives some credence to his dream of becoming a London comedy scriptwriter.

Does the novel, then, serve to expose 'the myth of opportunity and upward mobility' through Fisher, the deserving beneficiary-elect of a meritocracy that fails to deliver?[22] Certainly, there is an element of authorial enthusiasm for the freedom and opportunity London is made to symbolize, as the focus for an aspiring writer; but Fisher's choice to leave or stay is not really worked through in terms of a restrictive class structure. Fisher's dream of escape is really a fantasy by which he would *avoid* the class choices that define life in Stradhoughton. Neither is he truly a thwarted talent: his club turn reveals his inadequacies as a performer, whilst his desire to write is not backed up by the willingness to apply himself (pp. 124, 27–8). The larger social and political frameworks recede, since their contingency on Fisher's predicament hinges upon the integrity of his aspirations. In the absence of such integrity, the career of Billy Fisher is reduced to a tale of adolescent self-enlightenment. Indeed, the most affecting moments in the novel are those episodes where the alternative perspectives of other characters – Liz, Councillor Duxbury, Fisher's mother – serve to expose the arrogance or impercipience of Fisher.

The class issue, then, is often clouded in those narratives where youthful rebellion overlays perhaps more legitimate desires for social change. The more serious obfuscation, however, emerges from the contradiction between ideological and economic definitions of class standing, such as are revealed in Storey's *This Sporting Life*. In other forms of social analysis, the categorization of class levels and distinctions is often conducted, as in the national census, on the basis of income and occupation, factors that are subject to objective measurement. This understanding of the differentials that might underpin class distinctions is purely descriptive, sociologically neutral, and quite different from the sense of self-conscious affiliation implied in the process of class formation. The objective measure of social strata used in market research – categorized as As, Bs, C1s, C2s, Ds and Es – establishes a six-stage rank order according to occupation that might support a simpler hierarchical class model for wage earners, with the middle classes distinct from the working classes.[23] Evidently this descriptive approach is in tension with the idea of the self-aware adoption or promotion of class interests, an impetus that implies a challenge to the 'given' hierarchy, but sometimes, paradoxically, does so by reinforcing the basic opposition.

## Education and Class Loyalty

The conflicting and contradictory perceptions of the social order, which are often unresolved in discussions of the British class system, are particularly evident in the fictional treatment of education and its effects. The dominant strand in the development of this theme has comprised those novels that investigate the ambivalent effects of educational opportunity. It is worth remembering, however, that the impression of opportunity for everyone can be overstated. In *A Kestrel for a Knave* (1968) Barry Hines's theme is the lack of prospects for working-class school-leavers, let down by their schooling. The only meaningful focus for Billy Casper, mistreated at home (on a northern housing estate), is the kestrel he has captured from its nest and trained. The kestrel becomes an object of devotion for Billy – a living talisman – on account of its fierce independence (pp. 118–19).

The kestrel ('Kes') is eventually killed by Billy's vicious elder brother, as a punishment to Billy for failing to place a bet on his behalf; but when Billy returns home at the end of the novel, having earlier fled the house in a 'final' gesture of anger and despair, there is a sense that he has adopted the world-view he had assigned to the kestrel: to appear 'not bothered about anybody' (p. 118). But despite this closing mood of implied self-reliance, it is the sense of Billy's predetermined and circumscribed future that prevails. In a perfunctory interview, the Youth Employment Officer soon decides that Billy should be put down for 'manual work' (p. 138), indicating the likelihood that he will follow his brother down the pit.

The bleak mood I have illustrated in *The Day of the Sardine* is linked to its pessimism about education. In this connection, Chaplin cultivates a sense of class defeat in his depiction of post-war Newcastle upon Tyne. This element of self-defeat is most visible in the episode of the schoolteacher pelted with rotten fruit, a plot hatched by Haggerston himself (p. 61). He later discovers that the teacher was George Flack's nephew, whose university education Flack had helped to finance (p. 111). Flack puts his nephew's eventual suicide down to something more metaphysical than the torment of his work (p. 234); but the suspicion remains that the cruelty meted out by his pupils has been a factor, and the tale of his persecution is one of self-advancement through education unwittingly destroyed by working-class children. The class point is underscored by the nephew's adoption of the name 'Carruthers-Smith' as part of his pursuit of social superiority. More importantly, the schoolteacher's plight is associated in Haggerston's mind with Flack's tortured memories of the First World War trenches (p. 88). As a coal-miner, Flack had been drafted to assist the effort of 'undermining' the German trenches in an operation of mass devastation that leaves him feeling 'dead' (p. 88). The specific mineworker's knowledge facilitates the operation, and the killing of other workers *en masse* in the opposing trenches: it is the same dynamic of self-defeat that structures the novel and that is Chaplin's main concern.

Despite these examples of the unavailability of advancement through education for working people, there is still a general sense that the 1950s is the decade in which the traditional working class begins to be absorbed into an expanding middle class, and many novelists have sought to examine the ways in which educational opportunity participates in this process. The distinctive feature of this development, and the reason why class becomes a central and compelling issue in British culture in the late 1950s and the 1960s, is that the novel of working-class life is being eloquently written by members of the working class themselves.[24] The paradox is that the individual who becomes a writer also becomes something other than working-class. The ideological tussle then centres on whether to designate that individual a figure of transition, or a figure of betrayal. The new generation of working-class novelists were often beneficiaries of the Butler Education Act of 1944, which had given them access to grammar schools, and had opened the door to a university place for some. Education remained class-bound, it should be stressed – only one in ten children of unskilled manual workers was successful in the eleven-plus examination – so the working-class novelist is an exceptional figure, moving beyond her or (usually) his roots in the process of establishing himself as a writer.[25] It is this which sharpens the dilemma of the working-class novelist or intellectual, and which makes the popular perception of betrayal difficult to repudiate.[26]

This dilemma, with its accompanying discomfort and resentment, is a recurring theme in David Storey's work. In his second novel, *Flight into Camden* (1960), a settled, northern working-class existence is threatened by the disruptive effects of education. Margaret Thorpe and her brother Michael provide anguish for their parents, the father a miner and the mother an obsessively house-proud housewife, by virtue of their new (but unfashioned) attitudes. Margaret is a secretary for the Coal Board, a representative of a generation moving beyond manual labour. The big disruption for her, however, is her affair with the married Gordon Howarth, a teacher of industrial design at the local art college. They run away to London together, but the relationship is doomed at a time when the permissive freedom of the 1960s has not yet taken root. They are pursued by Margaret's father and her brother, and eventually Howarth is persuaded to call off the affair, and return to his family.

It is the brooding and inconstant nature of Howarth (in particular) that enriches the book, and complicates this period of transition. In the first meeting between Margaret and Howarth, he emphasizes the attractions of London in comparison with the provinces (p. 20); later, Margaret tries to persuade her mother that no one in London judges her, that 'people take you as you *are*'. Her mother is dismissive: 'they haven't done round here', she says, 'they couldn't have been more shocked' (p. 224). But this is no simple opposition of metropolitan and provincial standards. The characters on the cusp of change seem uncertain in their desires. This is true of Margaret's sometimes lukewarm feelings for Howarth, as well as, more obviously, of his mercurial moodiness. It is Michael, however, the university lecturer, who epitomizes this difficulty. He is by turns manipulative and aggressive, and actually creates Margaret's problems by turning parental opinion against

Howarth. In a powerful scene, his father turns on Michael, lamenting his 'great educated emptiness' (p. 128).

This theme of 'educated emptiness' resurfaces in the later *Pasmore* (1972), a chilling account of the nervous breakdown experienced by another young university lecturer Colin Pasmore. His disaffection from – and abandonment of – wife and family is made to seem as unmotivated as the affair he embarks on is desultory. Storey's method in this novel is to pare down the writing to simple dialogue and flat description of events, thus emphasizing the inexplicable *Angst* of Pasmore, and the nullity of his identity. At the height of his breakdown, this sense of absence is described as a bottomless black pit that is felt to be without dimension, both within and without (p. 145). Even at the end, when Pasmore has been accepted home by his wife Kay, apparently wiser, he still dreams of the black pit that 'existed all around him, an intensity, like a presentiment of love, or violence: he found it hard to tell' (p. 171). It is a depressing conclusion, which suggests that Pasmore has been wrenched from his roots, and is unable to make properly nuanced human responses. The pit image, fairly obviously, ties him to his father (again, a miner), who claims to have sacrificed his life for his son. Education is here articulated as the route of escape from working-class hardship, for Pasmore's father: while his son was at school, job satisfaction at the coal face consisted of reminding himself that every piece of coal that he dug was a piece his son wouldn't have to dig. The self-sacrifice is acutely felt:

> 'Nay,' he said. 'Do you know how high it is where I'm working? Thirteen inches.' He measured out the distance between his hands. 'If it shifts as much as an inch I'm done for. I can feel it riding on my back. Why, you've got to make it add up to something.' (p. 86)

Alan Sinfield points out that the misunderstandings that education produces 'are offered mostly from the point of view of the upwardly mobile, the one who writes'.[27] Storey's achievement here is to convey the father's perspective most tellingly, even to imply it colours the son's, particularly in that oppressive metaphorical pit that haunts his dreams. The father feels that all his efforts have been wasted when his son's marriage breaks up. Again, the inability to cope with social transition destroys the hopes of both generations. The father here is desirous of social mobility, but cannot conceive of an existence that is not defined by marriage and family. Pasmore's self-contradiction, premised on the divergent generational pulls, is encapsulated in the cracked mirror at his parents' house, which will not allow the two halves of his face to come together (p. 84). As a measure of Pasmore's failure, Storey seems here to allude to Hoggart's 'test' of a working-class boy's 'real education' that 'lies in his ability, by about the age of twenty-five, to smile at his father with his whole face'.[28]

In *Saville* (1976), David Storey's familiar autobiographical theme – the equivocal consequences of class mobility – is traced to its particular historical root. Colin Saville, a miner's son, is successful in the 'eleven-plus' examination, in its early days, and fulfils his father's hopes by securing a place at grammar school. As in *Pasmore* and *Flight into Camden*, the fulfilment of the father's ambitions ensures the son's alienation from his background. What Storey successfully dramatizes is the naivety surrounding the meritocracy that the Butler Education Act (1944) was supposed to usher in. On his first day at the grammar school Saville is publicly ridiculed by a master for his father's inability to spell (he has mis-signed his name with a single 'l' on his son's health certificate [p. 150]). In a protracted exercise in humiliation the master goes on to challenge the father's given occupation ('colliery worker') pedantically establishing that he is a miner, not a white-collar worker. Finally, Saville's ignorance of the school's Latin motto is exposed, and the master sees, in the occasion of his own prejudice and cruelty, reason to brand his pupil a 'rebel' (pp. 149–53). It is a powerfully rendered episode that distils the novel's treatment of class disjunction. In the face of such arbitrary and unthinking mistreatment Saville's stolid and unresponsive character is formed. What Storey presents is class disruption rather than transition, a violence that results in Saville feeling 'apart' from everything (p. 333).

In *A Serious Man* (1998), Storey's first novel for fourteen years, this theme of dislocation reaches a depressing conclusion. The protagonist Richard Fenchurch – like his creator, a once successful novelist, playwright, and painter – is recovering from mental breakdown. Part of the process of self-analysis involves a recognition that his motivation is divided according to conflicting notions of class identification: his artistic work has been 'energised' by the dynamic of working-class life, while his ambition has been driven by his middle-class social milieu (p. 279). There is a clear element of authorial identification with this, which is especially poignant given Fenchurch's sense of having betrayed his class (p. 297).

A writer who attempts a more positive treatment of working-class life, and the dilemma of the working-class scholarship boy, is Raymond Williams, whose first (autobiographical) novel *Border Country* (1960) is a complex deliberation on changing class identity and the loss of traditional community values, focused through the experience of a Welsh border village. Matthew Price, a university lecturer in economic history, is summoned home to Glynmawr, from his life in London, by news of his father's illness. Price thus begins a journey of self-evaluation, based on the troublesome negotiation between intellectual and working-class kinship.

Price (like Williams) completes his schooling before the Second World War, and goes up to Cambridge, so the displacement he feels on his return is not a consequence of post-war education reforms; nevertheless, given the date of publication, Williams's treatment of this theme contributes to those broader inquiries, from the 1950s on, about the effects of the supposed widening of educational opportunity. But Williams's interest is historically still more extensive: his method for much of the novel is to juxtapose scenes from the narrative present in the 1950s, with episodes from the past, centred around the impact of the General Strike of 1926.

In a lecture originally given in 1976 Williams indicates the importance of this event to the conception of *Border Country*, and in particular to the sense of rapid class transition that he seeks to uncover. The portrayal of the strike in the novel concerns the signal-box at Glynmawr where Matthew's father Harry works. Williams's own father was a signalman at Pandy, a representative of those new members of a 'modern industrial working class' who still operated 'in a small group within a primarily rural and agricultural economy'.[29] This is the most significant of the many 'borders' that the novel investigates, that which locates the demise of a settled rural working-class way of life, symbolized by these railway workers whose daily lives are structured by a village community, but who experience a different 'community with other signalmen over a wide social network'.[30] In another lecture Williams distinguishes the two types of community as 'rural' and 'industrial', seeking to imbue the latter with potential for a newly conceived working-class purpose.[31] This purpose, however, is hard to discern as the effects of the General Strike in *Border Country* demonstrate.

A crucial scene is the one in which young Matthew (known as 'Will' in Glynmawr) goes to the local shop on an errand for a neighbour, Mrs Lewis. Presented with Mrs Lewis's purse, the shopkeeper finds it to contain just a hairpin, and not the pound note that Mrs Lewis had claimed. When Will, fearful of being blamed, fails to return home, his father sets out to put matters right. He pays for the goods with a pound of his own – put by with great difficulty for rent money, whilst the strike is on – and returns home to find that the original pound has been discovered, still on the Lewises' table. Harry's pound is retrieved, but he remains withdrawn and angry, showing no relief; Will, for his part, angrily rejects the twopence that accompanies the returned pound, his usual payment for running this errand (pp. 106–13). The episode emerges as a parable of the pressures on the working man's pound, as a consequence of the looming class defeat of the General Strike. It is true that Harry's pride is slightly out of kilter with the community's own values, which ensure that needs are met by collective arrangement. (Mrs Hybart, in fact, refuses to accept the pound for rent, even though she disapproves of the strike (p. 122)); but the story of the lost pound reveals the pressures on the community that external interests are bringing to bear. Indeed, the railway company imposes punitive measures on the returning strikers, and Harry finds himself out of work for a while.

The key figure in this phase of transition is Morgan Rosser, the closest friend of Matthew/Will's parents. Rosser is the impassioned NUR branch secretary during the strike, and the staunchest upholder of those local values of collective support; but the strike leads him in a new direction, selling produce for himself. Rosser establishes his own factory, selling jam from local fruit, but the factory is sold to a larger concern shortly after the war (a fact he conceals locally), and becomes a depot in effect, 'labelling the pulp from abroad' (p. 330). Rosser is a complex character, but his actions denote him as an agent of class defeat, precisely because they allow external interests to take control of the community's economy.

## The Formal Challenge of Class

For Williams, the problem was to find a new form for the novel that might encompass the new social experience of class transition. Williams's first two novels seem, at first glance, traditional works of realism, far less innovative than the direction his fiction was later to take. However, since these early works engage closely with the problem of realism, this is an impression that is misleading. The alternative form he was seeking to devise had its roots in the working-class novel of the inter-war years, which, for Williams, had become 'a kind of regional form' (he cites Jack Jones and Gwyn Jones as examples). Williams seeks to develop this restricted type of genre fiction, retaining its capacity to describe 'the internally seen working-class community', but to combine this with a sense of 'a movement of people' away from those communities to which they nevertheless remain connected.[32]

If Williams the novelist seeks to innovate, he also looks back in his quest to find an authentic form for working-class fiction. Comparing twentieth-century fiction with the novels of the nineteenth-century realists, Williams finds an absence of history in the former, where a character's experiences may not appear to be determined 'by any larger forces'. Economic pressures – demanding speed and relative brevity in the novelist – are creating an ideological squeeze on the novel, demanding the omission of social history, and the exclusion of the kind of political embedding that would be necessary in a fully realized working-class fiction.[33]

An important text in Williams's theory of the novel is *The English Novel From Dickens to Lawrence*. Here Williams sees the crisis in the portrayal of a 'knowable community' as the central problem for the English novel since the mid-nineteenth century, since the meaning of community becomes increasingly uncertain with the rapid social change that accompanies a 'transforming urban and industrial civilization'.[34] He finds the locus of the formal problem this now poses in Lawrence: in *The Rainbow*, for example, Williams detects 'the experience of community. . . and then of its break-down'. Lawrence's lost 'community' is of the settled working class, and it is this kind of evocation to which Williams writes back. In Lawrence, Williams favours (in preference to the abstract language of the late work, epitomized in *The Plumed Serpent*) the language that captures that lost world, the 'ordinary words' that denote 'where the feeling still was'.[35]

Williams's aim in *Border Country* is, in effect, to achieve something like a reinvigorated Lukácsian realism that will reveal the public significance of private action and personal feeling. This also involves a new understanding of community, to gesture beyond the crisis, and to make it knowable once more. Necessarily, such a gesture can only be provisional, since the connections between the two different kinds of community – the older 'rural' kind, and the newer 'industrial', or even post-industrial kind, perhaps – have 'not been sufficiently explored'.[36] When, at the end of the novel, Matthew Price is seen bending to kiss his sleeping sons, bereaved after his father's death, Williams is pushing the novel to deliver a hint of this connection (p. 351). It is an affecting moment of positive sentiment and it is also the gesture of social continuity for a modern intellectual worker, specializing in Welsh social and economic history, who has latterly come to some kind of accommodation with his working-class roots (p. 307).

Thus, although the novel seems to enact the erosion, the dehumanization, even, of a working-class settlement (Glynmawr is now 'a place on the way to somewhere else' [p. 307]), it also seeks to establish the resources for rethinking community. There is no simple wistfulness or nostalgia, here. Williams understood that 'you have to go beyond the simple community' and that 'a phase of negation' characterizes this process of realization.[37] It is significant that Williams, in his lecture on the General Strike, chose to stress the 'element of victory' for the working class, amidst the defeat, 'the growth of consciousness during the action'.[38]

The formal problem outlined in *Border Country* becomes a crisis in its sequel, *Second Generation* (1964), which extends the inquiry into the nature of industrial community. The action centres on the interaction between the car industry and academia in a university city based on Oxford; and the principal burden of that nexus of class continuity and discontinuity is shouldered by Peter Owen, who feels acutely the tension between the two worlds. He senses the self-motivation of writing an academic thesis, in contrast to actual fieldwork, which might produce a genuine understanding of working-class identity. The car plant becomes a focus of class struggle, but the novel's most powerful image shows, effectively, that this struggle is couched in the wrong terms. Driving from Wales to England, Peter has a vision of a society structured by car production:

> An extraordinary priority had been given to it, in the economy and the society. This was normally understood as the priority of the machine, but it was no longer only this. What was central now was the fact of traffic: its kind of movement, its kind of signal, its inherent versions of what people were like and the ways to react to them. Everyone knew, in a private way, how much was left out, by these familiar definitions, yet still, in common practice, they seemed daily more absolute and more relevant. This was the network by which the society lived, and through which it moved and communicated. The rest, ineradicably, was private. (p. 234)

The class struggle conceived in classic Marxist terms, as a struggle over the means of production, becomes a diversion from the real social problem that is located here: the alienation of an industrial society that offers only one auto-mated network of communication, a structure that serves both to conceal and to perpetuate the underlying (and catastrophic) social atomization. It will not matter who controls this system of production, since the dehumanized network it depends on will remain unaltered. Of course, Williams's project in this phase of seeking to extend realism is somehow to embrace lessons of negation, and this does set him a problem in seeking to discover purposive class identities for this industrial community for which the negation seems absolute. There is a sense in which Williams has his characters settle for an older style of working-class existence, a movement epitomized in Kate Owen's disillusionment with sexual liberation, and her return to domestic married order. This can seem like an internalized defeat, and 'the betrayal of working-class aspirations'.[39] Yet Williams is really seeking a way of opposing the impersonal and divisive network that the characters encounter, rather than a retreat into nostalgia. Indeed, the repetitive Lawrentian insistence on 'settlement' is meant to imbue old social concepts with new meaning; but what remains telling is that pervasive motif of traffic, which seems to stand for a modern society that has bypassed the classic class struggle by removing the means of class identification and mobilization.

The challenge of class, at the formal level, often produces the effect of pushing against the frame, and this can reveal significant tensions. In 'The Loneliness of the Long-Distance Runner' it is the interrogation of what realism can deliver that makes the piece much more than a tale of commodity fetishism and class interpellation. What complicates the story is that Manichean struggle between 'us' and 'them', because Smith pointedly implicates the reader in his fight against 'In-law blokes like you and them' (p. 10). This arresting and frame-breaking accusation places consumers of literature, and defenders of literary culture, as partisan players in the contest.

The independence of Smith, and the challenge this embodies, is given a particular edge by this startling implication of literary culture. Much is made of the production of Smith's text: he is self-conscious about what he is 'scribbling down', as if his pretensions to write required some kind of apology (p. 13). At one point, an imaginative simile has to be justified as being inspired by something 'once heard on the wireless' (p. 19). If this suggests a desire to maintain consistency in the discourse of an ill-read narrator, the conclusion reveals a more interesting dimension to the self-consciousness. On the final page Smith announces that he intends to entrust his story to 'a pal of mine', with the instruction to 'try and get it put into a book or something' if he is caught again (p. 54). The existence of the story thus implies both victory and defeat: the victory of Smith as a published author, challenging the class expectations of literary culture, but the defeat of his repeated incarceration. But the conceit of the ending also requires us to rethink this notion of 'defeat'. In Smith's terms, confirmation of his continuing 'Out-law' stance signals his continual refusal to conform, and so must also be judged a victory. The confirmation of Smith's authorship thus serves to privilege a voice not normally heard, whilst dignifying and preserving a perspective beyond the conventional parameters of literature and society alike. Yet, if the notional achievement of Smith as a published author extends the parameters of the 'literary', he has also been assimilated by the mainstream culture that he renounces.

The closer one looks at the key writers of the 1950s and 1960s, the more one finds unexpected subtleties and complexities, especially in those texts that depend on an evocation of gritty northern working-class experience. The class entrapment that pervades *This Sporting Life*, for example, coexists with something less easily identifiable. Storey engages with the problematic nature of social realism in a novel where the solidarity of place and setting – the provincial element – combines oddly with a strand emphasizing 'the mystery of being human' and 'the misinterpretation of appearances'.[40] This paradox is not inconsistent with the illogic and brutality endemic in the industrial landscape. Ian Haywood detects a 'tone of existential bleakness' that might define the extreme mood generated by the pessimistic treatment of industrialism, and particularly the institutionalized machismo that defeats Machin's sensitive impulses, and for which Mrs Hammond – a really very remarkable working-class character – is sacrificed.[41] Rather than making the real problematic, perhaps Storey has discovered the point where provincial working-class realism tips over into fable.

Something equally interesting, technically, occurs in Sillitoe's *Saturday Night and Sunday Morning*, on account of the compelling vitality of Arthur Seaton. Carmen Callil and Colm Tóibín suggest that, were the novel written in French, 'Arthur Seaton would be an existentialist hero and the book an essential modern text'.[42] There is an implicit critique of critical fashion, here, which carries some weight; and Seaton's misdirected and uncontainable energy certainly requires some explication. The problem with elevating him to the status of existentialist hero, however, is that this involves an incomplete reading that overlooks the centrality of Seaton's sexism; but there is, certainly, an evocative description of factory machine-work in which the alienation is offset by the 'favourable rhythm' of automatic labour, which frees the mind for the pleasurable pursuit of 'pipe-dreams' (pp. 37–40). Yet this is productive of neither a philosophical disquisition on the human condition, nor a properly politicized account of working-class disaffection, since Seaton's rebelliousness manifests itself in purely individual concerns.

The book's main technical difficulty, and the reason for its inscrutability, concerns the narrative voice, which is closely bound up with Seaton's: indeed the method of free indirect discourse pursued involves the merging of character and narrator on occasions. Consequently, it is left to the reader to supply the vantage point of judging Seaton. This is significant in reading the conclusion, since an effort of resistance is required to uncover the implicit suggestion of the character's absorption in the system. The most uncomfortable aspect of this is the implication that his marriage to Doreen will be a union of conflict, a channel for the negative energy that has surfaced in his other relationships:

> Arthur held her murderously tight, as if to vanquish her spirit even in the first short contest. But she responded to him, as if she would break him first. It was stalemate, and they sought relief from the great decision they had just brought upon themselves. He spoke to her softly, and she nodded her head to his words without knowing what they meant. Neither did Arthur know what he was saying; both transmission and reception were drowned, and they broke through to the opened furrows of the earth.
> (p. 215)

This is a rare moment in which the narrator passes judgement on the couple that have just agreed their union. The quasi-Lawrentian language is used to imply an antagonistic misunderstanding that seems elemental. Neither is this simply a representation of a static working-class alienation. Doreen, who lives on an estate of 'nice new houses' (p. 150), is an inhabitant of the new suburbia emerging in an era of post-war prosperity (pp. 26–7), a prosperity defined purely in material terms.

What each of these instances demonstrates is the bemusement of the characters whose class-consciousness has not kept pace with social change.

This is the true source of the frustration or anger that characterizes this phase of writing, where the individual has no meaningful collective principle to rely on. The technical 'tinkering' with realism, to convey, for example, a quasi-existential helplessness for Arthur Seaton, demonstrates the apparent impossibility of regenerating a constructive working-class realism.

In later representations this technical point is still more evident. Pat Barker's *Union Street* (1982) is diametrically opposed to Raymond Williams's hopes for a fictional form that might fruitfully play off older perceptions of continuity with newer experiences of discontinuity. The title makes ironic reference to class solidarity and community spirit, for the action of the book is, largely, a catalogue of narrow-mindedness, poverty, and brutality, especially that which stems from male oppression and violence. Barker's method is cultivated to emphasize this social breakdown. The book comprises a cycle of seven short stories and, although some characters appear in more than one story, the dominant impression is of discontinuous and isolated experience. Even in those moments of linkage between stories, an apparent connection can reveal a grim significance. The clearest example of this is the loop that links the last story back to the first. At the end of the first tale, young Kelly Brown, who is brutally raped in the course of the story, is seen linking hands with an elderly woman she has chanced upon in the local park. Kelly cares little for the old woman, however, and the story ends with her walking purposefully home, apparently resigned to the dismal future that life in the locale of Union Street offers. The final story reveals that old woman to have been Alice Bell, in the process of giving herself up to death through exposure rather than submit to being put in the home she equates with a workhouse. Kelly and Alice are strangers to each other, and appear as anonymous 'extras' in each other's story. The cyclic organization implies continuity, but the legacy that Alice offers Kelly is one of isolation and despair.

James Kelman's *How Late it Was, How Late* (1994) is representative, formally, of the direction fiction has taken to treat questions of poverty and inequality. The novel is dominated by the interior monologue of the unemployed Glaswegian Sammy, who goes blind after a violent skirmish with the police, and whose story is a catalogue of oppression at the hands of the state. The novel's overwhelming sense of interiority imitates the oppression Sammy endures. There is something laudable in this voicing of experience that usually goes unheard; but the method serves to mimic the protagonist's ordeal. What is evoked here, as Cairns Craig notes of Kelman's earlier novels, is a world of 'economic deprivation' for which there is no 'possible salvation through the political or economic transformation of history'.[43] Kelman's dialectal form is a lament in which there is no trace of the traditional markers of working-class community, and in which suffering is a given state of being.

## The Waning of Class-Consciousness

The failure to achieve an authentic working-class form in the manner envisaged by Williams – in which continuity and discontinuity are fruitfully interwoven in the depiction of community – can be accounted for by the rapidity of social transition. In 1976, pondering 'why there is not yet socialism in Britain', Williams attributed this to the occurrence of 'mixed communities' that require that the 'struggle for class consciousness' now 'be waged on . . . more socially neutral ground'.[44] However, the emergence of this 'socially neutral ground' signals the waning of traditional class-consciousness.

The climate of political class loyalty – and its demise – is confirmed by the voting habits in general elections from 1974. Working-class support for Labour held up in 1974, but fell away in subsequent elections.[45] Through the 1980s and 1990s analyses of class have tended to be richer and more complex than the simple adversarial model, though this has still proved compelling, not least in the rhetoric of political campaigning. However, the tensions and contradictions between different understandings of class need to be kept in view. In his perceptive overview Cannadine shows how three mutually exclusive versions or models of the class system have recurred in British perceptions: 'the hierarchical view of society as a seamless web; the triadic version with upper, middle and lower collective groups; and the dichotomous, adversarial picture, where society is sundered between "us" and "them"'.[46] Understandings of class, then, are variously constructed, and in a way which militates against the production of coherent social identities.

The confusion this suggests actually applies to the entire post-war period. If the disintegration of traditional class affiliation – especially working-class solidarity – became fully visible only in the Thatcher years, there is a clear sense that available social models were becoming inapplicable much earlier. Nigel Dennis's satirical portrait of English identity in his *Cards of Identity* (1955) takes the era of the late 1940s and early 1950s as its target, a time of ration books and identity cards that, so Dennis implies, highlights the artificiality of imposed (and assumed) social roles. The action concentrates on the operations of the bizarre 'Identity Club' that decamps from London to the country for its annual meeting. The members of the club take over an empty manor house, and manage to staff it by persuading the locals to assume new social roles. In doing so they put into practice the club's cherished theory, that 'there is nothing that cannot be seen in terms of identity' (p. 100).

A perception of class lies at the heart of Dennis's comedy, and this is the symbolic function of the manor house, the kind of house that was 'once a heart and centre of the national identity', but that in the post-war era is 'one of the last relics of an age of established identities' (p. 100). Thus when the members of the club are able to interpellate the locals as 'butler', 'housekeeper' or 'gardener' they uncover a latent desire for an ordered class hierarchy, which overrides perceptions of inequality. This is most clearly illustrated in the new role assumed by Mr Paradise who, as the butler Jellicoe, willingly embraces a role defined by deprivation and pain: 'a reward would spoil everything', he feels (p. 105). There is certainly something cold, even vicious at the heart of Dennis's satirical vision. In the manner of Wyndham Lewis's tyros, Dennis's characters act in a ludicrous, predetermined fashion and, in the absence of any sustained analysis of the system that defines them, they become the butt of an essentially conservative comic mood. Yet, within this focus, there is something prescient in Dennis's satirical view, which quite rightly suggests that the English have continued to be enamoured of a traditional class hierarchy that is no longer applicable. The fluidity of identity celebrated by the Identity Club is thus tacitly shown to identify a hollow social structure in which class status depends primarily on assumed roles.

The waning of class identity, then, is a longer-term phenomenon than might be assumed. It is the Second World War, in fact, that locates the turning point in British social history. This is implied in the astute subtext of John Braine's *Room at the Top*. The rise of Joe Lampton is meant to be representative, but this representativeness is a little more involved than it appears. The death of Joe's parents, killed in an air raid (p. 16), is of particular importance in this connection. Ostensibly, this makes Lampton that staple protagonist, the rootless or orphaned individual making his way against the grain of social convention. But Lampton's rootlessness is the key, paradoxically, to his typicality. His parents (and his aunt and uncle) are the embodiment of traditional working-class goodness (p. 77), so their death severs Lampton from his class roots, and from the traditional community values of his lost family. Braine, in short, makes the wartime death of the parents symbolic of the death of traditional working-class values, based on the family hearth.

In cultural terms, Braine's class subtext is a fictional counterpart to Richard Hoggart's analysis in *The Uses of Literacy*, published in the same year. Hoggart's nostalgia for the working-class community values of the 1920s and 1930s is spurred by the consumerism and mass culture of the 1950s that displaces it; for Joe Lampton, the loss of class identity 'frees' him and makes possible an assault on society perceived as a hierarchy based on wealth alone (p. 28). As a consequence, Lampton becomes a 'Successful Zombie', detached and without emotion, whereas previously he had been able 'to live *among* the people around him' (p. 123). (There is something similar in Wain's *Hurry on Down* in Charles Lumley's sentimental feeling for the 'lovable' homes of the traditional working classes (p. 181).)

Hoggart's argument about mass culture is susceptible to over-simplification. It is not a simple polarization between 'good' old and 'bad' new working-class culture. The line of the argument, however, does trace a process of cultural dilution in suggesting 'that we are moving towards the creation of a mass culture; that the remnants of what was at least in parts an urban culture "of the people" are being destroyed; and that the new mass culture is in some important ways less healthy than the often crude culture it is replacing'.[47] This class-conscious corrective to the glib overview of the prosperous Britain of the 1950s is important, a necessary reminder that cultural wealth may be diametrically opposed to consumer wealth; what it fails to register fully is the rapidity of class change and the inevitable transformation of mass culture consequent upon it.

A number of novelists in the 1950s and 1960s concurred with Hoggart's analysis, often presenting the argument in stark terms. In *Saturday Night and Sunday Morning* the ubiquity of television is the principal marker of this new prosperity, and is roundly condemned, most notably in Seaton's feeling that this new cultural phenomenon serves to pacify the masses (p. 184). In 'The Loneliness of the Long-Distance Runner' the lure of consumerism makes the story, in part, a tale of class typification, and institutionalized criminality; whilst in Hines's *A Kestrel for a Knave*, social change is also measured in terms of mass culture. The grim headmaster Gryce (who canes a boy who has the misfortune to bring him a message when his mind is set on punishment) bemoans the advent of youth culture, and the disruption to the given social hierarchy that accompanies it. It is the disrespect he has lately encountered that particularly disturbs him, though his comment that young people are now 'just fodder for the mass media' (p. 56) implies, in the spirit of Hoggart, that popular mass culture is having a deleterious (but transformative) effect on working-class identity.[48]

In contrast, Vic Brown in Barstow's *A Kind of Loving* becomes an agent of the new mass culture. The son of a miner, Brown is the beneficiary of 'a golden age for young fowk' (p. 125): he works initially as a draughtsman for an engineering company, where a strong union secures good prospects (p. 158). However, he chooses to give up this career to work full-time in a music and electrical shop owned by a family friend (p. 160). Victor's expectation that he might one day inherit the shop – the efficiency of which attracts his critical eye – marks him out as an index of class transition, progressing from the provincial working-class world that produces him, to the class of entrepreneur and purveyor of those electrical goods (radiograms and televisions) that epitomize the new mass culture.

These great expectations point to the essential contradiction of Brown since his financial aspirations make him the conduit of the leisure culture he also despises. (Television is the focus of his antipathy, which at times levels out into an undeveloped opposition between 'high' and 'low' culture.) He rebels against a social world that continues to define him: as a shopkeeper – eventually a shop-owner, perhaps – he becomes an agent of the new materialism, which he recognizes as stifling in certain guises. The depressing compromise of the accommodation he finally reaches, engendered by the lukewarm 'kind of loving' that follows passion, has really to do with this more complex sense of domesticity, defined as a way of life controlled by larger economic forces in which he is unavoidably implicated.

## The Rise of the Underclass

From the perspective of 2000, the renaissance of working-class fiction in the 1950s and 1960s looks like the swansong of a literary mode with a backward-looking impetus. For a generation, this mode caught the anxiety of social transition (especially for those working-class writers caught up in the complex processes of change) by registering the contradictions that have surrounded the perception of class. The waning of class-consciousness, however, has brought with it the demise of the working-class novel in the naturally evolving form envisaged by Raymond Williams.

This does not mean, of course, that social inequality has been expunged. Nor does it make the perceived loss of community less pertinent as a literary theme. The ideal of 'classlessness' that has dominated political discourse in the post-war years is a serious distortion of this new reality. The idea of a 'classless society' was made popular by John Major, although this concept had been a tool in political campaigning since the Second World War. It is also associated with the political programmes of Major's predecessor (Margaret Thatcher) and successor (Tony Blair) as Prime Minister. Earlier, Harold Wilson (in opposition, in the run-up to the election of 1964) made his own populist appeal for a meritocratic classless society, in which socialism would advance the claims of scientific progress, for the general good.[49] There is 'an intriguing irony', as David Cannadine points out, that these recent attempts to manipulate public perceptions are anticipated in Karl Marx's own projected classless society, the socialist utopia.[50] However, the promotion of a classless ideal has not prevented successive governments from appealing to class divisions of one kind or another for political expediency. Thatcher, of course, showed herself to be very conscious of the familiar binary class model, most notably in her attitude to the miners' strike of 1984–5. Indeed, the confrontation with the trade unions was a central plank of the class war conducted by Thatcher, for whom a 'classless' society would be the outcome of the triumph of capitalism and the defeat of socialism, or organized labour.[51] Modernizing New Labour, having abandoned Clause Four, have slipped the chains of this old-style class war; but appeals may yet be made to a new version of an 'us' and 'them' binary opposition to advance the claims of ordinary citizens in the face of an older establishment (as in the restructuring of the House of Lords).

There is, then, a contradiction between the politicians' avowed goal of classlessness and the implicit appeal to different class models that is common in the cynical and manipulative discourse of political marketing. It is true that the changing nature of work in a post-industrial society (most visible in the decline of manual work) casts doubt on the continuing relevance of traditional class categories; but a new brand of inequality has been the consequence of this. On the one hand the post-war years have witnessed the development of a growing salaried middle class, covering a wide range of occupations, but tied together as consumers. On the other hand, a new 'underclass' has emerged to support the prosperity of the majority. If the dynamic of increasing prosperity has produced an expanded middle class, defined in terms of material comfort and docility, it has also produced this underclass of menial workers at the base of society.

The term 'Servant Class' has also been used to designate 'the army of cleaners and menial service workers, paid a pittance, often working only a few hours here and there, cash-in-hand, no questions asked, ministering to the world above in its homes, offices, hospitals and schools'. This Servant Class forms the peak of a new kind of lower class (with the growing ranks of the homeless still lower in the hierarchy), bypassed by technological change, and disadvantaged by the increasing rarity of unskilled manual labour. 'Underclass' seems to me to be the appropriate descriptor for the new phenomenon, that disenfranchised group for which 'unemployment and unemployability are the leitmotifs'.[52] The 'classless' society of Wilson, Major, and Blair, a notional meritocracy in which opportunity will not be restricted by traditional class, or 'old-school-tie' expectations, has thus brought with it a simpler model of social inequality, a new set of class distinctions for a population still often enamoured of the traditional divisions.

The rise of the underclass in the 1980s and 1990s, then, installs new levels of inequality, and a potentially more damaging kind of social disjunction. A writer who has responded fully to this development is Livi Michael: she has produced a narrative form that encapsulates the broader social failure to re-think community. Her first novel, *Under a Thin Moon* (1992), cultivates a self-conscious documentary feel in its depiction of life on a council estate in the 1980s. The narrative unfolds in a series of vignettes told in the present tense, the action jumping back and forth from one character to another.

Attention is drawn to the technique early on when the principal character Wanda 'imagines she is being filmed as part of a true-life documentary about the homeless' (p. 10). Imagining the pathos of her life, which a film crew might uncover, Wanda cries, unsure whether she does so for her own benefit or for the imagined camera (p. 11). The effect of this is to make a voyeur of the reader, and to mitigate the sentimentality of the writing, which becomes arch, as if colluding with the reader. Wanda's terrible experiences of poverty, which lead her into prostitution, child-beating and eventually suicide, are haunted by the sense of being filmed, so that her death 'seems like a natural end to the film she has always had running through her head' (p. 227).

Several of the characters have a perception of the distinction between middle-class and working-class 'credentials', but the experiences of Wanda demonstrate the irrelevance of such distinctions to the members of the underclass who are irrevocably disempowered. Several episodes feature Wanda's daughter Coral in her adulthood, at a future date. Her suffering is a depressing echo of her mother's, but she has at least come to some contemplative understanding of her situation: 'when you have no money it is like looking at the world through the chink of a door. She does not know if there is any other way of looking. Or maybe it is like looking by the light of a very thin moon; not just limited, but different' (p. 230). Coral then determines to begin writing, so, in a familiar novelistic gesture, the book ends with a metafictional projection of the writing persona; but her perspective, so the title image indicates, is diminished: the imprisoning poverty also restricts the point of view in Michael's studiedly restricted delivery.

Michael's third novel, *All the Dark Air* (1996), is an acute examination of the ideological misperceptions that surround class, and that help to maintain an underclass. In this novel she traces a matrix of underclass misperceptions, suggesting that the inability to perceive the rapid changes to the class structure is an additional disenfranchising factor. The novel's impressionable and well-meaning heroine Julie enters a relationship of sorts with class-warrior Mick. They conceive a child, having moved into Mick's uncle's dilapidated house. Mick progresses from his pitch selling the *Big Issue*, to hawking the *Socialist Worker*, and espousing militant socialism. Julie's interest in meditation and the activities of a local 'New Age'-style group then seems to set up a stark opposition between a rigid masculine socialism, and a middle-class (and almost exclusively female) 'alternative' culture. The novel proceeds to undermine the basis of this opposition.

Mick condemns Julie's 'Mind Power' meetings, feeling its main participants are egotistical individuals, people who have 'got on' and are, he feels, class enemies (pp. 157–8, 257). Livi Michael is not blind to the inequality that angers Mick, but she shows how his militancy is self-defeating: he cannot settle to the business of making a home at Uncle Si's (the building work he has commenced in lieu of rent remains unfinished) because he misses being homeless (pp. 286, 305). His dated perception of the class war prevents him from getting a purchase on, and finding a place in society. He seems condemned to a life of hard drugs and social exclusion on account of this ideological failure. Julie's New Age friends are, of course, materially privileged; and their social views can seem more benighted and unforgiving than Mick's, as when suffering is attributed to 'karma' (pp. 92–3). But the stereotype does not ultimately fit, as is demonstrated in the person of Julie's friend Josepha, originally of Caribbean extraction, and the great-great-great-granddaughter of 'one of the last slaves in England' (p. 71). Josepha epitomizes a post-imperial multicultural England, struggling to make sense of its complexities, where easy class explanations no longer make sense.

Julie's pregnancy progresses against a background of suffering and violence (especially directed against children), and the novel ends with the commencement of her labour, stressing the need for a new kind of humanism, based (in a verbal echo of Joyce's 'The Dead') on human continuity, on a unified perception of 'the unending labours of the living and the dead' (p. 322). This humanism might be produced by navigating past the ideological confusion that the novel throws up: New Age mysticism, religious quietism (pp. 254–5) and, especially, an anachronistic class war, which actually assists the installation of the new underclass.

## The Realignment of the Middle Class

Michael depicts a pernicious system of inequality that is misperceived. This state of affairs in society as a whole hinges on the larger middle-class group, which thus emerges as the crucial (and culpable) term in the post-industrial equation. The nature of what it means to be 'middle-class' is transformed in the post-war years, generating a crisis of identity no less problematic than that which surrounds working-class experience, and post-war novelists have not left the contradictions of middle-class experience unremarked.

Even Angus Wilson's novels of the 1950s, which in some ways offer a defence of liberal values, also locate this crisis, and in appropriate formal terms. The career of Meg Eliot, protagonist of Angus Wilson's third novel, *The Middle Age of Mrs Eliot* (1958), depicts in miniature a changing class structure. As in his first two novels, Wilson gives the liberal views of his central character a rigorous testing; but whereas Bernard Sands (*Hemlock and After*) and Gerald Middleton (*Anglo-Saxon Attitudes*) either retain or rediscover some kernel of conviction or belief (even if in the case of Sands it does not save him), for Meg Eliot the testing involves the forging of an entirely new identity.

The novel opens with a scene involving Meg Eliot's charity work for an organization called 'Aid to the Elderly'. As chair of the organization's committee she is able to indulge the domineering side of her nature in the name of altruism. It is true that her firm diplomacy is presented in a favourable light – for example in her ability to circumvent the prejudices of 'the few diehards' on the committee (p. 8) – and in this sense she seems, potentially, an agent for change. She makes an ally of the trained social worker Mr Darlington, brought in 'at the suggestion of the Ministry' to assist the work of a committee run by upper-middle-class volunteers. If Mrs Eliot is on the cusp of change, however, she is also, in part, one of Wilson's 'dodos', a fashionable wealthy lady, married to a successful barrister, dabbling in good work.[53]

In the opening scene the committee interviews a Mrs Crowe, whose grandmother is receiving support from the charity: pressure is brought to bear on Mrs Crowe to take her grandmother in, on the basis of moral obligation and 'duty'. Mrs Eliot seems unhappy with the moral overtones, but she does prepare the way for this line of argument, and Mrs Crowe, despite having a husband and twins, and regretting the necessary loss of 'the lodger's money', capitulates in the face of the pressure brought to bear by her social superiors (p. 11). The class-based paternalism of this committee embodies a misguided liberalism, which the career of Mrs Eliot will expose as anachronistic. (When, a few pages later, she has occasion to condemn a different 'moral bullying' [p. 17], the sense of her own hypocrisy is underscored.)

Her career is based on the perception of a necessary class shake-up in English fiction: very soon she has been widowed by a random act of violence, impoverished and disillusioned about her marriage, and forced to reinvent herself entirely. Finally, with new qualifications, Meg Eliot takes up a career as secretary to a (female) Labour MP. However schematically, the transition from meddling charity work to salaried employment in politics projects the emergence of a cohesive meritocracy sustained by personal effort and conviction.

Perhaps the most interesting chronicler of the dissolution of middle-class liberalism is Barbara Pym, whose own career also suffers as a consequence of the changes that impinge on her writing. These changes are acknowledged hesitantly, at first, but then explicitly in her later work. The scope of Barbara Pym's early social comedy is well illustrated by her second novel, *Excellent Women* (1952), with its concentration on the life that revolves around the clergy, the church hall, and the jumble sale. The narrator Mildred Lathbury, 'an unmarried woman just over thirty' (p. 7), seems older than her years, especially to the reader of a later generation. She is one of those 'excellent women' who can be relied upon to run a stall or arrange the flowers, who may have formed a secret attachment to the clergyman they serve, but who are 'not for marrying' (p. 176). Mildred Lathbury, involved in part-time charitable work on behalf of 'distressed gentlewomen' (p. 73), offers a limited challenge to this stereotype. In the manner of Jane Austen's *Mansfield Park*, the novel concerns the way in which a settled life is disrupted by the arrival of dangerous interlopers. The Napiers' marital difficulties present the principal dilemma for Mildred since, in assisting their reconciliation, she has to grow beyond her attachment to the dashing Rocky Napier, whose charm is based on a conscious projection of a dashing romantic stereotype.

Pym's social world reasserts itself at the end of *Excellent Women*: the inter-lopers are expelled, and Mildred returns to her reassuring role as excellent woman, facing the prospect of proof-reading work for the anthropologist Everard Bone (pp. 237–8), a 'reward' for excellence that is made to seem more like a burden. In general, the novel's structure of reassertion is partly undermined by the mood of disappointment that conditions the narra-tor's experiences: the alternative world of unfettered passion that has been glimpsed, but rejected, seems to retain its appeal. This mood is summarized in Mildred's reflection that her world is restricted to 'the small unpleasant-nesses rather than the great tragedies; the little useless longings rather than the great renunciations and dramatic love affairs of history or fiction' (p. 96). The plot and the mood of the novel combine to lay bare the paradoxical limits of this benevolent, Church-going, upper-middle-class Englishness, which seems irrelevant, stifled by self-denial, especially when confronted by the freedoms of an increasingly secular society.

In *A Glass of Blessings* (1958) Pym utilizes the plot of reassertion with greater conviction. The narrator and heroine Wilmet Forsyth, thirty-three at the outset, married, well-provided-for and bored, finds herself falling in love with the brooding Piers Longridge, oblivious to her husband's own incipient wanderings. It is a novel of self-discovery, as Wilmet uncovers various areas of blindness and self-delusion: it is, as Michael Cotsell observes, 'Pym's *Emma*'.[54] The discovery of Piers's homosexuality instantly reveals to Wilmet that she has misinterpreted their friendship, and this comedy of temptation and reconciliation is balanced by husband Rodney's owning up to a clandestine dinner, but nothing more (p. 245).

This traditional comedic structure, with its resolution of matrimonial harmony, seems to assert the primacy of Pym's Christian morality, voiced most explicitly by Wilmet as her personal lesson sinks in: 'it seemed as if the Church should be the place where all worlds could meet, and looking around me I saw in a sense this was so. If people remained outside it was our – even *my* – duty to try to bring them in' (p. 205). However, the qualifiers here ('should', 'in a sense') imply a loss of authority for this 'tall tweedy young Englishwoman' (p. 33). It is significant that her self-revelation is produced by the discovery of a homosexual relationship, thriving on a domestic harmony lacking in her own marriage. Moreover, Piers's partner Keith is initially judged by Wilmet as 'slightly common' on account of his telephone manner (p. 153). All of these details imply a process of social transition that neither Wilmet nor the novel's benign Christian morality can fully encompass. This is acknowledged in Keith's cheerful admission of atheism in the scene where Wilmet tries to bring him into the fold (p. 215).

In a sense the dwindling class relevance of this kind of English social comedy is confirmed by the way in which Pym was bypassed by literary trends in the 1960s and 1970s. Although she had published six novels between 1952 and 1961, her seventh was rejected by Jonathan Cape in 1963. Several novels then went unpublished initially, including *Quartet in Autumn* (1977). When this novel had finally been accepted for publication, Pym's reputation was on the verge of being dramatically revived: in a *TLS* special edition of 1977, Pym was named by both Lord David Cecil and Philip Larkin as one of the most underrated novelists of the century.[55] The late flourishing of her career saw *Quartet in Autumn* shortlisted for the Booker Prize in 1977, and this novel is particularly significant for the ways in which it updates Pym's perception of her favoured social stratum.

That sense of being bypassed is the explicit focus of a novel that traces the progression of four office co-workers towards or into retirement. The lack of passion in the lives of this quartet, their inability to forge lasting bonds, even with each other, is the source of the book's elegiac tone. Where *Excellent Women* and *A Glass of Blessings* attempt to ameliorate the effects of thwarted passion, *Quartet in Autumn* repudiates the denial of life and finds no stable church-based community as a surrogate for the emotionally undeveloped existence. Of the four principal characters, it is the predicament of Letty Crowe, a typical Pymian spinster, that draws the reader into the topic of social relevance, initially when she cannot find a library book to her taste: 'she had come to realize that the position of an unmarried, unattached, ageing woman is of no interest whatever to the writer of modern fiction' (pp. 6–7). As a self-conscious aside this is a provocative 'realization', belied by the novel's success (and the later popularity of Anita Brookner), but it is very much in tune with the novel's theme. Letty, whose narrow, middle-class origins are twice referred to (pp. 25, 56), bears the brunt of the culture shock endured by the ageing gentlewoman.

The tone is set in an early episode where Letty observes a destitute woman on an Underground platform, and wonders whether or not she should offer help; and whether or not this destitute figure is not in fact her old school contemporary Janet Belling. Another passenger makes an enquiry of the slumped individual, at which point the most violent invasion of Pym's genteel fictional world occurs: 'the figure reared itself up and shouted in a loud, dangerously uncontrolled voice, "Fuck off!" Then it couldn't be Janet Belling, Letty thought' (p. 18).

Barbara Pym's editorial work at the International African Institute, an anthropological institute for the study of African languages and cultures, gave her inspiration for both the form and the content of her novels.[56] Anthropologists appear frequently in her work, and her own anatomy of a fading, genteel, church-going England amounts to 'an anthropology of the middle-class England of her time'.[57] The anatomy is gentle, governed by the 'quality of reticence' that Penelope Lively discovers in Pym, though it is a little curious that Lively denies the class element to the 'sexual conflict' that, she feels, preoccupies Pym.[58]

Lively herself is noted for creating heroines that are 'middle-class, middle-aged inhabitants of middle England', and thus 'icons of normality'.[59] In *Spiderweb* (1998), an apparent *hommage* to Pym, Lively creates an anthropologist heroine to frame her own survey of a fractured English society. Cool, detached Stella Brentwood retires to a cottage in Somerset and finds confirmation that her profession has made her a 'voyeur' with an 'interest in community' that is 'clinical' (p. 75). The spiderweb image, in its most prominent appearance, underscores the self-containment that has prevented Stella from forming a lasting relationship: she imagines lines netting the globe, tracing 'her own progress through time and space', and forming a complex web in four dimensions. There are 'portentous nodes' where places have been revisited, and where, thinks Stella, 'you walk blindly past the self that is to come and cannot see her' (p. 19). Here the alienating (and ironic) effects of anthropological work are uncovered, where the notionally privileged knowledge of social structure and integration isolates the individual.

A general point is being made here about the rootlessness produced by certain kinds of specialized professional knowledge; but the more telling 'webs' for the novel's immediate plot are the emotional traps that Stella encounters. Her best friend, the lesbian archaeologist Judith, wants them to set up house together, and this proposition coincides with a grimly pragmatic proposal of marriage from the former husband of Nadine, Stella's Cambridge contemporary who has recently died. These traps highlight Lively's own presentation of the 'sexual conflict', and the tendency of others to seek to appropriate a single woman according to their own designs. Finally, however, the most pressing danger comes from Stella's neighbours, a dysfunctional family with two teenage sons apt to express their disaffection through arson and violence. At the end of the novel Stella has put her cottage on the market, and fled from the various invasions of her solipsistic personal space. She remains 'on the outside looking in', having failed to fit in to her new environment. The crucial point, however, is that this is no real community:

in contrast to those she has studied, which are 'integrated', with 'a shape, a structure', the contemporary Somerset she flees is 'a late twentieth-century melting pot', 'a web' containing 'mutually exclusive groups co-existing after a fashion' (p. 208). The old rural order has passed, leaving a social vacuum. Stella's flight is an admission of defeat, a demonstration of the ineffectuality of purely theoretical knowledge.

## The Role of the Intellectual

In *Spiderweb* (1998) Lively shows, implicitly, that traditional notions of class have become irrelevant, and (through Stella) that the professional intellectual class is without power or discernible function in the melting-pot that has resulted. If there is a post-war crisis of class identity this reflects a broader process of social restructuring in which intellectual work is repositioned. What we are witnessing is a response to economic globalization, or that version of postmodernity that equates it with the international movement of capital, the dominance of transnational corporations, and the consolidation of a global media system. These trends are promoted by the rise of a new kind of class, that which has been termed the 'new international bourgeoisie', the class whose interests are aligned with the transformative processes of globalization.[60] In this social model, the 'salariat', or salary earners contribute either willingly (if they are 'affluent administrators') or under duress of one form or another (if they belong to the group of 'increasingly poor and insecure professionals and clerical workers').[61]

Seen entire, this new structure, at the foot of which lies that growing servant class or underclass, further exposes the paucity of appeals to class-lessness. New divisions replace older ones (though these are complex and continually evolving), and a different kind of hierarchy is established, where real power lies in the hands of multinational companies, especially media (and latterly media and Internet) conglomerates. This is a global development, but it is one that has made thinking about class in Britain particularly problematic: novelists have often caught the mood of great uncertainty in which a culture based very much on its own internal systems of class differentiation is rapidly overtaken by an international economy that renders the national social explanations obsolete.

This state of affairs presents a problem of location for intellectual work, and, specifically for this discussion, the work of the critic and the novelist. How does the new intellectual class, defined in a world of 'professional' standards and expectations, perform the work of social commentary? Later in his novelistic career Raymond Williams sought to find ways of responding to this problem. His clearest critical statement on the new social model is *Towards 2000*, in which he describes how 'a scheme of production for the market has ... substituted itself for a society'.[62] The agenda in this book is to determine the grounds from which a generally accepted understanding of common interests can be established, interests to which capitalism is inherently hostile. This new global context necessarily demands new novelistic forms, and even Williams, despite his earlier intentions, demonstrated his understanding that realism could not meet the requirements of the end of the twentieth century. His political thriller *The Volunteers* (1978) represents an alternative solution to the problem. The novel is a future projection (to 1987–8), and describes a future in which there is no Labour Party, and in which the working class can muster only regional activism rather than collective action on a national scale. Underground terroristic activities seem to represent the only significant source of political challenge to the presiding national government.

Lewis Redfern, the novel's narrator, is a journalist working for Insatel, an international television satellite service. Once an activist in the political underground, he has been recruited as a consultant analyst, able to infiltrate what is called 'the active movement' (7). Part of Williams's purpose, as Redfern's background indicates, is to examine the ethics of putting pre-professional radical credentials in the service of 'professional' analysis in the information age.

There is another dimension to this analysis of motives, and an interesting self-conscious allusion to the cultural gradualism that is sometimes said to dilute Williams's political thought. The title refers not just to members of the active movement, but also to a group of Fabian-style intellectuals whose project is to advance the socialist cause through a slow process of infiltration of the state apparatus: through pursuing a career. This very long-term (and unannounced) revolution makes professionalism a kind of gradualist activism in itself, though it is constantly under threat of absorption and incorporation.

The figurehead of these volunteers in the novel, the politician Mark Evans, who initially seems a despicable careerist, finally emerges as a principled figure whose machinations are well-intentioned rather than sinister. Yet the book produces a tension in its conclusion. The experiences of the narrator are set against the ambivalent, but ultimately productive professionalism of Mark Evans; because, for Lewis Redfern, caught in a web of intrigue, committed action also involves giving up his job. Here Williams puts the dynamic of the political thriller to good use. The dominant mode of the novel, however, is a kind of first-person confessional in which Redfern repeatedly confronts his own motive. Built into the novel's style, then, is a demand for continual self-evaluation in the interests of rooting out the wrong kind of professional activity, or service, pointedly illustrated here by the influence of the multinational information industry.

The novel's prescience about the dominance of global media corporations, as well as the disappearance of the Labour Party's socialist principles, makes it seem far less futuristic twenty years after publication. Indeed, hindsight makes aspects of the novel's political vision seem irrefutably realist. At the time, however, Williams set out to move beyond realism. The style is also partly the result of commercial pressures. Explaining why certain aspects of the characters' motivation remains undeveloped, Williams mentioned some enforced cuts, but also seemed pleased not to have 'been driven back to more conventional or received forms, with their greater amplitude'.[63] Stylistically, Williams sought to dramatize the blend of discontinuity and continuity through linguistic juxtaposition rather than through realist exposition. It was this, he hoped, that would demonstrate the 'disjuncture of consciousness' between old notions of industrial disputes, and the experience of the workers depicted.

A potential problem with this stylistic principle is that the terse hard-boiled style of Redfern can seem to be at odds with the notional growth of his moral standing; and where the book adopts the clipped style of media short-hand there is a hint that it is being colonized by the homogenizing global culture it seeks to critique. Williams convincingly argued that Redfern is not really free as a moral agent, but is rather acted upon, a view that offsets these technical difficulties. Even so, the formal problems Williams set for himself – and does not quite resolve – highlight the enormous difficulty that now obtains in dealing fluently with class-based politics.[64] Yet there is a serious attempt in *The Volunteers* to examine the responsibilities of the intellectual in the post-industrial age, and to link that examination to the function of the novel, still evolving as it seeks to accommodate new models of work and social organization. The dizzying speed of these changes is only partially registered in a consideration of class formation and evolution. As the next three chapters demonstrate, gender relations and ethnicity accounted for some of the most dramatic social changes in post-war Britain, changes that inspired some of the most challenging fiction.

## Chapter 3

# Gender and Sexual Identity

One of the myths of the 1950s is that this was a decade of social stability, courtesy, and traditional family values. According to this view, it took the emergence of youth culture in the late 1950s, and the explosive impact of the promiscuous 1960s to shake up the status quo, and begin the process of dismantling the traditional family unit, rooted in marriage and sustained by the husband's wage, and the domestic travails of the wife. This is a narrative that locates modern, 'second-wave' feminism, taking root in the 1970s from the seeds sown in the 1960s, as the principal agent of transformation.[1]

This outline history of gender relations accurately describes the drift of change, though it perhaps makes too much of the eventual visible manifestations of longer-term adjustments. It is certainly true that once modern feminism had been fully articulated, its tenets installed in the popular consciousness, the ambitions and desire of the populace in general (and women in particular) could not be fulfilled by traditional marriage with its built-in inequalities; but it is probably an over-simplification to mark a sharp dividing line in the 1960s between the Old and New Woman. The sexual revolution of the 1960s was neither as instantaneous nor so widespread as is sometimes assumed. Within a longer historical perspective modern feminism is given an unstoppable impetus in the Second World War. The war effort had depended upon the toil of women in the workplace so that the gendered pattern of work was drastically altered. Even allowing for the readjustment of the immediate post-war years, with the returning male workforce, the culture had changed for ever.

## Out of the Bird-Cage

The impression that the 1950s epitomized a traditional British way of life is belied by the way in which some of the planks of second-wave feminism were being put in place. In 1955, for example, the Conservative women's conference made a demand for the reform of married women's tax. This early move for financial independence, from unlikely quarters, anticipates a central issue for feminism in the 1970s.[2] These gathering social forces were not articulated instantaneously, however, and serious fiction did not fully register the emerging feminist impulses until the beginning of the 1960s. Consequently, when the glimmerings of modern feminism are detected in the post-war novel, there is a sense of waking up to given and established truths.[3] Indeed, it is impossible to claim that the mainstream literary culture of the 1950s was fully responsive to changing gender roles: this is not an issue that is usually associated with the Movement or the Angry Young Men, for example. However, even the reputed 'Angry' writers were capable of some sensitive reflection on gender questions. A surface reading of a novel such as John Braine's *Room at the Top* (1957) reveals a wealth of sexist attitudes, which, a more involved reading indicates, may be condemned in important ways. The sexual immaturity of Joe Lampton is a central (and lamented) aspect of his character, for instance. The female nude, and particularly Manet's *Olympia*, is used to illustrate Lampton's struggle to circumvent his appropriating male gaze.[4]

The enlightenment that eludes Joe Lampton begins to coalesce for Bill Naughton's Alfie Elkins, narrator of *Alfie* (1966), a male protagonist in the mould of Alan Sillitoe's Arthur Seaton: he is a character whose self-definition manifests itself in the pursuit of sexual freedom. Yet despite being ruthless, and sometimes aggressive, in pursuit of his sexual conquests, Alfie is internally divided, and this is the feature that gives the novel its depth. When one of his girlfriends, Gilda, becomes pregnant, Alfie begins to develop a more sensitive side: he shows the signs of emotional investment in his son, even though he does not want to be tied. He resists Gilda's attempts to cajole him into marriage, and professes himself relieved to have got rid of her (p. 53), though he is later tormented by the loss of his son. Having repressed his emotional needs, however, he is on the way to a physical breakdown and a sojourn in a TB sanatorium.

Naughton makes this task of reading between the lines a simple matter since Alfie makes repeated references to his more caring qualities. The defining moment of the novel is Alfie's encounter with the dead foetus following the illegal abortion Lily has undergone in his flat. He is shocked by the sight of a perfectly formed infant, and by his complicity in this killing. The novel is set before the reform of 1967 that legalized abortion; but Alfie is concerned with a moral rather than a legal crime. The morality, however, speaks to his own particular circumstances. The experience of having to dispose of the child's remains – another son lost to him – provokes the hallucinatory sound of a child screaming, 'as if it would go on wailing to the end of my days' (p. 196). The moment encapsulates Alfie's self-division, and the consequences of denying his altruistic impulses.

This is an era, then, in which the certainties of gender relations are beginning to be questioned anew in serious fiction; in such a context the glimmerings of feminist assertion are significant. Such intimations are evident in *The L-Shaped Room* (1960) by Lynne Reid Banks, in which a dawning feminist consciousness is dramatized. The restricting factors are those lingering conventional views of social structure and gender relations that limit both the consciousness of the central character, and the design of the novel. The experiences of Jane Gardner, fighting social prejudice and paternal rejection, as a single mother-to-be, are presented as those of a middle-class woman 'slumming it'; but the novel demonstrates the incipient break-up of the class differentials it otherwise projects. On balance, however, the full implications of Jane Gardner's redefinition of the mother's role are diluted by the various acquired prejudices – concerning ethnicity and race, as well as gender – that she cannot fully relinquish.

Even so, the consciousness of narrator Gardner seems to be explicitly feminist, in several respects. She endures a series of encounters with men seeking to control her life: first, her father; then the doctor who assumes she seeks an abortion when she merely wishes to confirm her pregnancy; and then the hotel owner who forces her to give up her PR work in his establishment. These encounters make her want to groan aloud realizing that the 'junctures' of her life seem 'to be marked off monotonously by men at desks' (p. 123). After standing up to the profiteering judgemental doctor, however, she begins to cry, giving him the opportunity to become more supportive, though he is consistently condescending and she feels he has won their battle (p. 38). The same kind of defeat taints the reconciliation with her father, who earlier throws her out of his house at the news of her pregnancy. She comes to reinterpret his hostility as her own construction: 'had I, perhaps, *wanted* to feel ill-used, misunderstood?', she ponders (p. 289). The hotelier, we discover, had known of her pregnancy, and had forced her to give up work with the benign intention (as she later interprets it) of protecting her reputation. The novel seems to endorse this sense of re-evaluating the key paternal figures, but this implied authorial stance is not fully coherent. It embodies an inadequate apology for the patriarchal structures that have been exposed: the hotelier's 'kindness' (p. 207) tacitly reinforces the prejudice against unmarried mothers; the doctor's surface decency is belied by his power over the distraught female patient; and the father's overtures bring home the reformed and dutiful daughter he originally required.

As self-doubt dilutes the challenge Jane Gardner offers to this triumvirate of patriarchs, the novel seems to embrace the sense of compromise that results, supplying a timid reassertion of the status quo. The critique of misogyny seems ultimately to be weakened by attitudes that partially reinforce it. (The same is true of the treatment of homophobia, racism, and anti-Semitism.) There is also a reassertion of class differentials, which, in the form of Jane's legacy from her great aunt Addy, utilizes a hoary literary convention that spirits Jane away from her L-shaped room, and the social and racial mix that characterizes the dilapidated Fulham house.

There is, possibly, a rhetorical dimension to the limited challenge: an oblique attack on prejudice is sometimes more effective than the direct assault; but a more convincing reading suggests that the novel cannot quite recall the dissident energies it has released, and this is particularly true of its treatment of the male double standard, with its condemnation of the women who fulfil masculine desires, and its attendant confusion about the institution of marriage. Jane has an *alter ego* in the prostitute 'Jane' who lives in the basement of the Fulham house, and who articulates the moral high ground in her sympathy for her pitiful clients. Her experiences enable her to see clearly the absurdity of the traditional marriage vows, and the unequal institution they underwrite: 'fancy promising to love, honour and obey – some *man*. That's what'd stick in my throat' (p. 133). Jane's own spirit of independence, in its strongest manifestation, corresponds to this refusal of sexual subservience; and it is the L-shaped room itself that supplies the space in which her personal growth is nourished. The novel ends with the sentimental conceit of Jane's return to the house, and her encounter with the new tenant in the L-shaped room, reliving Jane's withdrawn defiance of male rejection. The story of acquired strength and female self-assertion is set to repeat itself (p. 319), implying the need for the fully independent feminism that *The L-Shaped Room* cannot adequately frame.

The limits of Banks's novel, it must be stressed, are contextual limits, rather than a failure of authorial imagination. It is important to bear in mind that, in the early 1960s, before the contraceptive pill, and whilst abortion was still illegal, female sexuality was greatly restricted. Although a number of organizations campaigned for abortion in the 1950s, it was not legalized until 1967 (and then only if there were medical or psychological grounds). However, although abortion was illegal in the early 1960s, there was a proviso of 'at risk', which some doctors interpreted freely.[5] With this climate in mind, it is the issue of restricted opportunities for Banks's protagonist that strikes the most resonant feminist chord.

In her early novels Margaret Drabble takes up the problem of the conflict between family and career, an issue laid bare by the predicament of the single woman, contesting a complex of prejudices. It was by virtue of these early works that Drabble came to be viewed as a 'women's novelist', a useful label, suggests Ellen Cronan Rose, if it is taken to indicate that 'her subject was what it was like to be a woman in a world which calls woman the second sex'. Rose emphasizes the influence of Simone de Beauvoir's *The Second Sex* on the young Drabble, who takes forward the 'practical implications' of de Beauvoir's analysis of what it means to be a woman in a man's world.[6] Sarah Bennett, narrator of Drabble's first novel, *A Summer Bird-Cage* (1963), faces a dilemma that is emblematic of women's changing role, that apparently stark choice between marriage and career after graduation. The novel sets out to test the confines of this female birdcage. It is Sarah's sister Louise who challenges convention by marrying for his social position a man she dislikes, whilst retaining her lover. Sarah comes to wonder whether this disreputable behaviour might, in fact, imply a reversal of tradition from within, 'a blow for civilization' (p. 180). These antagonistic sisters are both vain and self-deluded, however, and the most positive feature of the plot is their recognition of each other, a reconcilement that offers a glimpse of a more genuine sisterhood.

More significant, in terms of Drabble's career, is the identity of Sarah as a writer: she is a would-be novelist, who wants 'to write a book like *Lucky Jim*' (p. 185). There are, of course, marked differences between *Lucky Jim* and the novel that Sarah produces – the conceit of the novel is to assign 'authorship' to the character, 'typing this last page' at the close (p. 207) – and these uncover a challenge in Drabble's design. Whereas Jim Dixon's experiences expose the absurdities and pomposities of university life, and, finally, enable him to turn his back on academia, for Sarah Bennett, university life never emerges as a serious option. Sarah feels restricted by an imposed sense of her sexual identity: 'you can't be a sexy don', she says, in a reflection that locates a simple inequality: 'it's all right for men, being learned and attractive, but for a woman it's a mistake' (pp. 183–4). Jim Dixon, of course, is ill suited to academia, but operates as an outsider wreaking comic havoc from within institutional life. Sarah Bennett, by contrast, is an outsider who remains outside, trying to accommodate herself to inhospitable options, one of which is writing a book like *Lucky Jim*. The fact that she 'fails' in this objective is very much to the purpose in this alternative account of an educated woman trying to make her way in the world. The more subdued comedy of *A Summer Bird-Cage* fits the mood of the outsider trying to acclimatize, and gently rebukes the mode of farce, the luxurious option employed by Kingsley Amis.

Drabble produces a significantly disruptive feature in this novel: that of the intrusive narrator breaking the frame of an apparently stable narrative. This may not produce the kind of ambivalent dualism of protagonist and narrator that characterizes *Lucky Jim*;[7] but, given the greater restraints of a first-person narrator, Drabble does oblige her reader to ask questions of a narrator who interrupts her narrative to confess to the withholding of central information about her emotional life – her love for someone now on a scholarship at Harvard (p. 73). Even if this interruption was not born of a conscious decision on Drabble's part, it has an important technical consequence.[8] The narrator expects to marry the currently absent Francis (p. 74), thus placing her at a greater distance from the action in which she is no longer a central emotional player. If this does make Sarah into 'some sort of *voyeuse*', as she suggests (p. 73), it also has the effect of invalidating the integrity of her observations, obliging us to subject her judgements of others to greater scrutiny. Finding a voice as a woman's writer is here an exploratory and incomplete enterprise, involving the stratagem of spoiling the easy contract of a first-person confessional style.

Some advancement is discernible in Rosamund Stacey, narrator of Drabble's *The Millstone* (1965), who successfully begins an academic career, ignoring the expectations that attach to a woman's sexual identity. However, this management of how her identity is gendered produces other distortions. Her relationships follow a pattern in which she gives the appearance of having lovers whilst actually abstaining from sex. Thus she cultivates a 'raffish seedy' air (p. 20), whilst sliding further into a disabling insularity that seems to stem from the 'maladjustment with regard to sex' that she shares with Sarah Bennett and other Drabble protagonists (p. 165). Her first sexual encounter leaves her pregnant by George Matthews, the character she believes to be homosexual and therefore not a potential long-term partner (though there are hints for the reader that his attachment to her might be serious). The novel then sets Rosamund's accomplishments – her entry into motherhood, as well as her scholarly determination – against the flaw in her personality, her inability to connect with others.

The accomplishments, however, are considerable. Rosamund, as a single mother, prevails in her determination to contest those social codes by which she is judged adversely, and that put pressure on her to give up her baby for adoption. Her discovery of a deep maternal bond with baby Octavia combines impressively with her refusal to allow her career to be disrupted. Rosamund's experiences seem, then, to invite a triumphant feminist reading, in which the Holy Grail of motherhood combined with professional success is attained.[9] However, Drabble's narrative style is less conclusive than this, and produces a cultivated indeterminacy generated by the flaw in Rosamund's character.

In the concluding episode she encounters George by chance, for the first time since their evening together. After telling him she has a baby, she lies about Octavia's age when he pointedly enquires (p. 164). Rosamund continues to resist the urge to reveal to George his paternity, and accepts her inability to bridge the gulf between them. 'There's nothing I can do about my nature, is there?' she asks, and he replies, with the novel's final words, 'no, nothing' (p. 172). The millstone of the title is thus revealed to be Rosamund's nature – the novel's final negative – rather than the social stigma of an illegitimate daughter that it ostensibly denotes. In this way Drabble produces a novel in a more subtle feminist vein than is recognized in the celebratory reading, since for Rosamund gender expectations have produced an emotional deformity, and an irresolvable double bind. She combines independence with motherhood in the face of convention, only to perceive this as a pyrrhic victory, won by nurturing her deadening solipsism.

Rosamund's 'success' is also tempered by the sense of class privilege that compounds her insularity. This element of the novel demonstrates emphatically the still persisting ideological perception of class, which recedes towards the end of the century. As the novel makes clear, she succeeds as a single mother because of her class standing: at crucial moments (especially in the hospital scenes) obstacles are removed and prejudices are tempered because of her social position. Class and wealth often produce diverse experiences of pregnancy and birth, rather than the community feeling that childbirth is often assumed to engender. In an interesting demonstration of how this discrepancy impacts upon the novel, Tess Cosslett compares Buchi Emecheta's *Second-Class Citizen* (1974) with *The Millstone*.[10] Cosslett rightly shows how Rosamund singularly fails to bond with the other women at the clinic she attends, how a personal contact (the consultant Prothero, her father's friend) wins her some privileges at the hospital, and how the bond with her baby serves only to make her more withdrawn. (This is a deliberate feature of the characterization in my reading.)

In *Second-Class Citizen*, however, the protagonist Adah experiences an accreted sense of inferiority based on a new conjunction of 'class and race consciousness', which 'cuts across' any glimmer of 'female bonding'.[11] Motherhood becomes a millstone for Adah by virtue of the combination of forces that define her as a second-class citizen. This includes a depiction of the racial discrimination experienced by Nigerian immigrants in 1960s London, notably when naked prejudice drives Adah and her family, in their pursuit of accommodation, to the 'ghetto' established by settlers in the 1940s, when Nigeria was 'still a colony' (p. 81).

The comparison between Emecheta and Drabble further emphasizes the sometimes stubborn persistence of conventional class divisions, and the way in which these are often enforced by racial prejudice in the post-war era. This may be a class structure in a state of flux, but that does not prevent the recrudescence or, worse, the supplementation, of conventional divisions. To the extent that the British class system is registering change, the crucial question is how quickly that change is seen to make a difference to the poorest stratum of society. Nell Dunn's first two works, *Up the Junction* (1963) and *Poor Cow* (1967), find a way of relating the aspirations and disappointments of working-class women to the broader development in the 1960s of women's liberation and sexual freedom. This social focus, rendered principally in vernacular dialogue or interior monologue, was seen by Dunn's first readers to be fresh and challenging, though her work from the 1960s elicited both praise and disapproval for its frankness.[12] A potential problem with Dunn's class fiction, however, is that it is the work of an 'outsider'. Dunn moved to Battersea in 1959 and did her 'fieldwork' as 'a refugee from smarter and more moneyed circles'.[13] This is not to say that Dunn's tenor is patronizing; in fact, she achieves a distinctive tone that is sympathetic yet notably unsentimental.

With hindsight, Dunn's fiction might be seen to bridge the class divide, and to assist in the process by that it is substantially dismantled. In context, however, Dunn's position of external observer, writing across the class barrier, produced a fictional mood that is problematic. The narrator (a fictionalized Nell Dunn), perceived as 'an heiress from Chelsea' (p. 10), remains anonymous, her motivation inscrutable. She participates in the life described without passion, seemingly for the sake of the copy it affords. This is troubling in the section 'Out with the Boys', where the narrator rides pillion in a bikers' 'burn-up' that leaves one of the riders dead whilst she remains unscathed (p. 87). The reader is left to wonder how far the narrator is implicated in the death, since the boys are presumably showing off for her benefit. Throughout the book she gathers revealing data only whilst her own involvement in the sexual economy of this world is presumed to be greater than it is.

*Poor Cow* represents a considerable technical advance over *Up the Junction* in that its passages of first-person narration serve to lead us deeper into the social milieu of heroine Joy. Her reflections on her life, which sometimes achieve the immediacy of the confessional mode, seem frank, uncensored, and are all the more affecting for that. Moreover, Dunn often switches suddenly from these first-person reflections to the third-person mode, a process of juxtaposition that seems to preclude the establishment of a withdrawn omniscient eye. (Joy, in any case, remains the principal focalizer throughout.) Joy is the wife of a petty criminal, and represents a flourishing of *joie de vivre* in the unlikeliest of places, and against all odds: the cruelty of her hateful husband Tom, the prison suicide of her lover Dave, the danger of being lured into semi-prostitution. These seem insignificant in the face of Joy's assertion of her own sensuality and her powerful maternal bond with her son Jonny. Even Joy's pride in her success as a photographer's nude model seems genuine, impervious to the threat of exploitation (p. 80). In this sense Drabble is right to counsel readers of a later generation against the temptation to view Joy 'not as a symbol of liberation, but as someone to be liberated'.[14] In the conclusion, brushing aside the careless brutality of husband Tom, Joy realizes how she will seem to passers-by: 'if anyone saw me now they'd say, "She's had a rough night, poor cow"' (p. 135). The title image resonates, underscoring the character's self-knowledge, which is rooted in her revealed role as Mother Courage: all that matters is the bond with the child (p. 134).

There are moments in *Poor Cow*, however, where that externalized view-point that hampers *Up the Junction* resurfaces. In Joy's letters to her imprisoned lover Dave, for example, Dunn's attempts to render Joy's semi-literate mode of expression can seem condescending, as when she recounts a plan to attend 'aleycustion' (elocution) lessons (p. 49), or when she sums up her feelings: 'I'm so raped up in Your love I never wont to be un raped' (p. 44). The mistake implies delusion, a sexual oppression that Joy cannot perceive. But this is not appropriate in connection with the genuine mutual passion of Dave and Joy, and there is an uncomfortable sense that the author is being unfair to her creation. The occasional arch misspelling in Joy's letters, which are otherwise properly punctuated, and constructed with due attention to correct syntax, reveals the presence of the knowing author, not the 'orthography of the uneducated' (in Raymond Williams's phrase).[15] Sexual freedom in Nell Dunn's fiction, then, is heavily qualified by contextual factors, not least of which are those with a bearing upon the author's own situation.

The issue of gender often suggests restrictions that are concealed in the popular accounts of new social energies. It is difficult, for example, to find serious fiction that endorses the ideal of the counterculture that, in the late 1960s, promoted 'a passionate desire to meld Utopia with everyday living', in the hope of fostering a sense of common humanity through the expression of universal love.[16] For the feminist movement, the contraceptive pill is generally perceived to have placed the power of reproduction in women's hands, enabling them to choose sexual experience without the fear of becoming pregnant. The images of female sexuality in the 1960s were contradictory, however, 'communicating blatantly opposing messages of freedom and subordination'.[17] There was a 'double oppression' of women in the libertarian talk of the 1960s, where sexual liberation and freedom were a convenient way of facilitating predatory male desires.[18]

The foment for social change, and the distinctiveness of women's unrest, is succinctly conveyed in Jill Neville's *The Love Germ* (1969) set in the Latin Quarter of Paris in 1968. The novel conveys the revolutionary idealism of May 1968, but also expresses the arrogant mistreatment by male militants of the women that they depended on. Neville uses the metaphor of a sexually transmitted disease both to evoke the dangerous excitement of the times, and to satirize the more earnest revolutionary ambitions. Free love and beneficent social change are ideologically yoked in the mind-set of the times, and the 'germ', which is both revolutionary and sexual, spreads dramatically. In this there is an obvious puncturing of anarchist Giorgio's intellectual self-importance. Finding himself infected with an STD, he withdraws some of his postgraduate grant and flies to London to avail himself of reliable free treatment, and feels gratitude for the society he purports to hate (p. 79).

The association of the 'love germ' is not wholly ironic, however. Polly's attraction to the dark, unkempt, and promiscuous Giorgio is also a reaction against the small-mindedness of her parent's generation. Giorgio, who does most of the 'infecting', biological and intellectual, is, thinks Polly, 'a man that would make her father want to fumigate the room' (p. 138). The ambivalence about the love germ tips towards cautious celebration, endorsing a sense of libertarian generational change. Giorgio progresses beyond Anarchism, and affiliates himself with the Situationists, and a sense of personal revolution: 'let us start our pleasure and the castle of sadness will crumble' (p. 145). This is an expression of the Situationists' challenge to the society of the spectacle, a challenge mounted through the construction of situations in which individuals would seek out their desire, effecting an imaginative transformation of daily life, turning it into something passionate and dramatic.[19] The novel's conclusion, which reunites Polly and Giorgio in their sexual passion, catches something of this liberating personal politics.[20]

Yet the novel's strongest impression, despite this ending, is the assumed superiority of the male characters, and their condescending and exploitative attitude to women. Underneath the mood of political revolution, Neville discovers the discontent that will fire the organized political feminism in the 1970s. The problem is succinctly expressed in the attitude of the 'professional revolutionary' Gottlieb who reflects: 'maybe we ought to protect women a bit after all. If they go out into the blizzard on their own, they develop marvellous characters, but you can strike matches on their personality' (p. 112). Within Neville's semi-satire one can see, in Fay Weldon's terms, 'the forces of Praxis converging', but for the 'gender revolution' and not the Communist one.[21] Such forces would celebrate the right to develop marvellous character, with scant regard to the offended male sensibility.[22]

The last of my examples from the 1960s, illustrating those feminist impulses that were soon to be consolidated, is innovative in its efforts to extend the realist mode in establishing an alternative approach to the re-evaluation of gender. This is *The Magic Toyshop* (1967), a transitional novel in Angela Carter's *oeuvre*, anticipating the fantastic elements of her later work, but utilizing realist codes to engage the reader. It is through her use of fairy-tale components that Carter disrupts the realism that the novel otherwise cultivates. Carter recognizes the misogyny of the conventional fairy-tale, as well as the amenability of fairy-tales to being rewritten and disseminated in ways which enshrine particular (especially patriarchal) social codes; but it is through this realization that Carter reclaims the fairy-tale as a medium for the feminist writer.[23]

In *The Magic Toyshop* the challenge to the fairy-tale is conducted in an ambivalent spirit. Where the fairy-tales of the brothers Grimm or Perrault suppress their subtext of sexuality, Carter makes the emerging sexuality of her fifteen-year-old protagonist Melanie the narrative's driving force. The novel opens with her celebration and exploration of her newly awakened body (p. 1), and makes this sensuality responsible for instigating the causal chain of events. Melanie's parents are absent, abroad, and one night her restlessness inspires her to an act of transgressive usurpation. Unable to sleep, she tries on her mother's wedding dress, and contrives to lock herself out of the house. The apple tree by her bedroom window supplies the only route back in, but the climb leaves the dress blood-stained, and in ribbons. When, the next morning, a telegram announcing the parents' death arrives, Melanie is convinced that the donning of the dress has caused the tragedy (pp. 9–24).

The preparatory element of a folk- or fairy-tale often requires an interdiction to be violated, and Melanie's transgression serves this purpose.[24] However, Carter's mixed mode also casts doubt on this principle of poetic causality. The overt symbolism of the opening episode denotes Melanie's desired passage into sexual adulthood (the bloodied dress), as well as the assertion of womanhood through the usurpation of her mother. However, the persisting realism also makes the reader baulk at this unequivocal symbolism, and at the idea that the death of the parents is causally connected to Melanie's midnight adventure. These opposing effects function together to make female bodily experience the central issue, and to undercut the guilt associated with its expression.

The novel shows, however, that female sexuality can be channelled in different ways, and Melanie's own self-image as an object of desire, as when she imagines herself as a model for Toulouse-Lautrec (p. 1), shows her to have imbibed male constructions of the female. This makes her vulnerable to Uncle Philip, the toyshop owner, to whom Melanie and her orphaned siblings have to go to live. Another symbolic set-piece in the novel is Uncle Philip's puppet-show of Leda and the swan, in which Melanie is obliged to play Leda against her uncle's puppet-swan. Uncle Philip, the clinical puppet-master performing the 'rape' vicariously, demonstrates his inner nature, which is the very embodiment of patriarchal tyranny.

The oppression of Aunt Margaret and her brothers Finn and Francie is partly overturned as the ogre is confronted. Discovering the incestuous relationship of Margaret and Francie, a libidinous energy that subverts his patriarchal order, Uncle Philip sets fire to the shop, leaving just Finn and Melanie to survive the conflagration. 'Nothing is left but us', says Finn, and grappling with the significance of their new start 'they faced each other with a wild surmise' (p. 200). Eschewing, now, the conventions of fairy-tale, Carter turns the resolution over to the interpretive work of the reader. The self-consuming energies of the patriarch have been violently unleashed, leaving the vertiginous possibilities of a different kind of order, a matter indeed for the 'wild surmise'.

## Second-Wave Feminism

In *Nights at the Circus* (1984) Carter makes that wild surmise, employing fantastic elements in a way that demonstrates the political reality of second-wave feminism, and the changed collective consciousness it has, by this time, brought about. The protagonist Fevvers is a trapeze artist who claims to have 'hatched out of a bloody great egg' (p. 7), and to have wings and the ability to fly. As a freak, she is a stage and circus attraction whose otherness the reader is asked to ponder: is this otherness genuine, or is she a con artist? The novel thus makes the plausibility of its own fantastic elements a matter of internal debate, a debate that leads the reader, by analogy, to consider the principal theme: the treatment of woman as object, and the means by which female self-identity can be asserted beyond the appropriating male gaze. The setting of 1899, the time of parliamentary debates about women's suffrage (pp. 78–9), puts the novel in the broader context of twentieth-century feminism, but with the certainty of hindsight.

Carter's method is to render Fevvers less of a freak, and more of an achieved empathic character as the novel progresses, even though her status as a bird-woman hybrid seems also more convincing. This empathic enhancement is assisted by the technical shifts of the third and final section, which contains passages of Fevvers's own narration in the first person. The reader's response is also guided by the response of Walser, the male journalist who decides to follow Fevvers on her circus tours. Initially he sees her as an object of intrigue, but there is also the germ of a more involved response in his first perception of her act: 'he was astonished to discover that it was the limitations of her act in themselves that made him briefly contemplate the unimaginable – that is, the absolute suspension of disbelief. For, in order to earn a living, might not a genuine bird-woman – in the implausible event that such a thing existed – have to pretend she was an artificial one?' (p. 17). The double bluff underscores the novel's feminist vision, revealing a general significance in Fevvers's predicament. Walser recognizes that *subsistence* for a 'freak' would depend upon the concealment of the exotic under a disguise of artificiality. The paradox of such a situation would be produced, not by the behaviour of the bird-woman herself, but by the contradictory desires of the observers.

The eventual romantic union of Fevvers and Walser consolidates a more propitious understanding of woman. This is clinched in the significance of Fevvers's infectious laughter at the novel's close, a response that gently mocks Walser's original fascination with Fevvers as a fascinating oddity. The laughter, which is said 'to twist and shudder across the entire globe' (p. 295), is a sign of the carnivalesque debunking of the male gaze that the novel promotes. This is a global feminist possibility, demonstrated through the 'confidence' that enables Fevvers to undermine her status as object by seeming to cultivate it. This apparent ambivalence is matched in the deployment of fantasy: despite the debunking of illusion, fantasy is utilized as a positive strategy of subversion. The underlying point is that the feminine remains other – in the same way that Fevvers's fantastic origins are made credible – but that this otherness needs to be self-defining, and so 'fantastic' only from a hostile perspective, in the final analysis.

To understand the context in which such an assured imaginative rendering of female otherness is possible, it is necessary to review the achievements of second-wave feminism in the 1970s. For many women, feminism in the 1970s had 'the force and attraction of a profound explanatory system', galvanizing and empowering women already experiencing the benefits of post-war education reform, and the consumer boom, and now feeling liberated from the crumbling traditional family structure. A double standard often still operated, of course, despite the general trend of reform. Michèle Roberts conveys this economically in *The Visitation* (1983) when protagonist Helen Home is made to feel she has 'failed' by passing her 'eleven-plus' exam while her twin brother Felix does not (p. 16). As the metamorphosis gathered pace, however, it was women who found themselves 'in the driving seat of these profound social changes'.[25] The 1970s, in fact, witnessed a dramatic change in gender relations – far more significant than the 'sexual revolution' of the 1960s – as the accumulating shifts in attitude broke through into popular consciousness.

This sudden visibility of longer-term changes can be measured not simply by the new intellectual climate, and the rise of 'Women's Studies' in universities, but on the basis of practical political measures. The initial demands of the Women's Liberation movement in the early 1970s, as approved by the early women's conferences, were material ones: 'equal pay, equal education and opportunity, twenty-four-hour nurseries, free contraception and abortion on demand'. In 1974 the movement added two more demands to this list: the right to 'legal and financial independence', and the right to self-defined sexuality. Legislation which, on the face of it, went some way to meeting these demands was passed by the Labour government that came to power in 1974: Acts were passed in 1975 covering Sex Discrimination and Equal Pay, as well as paid maternity leave, which was made a statutory right. However poorly this legislation operated, its instant appearance on the statute book indicates the extraordinary success of the Women's Liberation movement in achieving its headline demands. (Free contraception had been made available in 1974.)[26]

The writer who perhaps best catches the mood of second-wave feminism is Fay Weldon. The characteristic mood of righteous outrage and practical determination is evident in one of Weldon's best novels, *Praxis* (1978), coming from a 'middle period' in which her feminism is consolidated. *Praxis* is representative of Weldon's art in depicting the slow process of enlightenment that enables an exploited female character to assert herself, and break free from the shackles of patriarchy. In Weldon's presentation, patriarchy is a system that exploits biological difference to produce and substantiate social inequality as a 'natural' state. Praxis Duveen learns this lesson through her relationship with Willy, a university contemporary who privileges his own education and career over hers, making her his drudge.

Praxis eventually puts the failure of her relationship with Willy down to her inability to conceal the fact that she 'was too nearly Willy's equal', the sin that provokes the repression. Praxis' husband Ivor enshrines the principle of a dominance asserted on the basis of insecurity: he has no interest in her past, or in her principles, and merely 'wanted her life to have begun the day he met her, and his opinions to be hers' (p. 178). Such inequality is abroad as a religious principle for many, who 'predicate some natural law of male dominance and female subservience, and call that God' (p. 13). At school, the principle is formalized for Praxis and her sister, who are taught that they are the daughters of Eve, and responsible for original sin (p. 18).

The novel's title implies the political changes that are abroad, 'the forces of Praxis converging' for the 'gender revolution';[27] and we are duly informed that Praxis' name means 'turning-point, culmination, action'. But Weldon extends the definition to connote, also, 'orgasm; some said the Goddess herself' (p. 9). This enriches the feminist challenge the character embodies, serving to reverse and supplant the false religion of patriarchy through positive action, and sexual assertiveness. This is not, however, presented in the manner of a feminist tract, and is subject to doubt and uncertainty, an emphasis that is especially clear in the episode of Praxis' experience as a prostitute when she unwittingly takes as a client the father who had walked out on his family years before. She accedes to sex a second time, having worked out his identity, and having satisfied herself that 'incest' is a social construct, referring to something that happens within families (and so inapplicable to a father who abandoned the child). This time her orgasm, a mixture of 'bitterness and exultation', elicits from him a reverent response. She is said to have 'altogether demystified him', turning him from 'saint to client, from father to man' (pp. 143–4).

Through transgression, patriarchy is dismantled as the father is de-fathered, and the sexual power – along with the religious aura – passes to Praxis. The ambivalence, the 'bitterness', stems partly from the sense that this self-assertion is a reversal of power, rather than a deconstruction of the power relationship itself. Recognizing the pragmatism of arrogating power to oneself, the feminist will move through bitterness to exultation. Another source of the ambivalence, however, is the later revelation that the father, knowing Praxis' identity, may have sought the incestuous encounter (p. 260). Again, Weldon makes the struggle of feminist assertion a difficult and con-tradictory process.

However, when Praxis employs her skills (acquired as an advertising copy-writer) as editor of a newspaper for the Women's Movement, the novel courts a more programmatic feminist message.[28] Praxis makes her conver-sion through the writing of her 'rousing editorials' (p. 261), which are received by others as 'the stuff of revolution: the focusing of a real discon-tent' (p. 270); but Weldon distances herself from the easy circulation of ideas, and returns us to the difficulty of action in a conclusion that explains why Praxis has spent a period of time in prison. She chose, we discover, to smother an unwanted Down's Syndrome baby, a decisive act of sisterhood that seems 'like the rectifying of a mistake', and that finally grants her access 'into the real world, where feelings were sharp and clear, however painful' (pp. 272–3).

For the reader, however, it is not so much the actual event described that forms the challenge, as the realization that positive feminist action depends on a difficult and subversive overturning of accepted social codes. In *Praxis* the locus of this is the challenge to 'Nature'. In a section of first-person narrative Praxis appeals to her 'sisters' to see 'Nature' as 'on the man's side', producing a catalogue of illnesses related to pregnancy and birth, and consigning women past child-bearing age to the scrap-heap: 'it seems to me that we must fight nature tooth and claw' (p. 147). In this, the voice of Praxis seems to correspond with Weldon's.

If Weldon does write 'survival manuals for women', as one critic suggests, this practical element stems from the quality of the debates she encourages.[29] A seminal aspect of this is the resistance of easy or obvious positions, and Weldon is especially wary of the unthinking or fanatical stance. Groups of women acting in concert are sometimes lampooned in her fiction. The most startling instance in *Praxis* is the encounter with the 'New Women' on the bus, confident, sexually provocative, and satiated; Praxis recognizes these women as reaping the rewards of the feminist effort, but having progressed to an empty freedom that is 'heartless, soulless, mindless' (p. 14). Weldon is seeking to prioritize an independent, experiential effort, and to demonstrate that glib notions of sisterhood are inherently damaging. But this can also make her work appear to oppose received feminist ideas, and to install compromised solutions to the fact of gender oppression. This issue lies at the heart of *The Life and Loves of a She-Devil* (1983).

In *Praxis* the external 'control' of the woman's body, whether through natural forces, or the patriarchal control of those forces, is the focus of feminist resistance. In *The Life and Loves of a She-Devil*, where the desire of 'she-devil' Ruth Patchett is to refashion herself as an idealized object of male desire, the resisting gesture seems oddly to collude with the oppressive system. Structurally, the feminist impulse is more systematic than in *Praxis*, where the protagonist endures exploitation of various kinds for much of the novel. Here, Ruth Patchett puts her plan of revenge on her unfaithful husband into swift motion, burning down the family home, and depositing her children with the wayward spouse and his mistress whilst she hatches a plot that will destroy their lives. In the process of framing her husband for embezzlement, she accrues the funds that will enable her to undergo the extensive surgery to transform her appearance from seeming 'rough-hewn in granite' (p. 87), to a replica of the mistress, romantic novelist Mary Fisher.

The values of popular romantic fiction are easily exploded, as Mary Fisher is given a lesson in 'the nature of love' (p. 105) that exposes the lies she has been telling to the world (p. 7). Ruth, in the guise of housekeeper Molly Wishant, is unequivocal in her repudiation of women's pulp fiction, and the ways in which it restricts the 'emotional maturity' and 'moral sense' of the women who consume it (p. 204). Having supplanted Mary Fisher, she writes a romantic novel that Fisher's publisher wants to publish. She establishes her moral superiority by refusing permission: the point of the exercise is to reveal that writing such material is 'not so difficult' (p. 256).

The main interpretive puzzle concerns Ruth's desire to undergo the extensive and dangerous 'remaking' that will render her an imitation of her rival, and 'an impossible male fantasy made flesh' (p. 239); but what appears to be a simple capitulation to the male perspective is in truth more complex and more interesting. The process of surgery at first seems the epitome of controlling male desire, confirmation of cosmetic surgeon Mr Ghengis's feeling that his occupation was 'the nearest a man could get to motherhood' (p. 229). However, Ghengis and the other surgeon Black fall in love with Ruth, a devotion necessary for the generation of her beauty (p. 245). Moreover, they are squeamish where she is resolute on the matter of shortening her legs (p. 242), and this indicates that she has pushed beyond the surgeons' intellectual limits, accruing to herself the psychological control of her own remaking.

In a development of the attack on nature in *Praxis*, Ruth demonstrates the principle that 'she devils are beyond nature' (p. 142) so that when her project is complete, she feels that 'even nature bows to my convenience' (p. 255).

The Frankenstein motif is overtly signalled, and the major operations Ruth undergoes take place in the midst of violent electrical storms. Ruth, as the author of her new self, is both Frankenstein *and* Frankenstein's monster, in a gesture that reverses the sense of Mary Shelley's cautionary tale. As she-devil, however, Ruth is actually pushing through to a position that is beyond gender opposition: the struggle simplifies itself to a question 'merely of power' (p. 256).

For many feminists, this will seem a worrying conclusion, an appropriation (and so a confirmation) of given power relations. Even here, however, Weldon supplies an element of resonant uncertainty for the reader's reflection. By reconstructing herself as the object of desire, Ruth demystifies that object, stressing its artifice. At the same time, she fulfils that dream of taming nature, reversing its assault on the female. But the position of power thus secured, in Mary Fisher's tower on a crumbling cliff-top, is precarious, still vulnerable to the actions of nature; and in its artificiality it seems a dubious position for moral authority. There is certainly something unresolved in Weldon's assault on 'Nature'; but in another sense the limited feminist message seems deliberate. Implicitly, the novel is demonstrating that this is no enduring victory, but rather the imperfect pinnacle that a woman can achieve in the structures of patriarchal power.[30]

In both *Praxis* and *The Life and Loves of a She-Devil*, Weldon's characteristic technique of combining sections of first- and third-person narrative serves her purpose well. The effect is to juxtapose an external view of her central characters, with an evolving account of their personal struggles. It is a technique that demonstrates the discrepancy between a woman's sense of self, and the world's perception of her, a kind of feminist technique-as-discovery that elicits the reader's sympathy for the individual's motivation whilst slowly invalidating the external, hostile view. But that hostility has remained a focus of opposition for feminist writers, especially in their attempts to promote a broader understanding of gender roles. Jeanette Winterson has been a key figure in shaking up that conventional mind-set, and in advancing more fluid representations of gender, especially through her treatments of lesbianism and androgyny.

Winterson constructs her fictions as quests for self-knowledge, specifically concerning the way in which the desire of the individual resists given patterns of behaviour or understanding. Her first, autobiographical novel, *Oranges Are Not the Only Fruit* (1985), established her as a key exponent of feminist fiction. The novel's focus is the burgeoning lesbian identity of narrator Jeanette, perceived as demonic by the evangelical Lancashire community in which she is raised.

Jeanette's task is both to resist the repression that she encounters, and that has been suffered by the preceding generation, and to establish the grounds for a co-operative sense of sisterhood, beyond the judgemental antagonism of the society she knows. Miss Jewsbury, who opportunistically comes to Jeanette's aid when she is denounced for her sexuality, has learned to keep quiet about her own homosexuality, though she is suspected of being 'not holy' (p. 105). There is even a hint that Jeanette's foster-mother may have had lesbian leanings. In her photo album the photograph of an old boyfriend's sister is situated in a section devoted to 'Old Flames', though it soon disappears (p. 36). Jeanette, armed with the orange 'aura' and the 'orange demon' (p. 106) of her resistant imagination and defiant lesbianism (the two are linked), will neither conceal her feelings nor allow them to be rechannelled in the expression of religious devotion.

In the manner of Angela Carter, the realist code that governs Jeanette's narrative (the story of growing up in an enclosed community), is combined with narrative strands drawn from or inspired by fable, myth, and folklore. The combination of these disparate approaches to story is characteristic of Winterson's technique in which the reader's hold on normative social reality is shaken up by the appeal to a higher kind of psychological 'truth'. Consequently, a readjustment of how that social reality is perceived is demanded. This method is announced in the discussion of story and History, where emphasis is placed on the relativity of narrative. The narrator insists that the separation of fact and fiction in the dichotomy of storytelling and history is 'curious': rather, it is suggested, history should be celebrated in its complexity, 'like string full of knots', so that 'the best you can do is admire the cat's cradle, and maybe knot it up a bit more' (p. 91). The technique that results from such a conviction is also a challenge to the stereotypical tramline thinking of patriarchy, and historical teleology.

The alternative visual metaphor that Winterson employs to describe her technique is that of the spiral, a form that 'is fluid and allows infinite movement' (p. xiii). Something of this movement is shown in the fantasy story of Winnet, adopted by a sorcerer who subsequently banishes her. (If she stays, she will lose the powers the sorcerer has bestowed upon her [pp. 137–43].) She chooses to find a different way of utilizing her powers, and sets out on a journey towards a 'beautiful city' (p. 149), determining that it will be 'a place where truth mattered' (p. 154). Winnet's quest thus becomes a metaphor for the writer's search for a style with access to a heightened psychological truth.

If the metafictional aspect of the fantasy story is straightforward, the economy with which it anticipates the novel's conclusion, and the surprising return of Jeanette to her foster-mother, is more subtle. In the final pages, Winnet's narrative is incorporated into Jeanette's as she ponders on her life away from home, in a metaphorical city 'full of towers'. This is the locus of escape, but it makes her long 'to sit on the ground again' (p. 157). The city of towers denotes the work of the unfettered imagination, which also needs to be grounded in social reality. The quest of Winnet (whose name combines first and last syllables from the author's surname and Christian name) defines the limits of the writer's detachment. In this autobiographical work, the quest of Jeanette the narrator is linked to Winterson's search for her identity as a writer, so that when Jeanette claims that she is a 'prophet' (p. 156) this is also a definition of Winterson's desired role as the producer of a new feminist mythology.

The chapter titles are taken from the first eight books of the Bible, and the most interesting reference is to the Book of Ruth, which resonates in the final chapter. Here Winterson makes use of biblical Ruth's extraordinary loyalty to her mother-in-law Naomi as a point of reference for Jeanette's return to the foster-mother who had denounced and betrayed her. The need to return, previsioned in Jeanette's adoption and completion of Winnet's quest, suggests also that the foster-mother may have something of the sorcerer about her after all, inspiring/bestowing Jeanette's gift of imagination. In a breathtaking manoeuvre Winterson subverts a text from the Bible, the seminal patriarchal text for some feminists, discovering within it a lesson of sisterhood or female loyalty that might acknowledge the lesbian within the fold, not as an outsider, but as the *instigator* of a non-antagonistic feminist ethos.[31]

Much of Winterson's work offers a corrective to the extreme feminist position that emerged in the late 1970s, misanthropic in its implications, and that branded all men as potential rapists, and advocated 'political lesbianism' as the only way forward. A crisis point was reached at the Women's Liberation conference in 1978, which 'divided so acrimoniously on the question of inherent masculine violence', reports Sheila Rowbotham, 'that no one was ever prepared to call another one'. Perhaps this internal dispute and collapse is partly a tribute to the movement's achievements: having delivered practical political change in key areas, and having contributed to a sea-change in public perception, its purpose had been served. The loss of consensus, however, also took its lead from the broader political climate, and stands as another indication of the confrontational politics of the late 1970s.[32]

Opposing forces were in play in the wake of Women's Liberation and the transformation of gender identity it helped to expedite. The loss of faith in the institution of marriage in the 1970s is demonstrated by a rising divorce rate, which meant that there was one divorce for every three marriages by the end of the decade. Significant changes in sexual behaviour and attitudes were abroad, marked especially by an increasing tendency for young people to live together, and a greater tolerance of lesbianism. Yet the new political mood of the 1980s, with its emphasis on personal attainment, effected a disruption of feminism's collective goals. On the one hand, 'the individual-istic emphasis of the 1980s' seemed to help women slip the chains of their traditional inhibitions and confinements; but on the other hand, personal gain seemed to be an arbitrary matter: 'a few might rise, but many didn't; this was the downside of individualism'. A new dichotomy emerged along political lines in response to the self-advancement that characterized the 1980s. Women on the right promoted the discourse of individual assertion, whilst women on the left expressed 'a thwarted yearning for a longer-term responsibility for conserving – communities, human life, resources.' The most memorable symbol of female protest in the 1980s was the Greenham camp, based at the Greenham air base, and founded in protest at the presence of Cruise missiles. In 1982 30,000 women joined hands and encircled the base. In promoting peace, and also situating themselves against the free mar-ket of Thatcherism, the Greenham women 'symbolized a web of human life' for many people.[33]

In *Sexing the Cherry* (1989) Winterson's exuberant magic realism delivers some pointed connections with her contemporary context. Dog-Woman, the supernaturally powerful seventeenth-century giantess, is partly a magnif-icent figure of female vengeance, a fantastic development of Fay Weldon's she-devil, Ruth Patchett. There are obvious limits to Dog-Woman's lib-erating potential, however, contained within the patriarchal institutions of seventeenth-century England; her *alter ego*, the twentieth-century chemist and ecological campaigner, draws strength from the hallucinations in which she imagines herself empowered to gather together the agents of ecolog-ical destruction in a huge sack. These financiers and world leaders are forced to redistribute resources, and to undergo 'compulsory training in feminism and ecology' (pp. 121–3). Yet this is not a simple extension of the fantastic impulse of Dog-Woman's tale. Winterson closes down the fantasy, and insists on a realistic interpretation of the contemporary echo, where the campaigner's hallucinations are linked with a protest in which she was exposed to mercury pollution (p. 123). This raises the possibility that Dog-Woman's entire narrative is the heroic campaigner's invention, a prod-uct of mercury poisoning. The fantastic creation is thus redefined as an imaginary mutant, the polluter's nemesis.

The tension between referentiality and fantasy in Winterson's work is often productive, but it is also a formal correlative to the conflicts that attend the fate of feminism. In this interplay between referentiality and fantasy, *Written on the Body* (1992) stands as a limit case. It is an expression of lost love, and the emotional suffering it begets; but it is also a demonstration of the impossibility of fully communicating such intensely personal emotion without having recourse to cliché, or conveying a sense of delusive fantasy.

The novel's title indicates its chief stylistic innovation, the attempt to fuse the physical and the textual, to infuse language with the sensations of erotic love. One's essential self, the novel suggests, is found in a secret code 'written on the body', and decipherable by the sensitive lover's hands reading the body of the other like braille (p. 89). In a consciously overwritten sequence Winterson extends this idea of intimacy, and attempts to reclaim the description of the body from the deadening clinicalness of medical discourse. A sequence of erotic celebrations of the (androgynous) narrator's lost lover's body is given, each a response to a technical description of a bodily part or attribute (pp. 115–39). The narrator pushes through and beyond the technical detail in the attempt to discover a visceral sensuality (that also embraces disease), and in this novel such a sequence inevitably appears to be gendered, since it is a repudiation of the objective and patriarchal clinical view.

The significant 'fantasy' or imaginative element of the novel thus involves a sustained deliberation about the details of physicality. In another key passage, a simplistic computer culture is equated with an alternative and dangerous kind of fantasy, exemplified in the possibilities of Virtual Reality. Rejecting the possibilities of Virtual sex, the narrator states a preference for 'a real English meadow' (p. 97) as a site for romance, thus renouncing the solipsistic fantasy world of the computer.

Winterson's use of magic realism, a blend of purposive fantasy with verisimilitude, stands in opposition to the reductive culture of postmodernity, as she sees it. The problem for the narrator of *Written on the Body* is that the overwhelming negativity of lost love can be overcome only by a kind of dubious fantasy projection. Accordingly, at the very end a 'Virtual' image of the lost lover Louise is conjured up in the mind's eye of the narrator, who then introduces the conundrum of whether or not this is a happy ending (p. 190). The reader, witnessing this retreat into the kind of fantasy in which the real is distanced, is implicitly invited to think the ending a dismal one. The defeat of love, and the life-denying ramifications of the defeat, produces a narrowing of narrative possibilities. The way in which the gesture towards androgyny is subtly undermined by the novel's more polarized lesbian sentiment speaks also to this perceived impasse.

The mood I am tracing is one that anticipates the revisionary energies of post-feminism, and it is very well illustrated in Angela Carter's final novel, *Wise Children* (1991). Here, the exuberance of *Nights at the Circus* is evident in a tempered form. The novel is presented as Dora Chance's autobiographical account of the lives she and her identical twin Nora have led as music-hall performers. Dora looks back on her family history from the perspective of her seventy-fifth birthday, a post-war vantage point from which the twentieth century can be judged. Notionally, Dora is garnering the materials for her memoirs and her family history; but the idiom catches the freshness of unpolished spoken memories, and this lends a vitality – and a consequent authenticity – to the female voice offering an informal 'history'.

If there is an implicit feminist challenge to patriarchal codes in the self-asserting impetus of female autobiography, Dora's narrative makes full use of that potential. The context is that of a declining, post-imperial Britain, a decline that is directly associated with the cultural scene. Dora and Nora are the illegitimate daughters of Sir Melchior Hazard, 'our greatest living Shakespearean', and the last true proponent of 'the imperial Hazard dynasty that bestrode the British theatre like a colossus for a century and a half' (pp. 89, 10). The low-brow music-hall careers of the Chance sisters contrast with Melchior Hazard's theatrical reputation, built from playing Shakespeare's great tragic male heroes (except Hamlet [p. 89]), and this indicates a significant opposition: tragedy is associated with patriarchy and cultural imperialism, whilst comedy nurtures the corrective, feminine impulse. In fact, the comedic force is less programmatic than it sounds in summary. This is clear in the central comic episode, the Hollywood production of *A Midsummer Night's Dream*, in which Nora and Dora appear. Far from benefiting from a positive influx of the joyous singing and dancing Chances, the production is vulgarized by the demands of mass media appeal and turns out a 'disaster' (p. 148).

The ambivalence about comedy, and about the efficacy of the debunking female spirit, is announced in Dora's assertion that 'there are limits to the power of laughter'. She goes on to say that 'though I may hint at them from time to time, I do not propose to step over them' (p. 220). This is an apt account of the novel's muted ebullience, which stems from a number of blurred distinctions. Carter structures her novel in the manner of a Shakespearean comedy, revolving around the mistaken identity of twins, and the confusion about paternity. Yet Melchior Hazard's failure properly to acknowledge his true daughters is a continuing source of anguish for them (though they do ultimately succeed in inveigling their way 'into the heart' of the Hazard family [p. 226]). More importantly, there are significant limits to the carnivalesque debunking the sisters can indulge in.

This is illustrated in the novel's most transgressive moment, the coupling of Dora and Peregrine, her uncle but publicly known as her father, on the occasion of her real father's one hundredth birthday party. In the apparent attempt to 'fuck the house down' (p. 220), the pair break several taboos: sex between the elderly (Peregrine is 'a centenarian', Dora is seventy-five); sex in the father's bedroom; and on the occasion of a celebration in his honour. However, this is not the straightforward debunking of patriarchal authority it appears to be (though it is partly that). In the middle of the act, Peregrine (the illusionist) exclaims 'life's a carnival', and Dora soberly points out that 'the carnival's got to stop, some time' (p. 222). Carter here signals the limits of Bakhtinian carnival, which has sometimes been misappropriated as a model for the radical social challenge: but when carnival ends, the status quo is reasserted.[34] During sex with Peregrine 'everything seemed possible' to Dora, but the episode also occasions the memory of her earlier seduction by him at the age of thirteen (pp. 221–2).

The apparent assertion of transgressive female sexuality is thus reconfigured as the flipside of the uncle/father's abuse, and this revelation takes its place in a pervasive incest motif, which serves to make the novel's title profoundly double-edged. Earlier in the novel Peregrine, in a Shakespearean paraphrase, gives 'the gypsy's warning' that 'it's a wise child that knows its own father', continuing 'but wiser yet the father who knows his own child' (p. 73).[35] Such wisdom is hard won amidst the confusion about paternity, and the incestuous predation of the patriarch, which taints sexual 'knowledge'. (Both Melchior, and his father Ranulph before him, have married their 'stage' daughters.)

In the final pages Dora and Nora become the guardians of three-month-old twins, offspring of Melchior's son Gareth, with the true potential to 'be wise children all right' (p. 230). It is an archly constructed conclusion, since a full explanation about the babies' origin is said not 'to belong to the world of comedy' (p. 227). But also missing from the comedic world constructed here is the father figure. Wisdom for these children seems to hinge on *not* knowing their own father, and this seems to be a retreat from the engagement with patriarchy that orders much of Carter's fictional world.

## Post-Feminism

In the climate of post-feminism the explicit critique of patriarchy has become an anachronism, as more complex and self-conscious gender identities are taken for granted. This situation was not established instantaneously, of course, and it is now possible to see more hesitant or inconclusive treatments of gender to have participated in the intellectual milieu in which feminism is re-evaluated.

A writer whose work corresponds to the climate of transition or incompletion is Anita Brookner. Initially, this connection may seem improbable. It may also appear curious to include Brookner under the heading of 'post-feminism', since her writing might be said to be impervious to feminist ideas; indeed, to many readers Brookner's fiction promotes a conservative view of women's lot that colludes with traditional models of gender inequality. In a review of *Altered States* (1996), Natasha Walter went further and found occasion to condemn Brookner's writing as representative of a more general literary failure. Walter criticizes Brookner, not just for her repetitiveness, but also for the perceived 'torpor' that governs her prose style and her outlook. Walter sees the inertia and passivity she associates with Brookner as embodying 'the dead end of English literature' in contrast with 'other, altogether livelier [though unnamed] British writers'.[36]

This broadside, however, is worryingly normative, effectively invalidating a certain manner of writing. This is to deny Brookner a voice, since both her style and her subject matter are branded inherently reactionary. It is also to dismiss Brookner's extensive appeal: her popularity suggests there may be something of value beyond the attributed failure to innovate. To privilege the most obvious attempts at innovation is, in any case, a dubious critical practice. It is important to realize that where there is apparent continuity, there may be a more subtle challenge that bypasses immediate and evanescent literary fashion.

Brookner's typical plot, in the manner of Barbara Pym before her, concerns a middle-class spinster of means, disappointed in love and coming to terms with narrowing life options. Thus summarized, Brookner's *oeuvre* does indeed appear both restricted and repetitive, but this is to conceal the implicit challenge she offers to fashion and to convention, particularly to the conventions of romantic fiction. This challenge is particularly evident in Brookner's most famous novel, *Hotel du Lac* (1984).

Brookner incorporates an implicit deliberation on her own writing practice in *Hotel du Lac* by making her heroine Edith Hope a writer of romantic fiction, and a character who partly resembles her creator. In doing so, she dramatizes her own concern that she may be taken as a writer of trivial entertainments: the ideological limitations of formula romance writing are ridiculed, even whilst feminism's supposed progression beyond gender stereotyping is made subject to doubt. Edith is aware that her novels, in which the reticent unassuming girl always gets the hero, perpetuate a social lie, since it is not the tortoise, but the hare that wins in real life (p. 27). She is aware that her work deals in 'fantasy and obfuscation' (p. 50), and, for the major part of the novel she shows herself to be a bad judge of character, slow to read her fellow guests at the Swiss lakeside hotel, in which she is enjoying a brief 'exile'. (She has been persuaded to go abroad in disgrace, having left her groom standing at the Register Office.)

Edith also has a married lover, and she expends her emotional energy composing her letters to him. On the verge of entering into a loveless marriage of respectability with a fellow hotel guest, the wealthy Mr Neville, she realizes that such a marriage would be based on his terms (p. 178), and that by accepting them she would lose the hope of romantic fulfilment on which her life has been based. Consequently she decides to go back to the one-sided affair with married David Simmonds, deeply unsatisfactory to her, aware that this is not the fulfilment she seeks, either: she is not 'coming home', but merely 'returning' (p. 184).

The novel Edith inhabits is thus markedly different from the novels she writes. In contrast to these romantic fantasies, her own story stresses the limits of passion, offering the choice between two unhappy situations, merely. It is not a feminist position (not least because the fantasy is not fully relinquished) but one that soberly assesses the curtailed opportunities for women of Edith's class and generation. In this respect, Brookner is in tune with Edith in the refusal to write what *Cosmopolitan* readers, the 'multi-orgasmic girls with the executive briefcases', want to read, the novel in which the 'hare', the 'scornful temptress' is the winner (pp. 27–8).

Edith's morality is akin to Brookner's in its focus on the meek and unassuming woman, even if the treatment is different. Edith also anticipates the concern that reviewers of Brookner's subsequent fiction have often voiced, that her story of the disappointed life is one that she re-tells over and over again. Seeing the paperback edition of her best novel in a bookshop window, she is chilled by 'the prospect of doing it all over again, for the rest of my life' (p. 150). The sense of an unchanging situation has a larger philosophical purpose, however. In a more temperate account of Brookner than Walter's, Kate Fullbrook explains her focus on failure and loss in terms of her academic influences and predilections. Thus Brookner the novelist is also Brookner the historian of ideas, pondering the long-term consequences of the Enlightenment, and the subsequent legacy of Romanticism that together generate 'the promise of strictly secular fulfilment'. Thus, argues Fullbrook, the question Brookner repeatedly addresses is 'whether the state of personal and cultural exhaustion' experienced by her characters 'inevitably follows from great eighteenth-century shifts in the cultural formation of European thought'.[37]

Such an understanding of Brookner's inspiration makes her exploration of failure and loss necessarily unavailable to a feminism defined in narrower historical terms. In this sense Walter's complaint about torpor and inertia may locate Brookner's intellectual strength, rather than identifying any technical weakness. Indeed, the exhaustion of the Enlightenment ideal seems to be expressed – quite consciously – in an 'exhausted' literary style (though one might ponder how many such novels are needed to make the point). In the key image of *Hotel du Lac*, Edith Hope, whilst aboard a pleasure steamer, is struck by 'the empty lake' with its 'allegorical significance':

> Ships, she knew, were often used by painters as symbols of the soul, sometimes of the soul departing for unknown shores. Of death, in fact. Or, if not of death, not of anything very hopeful. Ship of fools, slave ship, shipwreck, storm at sea . . . Edith, once again, felt unsafe, distressed, unhoused. (pp. 159–60)

The art historian Brookner here eschews direct allusions to particular painters or schools, the better to imply the kind of historical continuum that Fullbrook claims for her. Significantly, Edith's reflections move from allegorical depictions of death and the afterlife to altogether more secular anxieties. This lake, the site of her limited personal growth, here reveals the post-Enlightenment secular emphasis that Fullbrook puts at the heart of Brookner's tragic vision, and that does, indeed, seem to be Edith's unsettling legacy.

Whatever one thinks of Brookner, the direction of her work has come to coincide with the post-feminist determination to fly by the nets of gender opposition, and to promote a world-view that is not required to be partisan in gender terms. In its more conscious forms, this spirit of re-evaluation is the intellectual legacy of the 1980s when definite shifts in gender relations and in the codes and mores of sexual interaction were occurring. Sexual control was wrested from the male in a period marked by 'a certain androgyny in style', but also by a developing fear of gender disconnection.[38]

In the 1990s the shift in gender relations began to seem dramatic in some quarters, provoking a reassessment of feminism, its effects, and its objectives. The notion that the tenets of feminism, insofar as they relate to British social life, need to be re-evaluated has been persuasively put by Rosalind Coward. In a brave, and quietly radical gesture, she has called for feminists to give up their 'sacred cows', and recognize that the successes of feminism, coupled with economic change, make the restatement of original feminist goals sometimes inappropriate. More complex gender relations, the rise of the underclass, the increase in violence – these are the 'changing realities' that require 'an audit' of feminism, an acceptance of the new need 'to see gender as just one possible reason for social and personal conflicts rather than an all-encompassing cause'.[39] Crucial to this sense of change is the changing workplace of the 1990s, the 'feminization' of the economy, characterized by a huge shift towards part-time or hourly paid work, that found women 'more prepared' than men for the casualization of labour.[40] Evidently this development brought with it different kinds of exploitation, but the gender implications have altered, since these are changes that accompany the loss of traditional male work in the declining heavy industries.

The impulse to re-evaluate female experience inspires Nell Dunn's *My Silver Shoes* (1996), in which the character Joy is resuscitated twenty-eight years on from the opening of *Poor Cow*.[41] She now lives in Putney in a council flat next door to her mother, and works at a job club where she has inspired many of the unemployed people seeking help. She also has a boyfriend (Jeff) who seems an ideal partner, responsive to her sensuality.

This is no simple celebration of the social and material gains of women, however, and almost at once this well-managed situation begins to fall apart. Joy's mother Gladys goes into the early stages of senile dementia after a fall, whilst her son Jonny deserts from the army, finding his posting in

Northern Ireland unendurable; he takes up residence at home awaiting his inevitable arrest by the military police. Joy gives up her work to care for the increasingly demanding Gladys, and Jeff, unable to tolerate these new pressures, eventually decides to leave her. Jeff and Joy are reunited after a cooling-off period in which Joy and Gladys, returning to an old haunt, take a holiday at a caravan park at Selsey Bill. Both women enjoy memories of particularly lurid sexual encounters in this episode of self-discovery, and this underscores the central theme: the continuity of these two women, linked by the need to assert themselves through their sexuality (pp. 191–4).

The sexual frankness of Joy is now put in very precise economic terms. If the sexual theme of *Poor Cow* had conveyed a hint of the liberating sixties, *My Silver Shoes* refutes the association. At the start of the novel Joy had appeared independent, constrained principally by a shrill mother with a narrow vision. But by the end of the book Joy and Gladys are revealed to have the same defining characteristic, the uninhibited sexuality that, in a situation of poverty, seems to be a woman's only reliable route to empowerment. In accordance with the shifting balance of power, the later Joy is significantly more assertive than she is in her earlier incarnation, whilst the latter-day men are inadequate, and betray an understanding that they are in need of guidance.

The real problem for feminism, however, has been the way in which the new gender relations are rendered meaningless by a media driven by the need for 'infotainment', and the consequent over-simplification of real issues. A case in point is the Girl Power of the 1990s, which was predicated on diverse role models, the idea of making something of yourself, whatever you are like. The range of types represented by the Spice Girls – 'posh', 'sporty', 'baby', and so on – rides on that wave of empowerment, though the bland stereotypes, and the exclusions they reinforce (what price a 'bookworm' spice?) signal the familiar impoverishment of diversity by commercial interests. There was also a perception, however, that Girl Power might signal a reversal of gender dominance in key areas; but such a banal celebration of a cult of power implied a problematic separation of the attributes of gender from the surrounding political and historical context: female achievement could be praised for its own sake. Thus Natasha Walter, in a notable instance of historical amnesia, felt able to acclaim Margaret Thatcher as 'the great unsung heroine of British feminism', though other commentators were less willing to overlook Thatcher's 'overt hostility to feminism and her lack of support for women in general'.[42]

In the late 1990s Fay Weldon became associated with a feminist backlash, the critique of a perceived 'girls on top' culture often now being voiced by prominent feminist proponents of earlier decades. The novel that most clearly conveys this spirit of revisionism is Weldon's *Big Women* (1997). Here

Weldon examines elements of contradiction and hypocrisy in the feminist movement, by tracing the fortunes of a women's publishing house (based on Virago) from the early 1970s through to the era of publishing conglomerates and the death of the small press. The novel suggests that this is the logical consequence of the profit motive, and that a new breed of woman now appears, in the wake of feminism, to take up the reins of commercialism.

By taking Virago as her satirical model Weldon attacks one of the sacred cows of feminism. Virago was famed for rescuing important women novelists from obscurity, such as Rosamund Lehmann, Rebecca West, and Edith Wharton, and for publishing key contemporary writers such as Maya Angelou, Margaret Atwood, and Angela Carter. It was a publishing house that managed to combine principle with profit. In the mid-1990s, however, Carmen Callil, one of the founders, decided to put Virago on the market, and after a bitter boardroom struggle, it was sold to Little, Brown.[43] This arresting conflict between feminist principle and high finance seems to locate a defining moment in the transition to post-feminism, provoking Weldon's reflection that the rise and fall of Virago as an idealistic women's press 'more or less coincided with the rise and fall of feminism as a special case'.[44]

*Big Women* opens in 1971, the year of the *Oz* Trial, with the scene in which the 'Medusa' publishing house is born.[45] A woman's meeting in Primrose Hill culminates in drunken, naked dancing to mark the birth of Medusa, whilst a squeaking bed announces the husband's infidelity with one of the women who has slipped quietly away. Weldon thus encapsulates the dilemma for feminist activism, besieged by the predatory male on one side, and the internal betrayal of the sisterhood on the other. The revelry is broken up by the arrival of Zoe's husband Bull, the truly demonic patriarch of the novel, suspicious of his wife's independent spirit; however, it is Saffron, the daughter of Zoe and Bull, who emerges as the emblematic figure of the 1990s, and her memory of this episode is crucial to Weldon's portrait of 'a child who starts going to women's meetings at three and ends up as a journalist, hard as nails, running the world'.[46]

The schematic psychology of Saffron is thus framed as a reaction against idealistic feminism, coupled with a willingness to embrace its material advances. The other determining factor, however, is the manipulative father who oppresses the tragic Zoe, denigrates her writing, and finally drives her to suicide. Another formative childhood scene for Saffron is the one in which Bull burns the manuscript of Zoe's book 'Lost Women' (pp. 141–3), concerning the lamentable fate of the female graduate (p. 117), written over a period of five years in moments stolen from housewifely duties. Bull's mistress claims to be the real cause of Zoe's suicide; but it is Saffron's perception of her mother's fate that is important, and her quest to uncover the truth leads her to conclude that Zoe was driven to her death by Bull (p. 262).

The formation of Saffron as the unsentimental media whizzkid of the 1990s, presiding over a magazine in which advertisements take priority over copy, and where high profits are the only duty (p. 279), thus has twin parental sources. This ethos of self-advancement has its roots in the less coherent, but equally manipulative and self-serving actions of the father; but it is the opportunities created by her mother's generation of feminists that enable the ruthless young woman to make the instruments of oppression her own.

The novel's analysis thus imputes men and women alike in the formation of a world in which profit takes precedence over principles. Saffron is instrumental in the boardroom tussle that sees Medusa sold off to the media giant 'ComArt' (pp. 342–4), marking the demise of Medusa's function. Disempowered, the incorporated Medusa 'turns no one to stone' and 'could be any gender at all' (p. 345). In another sense, however, 'de-gendering' summarizes the novel's more hopeful implication. An essential aspect of Weldon's revisionist critique is the insistence that 'some qualities are simply human, not specific to one gender or the other' (p. 69). The narrator summarizes this hope that 'gender, like the state in Marxist aspiration, might in the end wither away' (p. 338). Having tracked the demise of the idealism of the 1970s, Weldon seeks to replace it with her own post-feminist idealism. This spirit of re-evaluation seems to be akin to other, non-confrontational instances of post-feminism. In asking the question whether or not feminists 'want to continue special pleading for women's interests or defending women's "rights" as greater or more pressing than men's', Coward poses a further question: 'would it not be more helpful to be looking at human rights and at the rights of all members of society?'[47]

However, in the renegotiation of feminism there is by no means consensus on the desirability of gender withering away. In *The Whole Woman*, for example, Germaine Greer is confrontational to the point of caricaturing masculinity, suggesting that while 'women change', 'men become very early set in their ways as lifelong Arsenal fans, lager drinkers, burglars, bankers, whatever' sticking to these 'chosen tramtracks for the rest of their lives'.[48] The rhetoric is deliberately provocative, but it bespeaks its own unwillingness to adapt. Yet Greer, too, is dismissive of 'lifestyle feminism', which she sees as a 'sideshow' to 'the main event, the world-wide feminization of poverty'. This is a sobering view, which means that 'the second wave of feminism' has not yet reached the shore, but is 'slowly and inexorably gathering momentum'.[49]

From the perspective of serious British fiction it is the shift away from women's rights and towards human rights that seems to be the dominant trend of the 1990s, a direction illustrated in the novels of Shena Mackay.[50] From the second phase of Mackay's career, the high moral stance of *The Artist's Widow* (1998) is an exemplary instance of the post-feminist novel.

The widow in question is Lyris Crane who, an artist herself, and 'pushing eighty' (p. 6), hangs on to the ethical conception of art she has fashioned in an earlier era. The novel begins with the private viewing of the deceased husband's last paintings at a Mayfair gallery. The satire of the nepotistic and self-serving contemporary art scene that this scene launches is developed most fully in the portrayal of Lyris's great-nephew Nathan, a would-be Damien Hirst who is lazy, untalented, and unscrupulous. The rumour that Charles Saatchi is in the process of launching the career of one of Nathan's female contemporaries is a particular source of bitterness for him.[51] Indeed, Nathan encapsulates the view that Mackay projects about the 'sensational' world of contemporary art: publicity is the primary factor (p. 140).

Lyris's world-view, by contrast, is public-spirited and without affectation. But she has a direct encounter with the new values in the form of Zoe Rifaat, a feminist film-maker who wants to include Lyris in a documentary about neglected women artists. Zoe is a careerist with a predetermined agenda, and no intellectual substance, and Lyris has no intention of colluding with her insincere feminism, which is also an insult to her marriage and her dead husband's memory. Lyris's own conception of work, rooted in the quiet pursuit of traditional, painterly values, is paralleled in the ethos of Mackay's post-feminist fiction-making.

There are two aspects to Lyris's convictions about art. First, the importance of recording aesthetic beauty, especially as manifested in particular objects, both natural and man–made; and, second, the recognition that such a record is made on behalf of others (p. 159). This principle of reaching out through artistic expression is typified in Lyris's painting 'The Blue Bead', in which she addresses the question of how a prisoner, or an orphaned refugee child might retain a sense of self with only the simplest possession, such as a single blue bead, to form a link with the past. This 'terrible poignancy of our possessions', which both 'define and console us' (p. 94), suggests also Mackay's view about the potential of the novel, a commodity that might aspire to make meaningful social links, and that offers the balm of consolation when it achieves something like a definitive analysis.

The novel ends with the deaths of Princess Diana and Dodi Fayed, and a bemused response to the inexplicable outpouring of public grief, the empathic engagement with the plight of another that is implicit more quietly in the method of both Lyris and her creator. Seeking to understand the 'extraordinary . . . pain at the fairytale gone rotten', Lyris worries that 'we're in danger of genuine grief being whipped up into something ugly' (pp. 167–8). Concerned at the unreflective sentimentalism of the public reaction, Mackay seeks to co-opt this general capacity for empathy to mesh with her own principles of artistic communication. But this suggestion about the sensitivity to the other cuts both ways: Mackay's satire, peopled by hard 1990s careerists, is put on pause, its harsh mood dissipated through this acknowledgement of shared, mysterious grief.

The death of Princess Diana encapsulates a number of dilemmas that surround the perception of women's role at the end of the century. Diana, of course, was an extraordinary and privileged figure, so her 'ordinariness' seems, initially, rather far-fetched. Yet the spectacle of a nation in mourning suggested that she touched something deeper in the public's collective subconscious. Sheila Rowbotham convincingly ascribes this to 'the contradictions of class and gender which Diana embodied'. She suggests that the mood of the 1990s encompassed pleasure at extravagance, but also a sense of remorse at the (global) inequality this denotes. Diana, the Princess involved in humanitarian works, was perceived to have embraced these conflicting impulses. She also 'lived out several familiar contradictions of gender', showing herself to be simultaneously caring and tough, and to combine passive and active aspects of femininity. As the embodiment of these social contradictions, Diana represented the ordinary, or the everyday in a kind of 'concentrated essence', so that 'her sudden death gave her a quasi-religious significance'.[52]

Shena Mackay's Lyris, in the spirit of much post-feminism, seems to be working towards a similar understanding of Diana's death in the 'paused' moment at the end of *The Artist's Widow*. What is required is an explanation of the collective empathy, a realization that the 'contradictions of gender' have been generally internalized, producing something that approaches an androgynous populace, with individuals hailing each other in a fleeting moment of recognition.

## Repression in Gay Fiction

If there are elements of retreat in some of the more significant feminist texts, gay writing has had to negotiate a still more restrictive atmosphere, and without the kind of reinvigorating impetus that characterizes successive phases of feminist (and post-feminist) expression. The fact of repression, especially earlier in the period, enforced some notorious compromises. The representation of gay experience in the post-war novel has been both more self-contained and defensive than the treatment of lesbianism, for example. Prior to the legalization of homosexual acts in 1967 the defensiveness and the reticence had an obvious legal explanation. The later self-containment often seems born of the need to strengthen the independent tradition of gay writing.

The extent to which the social and legal taboos of the post-war era restricted the expression of gay experience is clearly visible in Angus Wilson's

*Hemlock and After* (1952) in which esteemed novelist Bernard Sands has secured a government grant to help set up his centre for talented young writers at Vardon Hall. However, Sands experiences a personal dissolution as self-doubt overtakes his conviction about the Vardon Hall project. For the reader, too, doubts begin to surface about Sands's integrity, and these doubts are uncomfortably linked with his sexual identity.

Locked in a sterile marriage, Sands has begun, late in life, to have homosexual affairs with younger men; it is his wife, however, who seems the principal victim of the failed marriage (she has endured a breakdown). More problematic in the assessment of Sands is the way he articulates his own collapse, most particularly after the scene that closes Book I. Here Sands witnesses the arrest of a young man for 'importuning' in Leicester Square, and is overcome with a sensation of 'sadistic excitement' (p. 109). Although this is articulated as a crisis of humanism, it is also the turning point in the treatment of the sexual theme, for, hereafter, the expression of Sands's homosexuality seems less an unlocking of repression, and more a route for the sating of his egotistical desires.

Wilson's treatment of homosexuality here is clearly problematic: even if Sands's inner corruption need not *necessarily* be linked to his particular sexual leanings, there is still something uncomfortable in the association. In Alan Sinfield's analysis, the novel colludes with a legal system that outlaws homosexuality, and the story is arranged 'so as to exonerate the law and incriminate Bernard' (p. 75). As a consequence, concludes Sinfield, there is an internalization of homophobia in the novel that is masochistic: 'the "evil" of *Hemlock and After* is self-hatred'.[53]

Whilst allowing for a measure of descriptive accuracy in this account, one must also consider what it is reasonable to expect of Wilson. In fact, his novels of the 1950s are extraordinarily frank, given that homosexual acts were then illegal in Britain. It seems clear that he was obliged to find a compromise, and, in this connection, perhaps there is an acknowledgement of a personal 'hemlock' in the title. Yet the flexibility produces something more radical than Sinfield allows. The reader, in fact, is apt to be surprised by the self-disgust of Bernard Sands and at the nature of his dissolution.[54] The questioning that such surprise engenders is then squarely directed at the social mores and legal injunctions that generate Sands's repression and confusion. In this oblique manner Wilson's novel mounts the kind of attack on the homosexuality laws that he would have been unable to make directly.

Later in the period, as obliquity was replaced by assertiveness, gay writing gained a distinctive character; and yet, paradoxically, this results in a manner of expression that stands in marked contrast to the attempt by Angus Wilson to place homosexuality within mainstream social experience. An exemplary instance of this combined mood of withdrawal and assertion is

*The Swimming-Pool Library* (1988) by Alan Hollinghurst, which cultivates a
telling ambiguity in his representation of gay life in 1980s London. William
Beckwith, the central character and narrator, is an aristocrat with time on his
hands, in pursuit of frequent, and sometimes violent sex with men picked up
in a variety of places. (His haunts include a pornographic film club, public
toilets, and the London Underground.)

Sex with his more permanent partners is also charged with violence and
testosterone; and the dominance of this element of the novel can be alienating, especially to women readers; female characters, in fact, are almost
entirely excluded from the narrative, and women are always spoken of dis-
paragingly. Hollinghurst, however, is creating something more artful than
a novel that is merely shocking, though the shock value contributes to this
purpose. Fundamentally, he is announcing an appropriation of the tradition
of English fictional gay writing, a determination to deal frankly with that
which was concealed in previous decades. Both E. M. Forster and Ronald
Firbank (who supplies the epigraph) receive several mentions as key figures
in a more reticent tradition that this novel shakes up and emboldens. But
the explicit sex is not just a celebration of the breaking of taboos (though
it is partly that). It is also meant to be seen as a violent (and potentially
damaging) extreme of experience, held in tension with its opposite.

Beckwith, in fact, is conscious of his own brutality, and of the duality
of his nature, sometimes hedonistic, sometimes scholarly (p. 4). Passion and
cruelty can go together (p. 105), and this duality applies also to the appraisal
of the gay scene. He is aware, for instance, that the making of hardcore gay
pornography might be demonic to the outsider, even whilst seeming normal
to the participants (p. 187). Gradually, a learning curve is discerned that
sees Beckwith's reflectiveness displacing his hedonism. This has partly to do
with the recognition that the traditional (and increasingly anachronistic) class
structure that he inhabits has protected him from the ravages of prejudice.
Beckwith, of aristocratic stock, is a product of Winchester College. It is
here that he becomes Swimming-Pool Librarian (or prefect), and presides
over clandestine midnight sex sessions in the changing-room, known as the
'Swimming-Pool Library' (p. 141). In London, at the Corinthian Club, the
swimming pool and showers are a site of ritualized male display, completing
the impression of Beckwith's life as one in which his homosexuality has
been nurtured by powerful institutions.

Two elements of the novel serve to disrupt this enclosed and protected
world, and the brutal, self-serving underside it has encouraged. First, there
is the beating Beckwith receives at the hands of a gang of skinheads whilst
looking for Arthur on a tower-block estate at Stratford East, an episode that
obliges him to revise his perception of skinhead masculinity as iconically
gay (p. 172). The central plank of Beckwith's personal growth, however, is

the second element, his experience with the elderly Lord Nantwich, who settles on Beckwith when looking for someone to write an account of his life. In reading Nantwich's papers and journals, Beckwith uncovers many contemporary parallels in the homosexual experience of earlier periods; but the most significant discovery is that Nantwich had been a victim of police entrapment, and had been sent to prison for soliciting in 1954. As Director of Public Prosecutions, Beckwith's own grandfather Sir Denis (subsequently Lord) Beckwith had been responsible for the 'gay pogrom' (p. 278) that had resulted in the high-profile arrest of a lord.

In offering young Beckwith the chance to be his biographer, Nantwich is also giving him the chance to right his grandfather's wrong, to express his homosexual identity in a public-spirited denouncement of the power structures that foster oppression and inequality. Of course, it is the same system that has produced Nantwich, and the hedonistic and brutal homosexuality of Beckwith himself; but here he has the chance to marry the passionate hedonist and the reflective scholar within, and become the true librarian of the swimming pool. The invitation is declined, but Hollinghurst goes to some lengths to stress the partial moral growth of Beckwith, his identification with a wider gay community, and his new distaste for unthinking priapic lust. At the same time, however, the liberatory claim inherent in the explicit representation of gay life is sustained, and in the final sentence Beckwith's eye is caught by a youth in the showers at the Corinthian Club (p. 288). The sense of repetition is ambivalent, suggesting both solidarity through continuity, but also the possibility of Beckwith's lapse.

A different kind of self-containment was occasioned by the onset of AIDS. In *The Waters of Thirst* (1993) Adam Mars-Jones registers the way in which AIDS curtails gay experience from the early 1980s on, with 1982 the dividing line between promiscuity and a new (enforced) fashion of patient courtship (p. 4). William, the protagonist, practises sex 'exclusively in its safest forms, fidelity and fantasy' (p. 17). Fidelity is ensured by a monogamous relationship with partner Terry, whilst the fantasy is fulfilled by his 'archive' of pornographic material featuring a gay porn star and entrepreneur, Peter Hunter. Gay pornography is here a manifestation of turning inwards, a point underscored when William begins to wonder if Peter Hunter is concealing the signs of disease: he scours the new material he receives not for stimulation, but for evidence that Hunter, as the 1980s progress, is concealing more and more of his body in an effort to cover the stigmata of illness. Finding no evidence to disprove this hunch, William begins to file away the packages of new material unopened (p. 121).

The material success of pornographer Hunter, undermined by the shadow of AIDS, is paralleled in the more bourgeois advancement of William and Terry, moving up the property ladder in the housing boom of the 1980s (p. 27), a momentum which is eventually undercut by William's illness. Here, however, Mars-Jones widens his scope to embrace a predicament that is not specific to the situation produced by AIDS. William, in fact, suffers from kidney disease, which, rather than appearing solely as a metaphor for AIDS, opens up the novel's broader concern with the question of 'thirst'. This is the novel's central metaphor, projected by the term 'tantalus', which the narrator glosses as 'anything that you must have, and may not. Anything that your body craves and your mind knows you must do without' (p. 28). For the kidney patient, dependent on dialysis, alcohol and salty food are forbidden, and the daily intake of fluid is restricted to a pint and a quarter a day (pp. 67–8). The 'tantalus', initially introduced as the term for an antique case for decanters (p. 28), links the bourgeois world in which William and Terry have risen with the limits imposed on William through illness. It also suggests the limits and restrictions placed on gay, and especially English gay, experience more generally.

After his operation, William develops a form of pneumonia normally associated with AIDS, and the novel closes in a hallucinatory style that serves to stress its metaphorical connotations. There is a suggestion that William may now be succumbing to AIDS himself, and we are tacitly cautioned that morphine, which 'seems to go in for some embroidering on its own account' (p. 165), takes his account beyond verisimilitude. *The Waters of Thirst* evokes the cultural and social restrictions on gay life, the process of recoiling from physicality and accepting a narrower range of experience. Although this is a prominent manifestation of life post-AIDS, Mars-Jones also makes this speak to the circumscribed possibilities of gay experience more generally, in the face of prejudice and intolerance.[55] In the manner of Hollinghurst, however, he produces a novel that replicates the limits it anatomizes, and that contributes to a developing niche of socially withdrawn English gay writing.

## Chapter 4

# National Identity

Nationalism is a concept customarily treated with caution, if not deep suspicion, in intellectual circles. Eric Hobsbawm's analysis of the violent and destructive tendencies of nationalism over the past two hundred years, with an emphasis on the territorial imperative, and the mistreatment of minorities, leads him to conclude that 'no serious historian of nations and nationalism can be a committed political nationalist'.[1] Since the late 1980s, however, new nationalistic energies have been unleashed – following the collapse of communism in Eastern Europe, for instance, or the demise of apartheid and the birth of a new South Africa. The status of nations has begun to seem more volatile, and less easy to interpret.[2] Consequently, the received wisdom of viewing nationalism as inherently reactionary has been the focus of a revisionist view, especially in the field of postcolonial studies. Neil Lazarus, for example, questions the portrayal of national feeling as intrinsically undemocratic, suggesting that the nationalism of emergent states might rather be seen as tending towards new forms of social organization, especially where the emerging state can be seen as 'a relatively open site of political and ideological contestation'.[3] The most persuasive aspect of this claim is that new forms of nationalism might represent a way of resisting the encroachment of economic globalization, specifically where existing nation-states are seen to co-operate too obligingly with the objectives of multinational companies.[4]

Here, then, are two competing views of nationalism, perceived either as the false resuscitation of traditional self-interest, or as the route to a more equitable, negotiated future. The treatment of British national identities in post-war fiction has tended to fall somewhere between these two positions, wary of an uncompromising tradition on the one hand, whilst tentatively contemplating the reinvention of nationality on the other. A third position emerges as a consequence of this dialectic: a kind of post-nationalism built on reappraised symbols and traditions that implicitly acknowledges the mongrelized nature of most British identities. The hesitancy about national identity is, inevitably, most pronounced in refigurations of Englishness, where the legacy of imperialism remains a dominant presence.

## Reinventing Englishness

It has not been fashionable in the post-war era to contemplate the more stable elements that might comprise an English national character. Two effects of the end of Empire in particular suggest the reason for this reticence: first, the assertion of Englishness is still tainted with imperialism, in some quarters; and, second, the end of Empire and the period of postcolonial migration begins a new process of cultural (and biological) hybridity that makes stable national identities problematic. Even so, the development of a genuinely multicultural society will be a very long-term project, a fact that makes the reticence over the persisting 'Englishness' regrettable.

John Fowles is one writer who has bucked this trend of silence; and, interestingly, he has written of reticence as a national characteristic, a sign of 'ethical sluggishness'.[5] In *Daniel Martin* (1977) the English trait of reticence or withdrawal is treated ambivalently, as an indication of positive potential, but also of failure. Fowles links this moral conundrum to the 'archetypal national myth' of Robin Hood (p. 303), the myth, that is, of moral rectitude facilitated through withdrawal to the 'sacred combe' (p. 306). In the figure of the 'Just Outlaw' the personification of justice is held in tension with self-righteousness and asocial aloofness. Screenwriter Daniel Martin's decision to write a novel to investigate his own Englishness is associated with this idea, since he senses 'a far greater capacity for retreat in fiction': the novel, 'in Robin Hood terms', represents 'a forest, after the thin copses of the filmscript' (p. 308). This intriguing association of genre, myth, and nationality is demonstrated practically in the seven hundred pages of Fowles's novel, a veritable forest of a book, which concerns itself with Martin's quest for authenticity, finally hinted at through an appreciation of the historically contingent relationship between person and place.

The role of contingency in Fowles's investigation of Englishness reveals a glimpse of the relativity that usually has a more central place in treatments of English identity. 'The trouble with the Engenglish', stutters Mr 'Whisky' Sisodia, in Rushdie's *The Satanic Verses*, 'is that their hiss hiss history happened overseas, so they dodo don't know what it means' (p. 343). Rushdie demonstrates the dramatist's trick of giving a vitally important line to a stuttering character, thus embedding it in his readers' minds; and the trouble that Sisodia has with 'Engenglish' is significant since he inadvertently defines a race who are meta-English, English raised to the second power. This suggests both a self-importance and an inner vacuum, the two features that Rushdie identifies as the legacy of imperialism: the Empire, perceived as English rather than British, has cultivated a self-conscious arrogance in the national character, but has also displaced English identity, making the relationship between modern England and the construction of Englishness mysterious.

A suggestive novel in this connection is Julian Barnes's *England, England* (1998), which contains both a meta-England, and an investigation of the manner in which the national identity might be constructed. Barnes imagines the essential features of England reduced to a theme park on the Isle of Wight, with all the major tourist attractions reproduced in convenient proximity.[6] Entrepreneur Sir Jack Pitman buys the island for the establishment of his theme-park England, and supplements his simulacra of architectural landmarks – Big Ben, the Tower of London, Buckingham Palace – with injections of reality, for example in the part-time employment of actual Royals. 'England, England' comes to supplant 'old' England, but the confusion of the authentic and the bogus unleashes unintended effects. Robin Hood's Merrie Men, for instance, tired of their fake 'roast ox', go poaching in the Animal Heritage Park (Dingle the Woolly Steer is their quarry). In similar fashion, the actor playing Dr Johnson begins to fail in his duties as dinner host to visitors when his bad dining habits, bad odours, and his tendency to depression (in the sprit of the real Dr Johnson) begin to elicit complaints. But Barnes's serious purpose, in a book of conflicting moods, is to offer a more philosophical (yet accessible) deliberation on how the culture of the replica impacts on national identity, where the replica supplants the original.

This serious strand is structured around the life experience of the novel's central character Martha Cochrane. Whenever confronted with the query 'what's your first memory?', Martha, in a significant lie, summons the recollection of doing her Counties of England jigsaw puzzle. The memory has great personal significance as her father had the piece for Nottinghamshire in his pocket when he walked out on his family. Initially, Martha imagines he must have gone in search of Nottinghamshire, but when the fact of abandonment begins to sink in, Martha disposes of the remaining counties, a piece at a time.

The loss of faith in the Counties of England jigsaw, with its bald certitude about the composition of England, signals a haziness about origins. But it is also emblematic of a central emotional absence in Martha's life, a distrust of men that has a crucial bearing on her dealings with Sir Jack. Formerly one of his lackeys, Martha eventually takes control of the 'England, England' project, after acquiring incriminating evidence of Sir Jack at his 'Auntie May's', a brothel specializing in infantile fantasies. (Sir Jack has been filmed defecating in an outsize nappy, whilst being stimulated by his 'nurse' [pp. 153–8].) This episode serves emphatically to underscore the novel's point that the pursuit of unshakeable origins is entirely dubious. The project's historian points out that 'there is no prime moment' (p. 132), some pages before we witness Sir Jack's own 'primal moment' in the brothel.

There is, however, a dynamic in the book that is at variance with this insistence on the false or artificial elements of history and identity. In the final section we see an elderly Martha back in old England (now known as 'Anglia'), which, in the economic shadow of The Island, has degenerated into a parody of its preindustrial self. Yet this regression to village quaintness is not without its attractions. The final scene of the village fête, with its May Queen, its four-piece band and village bobby, its seed cake and preserves, pickles and chutneys, approaches a pastoral idyll. What is significant is how Barnes pushes the cliché – and in this sense the conclusion is a self-conscious fabrication like the rest of the book – until we begin to expect that it may deliver something of value after all. Martha has come here in search of a traditional churchyard where she might be buried (p. 241), and this Hardyesque resolution to her restless personal history infuses the final episode with a serenity that is surprising, given what has preceded it.

Yet these dissonances, in the tone of different sections, and in the contrast between the denial of originary myth and the pursuit of tradition, highlight the seminal feature of the novel. It is an 'idea of England' rather than a 'state of England' novel;[7] this suggests something inconclusive in the design, that what might be a stabilizing force for Martha is not fully endorsed. Indeed, the artificiality of this village life is insisted upon. However, what is authentic in this conclusion is the response of children to a dressing-up competition at the fête. Unlike Martha, losing interest at the sight of the local publican Ray Stout happily making a fool of himself dressed as Queen Victoria, the children are able to believe in both Queen Victoria and Ray Stout at the same time, thus displaying a 'willing yet complex trust in reality' (p. 264). The stress on dualism in inhabiting the present promotes also an idealized conception of identity, the capacity to make conscious use of the past in embracing the present. This might be said to sidestep the question of what an English national identity should actually comprise; but it does indicate the spirit, complex and contradictory, in which such a project would need to be conducted, and which Barnes's novel, with mixed modes and counterpointed moods, nicely emulates.

Barnes's novel is very much in tune with those recent theories of nationalism in which the constructed nature of national feeling is emphasized. The more encouraging formulations call for a conscious, responsible approach, in the spirit of Barnes's 'complex trust'. Without doubt the most influential theorist of national identity for critics of the novel is Benedict Anderson, who has persuasively linked the rise of the novel as a form with the emergence of the modern nation-state. In Anderson's reading, the nation is defined as 'an imagined political community', imagined as limited in geographical scope, and as sovereign in nature. The modern nation is thus an eighteenth-century concept, a product of 'an age in which Enlightenment and Revolution were destroying the legitimacy of the divinely-ordained dynastic realm'.[8]

For Anderson, the emergence of both the newspaper, and the novel are historically coterminous with the modern concept of the nation. This has partly to do with the sense of shared contemporary experience, or simultaneity, that is necessary to the consolidation of a national community. Anderson shows how this experience of simultaneity is emulated in the narrative technique of the novel, where the 'meanwhile' of narration connects characters (without their needing to meet) by embedding them in representations of particular societies; and where the reader, in whose mind the connections are realized, is granted an omniscient vantage point. What the novel produces, Anderson argues, is 'a sociological organism' moving through time, an idea that is 'a precise analogue of the idea of the nation', also 'conceived as a solid community moving steadily down (or up) history'. The argument is not simply that the novel emulates the imagined community amongst strangers, upon which the modern nation depends, but that it may have played a significant role in establishing the terms of the nation, and the confidence it breeds in 'steady, anonymous, simultaneous activity'.[9]

In a positive application of Anderson's, reading, the imaginary nature of the national community can be a constructive phenomenon to be interpreted, rather than merely a false entity to be condemned, and it is this that gives his theory its productive (and portable) applicability. Perhaps it is possible to overstate the role of the novel in the construction of national identity. Certainly, Anderson's observations about the 'mass ceremony' of newspaper reading might seem more convincingly applicable to post-war society. A newspaper is read in isolation, but in full consciousness that the private gesture is 'being replicated simultaneously by thousands (or millions) of others' who remain anonymous. The role of the novel may be apparently less tangible in generating and sustaining the shared national experience, because of its smaller readership and its lack of political immediacy; but the novel has a more enduring cultural resonance that allows the significance of a particular text to grow over time, so allowing it to play a more gradual, but perhaps more lasting role in 'creating that remarkable confidence of community in anonymity which is the hallmark of modern nations'.[10]

In his last published book Antony Easthope picked up the formative implications of the imagined national community, whilst rejecting any residual false/genuine opposition that might be implied in the emergence of an *imagined* national feeling that supplants an organic community of prenational culture. There can never have been a moment of genuine face-to-face community, argues Easthope, since 'immediacy, spontaneity and direct presence are necessarily deflected and betrayed by the universalizing, classificatory force of language'.[11] Having established the primacy of discourse in the formation of national identity, Easthope develops his main purpose, which is to identify the materials of Englishness. The critical approach is crucial in Easthope's argument, because he seeks to scrutinize the received idea that the English character, and the English intellectual tradition, are both governed by a common-sense empiricism, dismissive of continental theory. The main contention is that, if national cultures are shaped by particular discursive formations, an Englishness defined by empirical methods is questionable. The 'major limitation' of 'the empiricist method', writes Easthope, is 'its inability to interrogate its own epistemology, its own method'. Consequently, since 'empiricist discourse claims not to have a method or procedure for constructing knowledge of reality, it is not possible for it to question the very conceptual framework within which it works and on which its insights depend'. For a national culture based on such a purblind methodology the implications are ominous: an identity thus shaped is adopted as 'given', and is unable to identify the manner of its own construction. It cannot know itself.[12]

To my mind, the methodological opposition located here is a false one, since relativism can be usefully combined with empiricism. This book, for example, is empirical in conception insofar as it relies on a substantial sample of texts to demonstrate its findings. The analysis, meanwhile, seeks to identify the discursive contribution and composition of the selected novels. In relation to Englishness, however, the cautionary note about empiricism is prudent. The English are frequently characterized, as here by Jeremy Paxman, as failing to spend 'a great deal of time defining themselves because they haven't needed to'.[13] This arrogant refusal, the legacy of imperial self-confidence, does often seem to result in untheorized, empirical assumptions about the attributes of English identity, as witnessed in the frequent recourse commentators have had to listing the disparate ingredients of a presumed national character. John Betjeman's list included 'oil-lit churches, Women's Institutes, modest village inns' as well as 'the poetry of Tennyson' and 'branch-line trains'. This list originates in a wartime broadcast (1943), and has a special, understood patriotic purpose; nevertheless, Betjeman seeks to evoke a sense of national stability on the basis of *things*, rather than through the explicit statement of attitudes or beliefs.[14]

Paxman's own list of the components of Englishness includes 'country churches', 'Women's Institutes', 'village cricket and Elgar', as well as 'punk, street fashion', and 'drinking to excess'. The items on this list, admits Paxman, 'may not all be uniquely English'; yet, he claims, any three or four of them taken together will 'point at once to a culture as evocatively as the smell of a bonfire in the October dusk'. The striking thing about Paxman's updating of Betjeman's exercise is the divergent nature of the list he devises: 'punk' as well as 'Vaughan Williams', 'curry' as well as 'Cumberland sausages'. It points to a heterogeneous culture that does not lend itself to a single definition.[15] The empirical project, here – the expectation that the essence of Englishness can be evoked by the association of three or four sundry things – seems indisputably undertheorized. Such list-making is splendidly parodied in Barnes's *England, England*, which includes a list of the 'Fifty Quintessences of Englishness' ranging from 'ROYAL FAMILY', to 'WHINGEING' and 'FLAGELLATION' (pp. 83–5). But Barnes's satirical meta-England, rooted in the same kind of false metonymy, serves also to confirm the problem of national identity: the symbols of England, without meaning in themselves, are falsely taken as potent signifiers, theme-park or no. Barnes is most interested, however, in exposing the falsity of the pursuit of origins; and this suggests that the problem of English identity is not that it has been insufficiently articulated, but that the fluidity and uncertainty that surround any conception of national identity have not been fully embraced.

This puts a different complexion on the much-lamented lacuna presumed to be at the heart of English identity. Thus, if Mr 'Whisky' Sisodia in *The Satanic Verses* is right that the trouble with the English is that their history happened overseas, so they don't know what it means, he locates an absence that we should savour, without rushing to fill it with village cricket and Elgar. As my chapter on multicultural writing suggests, a great opportunity for national re-definition is the paradoxical legacy of this mood of imperial exhaustion. The vacuum is filled, in part, by the narratives of the 'children' of Empire, laying claim to their own postcolonial stories, and unleashing them in the 'parent' culture, which is subsequently transformed. Thus, the displacement of English identity is also a freeing-up, a process that makes England and Englishness potentially open to the multicultural moment that is the legacy of the imperial past.

## The Colonial Legacy

There have been some impressive novelistic attempts to investigate the meaning of that dissipated English history that 'happened overseas', and to assess its impact on the national character. The emphasis in this school of retrospective colonial fiction is often on an uncertain Englishness, strained to breaking point by the exercise of power. Here there is considerable affinity between the novel and some postcolonial critical analyses, as evidenced in the pertinence of Ian Baucom's discussion of Empire. Baucom shows how the conception of Empire as 'British' enabled England simultaneously to 'avow and disavow its empire' since by defining colonial places and people as 'British' they were made subordinate to England and to the English, whilst being held, simultaneously, as different. The schizophrenic 'Englishness' that promotes this contradiction is 'at once an embrace and a repudiation of the imperial beyond'.[16] 'Britishness', in this understanding, can be employed as a tool of subjection, but one that facilitates the evasion of responsibility. Baucom presents the post-war immigration legislation as building on this distinction, in effect, so that erstwhile British Commonwealth *subjects* are progressively deprived of 'British' citizenship by an English parliament seeking to preserve its home territory.[17] The retrospective colonial fiction of the post-war era is written in this climate of debate about immigration; but it looks outwards as well as inwards, its insights on the disappearing Empire being of particular significance to the ongoing domestic reconstruction of Englishness.

Paul Scott's *Staying On* (1977), for example, contains a subtle portrait of imperialism, and the Englishness that accompanies it, in terminal decline. Scott's earlier tetralogy *The Raj Quartet* (1966–75) is often seen as troublingly nostalgic for the days of the Raj, and gloomy about the prospects of postcolonial India. It is this air that leads Margaret Scanlan to brand it as 'a radically conservative novel that resonates with the conviction that human beings can do little to change their oppressive history'.[18] Richard Todd detects 'a retrospective air of nostalgia for Britain's Raj' persisting in *Staying On*, Scott's coda to *The Raj Quartet*; at the same time, he perceives 'a layer of gentle and at times surreal irony' that diffuses the nostalgia.[19] Building on Todd's observation, it is possible to see the undercutting of a still-persisting colonial Englishness, in *Staying On*, as undermining the source of nostalgia too.

*Staying On* is set in the early 1970s and concerns Tusker and Lucy Smalley, a retired Army couple, effectively forced to 'stay on' in India after Independence, given the difficulty of making a new start in England, and the need to eke out meagre funds that will go further in India. Tusker's bluff exterior conceals a psyche in confusion, apparently insensitive to the host culture. He calls his best friend Mr Bhoolabhoy 'Billy Boy', and frequently sacks the house-servant Ibrahim (who is subsequently reinstated, without ceremony, when the anger subsides). Yet Tusker is also a study in repression, and it is this that makes the Englishness he is made to represent intriguing. The novel opens with the news of Tusker's death from a heart attack, and then works in a temporal loop that arrives back at this death, its significance now fully disclosed. It is an effective narrative device that concentrates attention on the context of the event, which is emptied of its distracting element of surprise, whilst remaining a constant, brooding certainty.

The emotional charge that this framework enables is centred on the love of Tusker and Lucy, a love that is never explicitly stated, but that surfaces in a letter he writes to her in response to her fears of being widowed in a foreign country. In this missive Tusker makes reference to the personal crisis that surrounded his decision to 'stay on', and the sense of personal failure that induced what he calls 'the longest male menopause on record'. The apology, though brisk, opens a chink in his usually unemotional demeanour: 'Can't talk about these things face to face, you know. Difficult to write them. Brought up that way. No need ever to answer. Don't want you to. Prefer not. You've been a good woman to me, Luce. Sorry I've not made it clear I think so' (p. 232). Lucy puts Tusker's letter under her pillow: it is 'the only love letter she had had in all the years she had lived' (p. 233). What is being uncovered here is a repression of the personal life, which stems from a particular context. This is more than the stereotypical stiff-upper-lip Englishness it appears to be, since it represents a defensive move by which the former agents of Empire seek to preserve themselves in a post-imperial vacuum. Ibrahim's earlier observation of his ageing master extends this sense that a self-defeating principle may have been internalized as part of the national character: 'The English, once they began falling physically apart, did so with all their customary attention to detail, as if fitting themselves in advance for their own corpses to make sure they were going to be comfortable in them' (p. 29). This passage reveals the metonymic function of the Smalleys, whose increasing irrelevance in India stands for the broader postcolonial moment.

The death of Tusker obviously implies the simultaneous demise of imperial interests. But Scott also preserves a distinction between private experience and the post-imperial history with which it partially coincides. This method, by which private and public references are intertwined, yet simultaneously held apart, is amply illustrated in the business of the overgrown garden. The Smalleys live in The Lodge attached to the Bhoolabhoys' hotel, but have been deceived by Mrs Bhoolabhoy into relinquishing certain rights of tenancy (a prelude to their eviction), including the upkeep of the Lodge gardens (p. 36). Tusker's great distress at the humiliation (he is reduced to tears [p. 53]), prompts Lucy to employ a new gardener surreptitiously, hoping Tusker will assume he is in the Bhoolabhoys' employ. An absurd scenario ensues with the Smalleys refusing to acknowledge the new gardener, Lucy for fear that her ruse will be revealed, Tusker because he imagines the Bhoolabhoys are humouring him, and half expects a bill (pp. 67, 84). Scott thus produces the complex spectacle of an ex-colonial couple, behaving with apparent colonial imperiousness, even though they have been out-manoeuvred and deprived of their tenure. The fabrication of the colonial scene satisfies honour in the short term, but conceals the material facts of the situation. There is no nostalgia in this at all, but rather a sense of pathos at the folly and misplaced pride of the powerless English couple.

By the end of the century, the pathology of imperialism was subject to more explicit treatment. In *Pieces of Light* (1998), a Wilkie Collins-style supernatural story, Adam Thorpe conducts a more extreme analysis of that dynamic of colonial self-destructiveness. Hugh Arkwright, the principal narrator and focus, is a famous man of the Theatre, whose reputation is built on a notion of authenticity in the performance of Shakespeare; but he is finally destroyed by the truth of his colonial origins, revealed in a series of letters written by his mother, and finally discovered by Arkwright in his mid-sixties. His youth in West Africa, where his father was a District Officer in a forbidding outpost of Empire, is idealized by him as the source of a familial stability, of sorts. The final, devastating revelation is that his parents had adopted him, the illegitimate child of the previous District Officer, who had suffered a breakdown. His mother, the eighteen-year-old daughter of a missionary, had died giving birth. The son thus becomes an additional casualty of imperialism, someone whose personal and professional imperatives, more fantastic than the African fetishes he cherishes as a boy, are based on the doomed pursuit of indisputable origins.

The most important of these re-evaluations of colonialism are those of J. G. Farrell. The emergence of Farrell as a significant English novelist in the 1970s gives Bernard Bergonzi cause to qualify the pessimism that character-izes his treatment of English fiction in the first edition of *The Situation of the Novel* (1970). Bergonzi sees in Farrell a thoughtful reinvigoration of the his-torical novel that has the effect of redeeming 'the novel of traditional realism' often seen as inevitably linked to 'the epoch of bourgeois individualism'. On the strength of *Troubles* (1970) and *The Siege of Krishnapur* (1973), suggests Bergonzi, Farrell demonstrates that realism need not be slavishly linked with one ideological purview. A 'new realism' need not appear as 'an inevitable or habitual cultural mode', but rather as 'one possibility to be freely chosen'. Thus, the independent, sceptical spirit of postmodernism can be incorpo-rated within 'a reflective realism' that is 'aware of the conventionality of fiction' whilst remaining 'open to the world of experience'.[20]

In the spirit of this reflective realism, Farrell adopts the codes of the adven-ture narrative, and of the Victorian novel, without disrupting them overtly (as Fowles does in *The French Lieutenant's Woman* (1969)). Rather, he subjects such codes to ironic (and at times farcical) treatment in the process of un-dermining those imperial attitudes with which they may have affinities. *The Siege of Krishnapur* is set during the Indian Mutiny of 1857, and concerns a fictional siege partly based on the actual siege of Lucknow.[21] The focus is on the efforts of the Collector Hopkins and the British garrison in defending themselves against the attacks of the sepoys before relief eventually arrives.

The conventions of the heroic adventure narrative are gently mocked in the behaviour of the British who are confused about the spiritual and material bases of their civilization. This confusion is condensed in the image of the 'veteran assault force', a desperate reserve of elderly gentlemen, who, when the Residency is being stormed, are unleashed from the library to let off their shotguns and sporting rifles into the mêlée. Imagining themselves involved in engagements of Britain's military and imperial past, they burst forth 'with a querulous shout of "Yah, Boney!"' (directed at Napoleon), creating chaos and shooting down a chandelier (p. 315).

It is the conviction of rectitude, stemming from ignorance, that Farrell makes representative of the British presence in India. The imperial 'adventure' is most evidently ridiculed in the base use to which the opulent contents of the Residency are finally put, shoring up the improvised mud ramparts (p. 259). The Collector's faith in the artefacts of British civilization (he is a collector of these, as well as a collector of taxes) is rooted in his formative visit to the Great Exhibition of 1851. This faith is summarized in the marble bas-relief on view in his study, entitled 'The Spirit of Science Conquers Ignorance and Prejudice'. Later, chips from this artwork, together with sundry domestic metal and silver, make up an extempore blast of cannon-shot that wreaks havoc on the sepoys advancing in the Residency compound: amidst the carnage, one sepoy has his 'spine shattered by "The Spirit of Science"' (p. 307). The most telling such instance is the use of the heads of the Collector's 'electrometal figures': the bald head of Shakespeare reveals certain 'ballistic advantages' over the head of Keats, whose elaborate locks make for erratic flight (p. 323). This encapsulates what is, perhaps, the central tenet of postcolonial thinking: that cultural and imperial power are bound together in the operations of the colonizer.

When relief arrives and the siege is lifted the heroic model collapses, as the relieving forces are astonished by the appearance of the 'tattered lunatics' that the semi-starved survivors have become (p. 328). For Lieutenant Stapleton it is a romantic ideal that is also deflated. His fancied attachment to Louise Dunstable is checked by the high smell that prevents him getting near to her (p. 328). The relieving General, similarly affected by the bedraggled survivors, reflects that in the inevitable painting of 'The Relief of Krishnapur' he will have to place himself in the foreground, thus leading the eye away from the wretched heroes themselves (p. 330).[22] The colonial falsification of history here projects an Englishness studiously emptied of its corporeal frailty, precisely the hubris that Farrell anatomizes in the British imperial project, enamoured of its superior civilization, and convinced of its invulnerability. Here Farrell's formal project, the resuscitation of realism, dovetails with his analysis of colonialism. To Farrell, 'the real experience' is 'smoke in your eyes or a blister on your foot', individual suffering, personal lived experience.[23] His stance makes a particular claim for the realist historical novel, which is seen to recoup historical reality by virtue of its (fictive) imaginative projection, coupled with its stress on the personal.

In the brief final chapter, details of the marriages of various characters are given, in a parody of the Victorian novel's customary resolution. (Infidelity and bigotry feature in the lives of the 'heroic' survivors of the siege [p. 332].)

The most significant aspect of this resolution, however, is the humbling of the Collector, whose experiences in India have revealed to him the falsity of the imperial project. He comes to the conclusion that 'a people, a nation, does not create itself according to its own best ideas, but is shaped by other forces, of which it has little knowledge' (p. 333). This seems to anticipate Neil Lazarus's reconception of the nation referred to above, as 'a relatively open site of political and ideological contestation'; but it would be wrong to suggest that Farrell's novel is immersed in such contingency. Its self-conscious realism produces an effect that is still implicated in the perspectives of colonialism, which the Collector only begins to relinquish at the end of his life. Farrell, in fact, treads a fine line between complicity and independent critique, producing an ambivalent mode that is very much of its time. It may be true that 'postcolonial theorizing had already begun' when Farrell was writing his novel, but it is the more equivocal, provisional branch of postcolonial thinking to which Farrell subscribes. For all its irony, the novel retains its ambivalence (and even a hint of nostalgia) and falls short of the more overt 'postmodern parody' that is sometimes glimpsed.[24]

In the earlier *Troubles* (1970) Farrell had presented a related analysis of Englishness. As in *The Siege of Krishnapur* the focus is a liberal Englishman struggling to disentangle himself from the debilitating excesses of colonial thought, in another moral fable of national identity. The protagonist of *Troubles* is Major Brendan Archer, a victim of shell-shock in the First World War, who travels to Ireland in 1919 to meet up with his fiancée Angela, whose father owns the Majestic Hotel in Kilnalough. Neither party views the engagement with much enthusiasm: Angela, indeed, is dying from leukaemia, as the impercipient Archer belatedly discovers after her demise. There are ties that bind Archer to the Majestic, however; principally his foolish love for a local girl, Sarah Devlin. In the novel's design, moreover, the dilapidated hotel becomes associated with Archer, who seems unable to leave it. Thus, both building and character play a symbolic role in the treatment of fading imperialism.

Farrell's own comments on his intentions in *Troubles* indicate a serendipitous 'discovery' of his contemporary theme. Originally he chose the Irish troubles of 1919–21 'partly because they appeared to be safely lodged in the past', thus offering 'a metaphor' for the contemporary era. However, in 1969, during the course of the writing, the modern Troubles in Northern Ireland broke out, giving the work 'an unintended topicality'.[25] Farrell's historical dialogue, initially intended as a metaphorical parallel, was transformed by circumstances into a more literal echo, and this kind of consonance lends the treatment of national identity its particular importance in *Troubles*.

The Major, despite his traumatic war experiences, remains loyal to the objectives of the British military effort, and believes that 'the great civilizing power of the British Empire' was at stake in the Great War (p. 51). However, in the person of Edward Spencer, owner of the Majestic, he encounters an extreme version of this British nationalism bordering on madness. ('British' here denotes a union of Anglo-Irish and English interests.) On one occasion Spencer leads a party from the Majestic, including several old ladies, to Byrne's pub, for the purpose of 'harassing the natives'. Spencer's mission is to 'show the flag', and, accordingly, he leads the Majestic party in a rendition of 'God Save the King'. With restrained derision, the locals applaud, laugh, and finally join in the singing (pp. 86–9). But this extreme projection of Britishness emerges as the keynote feature of Spencer's identity, and of 'the face of Anglo-Ireland, the inbred Protestant aristocracy' over which he presides (p. 336). This adherence to the symbols of nationalism culminates in Spencer's use of a statue of Queen Victoria as a lure; and when a 'Sinn Feiner' duly arrives to blow up the statue in the hotel grounds, Spencer shoots and kills him.

This shooting is one of a series of incidents that causes the Major progressively to distance himself from Spencer (who is also his rival in love). The Major repeatedly shows himself to be liberal in his attitudes, and increasingly prepared to see the locals' perspective. In this he enjoys a learning curve, since his first impressions in Ireland serve to reinforce his stereotypical perceptions of Irish character; but Farrell (who was Anglo-Irish) is anxious to explode the Somerville-and-Ross-style portrayal of engaging Irish eccentricity. The undermining of this literary convention accompanies the gradual disabusement of the Major, who comes to realize that the true eccentricity is the dangerous lunacy of Spencer.

Farrell was of the opinion that his own ethnicity gave him a privileged vantage point: 'Being half Irish and half English . . . I'm able to look at the same thing from both sides – from that of the colonist and the colonised.'[26] Just such a balanced assessment is within the Major's grasp. Yet his qualities can also be defined as those (again stereotypical) attributes of Englishness that Sarah Devlin despises in him: respectability, seriousness, propensity to compromise, politeness, and desire for agreement (pp. 59, 115, 134, 248, 341). The characteristics that denote the Major's absence of sex-appeal for Sarah are also those virtues that make him the only character with moral presence. Finally, however, the Major does not live up to his potential. After Spencer has killed the would-be saboteur at Queen Victoria's statue, the Major decides he must try and make a gesture of conciliation. His motives are partly honourable, but partly political too: he wants to prevent the dead boy emerging as 'a martyr of the British' (p. 419). But as he talks with the local priest, his ambassadorial qualities desert him. He sees hatred in the priest's gaze, which seems to him 'blind, inhuman, fanatical' (p. 420). It is this that causes the Major to denounce the dead youth, and express the hope that his death will be an example 'to the other young cut-throats who are laying Ireland to waste' (p. 421). Having sought, in a spirit of conciliation, to prevent an anti-British mood flowing from the particular death, he ends up claiming the killing as a generalized message of British might.

It is a disastrous moment of private capitulation to broader forces. The Major finally chooses his tribe, as Sarah had told him everyone in Ireland must do (p. 34), and this collapse of reason gives a kind of logic to the burning down of the Majestic and the near-death of the Major at the hands of the IRA. Buried up to his neck in sand on the beach, he survives when the incoming tide fails to reach him. Delirious, facing death, the Major then subsides into a reverie based on a tale of romantic fidelity (p. 437); and, from the debris of the burned-out Majestic, he later retrieves a statue of Venus, goddess of fertility, to be shipped back to London (p. 446). Having failed to shoulder his designated moral burden, the Major redefines himself as the spurned lover of a more conventional kind of novel, nurturing the trophies that remind him of his emotional disappointment. The retreat signals the Major's ultimate failure, which is the failure to realize the full potential of those personal qualities that he has adopted as the components of his national identity.

Farrell is aware that there is nothing exclusively English about tolerance, compromise, and conciliation; and more so that these qualities can also be claimed in order to cloak more sinister imperial motives. Even so, the Major's failed effort to construct a version of Englishness rooted in these attributes reveals a more positive subtext about the post-imperial world, something that Farrell would scarce have dared to make more overt at the time of the new Troubles. What a good thing it would be, implies this subtext, if that myth of English identity, based on integrity and fair play, were to be fully realized. In this there is an implicit political plea, a laudable aim that validates Farrell's decision to concentrate the narrative perspective with the British (as he also does in *The Siege of Krishnapur*).[27]

## The Troubles

Since the Troubles were re-ignited in 1969, Northern Ireland has been the site of non-negotiable and antagonistic versions of national affiliation, a state of impasse that has restricted novelistic expression: the monolithic presence of the conflict dictates the writer's choice of topic. As if confirming the stagnancy this implies, Richard Kirkland's survey of literary culture in Northern Ireland since 1965 makes reference to just two novels (the earliest published in 1989). Kirkland's assertion that 'written expressions of cultural identity' have tended 'to favour poetry or drama' seems to confirm the sense of a moribund tradition.[28] Since 1969, the intractable political situation has produced a recognizable type of Troubles novel, often featuring a Catholic–Protestant love-across-the-barricades plot, where love and hope are extinguished by either the prejudices of the opposed communities, or by the temptation to become actively involved in the struggle. However, the more notable instances offer something more than the predetermined closure suggested by the type; and, in the 1990s, a new mood of political optimism appears to have sponsored a reinvigorated creativity in which social life in Northern Ireland has been accorded a more varied treatment.

The new mood follows in the wake of the Anglo-Irish Agreement of 1985 and the subsequent negotiations for devolved government and a long-term peace. In Eve Patten's account, a formal renewal begins to occur in Northern Irish fiction in the late 1980s, a resurgence marked by the ability of writers such as Robert McLiam Wilson and Glenn Patterson to develop innovative fictional modes that redeem the novel of the Troubles from the 'creative paralysis' that Patten detects in, for example, Jennifer Johnston and Bernard MacLaverty. Patten fears that these two writers 'reinforce for an international readership a compulsive literary stereotype – that of the Irish writer defiantly extracting the lyrical moment from tragic inevitability'. In Patten's view it is the cultivation of this lyricism that prevents both Johnston and MacLaverty from engaging 'with a multitextured and abstruse society'.[29]

Bernard MacLaverty's *Cal* (1983) falls into Patten's category of novels that, even if 'eloquent and well-executed', represent some kind of 'reductionist' imaginative failure, where 'wistful relationships' are 'swamped and severed by a faceless paramilitary machine'.[30] On the face of it, the bleakness of MacLaverty's novel seems to conform to this model of wistfulness faced with inevitable defeat, but it may be a little more complex than Patten allows. For Gerry Smyth, *Cal* places 'realistic political detail in ironic juxtaposition with a self-conscious and recurring motif of Christian imagery' and it is this significant tension that gives rise to the book's most interesting effects.[31] The plot is well conceived for the economic and unsentimental exploration of a tragic situation: a young Catholic, Cal McClusky, falls in love with the widow of an RUC reservist, whose killing he had been party to (as the driver in the raid). Guilt and anguish then become the dominant elements, which overlay a rites-of-passage story of first love. MacLaverty is careful to situate his character as victim of circumstance: work is difficult to find in a context of sectarian discrimination that results, ultimately, in Cal and his father being burned out of their home. Cal's involvement in terrorist action, moreover, is a matter of coercion. He wishes to extricate himself from involvement, and so finds himself on the run from both the security forces and the paramilitaries. The novel concerns itself with the depiction of a web of social and political forces that enmesh an average individual without political ambitions, like Cal. MacLaverty is not seeking a form that will deliver solutions; rather, his claustrophobic fable serves to underscore Cal's own bleak vision:

> To suffer for something which didn't exist, that was like Ireland. People were dying every day, men and women were being crippled and turned into vegetables in the name of Ireland. An Ireland which never was and never would be. It was the people of Ulster who were heroic, caught between the jaws of two opposing ideals trying to grind each other out of existence. (p. 83)

This jaundiced heroism denotes a climate in which tribal responses are predetermined. This is old-style nationalism, rooted in spurious perceptions of tradition, is oblivious to the flexible and transformative nationalist energies of the end of the century. The novel does not, however, simply offer a flat representation of an internecine Irish struggle (the popular British view); indeed, there are criticisms of British-sponsored violence, most notably in the first-hand account of Bloody Sunday, given by the (otherwise chilling) intellectual-activist Skeffington (p. 67).

There is certainly something claustrophobic, if not nihilistic, in the depiction of a situation in which love cannot flourish and suffering cannot be avoided; but the novel is complicated by its fabulistic element, which hints (falsely, as it turns out) at a broader dynamic of suffering and redemption, given meaning by the crucifixion motif. The novel closes with Cal's arrest, on Christmas Eve, and his sense of gratitude 'that at last someone was going to beat him to within an inch of his life' (p. 154).

Some kind of paradoxical renewal is implied in the embracing of suffering on the eve of the Christian festival celebrating the birth of Christ. It is the crucifixion, however, that is made to resonate as the novel's central symbol, reinforcing the sense of redemption through suffering, with Cal the Christ figure, taking upon himself the sins of his society. But this association is not consistently drawn; moreover, the crucifixion symbolism is so self-consciously realized as to provoke suspicion about its meaning. In the most startling use of the motif, Cal dreams he is in a railway station in Rome, faced by a crowd dressed in white togas, including the widow Marcella Morton. A man is on the track, face down, in the shape of a crucifix, his hands hanging over the edge of the rails. Cal signals to Marcella as a train approaches, but she seems unconcerned for the man, whose hands are severed at the wrist when the train passes, showering the crowd in their white togas with blood. They are impassive, and Cal screams at them until he wakes (pp. 106–7). The dream serves two functions: first, it contributes to our developing sense of Cal's guilt at his involvement in the murder of

Marcella's husband; and second, it juxtaposes two different responses to the suffering of the crucified man. Cal's fury is directed at the members of the crowd, including Marcella, who appear willing to embrace the symbolism of the scene, whilst Cal screams, not at the violence, but at the passivity of the others and their 'symbolic reading', as it were.

Two pages after the dream, Marcella tells Cal of her response, whilst on a School trip, to Grünewald's painting of the crucifixion, which had inspired awe in her on account of the terrible pain it conveys (p. 110). As a Christmas present Cal buys Marcella a book containing this image, which is given great prominence as the novel concludes:

> The weight of the Christ figure bent the cross down like a bow; the hands were cupped to heaven like nailed starfish; the body with its taut ribcage was pulled to the shape of an egg-timer by the weight of the lower body... She was sitting on the floor with her back to the couch, her legs open in a yoga position and the book facing him, just below her breasts. Cal looked at the flesh of Christ spotted and torn, bubonic almost, and then behind it at the smoothness of Marcella's body and it became a permanent picture in his mind. (p. 153)

That which etches itself on Cal's consciousness is, again, corporeal and literal rather than spiritual or symbolic: for him the actual business of killing is held in an arresting comparison with the object of his own physical love. Cal, effectively, ignores the religious symbol, a response that nudges us to do the same when we are invited to put Cal into the same frame of meaning on the following page. As in Cal's dream, an implicit stress is placed on particular rather than universal suffering.

Something similar occurs in Jennifer Johnston's *The Railway Station Man* (1984), another one of those novels that Eve Patten sees as 'reductionist' in 'retrieving the *condition humaine* from a complex, impersonal reality'.[32] Johnston uses a temporal frame to investigate the isolation of her artist-protagonist Helen Cuffe, installed in her makeshift studio on the northwest coast of Ireland as the novel opens. The narrative then unfolds as a sustained flashback that explains her sense of insularity. She had moved to the south after the death of her schoolteacher husband, shot by mistake in a paramilitary killing (pp. 8–10). A focus of her rehabilitation is her rediscovery of her skills as a painter, and this, together with her burgeoning relationship with the mutilated English war hero Roger Hawthorne implies a personal rebirth that, the opening forewarns us, will be curtailed.

The title alerts us to the importance of Hawthorne, Helen's neighbour, and obsessive renovator of disused railway stations. He claims previously to have renovated stations in Northumberland and Scotland, and now, eluding his family (who think he should be institutionalized), he is working on the station close by Helen's cottage. His plan is to get everything ready for the reopening of the line, in the absence of tracks, and then to involve Irish rail (p. 87). This behaviour, whilst both eccentric and naive, also implies something visionary, the rebuilding of community structures in the face of the overshadowing violence in the North.

At the same time, however, we cannot miss the dubious symbolism of Hawthorne's vision: 'I see my station working. Trains running through it. Goods. Not many passengers I admit. Most people have cars these days' (p. 133). The dream of an English war veteran, establishing in Ireland an infrastructure for the carriage of trade rather than individuals, is redolent of imperialism. The fact that this is contrary to Hawthorne's intention is very much the point: Johnston, like MacLaverty, is interested in a situation where actions are put into a contextual frame of meaning that may distort intentions. The explosion that kills four men, including Hawthorne and Helen's son Jack, produces an almost farcical conclusion. Jack, involved with an amateurish Republican paramilitary group, has earmarked Hawthorne's disused shed as an isolated storage site for the explosives, which are accidentally detonated in the fateful conclusion. Given the novel's broader vision, there is a logic to this denouement that symbolizes the clash between competing destructive ambitions in Ireland.

What remains is Helen's painting, and her friendship with Damian, a reformed activist. In the narrative present of the novel's frame, we discover that he has built a glass-fronted studio for her, and that she has begun to exhibit her work (pp. 1–2). This theme is expressed most forcefully in the series of pictures that Helen paints in rediscovering her talent. The sequence, entitled 'Man on a Beach', is inspired by an episode in which Damian comes upon Helen swimming naked in the sea, and then follows her example whilst she seizes the opportunity to sketch him (pp. 121–3). In the sequence of canvases, the figure becomes progressively less significant until, in the fourth and final image, all that remains is a pile of clothes. If this is a form of art that refines the human presence out of existence, it also lays stress on human potential: the clothes in the fourth canvas are 'the only colourful objects' in the sequence, its most visually significant presence, signifying both potential and absence (p. 187). This artistic achievement offsets the sense of defeat that characterizes the narrative action, and this qualified sense of hope through creativity applies to the position of Johnston as well as Helen Cuffe, the artist-figure in the text.

Published seven years before *The Railway Station Man*, Johnston's *Shadows on Our Skin* (1977) creates a similar mood, in which political violence disrupts personal relationships. Again, it is the possibility of artistic creativity that offers a slender prospect of an alternative future, in the form of the *Golden Treasury of Verse*, passed on as a gift to the budding poet Joe. These novels of qualified hope may seem partially to reinforce Patten's reading of a lyrical wistfulness in the face of tragic inevitability. My dispute really concerns what one can expect of novels at different times. It seems certain that political progression towards a compromise peace settlement had to be made before new fictional forms could be evolved to marry with a new mood of cautious political optimism. There is, of course, a limit to the capacity of literature to influence the direction of history, and the wistful lyricism of Johnston and MacLaverty might be seen to fit very well with an earlier mood of disappointed hope. This structure of historical correspondence explains the perceived significance of novels like *Cal* and *The Railway Station Man* as powerful imaginative interventions in the literary culture of the 1980s.

If MacLaverty and Johnston are harshly done by in complaints about their restricted vision, the Northern Ireland experience has, indeed, produced novels that convey a sense of stasis. In *Hidden Symptoms* (1986), Deirdre Madden produces a style of fiction with a confined atmosphere, which cultivates an aura of defeat and suffering that is quite distinct from the lyricism of MacLaverty and Johnston. At the centre of the novel is Theresa, the character whose brother Francis was the victim of a random sectarian attack, captured, tortured, and murdered for being Catholic. Theresa's embittered struggle is to reconcile her loss and the gratuitousness of sectarian violence, with her religious faith, and this results in a novel that is curiously inward-looking.

One strand of the novel privileges a pure kind of faith, or that which is hidden from view, but this pursuit of grace serves also to undermine the business of artistic representation, which, by comparison with religious certitude, can only obscure the 'truth'. Theresa's confusion in this area is emulated in the novel's form. However, if Madden is unable to articulate the required negotiation between art, politics, and morality, either through her characters or the form of her novel, she does alert us to a contradiction with ramifications beyond her own writing, and one that is particularly pressing for the novel in Northern Ireland.

A very different Catholic response is embodied in Martha Murtagh, protagonist of Mary Beckett's *Give Them Stones* (1987), a novel so structured as to make the experiences of one Catholic working-class woman representative of an oppressed life in Belfast. The book begins and ends in the 1970s, with a core narrative comprising an exploration of a family's experiences since the establishment of the province in 1922.

At the outset, Martha Murtagh, the narrator of this confessional novel, sees a boy shot in both legs against her wall by provisionals, prompting her to make a principled stand against the IRA activists in her area, in spite of her sympathy for the Republican cause. The novel thus stakes out a clear moral territory: the question of individual responsibility in public history, and the need to pay due attention to the justification of political means as well as ends. Martha's stand accrues authority to itself precisely because of the difficulty she has in relinquishing inherited nationalist views.

The novel ends with a celebration of a traditional identity of sorts in Martha: after she and her husband are burnt out of their home, she has plans to establish herself in proper commercial premises as a baker, offering her great aunts' legacy (for it is they who teach her to bake) in a modernized form (p. 152). In this way, the primacy of bread over stones is asserted, a reversal of the exhortation in the novel's title, and this is far from the apolitical solution it might seem. Martha's life is one of poverty and slight opportunity, conditions of the Catholic Belfast life she is made to represent. Her tenacity in reconstructing her life and purpose speaks to that experience in particular, demonstrating that material advancement is a prerequisite of integration.

A bleaker depiction of Catholic Belfast emerges in Kate O'Riordan's first novel *Involved* (1995), in which Catholic guilt, sexual repression, and sectarian violence are all inextricably linked. The stability of the book's symbolism, which emphasizes the closed system of religious violence in which all of the characters are caught, helps explain the book's dispiriting mood: the open-endedness that is a defining characteristic of much modern fiction is entirely absent from this work. Its lyrical qualities are thus defeated by the resolute closure of a narrower kind of thriller (in which the dream of escape into exile is crushed), and it is in comparison with this kind of narrative closure that one can appreciate more fully the lyricism of a MacLaverty or a Johnston.[33]

Of course, one does not always expect a sense of optimism or resolution in serious literary works. Indeed, the situation in Northern Ireland would seem to lend itself to a more fully realized *tragic* form, and one writer who has explored this possibility is Dermot Healy. In *A Goat's Song* (1994) a resonant sense of tribalism haunts the mixed relationship of Protestant Catherine Adams and Catholic Jack Ferris, especially in Belfast where his openness puts him in mortal danger. Their (mutual) drunkenness emerges as a defence against a world of terror, and it is this which gives the depth to the tragedy of their thwarted relationship. Jack explains to Catherine the etymology of 'tragedy' from the Greek: '*Tragos* – goat. *Oide* – song.' (p. 227) He goes on to propound the theory that the term arises from Greek agricultural practices, where Greek goatherds would rear bucks and nannies on separate islands: when the nannies were in season the scent would reach the stranded bucks on the breeze, and, in frustration, they would raise a mournful cry (p. 227). At the end of the novel (also its point of opening) this suggests a simple correspondence with the situation of the heartbroken Ferris, finally cut off from his Catherine. In the broader context, where a history of sectarian division is seen to sunder them, the tragedy is that of opposed cultures. In this sense, the novel presents a tacit plea for a united Ireland.

From the perspective of the 1990s Eve Patten astutely detects a new phase in fiction from Northern Ireland, marking the 'exploitation of literary strategies such as perspectivism, ambiguity and displacement' that are seen as 'attributes of a sustained constitutional and psychological identity crisis' that befits 'a contemporary Northern Irish self-image'.[34] A correspondence is proposed between a new experimentalism in Northern Irish fiction and the re-evaluations of identity, both psychological and constitutional, abroad in society – technical innovation as mimesis, in effect. The technical resurgence is perceived as *overdue* in a society experiencing an acute saturation in its conceptualization of identity, but this impatience may be unreasonable in the context of Northern Ireland: indeed, significant political progress towards a peace settlement was needed before alternative and exploratory depictions of Northern Irish identity could be expected to find broad public sympathy or recognition. But that moment seemed to have arrived in the late 1980s and early 1990s.

One of the earliest novels that contributes to this transitional mood of greater optimism is Glenn Patterson's *Burning Your Own* (1988). This is an initiation story in which ten-year-old Mal Martin begins to perceive the failings and prejudices of his own Protestant community. The novel is set in the summer of 1969, and culminates in the expulsion of Catholic families from the Protestant housing estate on which Mal lives. The focus for this tension is Mal's friendship with Francy Hagan, a Catholic teenager who is an outsider figure and a kind of guru to Mal. Francy, indeed, is the character who has an historical overview of the community's problems: he draws our attention to the improbable social solution intended in the building of 'a ready-made community' in the aftermath of the Second World War (p. 20), and ridicules the planning of a collection of streets 'trailing into a dump, at its arse end' (p. 18). It is the dump, the final ironic commentary on the estate and the social failure it embodies, that Francy has chosen to embrace. In a gesture of individual defiance, he has rejected the estate, and built his own den and inner sanctum at one end of the dump.

After Francy's family have been forced out, he returns to the dump to blow himself up in his booby-trapped den, after a tragicomic scene in which he conducts a satirical mock sale for the angry Protestant crowd that have gathered, kept at bay by Francy's braziers, and the occasional petrol bomb. The final item in Francy's 'sale' of items from his den is a Tricolour, which accidentally catches fire as he is in the process of cutting it up, a symbolic dismemberment producing 'a bit for everyone' (p. 248). The simultaneous burning of the Tricolour and of Francy establishes him as a martyr of the Catholic tradition, destroyed by the way in which the blight of urban planning colludes with sectarian intimidation. It is significant that Mal's uncle secures a Housing Trust contract to build a new estate, bringing the prospect of prosperity to the Protestant community, and employment to Mal's father. There is a crucial moment when Mal, alarmed by Francy's tendency to cynicism, kisses him with open mouth (p. 231). The embrace is confused and contradictory, expressing both the innocent desire for union and the inevitability of betrayal. The advance that *Burning Your Own* embodies is its withdrawn perspective. This facilitates a tentative (if thwarted) *rapprochement* between Protestant and Catholic, and the cultivation of a broader, contextual view.

Perhaps the most significant figure in the formal renewal of the 1980s is Robert McLiam Wilson, whose *Ripley Bogle* (1989) is an important transitional novel. It produces, centrally, both a re-evaluation of Northern Irish literary identity, and an associated alternative perspective on the Troubles. The eponymous protagonist and narrator Ripley Bogle is a young gentleman-tramp in the tradition of Joyce and Beckett, and the novel traces his decline over four days into increasingly desperate straits, whilst the story of his past, including the details of his Belfast Catholic upbringing, is revealed through (unreliable) recollection. Bogle's origins are established with farcical hyperbole: his home life is a parody of deprivation and cruelty, yet he manages secretly to turn himself into a genius from the age of five by the voracious consumption of stolen library books, subsequently buried in a neighbour's garden (pp. 27–8).

Bogle's learning eventually leads him to a place at Cambridge, so a more serious purpose is revealed in this, the path from the public library on the Lower Falls Road that connects the Northern Irish periphery with the supposed centre of English learning. The elusiveness of Bogle and his descent into trampdom is partly a refusal to engage with the solipsistic Englishness of the competitive 1980s, which he ruthlessly dissects. The difficulty is that the 'vitality of the Celt', which he claims for himself, remains unrealized (p. 202).

Even so, there is a sense in which Bogle's unconventionality, and the humour it generates, is productive. This is particularly clear in his recollections of Internment Night, when 'a massive West Indian Corporal' bursts into his room. In the *faux naif* manner of a Beckett character, Bogle fails to respond to the self-evident codes of the situation, and is instead moved by the 'exotic and dangerous glamour' of the soldier who causes his 'eyes to grow moist with love' (p. 33). This principle of defamiliarization, in which codes more conventionally associated with a bedroom scene displace those that push a greater claim, serves to heighten the sense of abnormality and disruption. This is the kind of principle that is used to convey the confusion surrounding Bogle's ethnicity. There is a school scene in the same vein where Bogle listens too literally to a Republican schoolteacher who inculcates the idea in her pupils that their names are 'Irish', even though some people will tell them that their names are 'British'. In a spirit of compromise, Bogle then dubs himself 'Ripley Irish British Bogle' (p. 16). Again, the adopted innocence underscores the disturbance of identity.

Bogle's narrative adopts strategies to conceal the real psychological damage he has endured, and in the final pages three central deceptions are revealed: first, the part Bogle has played in the murder of his school contemporary Maurice; second, the fact (hitherto denied) that he was the father of his former girlfriend Deirdre's aborted child; and, third, that his idealized relationship at Cambridge with the English Laura was pure invention. These revelations establish a new seriousness, and oblige us to reconsider the function of the humour, which now appears consolatory.

The final pages discover a level of trauma that explains the dislocation and exile of Bogle, haunted by the violence of the Troubles and the divisiveness of the religious divide. In this sense the book simultaneously contests and utilizes the twin conventions of Troubles fiction: the determining and truncating role of violence, and the doomed love-across-the-barricades scenario. McLiam Wilson conceals the full significance of these twin conventions, and then unfolds them in an exaggerated form to reclaim a novel in which they had apparently been diminished. This is a novel that thus announces itself as marking a period of transition, and, accordingly, Ripley Bogle appears in the final paragraphs on the brink of a new start, as if the novel has performed an exorcism of that baggage of inherited convention. Quite improbably the starving Bogle, also carrying an untreated stab wound, walks confidently towards the future with 'ease' and 'aplomb' (p. 326). At the level of realism, this must be read as a delusion; but, at the level of ideas, the exorcism we have witnessed strongly implies the emergence of a new literary identity.

Ripley Bogle makes a fleeting appearance in the later *Eureka Street* (1996), where his presence suits a mood of qualified optimism and reconciliation in the era of the ceasefires of 1994. Wilson's emphasis in this novel is on the 'magical' nature of Belfast, a quality produced through a simple humanistic celebration of its 'epic' citizens, both 'tender' and 'murderable' (p. 217). The novel has a popular-political function, but it also contains a number of inspired features, all of which demonstrate the moderateness it promotes. One is the character Chuckie Lurgan, a working-class Protestant strangely drawn to Catholicism, and whose name sounds like the 'supremacist republican slogan' *Tiocfaidh ar La* ('our day will come'), a coincidence that, through humorous misunderstanding, serves to undercut the 'supremacist' design (p. 150). An unlikely entrepreneur, Lurgan manages to secure vast sums of government money, initially for madcap schemes, but finally for plans centred on political and economic regeneration (pp. 380, 386).

Perhaps the most delightful feature of the book is the appearance of a new graffito, the letters 'OTG', in a city awash with the capital letters signifying political and paramilitary groups: UDA, IRA, UVF, and so on. The lesson of these letters, which could mean anything, is pointed out by one of the characters: 'I think someone's satirizing us' (p. 356). In the conclusion, it is 'OTG', mistakenly believed to be an underground organization, biding its time, that Lurgan seizes upon in launching his 'non-sectarian third force in Ulster politics' (p. 386).

## Irishness Extended

Another writer who contributes to the new mood in which humour is permissible is Patrick McCabe (indeed, McCabe has played a formative role in this phase). In both *The Butcher Boy* (1992) and *The Dead School* (1995), Patrick McCabe produces a remarkable narrative voice for the comic dissection of psychosis. The method is one in which the cadences and idioms of Irish-English serve to generate a unique blend of humour and pathos. (He attempts the same combination, with less success, in *Breakfast on Pluto* [1998], a treatment of the Troubles.) There is a gathering sense that creative efforts such as the linguistic innovation of McCabe, and the revisionist impulse of McLiam Wilson, indicate an emerging hybrid of national identity, a reinvigoration of Irishness in relation to Englishness.

'Irish Culture', writes Declan Kiberd, 'exists in a kind of parabolic relation to England's.' Consequently, 'the Irish, in renovating their own consciousness, may also be helping, wittingly or unwittingly, to reanimate England's'.[35] Irish migrants to England would seem to form a primary group for the development of this kind of cross-fertilization. However, much writing about the Irish experience in England, or Britain generally, concerns itself with the shedding of predetermined roles, and the relinquishment of shibboleths, in what amounts to a cultural ground-clearing exercise.

An acute problem of definition obtains in connection with those Irish writers living and working in Britain. Eamonn Hughes examines the (apparently oxymoronic) term 'Irish-British' in an interesting discussion that locates its usefulness and its limits. Hughes shows how it differs in its implications from other hyphenated terms such as Black-British. Afro-Caribbean writers, for example, are 'less easily assimilable' than Irish writers, due to distinctive social and cultural factors. This relative independence, together with an acknowledged and 'more conventionally colonial history', ensures that the term Black-British indicates 'the merging and/or yoking together of different social and cultural experiences'. Merging, however, appears the wrong word to use in connection with the Irish experience, because the relationship between Britain and Ireland is culturally more complex. The long-term contribution of Irish society and culture makes it 'a constitutive part' of the 'British socio-cultural entity'; whilst, at the same time, there is a sense that British and Irish cultural identities are irreconcilable.[36]

A key factor in distinguishing Irish from other migrant groups in Britain is the dream of returning home. Whilst this is a common aim for all migrant groups, the closeness of Ireland gives the dream greater plausibility. In practice this is often a delusion, but its persuasiveness can make the sense of temporary exile a defining conviction of the Irish-British; it might also explain, as Hughes speculates, 'the comparative absence of a fiction about Irish-Britain' as an identifiable and located community 'which requires cultural articulation'. The stigma of failure that often attaches itself, in the Irish consciousness, to those emigrating to England, suggests another reason 'for *not* producing an Irish-British identity'.[37] *Home From England* (1995) by James Ryan confronts and explodes the illusions that surround Irish emigration, which is not presented as necessarily temporary or as a source of great sadness. The (unnamed) narrator is entering his teens when his family move from rural Ireland to England in the early 1960s. The myth of return pervades the parents' attitudes to life in England, preventing them from a meaningful life in the present since 'going home stood at the centre of everything' (p. 59). The children, however, soon become acculturated to life in England, so that a generation gap qualifies the dream of return, and articulates it as a regressive myth of nostalgia, rooted in a debilitating nationalism.

The generational progression is clarified through the episode in which the family return to Ireland for a holiday that coincides with the fiftieth anniversary celebrations of the 1916 Easter Rising. The narrator's father is to be presented with a commemorative medal (even though he was too young to be involved in the 'war for independence'), and the celebrations will incorporate the unveiling of statues of two local heroes of 1916. The novel's defining moment is the arson attack on the wrapped statues, doused in paraffin and set alight through their protective straw layers. For the narrator, who is drawn into the vandalism by Hegarty, the tough-boy he admires, the action makes him feel 'fully convinced that I was reclaiming something that I had come to believe was irretrievable' (p. 135).

It takes the death of his father (after his retirement), however, for him to complete this process of reclaiming control of his own identity. The father is returned home for burial, and at the funeral the narrator overhears the abject local evaluation of his life: 'A harmless poor ould divil, home from England, God rest his soul' (p. 183). This is the concluding revelation. The final paragraph articulates the narrator's now complete disentanglement from his father's nationalism. He has arrived at a metaphorical 'vantage point from which I could see my fields becoming his fields', and from which 'his war for independence' comes to resemble the war games of boyhood (p. 184). This reverses the earlier image of psychic mapping, when, for the narrator, 'it was his fields that filled my landscape', together with second-hand memories 'like the part he had played in the war for independence' (p. 59). Divesting himself of the trappings of an anachronistic, falsifying nationalism, Ryan's anonymous modern Irishman reclaims the ground on which his identity might be based.

The reversal that orders *Home From England* implies an ambivalence, too, about the sources of nationalism, a progressiveness tinged with nostalgia. A related ambivalence emerges in Roddy Doyle's *Paddy Clarke Ha Ha Ha* (1993), the subtlety of which lies beneath its comic and convincing treatment of boyhood. (The novel is set in Ireland, but the theme of cultural interaction is central to it.) Surface toughness is the dominant code for the gang-mentality of ten-year-olds like Paddy Clarke; but his propensity to side with the underdog – he plays 'Indians and Cowboys, not Cowboys and Indians' (p. 147) – denotes an understated treatment of colonialism. Listening to the news, Paddy thinks the Americans are fighting 'gorillas' in Vietnam, and makes an instant allegiance: 'I was up for the gorillas.' When his mistake is explained, the instinctive allegiance holds: 'I was still up for them, the guerrillas' (pp. 227–8). In such a moment, Doyle seems to hold out the possibility of an oppositional theme, but his real purpose is to complicate simple understandings of influence and dominance.

Paddy Clarke, in fact, is a product of divers cultural influences, which are American ('The Virginian' television series) as much as English (the 'Just William' stories). His support of Manchester United, now one of the most famous of international brand names, underscores this transnational idea. Doyle is presenting an identity and a community on the cusp of change, inhabiting a world that is just emerging. (This is quite literal, since the 'Barrytown' that provides the setting for Doyle's earlier trilogy, set in the Dublin suburbia of the 1980s, exists here, in 1968, as just so many building sites, which comprise the playground of Paddy Clarke and his friends.) Neither are these disparate forces conducive to a settled existence. Paddy's family is eventually riven by domestic violence, and this casts a shadow over his own efforts to transcend the tribal brutality of his childhood. When the novel tips over from comedy to tragedy, the title is revealed as a taunt broadcasting the family's break-up as a source of public humiliation: 'Paddy Clarke – Has no da. Ha ha ha!' (p. 281).

If in Ryan's *Home From England* paternity symbolizes a nationalist myth of origin to be escaped, the loss of paternal stability for Paddy Clarke pitches him, less positively, into an implied post-nationalist world of unstable identities. The freedom from established patterns of nationalist affiliation, however, marks a significant historical moment.

## Welsh Resistance

The uncertainty that accompanies modern migration and the dissolution of traditional national symbols has had an acute effect on Welsh identity. Contemporary writers in Wales have been confronted with a crisis of identity that came to a head with the 'no' vote in the devolution referendum of 1979, a resounding defeat for separatist Welsh nationalism. The interest in devolution was to achieve a new head of steam in the Thatcher years, though that earlier popular assertion of connection to Britain was to colour later initiatives. The Welsh Assembly, inaugurated by Blair's government, tacitly acknowledges this history, and represents a diluted form of regional government in comparison with the new Scottish Parliament.

The political split between those identifying with Wales, and those identifying with Britain, is not reflected at the level of individual national identity, however. The conservative pragmatism that a referendum seems to encourage, masks the inclination of the majority of people living in Wales to consider themselves 'Welsh' rather than 'British'.[38] Indeed, a sense of national identity in Wales is more commonly predicated on a reaction *against* Britishness, and the political and cultural dominance it is perceived to represent. For Welsh Nationalists like R. S. Thomas, Britishness is simply another word for Englishness. In this view, incorporation into Britain supplies the means by which the essential attributes of Welshness – the Welsh language in particular – are swamped by an English cultural hegemony.[39]

The resistance of effacement at the hands of a colonizing Englishness brings with it certain problems, however. It often involves the attempt to define stable boundaries in the construction of national identity, boundaries that may have been surpassed by historical, cultural, and geographical change. In fiction, a retreat into a mythology of Welshness has been a frequent response to this challenge. In Alexander Cordell's *Rape of the Fair Country* (1959), for example, the family-saga form of historical romance employs, in a predetermined manner, a received history of English oppression in its cultivation of national pride and the love of place. The dynamic is retrogressive, in its dependence on a 'finished' and 'remembered past' that fails to address 'the openness of the present', or 'the will to a wider perspective'.[40] The inhibiting effect of the backward look is glaringly apparent in Richard Llewellyn's *How Green Was My Valley*, which has remained the most popular Welsh novel of the post-war period, even though it was published in 1939. Llewellyn's novel is 'widely and properly seen as the export version of the Welsh industrial experience', and it has latterly become infamous on account of its insular and sentimental appeal to place.[41] The revelation that Llewellyn was born in Hendon (as Vivian Lloyd), and not in St David's, Pembrokeshire, as a miner's son, serves to confirm the air of falsity that pervades the novel. The problem is not so much that 'Llewellyn' could not have cultivated his Welshness, in an emerging era of fluid national identities, but rather that the 'inside' version of Welshness his novel perpetuates seems to depend on a national identity more firmly rooted in place and lived experience.[42]

The case of Richard Llewellyn encapsulates the central problem for Welsh writers, where a turning inwards or (historically) backwards might stave off the process of assimilation to Britain, but only by cultivating a false, and so vulnerable, nationalism. What has become increasingly necessary is a form of cultural explanation that embraces the fact of migration, and heterogeneity, and that acknowledges that the insistence on origins is counterproductive.

The issue of internal Welsh conflict is memorably treated in *Resistance* (1985) by Mary Jones, in which the rootless, English-speaking Ann Thomas, suffering from cancer, retreats into a hotel in Powys. Her attempt to escape the material facts of her experience suggests also an attempt to 'lose herself', to evade the implications of identity. In its Gothic elements, the novel presents the oppressive hotel as a symbol of the nation's decline, and specifically its intellectual crisis of identity. At one point the hotel is compared to a brain, 'threaded with nerves that reached out from the central areas . . . their impulses growing weaker and weaker' (p. 36). The simile follows a passage in which Ann Thomas recollects the horror of seeing her skull X-rayed, and the doctor, seeking to reveal the effects of the tumour in her jaw, tracing 'the outline of where I had been eaten away' (p. 35). In this identification between the diseased protagonist and the dilapidated hotel, English influence is signalled as one source of national decay. But, as the site of other national antagonisms, the hotel stages the internal Welsh conflict between Welsh and English speakers, and harbours a militant Welsh nationalism that issues in a bomb blast, and an ensuing fire that kills the perpetrator, and damages the hotel.

The metaphorical elements of *Resistance* stress the sickliness of the Anglo-Welsh Ann, an internal exile within a nation in a state of self-destructive conflict and confusion. At the close, Ann is left shamefaced, clinging to her 'base instinct, the will to survive', whilst the other principal, the nationalist Aled, has been killed. The novel thus presents different connotations of 'resistance'. Aled's resistance of English colonization, emulating the militancy of earlier Welsh heroes, such as Llywelyn ap Gruffud, is self-defeating.[43] Ann's 'resistance', on the other hand, is more complex:

resisting the extreme nationalist perspective, she is also resisting the disease that, in its metaphorical meaning, is the English influence she carries with her. Thus her 'resistance' is Janus-faced (as her ambivalent response to Aled indicates), denoting an intermediary position between cultural capitulation and a regressive nationalism. Emyr Humphreys described the history of Wales as 'a history of unending resistance and unexpected survival', and this is also an apt summation of Jones's important treatment of Welsh identity.[44]

Emyr Humphreys's own *Outside the House of Baal* (1965), considered to be possibly 'the most canonical of modern Welsh novels', may be the definitive novel of Welsh national decline.[45] Humphreys employs a complex time-frame to juxtapose a post-war present with an unfolding narrative that traces his characters' pasts back to the early years of the twentieth century. This dual chronology, Humphreys hoped, would 'create a penumbra of meaning that would not otherwise be apparent'. A particular sadness for Humphreys is the waning influence of Welsh nonconformism, its values overridden, its authority ceded to the secular gods of progress. Yet the novel cultivates an air of ambiguity about progress, a factor indicated in the author's account of his interest in 'the splendours and miseries of the Welsh experience'.[46]

Preacher Joe Miles (J. T.) is the force of stability, a pacifist in the Great War, who seeks to uphold his religious principles even at the expense of personal anxiety or discomfort. But he is also an anachronism, a figure who stands opposed to the new kind of Welshman that is emerging. In the intellectual disagreement with his sociologist son Ronnie, this problem of national identity is underscored. J. T. believes that nationality is 'a question of loyalty' (p. 370), while for Ronnie this emphasis on 'living in the past', symbolized in the dream of resuscitating the Welsh language, 'lies on a new generation like a corrosive dust' (p. 371). Historically, speculates Ronnie, this stifling mood of 'dead-wood tradition' has required the talented Welshman to migrate in order to be liberated, in the manner of 'a Bevan, a Lloyd George' (p. 370).

J. T. may be the novel's most sympathetic character, but the logic of the migrant sensibility gathers momentum, together with the evocation of the 'corrosive dust' of tradition. For J. T., progress is summarized in the new neighbourhood public house, occupying a dominant corner position, and with an asphalt car-park that abuts his garden. Another character compares it to a cathedral, and J. T. dubs it 'The House of Baal' (p. 155). (Baal is the false, pagan god of the Old Testament.) Humphreys is acutely conscious of the assimilation of Wales to England, so the encroachment of commercial interests that negate Welsh culture (such as the modern pub, which is an assault on J. T.'s faith in temperance) are keenly felt. The careers of the next generation (Ronnie the academic, Bea the actress) are presented as part of that process of assimilation. But the new generation are moving through and beyond the phase of incorporation. Bea's career makes her an international migrant, and the novel's closing situation sees J. T. wishing to visit her at her Italian villa.

This reconciliation seems likely to be scuppered by Kate, the sister-in-law whose house the elderly J. T. shares. It is she who will not allow Bea's husband (who has had previous wives) into her house, and she who will not countenance the foreign trip (p. 183). In the novel's opening situation, which is extended through the novel, the one-eyed Kate, who has misplaced her glass eye, retrieves it from a bowl of prunes (p. 88). It is subsequently revealed that the eye was lost to a trailing hedgerow thorn, probably left by a neglectful farmer (pp. 173–4). The conservative Kate's limited vision is established as a consequence of a backward and self-defeating insularity, symbolized by the slapdash execution of traditional farming tasks. Kate also denies J. T. the opportunity of participating in the emerging transnational moment, by preventing the reunion with his daughter in Italy (p. 182). Pondering the future of the Welsh nation, Humphreys has written that 'it is always the past rather than the present that offers the best hope for a future'.[47] *Outside the House of Baal* suggests the reverse: that the adherence to a sickly tradition imposes a straitjacket on the present, cutting it off from its possible futures.

## The 'Possible Dance' of Scottishness

The more self-conscious expressions of postcolonialism have adopted an eclectic approach to fiction writing, sometimes producing hybridized forms that begin to do justice to the fluidity of national sentiment in some quarters of the contemporary world. In Britain, however, particular national literatures are often prevented from realizing this kind of heteroglot diversity by their own gestures of resistance. In both Scottish and Welsh fiction it is the dominant presence of English culture that represents the force to react against, but that remains present as a negative pole in the equation of nationality.

The problems of refashioning national identity in Scottish literature appear to be various. The inauguration of a Scottish Parliament at the end of the century may begin to offset Cairns Craig's concern that imaginative future projection has been delimited in a country where government is 'ceded to a British parliament'. There is still, however, a problem of dislocation that makes a settled tradition impossible to establish. In Craig's account, however, the difficulty emerges as the prelude to a re-examination of 'tradition'. Seeking to contest 'the "traditionless" thinking of a contemporary internationalism', Craig argues that 'traditions are heteroglossic'; they 'are not the unitary voice of an organic whole but the dialectical engagement between opposing value systems that define each other precisely by their intertwined oppositions'.[48] If it is an exaggeration to think of the dialectic of opposition as 'heteroglossic', there is certainly a useful anchor in the oppositional rethinking of tradition, which may be absent in some rootless or 'traditionless' versions of the postmodern.

A novelist who makes this dialectical engagement an appropriately formal matter is Alisdair Gray, whose novel *Lanark* (1981) has been highly influential in the development of modern Scottish fiction. The engagement with power in an experimental text actually lends *Lanark* the credentials of an exemplary postmodern work, in Alison Lee's definition. If Gray's 'primary concern is with structures of power', whether 'familial, governmental', or that which is derived from 'corporate control', he finds literary analogues in 'the manipulation of the reader and the character . . . by the very structure of the text'.[49] The novel's twin settings, Glasgow and the dystopian fantasy City of Unthank, suggest the two poles – realism and fantasy – between which Gray locates the impetus of his writing. The median position thus established represents a simultaneous challenge to the two fictional codes. The received history of the realist code is disputed in a famous passage in which Glasgow is said to be neglected in artistic representations, and so unavailable for imaginative inhabitation (p. 243). At the other extreme, the novel's fantastic elements suggest the dangers of the unfettered imagination, where escapism is in the ascendancy.

The experimental use of typography is one route for the investigation of textual power. The clearest example of this in *Lanark* is the split column epilogue which incorporates an 'Index of Plagiarisms' (pp. 485–99). Here different degrees of plagiarism in the novel are defined and acknowledged, an admission of the contestation of discourses throughout the text (which is reproduced in the epilogue's twin columns). A more general point emerges from this discursive play, since the resistance of 'type' is, at once, a challenge to the typicality of the realist character, and to the print medium that inserts the representative character within a broader historical dynamic. This is not, however, an instance of context-less postmodern playfulness. On the contrary, as Cairns Craig suggests, there is a very particular Scottish edge to this:

> For a culture whose whole existence since 1707 has been shaped by the medium of a learned written language which displaced its own oral cultures, and whose native languages were never properly standardized within the domain of type, typography becomes the symbol of its own culturally repressed condition: to overthrow the rule of type is synonymous with overthrowing the type of rule under which the culture has struggled for self-expression.[50]

Craig locates the cultural (and also typographical) colonization of Scotland by England with the Act of Union, which formalized the bond between the two countries. Certainly, it is possible to overstate the radicalism of the typographical experiment, which need not signify a defiant cultural oppositionalism. However, the experimental use of typography has become one of the distinctive features of the creative surge in the Scottish novel since the 1980s, and such gestures invariably have a relationship to the uncertainty of Scottish identity, even if the topic of cultural repression is not always an express concern.[51]

An experiment with typeface and layout is deployed, somewhat gratuitously, by Irvine Welsh in both *Marabou Stork Nightmares* (1995) and *Filth* (1998); but a writer who has made more accomplished use of typography is Janice Galloway, whose *The Trick is to Keep Breathing* (1989) uses various typographical devices to depict the emotional trauma of Joy Stone, whose partner has drowned in a swimming-pool accident. The dead man was married, but separated, but at his funeral Joy finds herself cast in the role of 'mistress', and so expunged from the collective consciousness by the words of the clergyman:

ESPECIALLY OUR LOVE

a split-second awareness that something terrible was about to about to

TO HIS WIFE AND FAMILY happen

Half-way into the silence for Norma Fisher, my arms were weightless. The rest came piecemeal as the moral started to compute.

1. The Rev Dogsbody had chosen this service to perform a miracle.
2. He's run time backwards, cleansed, absolved and got rid of the ground-in stain.
3. And the stain was me.
I didn't exist. The miracle had wiped me out. (p. 79)

The 'event' that interrupts Joy's narrating of it is her own effacement. This writing out of her emotional history is indicative of the character's inner vacuity, an absence reflected in the stylistic effect of leaving words incomplete where they appear to have 'spilled' into the margins of the page. This, together with the incorporation of a variety of discourses that fill the vacuum (postcards, advertisements, door-signs, speech 'bubbles') suggest the character's internal collapse. Galloway's technique, which emulates the frozen mental state of emotional trauma, has broader ramifications, too. Galloway exploits the capacity of the novel form to articulate the individual life in relationship with a larger social system, which may embrace (as is the case here) a national narrative. Joy's dissolution represents an uncertainty about national belonging, and the textual materials that might compose it. The title indicates the textual 'trick' that permits the breathing of life into a character, and the preservation of the sickly national self.

Repeatedly, what can be observed in the Scottish novel towards the end of the century is a metanarrative of national identity, often finely poised between imaginative reconstruction, and uncertain *Angst*. Alan Warner's *Morvern Callar* (1995) is a fine example of a complex deliberation on the relationship between nation and narration. The eponymous heroine and narrator is a twenty-one-year-old supermarket worker in a remote Highland seaport, whose education has been ruined by the exploitative nature of 'cash in hand' employment (pp. 10, 44). The novel opens with her discovery of the corpse of her boyfriend, whose suicide note bequeaths to her his unpublished novel on computer disk. The note contains a list of publishers, together with the request that Morvern should attempt to get the work published: 'I'LL SETTLE FOR POSTHUMOUS FAME AS LONG AS I'M NOT LOST IN SILENCE' writes the author. However, his further exhortation suggests that it is the silence of Morvern, whose surname 'Callar', in the resort she later visits, is glossed as meaning 'silence, to say nothing, maybe' (p. 125), that should be the real concern: 'KEEP YOUR CONSCIENCE IMMACULATE AND LIVE THE LIFE PEOPLE LIKE ME HAVE DENIED YOU. YOU ARE BETTER THAN US' (p. 82). In metafictional terms, Warner is seeking to liberate the silenced Scottish underclass (for which Morvern Callar stands) from the abuse of the neglectful novelistic imagination. Morvern's refusal to mourn the writer's death is thus a fitting response to his appraisal, as is her decision to publish his novel as her own. This 'dishonesty' reverses the displacement that the dead writer alludes to.

Morvern is released, if only temporarily, from the economic restrictions of her existence by the advance secured for the dead writer's novel (about which she is dismissive), and then, more substantially, by the inheritance from his father. This 'release' gives her the means to partake in the rave culture of an Ibiza-type resort. Overcoming the horrors of the philistine excesses of the Brits abroad on a 'Youth Med Tours' package, she finds her own way of relating to the hedonistic dance culture. In one description of a club scene, Morvern finds herself absorbed by the rhythm of the dance, and the contact with other bodies: 'you didn't really have your body as your own, it was part of the dance, the music, the rave' (p. 203). The moment is irreducibly ambivalent since Morvern's access to an independent celebration of rave culture is tempered by the anonymity of the dance, and the loss of self it demands.

Morvern's spirit of independence remains significant, however, particularly in the demonstration of her own aesthetic responses. She is particularly responsive to the natural beauty of her surroundings, though this sensitivity is pointedly distinguished from a conventional literary sensibility. Her camping trip to the mountains (pp. 85–107) demonstrates her affinity with place, her enjoyment of being 'in Nature', amidst the 'loveliness' that is 'just silence' (p. 104); but such trips have also been the occasion for her to dispose of her boyfriend's corpse, previously dismembered to facilitate a staggered burial 'all across the land' (p. 91).

The pastoral scene, symbolically, is the site for the disposal of the untrustworthy Scottish novelist with his more conventional mannerisms; but this is not a straightforward reclamation of the nation by Morvern on behalf of ordinary Scots. There is ambiguity here, too, especially when Morvern makes a pilgrimage to the dead man's revered childhood village (which he had represented in a railway model in their flat) in the final pages. She seeks out the 'Tree Church', a bower cultivated by generations of gardeners for the enactment of marriages and christenings, and pauses awhile, the melting snow falling on her, before she moves on to her uncertain future. As she is pregnant with a 'child of the raves' (p. 229), the scene offers some kind of benediction, and an acknowledgement of the dead writer's village, and the tradition it symbolizes. This 'holy' scene (which contrasts with the disrespectful amorous behaviour of the publisher's editor and designer in a London church [p. 165]), offers an image of a renegotiated tradition in which the insular and the global might come into meaningful contact. The gesture implies a more sensitive understanding of earlier versions of Scottishness than that demonstrated by the *de facto* renaming of the Caledonian Hotel in Morvern's home town, which became 'The Kale Onion Hotel' when the 'D' fell off and was never fixed (p. 57).

Part of Morvern Callar's progression is her refusal to take responsibility for the people who need her (p. 180); her apparent coldness, her refusal to submit to known standards of emotional engagement is her strength, the means by which her narrative signals a transcendence of the restricted literary past. Warner's second novel, *These Demented Lands* (1997), sees the itinerant Morvern on her travels again, once more negotiating the materials of her Scottish heritage (she is visiting the Hebridian island where her fostermother is buried). The novel is fragmented, and ambitiously avant-garde, with Warner making similar connections between his literary inheritance and contemporary culture in the pursuit of making sense of current Scottish experience. The two epigraphs – one from Robert Louis Stevenson, the other from the group 'Black Grape' – underscore the unexpected yoking of sources in the fashioning of a form that is both exploratory and studiedly contemporary, but which is conscious of its own dependencies, traditions, and limits.

Similar dualisms have characterized the work of many Scottish writers. Perhaps the most prominent example of such ambivalence is to be found in

the work of Muriel Spark. Ian Rankin suggests that the qualities of rationalism, detachment (associated by Spark with her Edinburgh upbringing),
and the pursuit of the distinction between truth and fiction are those which
might signify Spark's Scottishness. He concludes that her defining attributes
stem from the dualisms of 'a Christian with a belief in the Absurd', able
to express profundities without apparent seriousness, and who is 'the most
"European" writer whom Scotland has produced'.[52] At a formal level these
dualisms produce the tensions that are characteristic of her novels, particularly the withdrawal of realistic representation, which produces an emotional
distancing so that the reader 'is encouraged to evaluate, rather than identify
with, the characters'.[53]

Spark's technique has been subject to change over the years, but this
underlying effect of paradox has remained constant. In her most famous
novel, *The Prime of Miss Jean Brodie* (1961), the significant characters are the
eponymous schoolmistress Jean Brodie, and her pupil Sandy Stranger. Miss
Brodie, who cultivates her favourites as 'the Brodie set', is finally revealed
as an arch manipulator with fascist sympathies (the novel is set in the 1930s)
rather than the independent free spirit she initially appears to be. After
Stranger betrays Brodie, who is forced to retire 'on the grounds that she
had been teaching fascism' (p. 125), she remains affected by guilt, since her
intervention in the life of Miss Brodie emulates, whilst halting, the actions
of this self-styled Svengali. Even Stranger's conversion to Catholicism, and
her retreat to a nunnery fail to grant her a sense of grace: she is depicted
'clutching the bars of the grille' (p. 127), trapped by her own complicity.

The overweening control of Miss Jean Brodie, and the enforced imitation
by Sandy Stranger, are indicative of Spark's preoccupation with the authority wielded by the author of a fiction, presuming to play God. Here, as she
frequently does in her novels, she undermines this tendency, and allows her
characters the 'freedom' to fall and to fail. Joseph Hynes sees the paradox
that surrounds the problem of authority in Spark as a 'miracle of creativity'.
It is this 'miracle' that grants a measure of 'free will' to the creations that
inhabit an author's imagined world.[54] In a technical sense, this terminology
is appropriate insofar as it locates the balance that Spark is able to strike between artifice and illusion; and the religious connotation is applicable to the
moral underpinning of Spark's vision. Hynes associates Spark's conversion to
Catholicism with the beginning of her career as a novelist (the two coincide
in the 1950s), the conversion signalling her rejection of 'the world-bashing
determinism of Calvin and Knox in favour of a vaster inclusiveness that she
finds in orthodox Catholicism'.[55] Sandy Stranger can be seen as pursuing
this same objective. Like her creator, she desires 'the religion of Calvin' as
a 'birthright; something definite to reject' (p. 108). The rejection of a narrow Scottish Calvinism in favour of something more inclusive, the personal

choice of Stranger/Spark, is not entirely undermined by Stranger's entrapment in a nunnery. Indeed, the ambivalence of the character's position is an
irreducible metaphor for the author's own perpetual dilemma.

A. L. Kennedy's views on the nature of fictional composition exemplify
the provisional and creative nature of the national narrative as I have been
defining it: 'If I'm writing about (for example) love, murder, being a Scot [,]
and, if I am any good at it, I will redefine those things in my terms as I make
my fiction.' The claim is a modest one, which puts the question of national
feeling on a par with other themes, so that the investigation of Scottishness
is not established as a primary motivation or inspiration. Kennedy argues
that her 'nationality is beaten together from a mongrel mix of Scots, Welsh,
Scots-Irish and Midland English', and this (surely entirely representative)
instance of intra-British biological hybridity places emphasis on a collective enterprise that transcends narrow nationalist ambitions. 'By sharing my
intimate individual humanity – Scottishness included – ', writes Kennedy,
'I hope to communicate a truth beyond poisonous nationalism or bigotry.'[56]

By making 'humanity' her primary focus, Kennedy makes national identity, necessarily, a fluid quantity to be evoked only tentatively. This emphasis is illustrated in *Looking for the Possible Dance* (1993) where Margaret
Hamilton's quest for self-definition is set within the broader cultural problem of Scotland's subjugation to England. Margaret has endured the 'Scottish
Method' of education, which involves the complete neglect of 'the history,
language and culture of Scotland' (p. 15). As if in fulfilment of this bias to
her schooling, she finds herself as one of 'only two Scots on an English,
English literature course' (the other Scot becomes her boyfriend) (p. 38).
Both Margaret and boyfriend Colin become victims of the corruption
abroad in modern Scotland. She is unfairly sacked from her position as
assistant in the 'Community Link Centre' by the humiliated boss whose
advances she has rebutted. Colin, having exposed the activities of a loan
shark at the community centre, is punished with a beating, after which he
is nailed to a floor.

The dysfunctional social milieu is compounded, for Margaret, by the
stifling love of her father, whose death leaves her semi-functional, emotionally. After the crises – the 'crucifixion' of Colin, the engineered dismissal of
Margaret – she takes a trip to London to make up her mind about their future, and on arrival decides to return to Colin for good. Scenes from the train
journey, which are interspersed through the narrative, show Margaret be-
friending a disabled passenger, James Watt, misunderstood and mistreated by
his mother and aunt. The predicament of James, whose namesake, of course,
was a leading Scottish industrial inventor, comes to symbolize Scotland's
cultural self-denial. A bond is forged between Margaret and James, who
communicates with her via his note-pad, and she gives him her address as

he disembarks at Warrington. As he is manhandled from the train, however, he struggles to wave, and her piece of paper blows away (p. 170).

It is this experience of failed communication that seems to make Margaret resolve to return to Colin. In one sense the decision is a straightforward expression of alliance with Scotland, confirmation that neither she nor Colin truly belong south of the border. But this more obvious commitment to nation is overlaid by the personal aspect to the encounter with the stifled James Watt. Dependent on those who fail to recognize his emotional being, he embodies the conditioned solipsism that Margaret is finally shaking off in reclaiming her Scottishness. Looking for the 'possible dance' is the quest for a meaningful mode of living, that which Margaret discovers on the final page. Having made her phone call to Colin, promising her return, she 'sinks into brilliant air, becoming first a moving shadow, then a curve, a dancing line' (p. 250). The dance motif, figured in literal dancing, recurs in the book; but here, the movement of the dance of life has become an innate attribute of Margaret's being.

## Beyond the Isles?

It would seem that the novels that speak most eloquently to the problems of national identity for the four nations that comprise the British Isles are those that make the question of belonging a *process*, a matter of undoing past affiliations as well as forging new ones. In the light of this, Benedict Anderson's thesis about novel and nation requires some emendation. For Anderson, the modern nation-state is distinguished by its geographical finitude, which yokes together territorial unity with a sense of shared historical purpose for the inhabitants of a given domain.[57] The narrative procedures of the classic realist text, with its dense characterization, and teleological plotting, seem to correspond to the narrative constructions that the nation requires for its imagined cohesion. In this association, the function of the novel is simultaneously formal and political. It assists the consolidation of those processes of modernity that, particularly from the mid-nineteenth century through to the early decades of the twentieth century, generate the myriad confusions of the secular industrial world. Realism emerges as the literary mode that gives shape to the confusion, that facilitates the narration of the nation.

It is not clear, however, how the imagined community can exist for those nations that are not clearly bounded, historically. Imperial expansion, in fact, has been a significant factor in the histories of many European nations, suggesting that the modern nation is very often 'porous' where its notional boundaries are concerned. Imperialism also brings with it a legacy of diverse cultural influences, making the quest for national origins and traditional forms problematic. England is the obvious example of an imperial nation that is un-narratable without renegotiating its traditional cultural sources, though, since both Wales and Scotland are implicated in the British Empire, the issue of porousness has an impact also on the national stories of these nations. Wales, as part of Britain, is involved in the activities of Empire, whilst by the nineteenth century, Scotland 'had become an unbounded nation', the space of which 'extended tentacularly around the world'.[58]

If we adhere slavishly to the notion of geographical integrity in the modern nation-state, we might produce a seductively simple model of national literatures. According to such a model, the violence done to realism, through modernism and, later, postmodernism, might correspond to a progressive crisis of national identity that is particularly acute for post-imperial nations. The contemporary uncertainty about 'Englishness' might then be seen to fit a postmodern mood that cannot place faith in the contracts of realism and the more stable nationalism it sought to imagine.

On the other hand, it would be equally misleading to cultivate a facile celebration of a post-nationalist experimentalism. There may well be some affinity between postcolonialism and the self-conscious fictional forms of the post-war era; but the implication that needs to be resisted is that a contemporary form of narrative is more 'truthful' than the earlier forms it comments upon or extends. What is being disrupted by the multiple affiliations of postcolonialism is an earlier perception of national history, more narrowly defined, perhaps, but still faithful to the experience it records. But as the hybridity of nations becomes both more complex and more explicitly recognized, new kinds of narration may become necessary, capable of linking different perceptions of belonging – different territories, even – by means of mongrelized narrative forms. If the fictions of postcolonial migration have begun this project, as the following chapter suggests, the prominent interrogations of national identity in Britain and Northern Ireland have been more cautious, with one eye focused on the elusive issue of tradition and place.

## Chapter 5

# Multicultural Personae

In the postcolonial era, the question of identity and national affiliation becomes complex and indeterminate. This is nowhere more apparent than in a post-war Britain facing the challenges of the end of Empire and the process of national redefinition it brings with it, both in terms of international status and demographic composition. The novel has proved to be a fruitful site for investigating the hybridized cultural forms that might be produced in an evolving, and so *genuinely*, multicultural Britain.

This is not, however, a simple story of celebration. The migrant identities that are fictionalized in post-war writing are often embattled and vulnerable. This is sometimes due to the transitional nature of twentieth-century postcolonial expression, where postcolonial identity is properly conceived as *process* rather than *arrival*;[1] but the evocation of vulnerability has just as frequently to do with the inhospitable nature of British, and especially English society, often portrayed as unsympathetic to the goals of a living, interactive multiculturalism.

Kazuo Ishiguro's third novel, *The Remains of the Day* (1989), is a devastating portrait of repressed Englishness and an exploration of those national characteristics that must be expunged before an authentic post-nationalism can emerge. Even though the novel's present is 1956, and its key action occurs retrospectively in the 1920s and 1930s, Ishiguro is still concerned with perceived aspects of Englishness that retain an ideological force at the time of writing.

Ishiguro's own position, as someone born in Japan but brought up in Britain, gives him an intriguing 'semi-detached' or dual perspective. The first two novels, *A Pale View of Hills* (1982) and *An Artist of the Floating World* (1986), with their Japanese protagonists, utilize a reserve with its roots in conventions of Japanese politeness.[2] This preoccupation is developed in the style of Stevens, the ageing English butler who narrates *The Remains of the Day*; this reveals a parallel between two kinds of reticence, and implies some kind of broader global observation. The present of the novel, July 1956, is also the time of the Suez crisis, a disastrous episode of late imperial assertion that effectively marked the end of British imperial power. Although no reference is made to Suez, the mood of anachronistic self-importance that history attaches to it hovers over the novel.

Stevens is butler to the American Farraday, who has taken over Darlington Hall. Wealth and power have passed from English hands, and the traditions that prevailed in the time of Lord Darlington (now deceased) are consigned to the past: Farraday wants a theme-park simulacrum of a stately home, run with a skeleton staff, but complete with 'a genuine old-fashioned English butler'(p. 124). Stevens's true allegiance, however, is to the era of Lord Darlington (who had played a key role in the appeasement of Hitler), and the almost feudal pre-war class structure it represents.

Stevens's existence is dominated by the idea of what makes a 'great' butler, and he is centrally concerned with the 'dignity' that attaches to the office of a true professional in service. The idea of 'greatness' is pointedly related to the 'Great' in Great Britain, exemplified for Stevens in the undemonstrative rural English landscape (p. 28); but this restrained 'greatness' is actually code for repression or concealment. To illustrate the qualities of a great butler, Stevens cites his father's favourite anecdote of a butler in colonial India who discovers a tiger beneath the dining table. This butler then discreetly asks permission of his master, who is entertaining guests, for 'the twelve-bores to be used'. The employer and his guests hear gunshots, and when the butler reappears with fresh tea for them he reports that there will be no disruption to the dinner schedule, and that 'there will be no discernible traces left of the recent occurrence by that time' (p. 36). The colonized other, symbolized by the tiger in the dining room, becomes almost unmentionable, a real threat to the colonial order that asserts itself through the pretence of being unruffled. In this sense, the professional 'dignity' of the butler is an extension of the colonial system that conceals the repressiveness of its procedures beneath a veneer of order and decorum. The need to let off twelve-bores in the dining room neatly figures the violence that underpins this 'civilized' order.

Stevens recounts the episode in which he is given his own chance to emulate such 'greatness': this is the scene of the conference in 1923 at which Lord Darlington seeks to effect 'a relaxing of various aspects of the Versailles treaty' (1919) in his anxiety to promote accord with Germany. During this event, Stevens's elderly father (now an under-butler at the Hall) dies. Stevens defers going upstairs to see his father's corpse, preferring dutifully to continue serving the distinguished guests, despite his manifest emotional stress (pp. 105–6). For Stevens, the memory of the episode is triumphant, evidence of his possessing 'in some modest degree' the dignity associated with the great butlers (p. 110). This transformation of subjection into a spurious personal triumph indicates a complex thraldom that is emotional, ideological, and political; the condition has been thoroughly internalized, making him the ideal conduit for a ruling-class agenda.

If reticence, in one form, is a method of repression and concealment, in another form it is the adopted humility that allows exploitation to flourish. If Stevens's own taciturnity signals the degree to which he has embraced his master's ideology, and is the marker of his emotional retardation, it is also the characteristic that makes him sympathetic. It is in this sense that the novel's own undemonstrative style (presented as Stevens's narrative) can be defended. Within this subtly ambivalent style there is a utopian impulse, stemming from such features as Stevens's involvement of the reader in his situation of disempowerment (p. 199) (which inspires dissent), and from Ishiguro's overlaying of different cultural codes of 'politeness' (Japanese and English). He is hinting at a post-imperial, post-industrial world in which the individual must manoeuvre with ingenuity to retain ownership of those cultural codes that are subject to 'incorporation' in the world of multinational enterprise. This is the contemporary resonance of his observation that an older ideology of 'Englishness' served the purposes of Empire very well.[3]

## Jewish-British Writing

The themes and concerns of Jewish-British writing illustrate the problems of identity that are created where the means of cultural renewal are hard to establish. The neglect of Jewish writers, who are sometimes 'thought not to exist in Britain', indicates a cultural (as well as a social) process of marginalization, and produces an oppositional stance in the articulation of the Jewish-British experience, a felt need 'to write against the dominance of an oppressive Englishness'.[4] The antagonism and non-recognition that Bryan Cheyette is here identifying is responsible for the split stance in much Jewish-British writing, the feeling of 'simultaneously belonging and not belonging', that can prove to be disabling. One manifestation of this imprisoning schizophrenia, for Cheyette, is a 'culture of apology' in which the essential attributes of Jewishness are diluted, made to conform to the dominant norms of respectability.[5]

A more complex instance of this tendency is the combination of social aspirations with the conflicting adherence to traditional Jewish values based on the family. Bernice Rubens's *The Elected Member* (1969) is a notable investigation of the way in which traditional Jewish family values are distorted when the family also exhibits a simple desire for material advancement (the worst kind of 'integration'). Norman Zweck is the victim of this clash of values, a child prodigy whose development is manipulated and curtailed by the controlling love of his family. It is significant that the infant Zweck is found to be an accomplished linguist, and becomes fluent in a variety of languages by the age of twelve. This capacity for the growth of cultural fusion is symbolically arrested by Zweck's mother who, from misplaced pride, pretends he is younger than he is to make his achievements seem more impressive (p. 89). Once a brilliant lawyer, Norman Zweck has become insane, prey to drug addiction and hallucination. His decline is due principally to the family's repressive relations, which result in Zweck's incestuous relationship with one of his sisters, the suppression of his own confused sexual identity, and his catastrophic infantilization. Rubens borrows from Kafka's 'The Metamorphosis' to order her familial theme: the novel starts with Zweck incarcerated in his bedroom, tormented by his fears of crawling silverfish, and ends with the confirmation of his ejection as the family closes ranks.

Zweck's institutionalization marks him as the family's elected scapegoat, a status he initially resists, but finally comes to embrace (pp. 63, 221). The death of the father Rabbi Zweck, however, implies a loosening of the repressive first-generation values that have imprisoned Zweck and his sisters, and for which Zweck is sacrificed. Rubens intends the scapegoat motif to carry its full ritualistic load to connote the expiation of sins, and hope for the future. Such hope is implied in Zweck's final prayer, which begins in Hebrew, but which ends in a multi-faith gesture, suggesting the need for the adaptation of Jewish identity, a dilution that is not diminution (p. 224).

For Jewish writers the feeling of not belonging is, inevitably, shadowed by a history of persecution that is acutely felt. That history often encourages writers to widen their expressive scope in the treatment of international themes, and to experiment with fictional forms. In *Blood Libels* (1985) Clive Sinclair transforms a latent English anti-Semitism into a new Nazi pogrom (p. 186); but the revision of history in the novel is itself put into question. Narrator Jake Silkstone disputes the 'holistic' approach to history conceived as the 'synthesis of impersonal forces' (p. 7), arguing that 'one's view of history tends to be egocentric' (p. 10). In fact, the identification between Silkstone and Jewish ethnicity is pushed to absurd limits, as when his sexual possession of a woman is associated with arrival in Israel (p. 140). He is born in 1945 on the day of inception of the new state of Israel (p. 11), and a motif of bodily inscription, or 'dermagraphia', suggests that Silkstone carries the text of history on his person (p. 56). This is the 'psychosomatic approach to history' that proceeds without reference to facts, but on the basis of 'what people believed to have happened' (p. 188). When, on the final page, Silkstone is revealed to have been adopted, and to possess 'not a drop of Jewish blood', his function as personifying Jewish identity is exploded (p. 191). Sinclair thus enacts the sense of rootlessness common in Jewish-British writing, and makes a stark formal point in the process: he pushes the private–public identification – upon which narrative realism thrives – so far that it is revealed as problematic, if not meaningless for this purpose. The vacuum that is exposed has two aspects: first the unavailability of a credible international Jewishness; and, second, the lack of an agreed history for Jewish-British identity.

Perhaps the most positive strand in Jewish-British writing is, paradoxically, its leaning towards Europe, in response to the inhospitableness of the immediate cultural scene. This is not simply a question of asserting and interpreting a shared oppression after the Holocaust (though it is partly that): the more positive aspect to this European leaning is its shared artistic and intellectual project. If this is an implicit aspect of Rubens's reworking of Kafka in *The Elected Member*, it is an explicit thematic component in the work of Elaine Feinstein. Her novel *Loving Brecht* (1992) recounts the experiences of Frieda Bloom, a Jewish cabaret singer in Weimar Berlin, and her lifelong involvement with Brecht. By this means Feinstein establishes a historical frame that subsumes the rise of Hitler and the Holocaust. Thus, structurally, the novel 'contains' this great historical evil in a narrative that focuses on the ongoing difficulties of creativity in different arenas of political suppression: the Third Reich, Stalinism, and McCarthyism. In seeking to define the achievements of Brecht and his collaborators (with a critical eye alert to the personal failings of this fictionalized Brecht) the novel makes its identification with 'the literary, cultural and intellectual environment of Europe' that is its 'claimed inheritance'. Michael Woolf suggests that this claim, which is typical of 'much Jewish writing', is 'not emulated by the British and, particularly, the English novel'.[6] The (familiar) assertion of the latter's parochialism may be overstated, but the importance of a European cultural inheritance to Jewish creativity is well observed.

Central to *Loving Brecht* is the diasporic identity that Frieda Bloom acquires, and, by the end of the novel, is able to translate into a position of coherent and insightful cultural judgement. Bloom's life is also a representation of the intellectual quest of the migrant Jewish writer, a quest shared by those writers, like Feinstein, Sinclair, and Rubens, who were born in Britain. After a lifetime of displacement, Bloom finally settles in London, and acquires British citizenship, and it is from this position of relative stability that she visits Brecht, in post-war Berlin, for the final time. Forgiving the exploitative failings of the man, she concludes 'it is only what a man does that can be judged'. She further concludes that Brecht, whose poems 'will stand', will be judged favourably by history (p. 187). The novel is actually ambivalent about Brecht, but it is this willingness to privilege the centrality of *work* that is significant:

> I don't regret the shape of my own life. My work has brought me joy. I never feel lonely now, and rarely sad. In some ways I have been very fortunate. My house is . . . close to an area of London where several

generations of European refugees have made their home. I walk on the Heath with relish in all weathers, and watch the seasons change . . . and look forward to the visits of grandchildren. (p. 187)

This closing passage presents London as 'home' in a qualified sense, most particularly because, through its enclaves, it preserves the refugee sensibility that is an integral aspect of the European-Jewish identity. Bloom's distinction between the impersonality of work, and the intimacy of family is a crucial clarification that separates out the dynamism of a shared intellectual culture from the life-blood of a managed family tradition. Ethnic continuity is thus a combination of European cultural affiliation, and local non-integration.

## The Empire Within

The problem with 'integration' is that it often means 'assimilation' within a host culture that is insensitive to cultural diversity, and many novelists have been concerned by this new, internal form of cultural imperialism. Salman Rushdie, in an essay from 1982, alerts us to the ingrained problems of understanding race in Britain, where, following E. P. Thompson, he discovers 'the last colony of the British Empire'.[7] The problem of this new internal empire is its failure to stop seeking, whether implicitly or explicitly, to colonize or demonize aspects of racial difference. Rushdie is concerned about the failure of Britain to embrace the inevitable fact of its postcolonial future, and sees this as 'a crisis of the whole culture, of the society's entire sense of itself'. The misperception of racial and cultural difference extends to those apparently benign attempts at 'integration', which Rushdie sees as code for a nullifying assimilation. It is 'multiculturalism' that excites his particular ire, a term too often concealing mere tokenism.[8] The point, here, is that the identification of cultural difference does not necessarily entail the attempt to understand or embrace it: the reverse process of 'making exotic' may equally result. What Rushdie's essay implicitly requires is an approach to ethnic diversity that is situated between a glib multiculturalism and a flat assimilation. He is defining the space of the hybridized culture of the postcolonial migrant, of crucial significance to all inhabitants of the new emerging culture.

That term 'multicultural' need not be as anodyne as Rushdie suggests, however. A. Robert Lee indicates that 'hybridizations like "Asian-British", "Caribbean-British" or "African-British"', which can be further 'particularized into, say, Brixton-Jamaican, Cardiff-Bengali, Liverpool-Nigerian', contain also 'their own internal dynamics of heterogeneity and . . . tension'.[9] This cultural space of migrant and post-migrant writing is, necessarily, transitional, an interactive site in which multiculturalism must be redeemed as an active, conflictual process. In the post-war era we have witnessed an ongoing practice of redefining and rewriting the nation from within, and eventually, the emergence of what Homi Bhabha, a propos of Rushdie's *The Satanic Verses*, terms 'a hybrid national narrative'.[10] For most of the period, however, writers have had to confront the obstacles to this meaningful hybridity.

The prosaic and depressing fact of racism is, of course, the primary inhibiting factor to the more dazzling creative flights of multicultural expression. In Pat Barker's grim *Union Street* (1982) there is a dispiriting portrayal of racism amongst factory workers that is instructive. A 'West Indian woman' called Bertha tolerates in silence continued abuse from her fellow workers (p. 81); she ignores the complaints of the 'nigger stink' voiced by one particularly vile white woman Elaine, until one day Bertha's patience snaps and this repeated taunt from Elaine earns her a vicious beating. The onlookers, who had become uneasy at the extremity of Elaine's victimization of Bertha, now close ranks: 'Bertha's use of her fists, the silent ferocity of her attack, was something quite foreign to their experience. And they hated it. More even than the colour of her skin, it confirmed that she was an outsider amongst them' (p. 84). The antagonism, and the misrecognition – which permits the demonization of the apparent racial other – is presented as deeply ingrained, raising questions about its source.

The failure of connection is perhaps still more troubling when it is less tangible, not underpinned by explicitly racist views. Beryl Bainbridge's *The Bottle Factory Outing* (1974) is a tale of this more elusive kind of cultural misrecognition. The factory in question is a London wine-bottling concern, owned (and staffed) by Italian immigrants, with the exception of two English women, Freda and Brenda, who disrupt the cultural enclave, with disastrous consequences. Brenda is a focus of erotic attention for the manager Rossi, but it is the brash Freda, with her talk of worker's rights and her designs on the owner's nephew, trainee manager Vittorio, who emphasizes the cultural clash between a populist English feminism, and a traditional Latin patriarchy. The crisis comes to a head in the factory outing that Freda has planned, a picnic and visit to a stately home that, she hopes, will enable her to get closer to Vittorio. Freda perceives her Italian co-workers to be 'simple peasants', though with culture and tradition behind them (p. 11), a stereotypical appraisal matched by the sexually charged enthusiasm of the Italians: excited by the idea of the excursion with 'the English ladies', they have duly informed their wives and children that the outing is for the workers only (p. 9).

The outing begins in farce, but ends in a tragedy when the amorous Rossi, denied by Brenda, comes upon Freda in a wood, she having failed in her best attempts to seduce Vittorio. Overcome by a lustful urge, Rossi causes Freda to fall backwards, in the process breaking her neck as he falls on top of her (p. 175). Much Ortonesque business with the corpse ensues, until the workers decide to smuggle it back to the factory, and conceal it in a barrel of sherry bound for Spain in a consignment of empty barrels – if marked as tainted, Freda's barrel will be discarded at sea (p. 166). The death jolts the novel from its comfortable comedic mode – the unrequited lovers in the wood evoke *A Midsummer Night's Dream* – and forces us into a more systematic reading of ethnicity. The outing finds its way to Windsor Castle, on a day when the Queen is in residence, but the scene of English heritage is complicated by the characters' consciousness that they are also close to the family home of Mr Paganotti, the factory owner (p. 88).

There is a memorable scene in which some soldiers, exercising the Queen's funeral horses, allow Rossi, Vittorio, and Freda to take a turn on their mounts: Freda fancifully imagines herself at one with Vittorio, cutting a majestic figure (p. 108). This is not, however, tantamount to a national ritual reconfigured in a transcultural form. The English historical myth that resonates, in the plan to dispose of the unfortunate Freda, is that of the Duke of Clarence, executed for treason, reputedly by being drowned in a butt of malmsey. But it is not just English narratives that rebound, or are unproductive. Freda, an agent of the popular feminism of the 1970s, is unattractive to Vittorio because she upsets his expectation of taking the leading role (p. 91). According to the patriarchal story that shapes him, he is, in any case, promised to Rossi's niece, an impending marriage of commercial sense that will consolidate the Italian identity of the business, and so help preserve the isolated Italian community of thirty years' standing (p. 18). The despairing undertow of Bainbridge's farce is the clear implication that the popular forces of English social change have a long way to go to advance the cause of ethnic integration.

The pervasive misperception about 'race' has been compounded in the post-war era by the immigration policies of successive governments, making Rushdie's concerns well-founded. As he has pointed out, immigration is usually taken to signify black immigration, and is seen as a demographic and political problem, regardless of the fact that there are white immigrants too, or the fact that in any one year the number of emigrants from Britain may exceed those immigrating: 'immigration is only a problem if you are worried about blacks', concludes Rushdie.[11]

A glance at the post-war legislation on nationality and immigration is instructive in unravelling the sources of popular confusion. The British Nationality Act of 1948 confirmed the right of entry to Britain for the citizens of Empire, who were deemed British subjects; since then, however, there has been a steady attrition of these rights. The post-war 'open door' policy was ended by the 1962 Commonwealth Immigration Act, which introduced a system of employment vouchers, subject to quota, for Commonwealth immigrants. Further restrictions on East Indian Asians (1968) were followed by the Immigration Act (1971), which limited domicile to those born in Britain, or whose parents or grandparents were of British origin. Perhaps the most significant redefinition of nationality and citizenship was enshrined in the 1981 British Nationality Act, which abolished the automatic right to British citizenship for children born in Britain. This Act was designed to restrict the naturalization of immigrants' children, but in the process it removed from the statute book an ancient birthright.[12]

This sketch of the legislation demonstrates a number of things: first, that the post-war acceptance of the subjects of the former Empire – who were in some cases positively encouraged to migrate to the 'mother' nation – rapidly evaporated in the light of economic change and political expediency; and, second, the shifting policy shows that identity based on national affiliation is a mutable, political construction. A corollary of the constructedness of national identity is the kind of public confusion that allows racism to thrive. The Janus-faced response to the citizens of Empire is the most glaring instance of how policy, however pragmatic in intent, has colluded with public misperceptions of nationality, and has helped to foster a denial of postcolonial obligations and a rejection of the postcolonial heritage.

## 'Windrush' and After: Dislocation Confronted

Successive novelists have contributed to an ongoing challenge to this culture of denial, gradually expanding the ways in which fiction might treat of migrant experience and the tensions that attend it. These tensions became visible with the arrival of the 'Windrush generation' of West Indian immigrants in the late 1940s and 1950s, named after the *Empire Windrush* which docked at Tilbury in 1948. This is usually taken to denote the beginning of multicultural, or, as it is sometimes called, 'multiracial' Britain.[13] Black people had lived in Britain for generations, of course, notably in well-established communities in port-towns like Liverpool and Cardiff. But the docking of the *Windrush* signifies, metonymically, a new generation of Commonwealth migrants recruited to a labour market in need of workers to fill unskilled vacancies.[14] The naive sense of hope that this invitation fostered is caught in the response of Harris in George Lamming's pioneering work, *The Emigrants* (1954), who espies England from a ship's porthole and reflects: 'there was life, life, life' (p. 106). Immigrants from the West Indies viewed England not merely as a land of opportunity, but also as a kind of home, a mother country whose history, culture, and literature were familiar to them from their school textbooks. In close-up, however, things looked very different.

The experience of disillusionment is artfully rendered in the technically exuberant fiction of Sam Selvon, who migrated with Lamming to England in 1950. If the arrival in the inhospitable mother country was demoralizing, the literature that evolved out of this experience began to transform 'English literature' by appending to it a form of migrant postcolonial expression that rewrites the cultural centre. This is especially true of the London novels of Sam Selvon.

Selvon's fiction encapsulates that imaginative freedom of the novel, its ability to anticipate modes of living that are yet to materialize. In essentially realistic fiction, like the Selvon novels considered here, this freedom becomes a question of style, 'a linguistic as well as a social or political quest for freedom'.[15] In such a quest, the writer must find a provisional way of challenging dominant cultural forms. In this procedure an overwhelming sense of displacement – familial and cultural as well as geographical – must be turned into a positive force, an occasion to redefine the identity that might otherwise be overwhelmed.

Selvon's crucial innovation has to do with the rendering of Trinidadian dialect. In an earlier draft of his novel *The Lonely Londoners* (1956), the dialectal form was confined to the sections of dialogue, with the linking narrative written in standard English. Selvon's stylistic accomplishment is to have found a way of making the two interact. Refusing to render dialectal speech forms phonetically (a solution that implies that standard English is the norm) Selvon ensures that the language of narration merges with the language of his characters, and that different stylistic registers do not remain distinct. He embarks, in short, on a creolization of the English novel.[16] Another key source of inspiration for Selvon is Caribbean folk-tale and calypso. The tradition of Trinidadian calypso supplied much inspiration for Selvon's narrative method, since its distinctive features, 'subversive irony . . . farcical anecdotes, racial stereotyping . . . and the inclusion of topical political material' are all staples of Selvon's method.[17]

In *The Lonely Londoners* Selvon brings these stylistic innovations together in a work that addresses the difficulty of creating a community in a hostile social setting. The central character Moses Aloetta becomes a filtering consciousness for the disillusioned life of the West Indian Briton, and the apparent impossibility of achieving an equal standing in the economy (p. 129). Formally, however, the seeds of cultural hybridity are sown. The novel's narrator speaks a hybridized form of discourse that combines Trinidadian dialect and standard English (as well as, in its allusiveness, literary English). This results in a kind of vacillating narrative stance, by turns withdrawn from and engaged with the characters' experiences. The duality of the book applies also to the characters' attempts to colonize London. When, for example, Henry Oliver (dubbed 'Sir Galahad' by Moses) attempts to speak about 'the colour problem' at the Marble Arch Orator's Corner, he is heckled by fellow Trinidadian Big City (p. 99). It is also made clear that 'the boys' are attracted to such gatherings on summer evenings, not out of political commitment, but in the hope of seeing the exposed flesh of white girls (p. 98). Selvon's inspiration in traditional oral sources supplies one explanation for the chauvinistic attitudes of his characters, which parallel those of 'the urban trickster figures of calypso';[18] but sexual assertiveness is also the assertion of cultural identity in this novel. When Galahad waits for his white date at Piccadilly Circus, he is overwhelmed by a sense of being at the centre of things, since 'that circus is the beginning and the ending of the world' (p. 90).

At the end Moses is identified with the narrating consciousness, a familiar novelistic device that in this case suggests a fusion between the character and the author in a shared 'urge towards articulation and writing'.[19] The implications of this fusion are taken up in *Moses Ascending* (1975), which is a sequel of sorts to *The Lonely Londoners*. It is narrated by a Moses whose experiences are continuous with those of Moses Aloetta in the earlier novel; indeed, this later Moses also alludes to the previous book inviting the connection (p. 44). There are, however, major technical differences between the two works, and since these impinge on the construction of Moses's character in each case, the later Moses is, in important ways, discontinuous with his earlier incarnation.

The new Moses is a self-conscious narrator, an older immigrant who wants, in effect, to disengage from the 'new generation of Black Britons' (p. 15), and to withdraw into a world of literary creativity. He buys a house that (though it is due for demolition) enables him to ascend from the basement flat he has always inhabited to his own attic apartment (or 'penthouse' as he prefers to call it). Here he indulges his literary pretensions, through the writing of his memoirs, aided by his 'man Friday' Bob, a 'white immigrant' from the Midlands' 'Black Country', in Selvon's playful inversion of *Robinson Crusoe* (pp. 4, 31). However, in the course of the novel Moses discovers the impossibility of withdrawal: his house becomes the local headquarters of the Black Power movement, as well as a staging post for illegal immigrants. By the end, the tables are turned on Moses, partly on account of his own cynicism and misguided opportunism: Bob has taken over the penthouse, and Moses is back where he started, in the basement flat. Superficially, the novel's action appears to expose the fantasy of social withdrawal, and to endorse the need for committed action in the spirit of the Black Power movement, which developed significantly in Britain in the 1960s and 1970s. Indeed, Moses's desire to write is ridiculed by those characters,

Galahad and Brenda, who are directly engaged with the movement. However, Moses counsels against such a reading:

> One final word. It occurs to me that some black power militants might choose to misconstrue my Memoirs for their own purposes, and put the following moral to defame me, to wit: that after the ballad and the episode, it is the white man who ends up Upstairs and the black man who ends up Downstairs. (pp. 139–40)

This establishes that the episodes that comprise the novel are the stuff of Moses's precious memoirs. The writing project, rather than a castle in the air, is thus in harmony with this problematic novel of multicultural life. In this there is a tacit endorsement of the writer-figure's own (withdrawn) approach to questions of culture and politics. It is significant, in this connection, that Brenda's critique of Moses's writing is based on a spurious notion of grammatical correctness, a view which Selvon's fusion of registers implicitly contests (p. 104). As with *The Lonely Londoners*, the novel's significance lies in its stylistic creativity, rather than its ability to represent harmonious community life. It is in this literary sense that Moses, who is no leader by conventional standards, might be seen as someone who can lead his people to freedom.

Moses, however, is characterized by an engaging roguishness, rather than piety, and in Selvon's last novel, *Moses Migrating* (1983), Moses goes back to Trinidad as a tourist, and is shown to betray some of the habits of the Englishman abroad. This is not a heroic return from exile, but rather a demonstration of the colonization of identity, and in this appearance, Moses is in limbo between England and Trinidad. The novel opens with Moses planning his journey to the West Indies, and penning a letter of support to Enoch Powell, from whom he hopes to acquire funds for the return home (p. 1). Powell, whose attitudes are here linked to the alienation and self-division of Moses, figures frequently as a satirical butt in Black-British writing. In his infamous 'Rivers of Blood' speech of 1968 Enoch Powell spoke of his vision of 'the River Tiber foaming with much blood' in emphasizing the impossibility of racial integration. Specifically, Powell sought to foment popular support for anti-immigration legislation.[20]

'Powellism' certainly contributed to an atmosphere in which an anti-Black nationalism could flourish, even though his arguments about immigration were exaggerated (even taken on their own terms). The tightening restrictions of the 1960s meant that the fuss caused by Powell was out of kilter with government policy. As Peter Clarke wryly observes, 'immigration hit the headlines at just the moment when its tap root had already been severed'.[21] It is also important to remember that, despite its significant cultural implications, immigration has had only a small impact on the composition of the population overall. In the 1991 census (the first to collect data on 'ethnic' identity) just 5.5 per cent of Britain's total population is recorded as belonging to non-white 'ethnic groups'.[22]

The racial tensions and hostilities that were manifest from the late 1960s onwards, then, were built on iniquitous perceptions of race, that were sometimes exacerbated by government policy. The government legislation of 1968, in particular, seemed to indicate a racial bias in immigration policy. The Commonwealth Immigration Act of that year deprived East African Asians holding British passports of their right to stay in Britain. (The Act was subsequently deemed to amount to racial discrimination by the European Commission on Human Rights.)[23] This atmosphere of racial tension is a powerful background presence in Buchi Emecheta's first two novels, published in the 1970s, but a presence that the writer struggles to circumvent. Both novels are autobiographical works that fictionalize Emecheta's experiences as a Nigerian immigrant, trying to make her way in the London of the 1960s.

The arrival is actually treated in the second published novel, *Second-Class Citizen* (1974), but it is the first book, *In the Ditch* (1972), that really focuses on the context of inequality. At the outset of *In the Ditch*, Adah Obi has recently separated from her husband, and attempts to juggle her work, her evening classes, and the care of five small children. This situation of thwarted ambition and intolerable poverty is exacerbated by Adah's ruthless landlord, himself a Nigerian, who seeks to evict her. In desperation he resorts to witchcraft, or 'juju', in his efforts to banish Adah and her family.

On the basis of such scenes, it is easy to misread Emecheta and to assume that her first two novels, both set in England, are flatly critical of African culture. For example, it is tempting to compare Emecheta's treatment of the cynical landlord with the most famous treatment of Nigerian belief systems by a novelist writing in English: Chinua Achebe's *Things Fall Apart* (1958). An instructive contrast is suggested in Achebe's scene of the 'egwugwu', that is, the village elders dressed up as dead ancestors in order to preside over legal disputes. Achebe shows his English readers (especially) that theirs is not the only culture in which old men dress up in the absurd showy garb of legal authority. The village onlookers may recognize the men beneath the masks, but are engaged in a necessary contract of 'belief' in the egwugwu. The distinction between the mystical and the rational is not always what it appears, and traditional Nigerian – specifically Igbo – culture, we realize, had a coherence that the missionaries failed to appreciate.

After her first two autobiographical novels, Emecheta changed tack, and took as her subject the damaging impact of European imperialism on traditional Nigerian societies, in the mould of Achebe. *In the Ditch* makes the issue less clear-cut, however. Emecheta's description of the landlord practising juju is meant, of course, to emphasize his exploitative nature. The episode appears to invite assumptions about Nigerian men, thus encouraging (in particular) 'western feminists . . . into false generalizations about Adah's patriarchal culture'.[24] But the important point about the juju is that Adah remains impervious to it, even though she is aware that such disbelief would have been impossible in Nigeria.

In effect, Emecheta uses this conflict of cultures to cut through to specific social questions. Adah and her landlord are both members of a sub-class in 1960s London, and it is the complex of deprivation that this position implies that drives his cruelty, and that results in a distortion of Nigerian culture. The implication is that whereas juju would be unquestioned in Nigeria, as an integral part of a coherent social order, the opportunistic deployment of it elsewhere serves only to uncover those social relations that are inhospitable to the culture (p. 3). It is an implicit understanding of this that enables Adah to keep solidarity with her cruel landlord when his ruse is discovered by neighbours (p. 5). Emecheta's presentation, then, has a greater affinity with Achebe's celebratory nationalism than it appears to have.

Adah's experiences centre on her life in her council flat in the 'Pussy Cat Mansions', and the solidarity she comes to feel with the other women living here, 'in the ditch' of social marginalization. The narrator summarizes Adah's perceptions of a poverty-trap in which single mothers are obliged to stay single for fear of losing their dole money. This institutionalized sexual deprivation is offered as an explanation both for successive 'generations of unmarried mums', and as the reason 'why places like the Pussy Cat Mansions were usually a fertile ground for breeding hooligans' (pp. 60–1). A simple conservative philosophy of the family and social stability is hinted at, here, but the more sustained and coherent aspect of the critique is directed at the systemic problem. The institutionalization of poverty is embodied in Carol, the Family Adviser with a vested interest in retaining her 'problem' families (p. 94).

The foregrounding of the (inadequate) class analysis is a strategy for concealing the extent to which racism is an ordering experience for Adah. This displacement is *strategic* in the sense that the implicit denial of racial discrimination is also a means of transcending its more debilitating effects. Racism *is* a recurring topic in the novel, but it is often unconscious, an expression of ignorance. Emecheta seems more interested in the basic spirit of community that emerges in the extremes of poverty. It is this spirit that cuts across racial difference, and that mounts a challenge to the systemic preservation of inequality. This is not, however, presented as a solution to social fragmentation; rather, the solidarity is merely an expedient measure. At the end of the book, the community in need emerges now as a staging post for the migrant author-to-be. Looking back on her days at the Camden council flats that were her model for the Mansions, Emecheta stresses especially the importance of her eventual 'freedom from private landlords': the episode takes its small place in a narrative of self-help and personal advancement.[25]

## The Quest for a Settlement

My examples thus far represent variations on the theme of dealing with an inhospitable culture, and it is true that much of the most notable migrant writing in the period has been pushed to the expedient of establishing the standards and values of the enclave, thus leaving the mainstream culture intact. Even so, a marked difference in attitude is discernible in the generation of writers that followed the first wave of post-war immigrants. With hindsight, Sam Selvon now seems representative of a generation for whom *transience* was the defining condition. The unattached Moses Aloetta of *The Lonely Londoners*, with his conviction that he will inevitably return to Trinidad one day, is a self-appointed transient. Of course, his self-designation as 'exile' is ironically undercut; but this defensive strategy bespeaks a refusal to address the availability of Britain as a permanent home.

For a later generation, the mood of transience is replaced by an attempt to come to terms with the implications of permanent settlement. The title of Caryl Phillips's *The Final Passage* (1985) encapsulates this ambivalent moment of migrant experience. The recognition of the 'final passage' is a key psychological turning point, and one that is far from celebratory.[26] From Phillips's vantage point in the 1980s, the retrospective treatment of 1950s Caribbean migration uncovers a truth sometimes concealed, hitherto: the probability of having to make a home in a hostile country.

Another treatment of the settler's struggle for permanence is Timothy Mo's *Sour Sweet* (1982), which is the epitome of the tradition of enclave writing. Mo traces the experiences of a family of migrants from Hong Kong, fighting to make their way in 1960s London, despite the restrictive effects of their own cultural heritage, and the controlling influence of the Triads.

Mo's Lily is a force for tradition, insisting on sending financial assistance to her husband Chen's parents in southern China, and gladly welcoming the father into her home when Chen's mother dies. The novel draws a parallel between Lily's traditionalism, and that of the Triads, whose fighting methods are detailed in a particularly brutal attack on a rival gang (pp. 130–4). Lily as a child is forcibly trained in a savage form of Chinese boxing by her proud father, and later imparts some of the techniques to her son to help him deal with school bullies. The more important parallel, however, is the shared sense of duty to the Chinese community. The Triad philosophy is based on building power through allegiance (though fear and coercion are always present), and in feeling 'no responsibility to outsiders' (p. 181). The reliance on the family structure to preserve migrant identity is treated with irony in the novel, however, even whilst this reliance is seen as necessary. At one point the Chen household is compared to an amoeba, dissolving or absorbing the problems it must confront (p. 228). In its isolation, the family must resort to basic and reductive principles of survival: the failure of acculturation produces, of necessity, an uncultured response.

Chinese culture, such as it is, is represented by the takeaway restaurant that Chen, Lily, and her sister Mui open in south London. Emblematic of the crude nature of the interface between English and Chinese cultures, the restaurant is named 'Dah Ling' after Lily and Mui's home town, and the two women soon become known as 'the two Darlings' (p. 95). Mo articulates this tendency to anglicize names as an act of cultural colonization, the misrecognition and appropriation of the girls' place of origin. Chen constructs three rudimentary benches at which the English customers sit, in rows, a philistine audience facing the counter and the hatch through which the specially tailored food, which 'bore no resemblance to Chinese cuisine', emerges (pp. 94, 105–6). It is an image of blank exchange in which cultural heritage is sacrificed for material necessity.

The staple dish for the English customers is sweet and sour pork, and throughout the book the 'sour sweet' motif suggests the failure of the two cultures to interact meaningfully. The (related) Chinese concern with balance, with yin and yang, holds out the possibility of a productive fusion. But that which is 'sour sweet' is usually so because every apparent success or advance for the Hong Kong migrants also reveals a compromise that is deleterious to their identity.

Mui, in particular, is an ambiguous figure of cultural transition. She is the one who is able to deal most effectively with the truckers that frequent the Dah Ling restaurant. She is also the one who is shown to be able to negotiate with official agents of English culture, most notably when she manages to secure legal entry for Chen's father in the face of tightening immigration controls (p. 208); and it is Mui who marries and decides to apply for citizenship at the novel's close (p. 276). However, Mui has acquired her social literacy from television, and specifically through her addiction to soap operas. This, together with the fact that she bears an illegitimate child (possibly to an unknown lorry driver), makes the diminution of her own cultural identity seem an act of capitulation. Mui is also pragmatic, however, and here Mo is indicating the hard bargain that is available to the impoverished migrant, where assimilation and conformity are the price of a grim survival.

Chinese culture also presents a threat itself, since Chen, who is embroiled in gangland operations, is eventually killed by the Triads. As they send an anonymous monthly allowance to Lily, however, she assumes that Chen has simply run off, but continues to support his family. It is this delusion that governs the reception of Lily's reflections on the final page, where she wrestles with her guilt at enjoying Chen's absence, whilst investing her hopes in their son (p. 278). The Triads, however, are already controlling the life of this family, allowing Lily to feel an illusory sense of equilibrium. She is buoyed up by a hidden tradition of loyalty and obligation that makes it impossible for her to establish a new cultural space. Mo's method serves his purpose well. The concentration on his Chinese characters conveys a sense of claustrophobic insularity as well as an impression of rootlessness. The English characters, by contrast, are wooden and lifeless, suggesting the hostility of a culture in crisis.

## Ethnic Identity and Literary Form

The traditional bias of the fiction I have been discussing, with its reliance on the codes of realism, indicates that the transformation of the mainstream literary culture is a gradual process of supplementation. This long *formal* revolution is also something that can be detected where the subject matter seems entirely inimical to cultural hybridity. Such an inverse relationship between form and content is spectacularly apparent, for example, in Sam Selvon's first novel. This gradualism needs to be stressed, especially because a productive cultural hybridity is commonly (and erroneously) perceived to go hand-in-glove with overtly experimental forms. In such a view, you either have a startlingly innovative style *and* a rapturous presentation of multicultural energies, or you have neither. Rushdie's exuberant magic realism is thus sometimes seen to exemplify the kind of formal reinvigoration of the novel in Britain that the postcolonial era makes possible. There are certainly grounds for seeing particular instances of formal innovation in this light. However, such an easy equation between experiment and cultural hybridity can imply a simple opposition between experiment and tradition that is inappropriate, with traditional realism coming to embody a reactionary conservatism. Two novels that offer a corrective to this view are Andrew Cowan's *Pig* (1994) and Meera Syal's *Anita and Me* (1996). Both of these first novels won a Betty Trask award for traditional fiction, and both employ the realistic childhood initiation plot to examine questions of ethnicity and identity.

Set in the late 1960s, *Anita and Me* is a familiar bitter-sweet tale that traces a formative year in the life of Meena Kumar, from the age of nine to the time of her eleven-plus examination. Her civilized home life jars with the harsh environment of village life in Tollington, a former Midlands mining village, where the villagers, feeling their enclosed milieu to be under threat from external development, begin to close ranks, precipitating the growth of an overt racism from the seeds of unconscious prejudice. In Anita, the prepubescent local bad girl, Meena recognizes a kindred spirit, so that her rites of passage are fashioned on the experience of outgrowing the attractions of Anita.

If the initiation plot structure is commonplace, Syal is still able to modify her more recognizable materials for her own purposes. Homi Bhabha's account of how existing cultural forms can actually be contested and altered through the process of supplementation is directly relevant to Syal's novel in which the *faux naiveté* of the child protagonist is fully justified by the cultural rootlessness she is trying to move beyond.[27]

At the symbolic heart of the novel stands the (seemingly) deserted village Big House, home of the mine owner, and a place of intrigue and fascination for the local children. Its reclusive owner had presided over the pit closure, a procedure managed through 'faceless officials' (p. 15). When, however, Meena discovers a statue of the Indian elephant-god Ganesha in the grounds of the house (god of wisdom and good fortune), a mysterious appropriation of this relic of imperial days is suggested (p. 127). This unexpected cultural find signifies an inhabitation that turns out to be literal: the Big House is owned by one Harinder P. Singh, an Indian of some stature, who spent his wealth buying up the house and the local mine. But this is not a tidy instance of the postcolonial transference of power: Singh was duped into buying a mine that 'was almost dead', and he and his French wife feel themselves to be failures (p. 319). They have, however, taken a particular interest in the fortunes of Meena's family, and have even felt a sense of pride through this remote identification. Syal's overt allusion to *To Kill a Mockingbird* (a book that Meena found 'too dense' [p. 296]) signals a significant debt. Like Boo Radley in Harper Lee's novel, the owners of the Big House, demonized in local folklore, are revealed as benign reclusive figures, taking a vicarious pleasure in the endeavours of others.

Despite this dependence on an available fictional model, Syal complicates the process of Meena's initiation so that these recluses are re-demonized as cautionary figures. If Meena's advancement involves the recognition of Harinder and Mireille at the Big House, it also involves a disappointment with them, a failure of cultural kinship. Acting on a tip-off from the Big House, Meena's father is able to effect the removal of his family from Tollington as it is about to be engulfed in suburban development. The reader shares Meena's disillusionment with these English-Indians, newly revealed as neighbours, who simply discuss 'property and money' (p. 326). In fact, Harinder and Mireille are pariahs in a new sense, representative dupes of the first wave of post-war migrant settlers, whose susceptibility to exploitation is a wholly negative example.

The novel thus ends on an ambivalent note, with Meena and her family about to flee the English village that has failed to provide them with a lasting home. But there is also a sense of their escaping a peculiarly English cultural implosion, signified here by rapid suburbanization. Even the skinhead Sam Lowbridge recognizes that ten-year-old Meena 'can move on' whereas he can not (p. 314). Beyond the question of class difference, which is a factor in their relative degrees of mobility, Meena's wider horizon has also, and more importantly, to do with her migrant identity, for it is this precious commodity that enables her to 'move on'. It is both the true source of her ambivalent initiation, and the sign of her liminality.

Similarly, the difference between Meena and Anita Rutter is a cultural difference. Syal's novel implicitly contrasts the vibrant extended family activities of Meena's home with the dysfunctional home life of the Rutters. Andrew Cowan's *Pig* bases its family drama around the same distinction, and the complexion this puts on the fate of fifteen-year-old Danny's grandfather. After the death of his grandmother, Danny assumes that his grandfather will be able to move in next door, to the empty bungalow on their council estate. His mother is insistent that he will stay in a home, until the council plans to house a Muslim family next door, at which point she changes her mind, now arguing that her father has the greater claim to the bungalow (p. 88). The grandfather thus becomes a pawn in a hypocritical (and futile) attempt to oust the non-whites. The racist motive is poorly concealed beneath the false assertion of family feeling.

The vacuum at the heart of the white community is exposed in various ways, and it determines the limits of adolescent Danny's initiation. The comparison with *Anita and Me* is instructive particularly on the basis of the restrictions operating on Danny. Within the dominant racist structure of the town – and especially of the council estate – Danny's relationship with Surinder is doomed, and the novel poignantly suggests that their adolescent love is poisoned by this external frame.

Cowan puts this deceptively simple tale of the youthful loss of illusion in a broader socio-political perspective. The estate is run-down, following the closure of the local steelworks, and the stalled plan for the 'LeisureLand' complex to be built in its place indicates that the promise of regeneration is a false one. In later plans, the theme-park is to feature an imitation iron foundry, a parody of the livelihood of which the community has been deprived (p. 144). Danny's father, having been laid off at the steelworks, becomes a night security guard at the factory where Danny's mother also works (p. 13), and Danny, too, is being inevitably drawn in to this underclass, exhibiting no enthusiasm for continuing his schooling. He has no great aspirations, and may pursue unspecified work at the 'LeisureLand' complex (p. 191). Surinder, on the other hand, works diligently at her studies, and has confidence that she can rely on her parents' pride to support her ambitions for a professional career, possibly as a history teacher, thus eschewing an early arranged marriage (p. 139). Significantly, her preparatory summer reading supplies her with a knowledge of Victorian social history, and the squalor and poverty of working-class life in nineteenth-century England and Scotland (pp. 125–8). Surinder, who retains a strong sense of affinity with her Indian roots, is amassing the intellectual components of a hybridized cultural identity. Indeed, it is Surinder who takes possession of British industrial history, whilst Danny, in ignorance, seems set to relive the deprivations of the past. In this sense, Danny epitomizes a defeated community and an exhausted culture, and his 'initiation' serves simply to illuminate the cul-de-sac in which he finds himself.

The killing of his grandmother's ageing pig, the care of which Danny has taken upon himself, emerges as a complex act. It is a moment of gathering maturity, as he takes responsibility for the dying animal's welfare, and accepts the irrelevance of his nostalgia for his grandparents' domestic stability. Simultaneously, it is a rejection of the crass (and confused) racism that surrounds him: his action is precipitated by the discovery of a pig's trotters nailed to the door of the Muslims' bungalow next door. Relieved to find his 'own' pig 'Agnes' still intact, he decides to steel himself for the humane killing, thus ensuring that Agnes cannot be desecrated in this way.

Like Meena in *Anita and Me*, Surinder has no particular investment in place. She is the one who acquires the means of moving on, whilst Danny is left brooding in his grandparents' empty house, clinging to his memories of Surinder, and their ephemeral moment of harmony that circumstances conspire against (p. 213). A simplistic reading of Cowan's realism would be to equate it with the cultural exhaustion that he uncovers in his narrator; but it is the same elegiac style that celebrates the spirit of Surinder, and the fleeting possibility of a new cultural identity. Ultimately, the restricted style goes far beyond the depiction of the narrating persona: it serves the larger purpose of dispassionately depicting industrial decline, and the collapse of social possibility that that entails.

## Putting Down Roots

In *Anita and Me* and in *Pig*, rootlessness is transformed from an inner lack (as keenly felt, for example, by Selvon's Moses Aloetta) into a personal strength, enabling the migrant to remain untainted by surrounding social decline. This strength, however, merely denotes the potential for moving on to a more propitious environment, and beginning anew. But does this also imply the impossibility of geographical identity? The way in which Selvon's characters lay claim to the key landmarks of London suggests a remaking of urban space, and this has been a recurring motif in post-war writing. However, treatments of rural or pastoral topics, rare in contemporary British fiction generally, have been still scarcer in migrant writing.

A writer who has sought to challenge this apparent divorce between landscape and migrant identity is V. S. Naipaul. His novel *The Enigma of Arrival* (1987) is a compelling, brooding, and complex deliberation on postcolonial rootlessness that seeks to lay claim to the pastoral in defining a cultural niche for the migrant. The quest for self that orders the book is directly autobiographical; so much so that a reader can be forgiven for feeling that the text breaks its fictional frame, that it becomes 'an autobiographical text occasionally disguised as a novel'.[28] The narrator certainly 'stands for' Naipaul in his quest as a writer, but the journey is enriched by its self-conscious (and ambivalent) literariness, as well as by the cultivated confusions of the narrating persona, and the piecemeal, achronological manner in which his personal growth is detailed. These are the studiedly novelistic features of a book that pushes at the boundaries of the genre whilst remaining within them.

The 'Naipaul' figure is from the Indian community of Trinidad, and has grown up steeped in images of Englishness from school textbooks and classic English literature. The novel is centrally about how this 'Naipaul' frees himself from the fantasy of colonial English self-identity, but manages, at the same time, to salvage something of this nostalgic Englishness in the construction of a new self-image. This apparently paradoxical procedure is what rescues the writer whose sense of self is dependent upon a version of England that never was.

The idea of journey is both literal, pertaining to the fact of migration, and metaphorical, illustrating the writer's process of maturation. The two journeys are intertwined, since coming to terms with his past self is the process by which the migrant postcolonial writer establishes his sense of vocation. The writer's material, indeed, comprises the significant personal developments centred on his journey from Trinidad to a new place in the English landscape, and in English literature.

The 'Naipaul' character's defining reflections occur whilst he is the tenant in a cottage in the grounds of a manor house in Wiltshire. The house and grounds, which are in decline, stand for the post-imperial moment that the arrival of 'Naipaul' also heralds. In a pointed parallel, the manor's owner withdrew from the world in 1949 or 1950, his symbolic illness coinciding with the departure of 'Naipaul' from Trinidad, bound for England, in 1950 (p. 197), a journey that is emblematic of the waves of inter-continental migration in the second half of the twentieth century (p. 130). But this is not a simple instance of symbolic transition, with the migrant writer ascending whilst the English landlord fades away. Both characters are intrigued by decay, and both are affected by the dissolution of imperial England.

For 'Naipaul', this is a literary-historical problem, since, for him, the acquisition of self-knowledge invariably involves the relinquishment of cherished pastoral images, as when the 'country-cottage effect' of a neighbouring property is revealed as the imposition of one owner's taste (p. 35). Such revelations begin to unsettle the writer's habit of viewing the rural scene – its inhabitants as well as its dwellings – as 'emanations' of 'literature and antiquity' (p. 25). Indeed, the rural scene is initially interpreted entirely on the basis of divers earlier cultural readings: Hardy, Wordsworth, Constable (among others) are used to mirror (and so misread) the contemporary moment.

For some, Naipaul's presentation of a complex 'homecoming' fails to register the connection between the exercise of colonial power and the maintenance of traditional English tranquillity. David Dabydeen's *Disappearance* (1993), for example, has been read as a reply to *The Enigma of Arrival* that reveals this omission.[29] There is, however, a strand of self-consciousness in Naipaul's book that takes the investigation in a different direction. The problem for 'Naipaul' is that the recognition of the constructedness of rural England is self-negation, too: as Ian Baucom remarks, the character is one of the 'strange creatures' produced by the British Empire, 'a colonial subject more rigorously English than the English'.[30] Thus, if there is an element of contradiction in the writer's tendency to cling nostalgically to the version of England he also exposes as fantasy, this is also, in a further paradox, a kind of self-assertion. It is also an integral part of the novel's method, which relies on an element of inconsistency in the writing self.

The writer laments his youthful impercipience, dazzled by a romantic idea of writing, and too immature and self-absorbed to notice or record the really interesting or significant things happening around him (pp. 130–1). Something of this self-absorption persists, however, in the mature writer, who is curiously uninformed about life in a small Wiltshire village where, to him, 'so many big events . . . seemed to happen off-stage' (p. 41). Naipaul subtly creates a character whose judgements seem based on speculation, and whose vocation as a writer is seen somehow to depend upon his aloofness. Partly, the writer is locked in an earlier version of the rural; but his task seems to be to inhabit this nostalgic pastoral and undermine it from within. If, therefore, the narrator creates the kind of melancholic mood that is sometimes attributed to Hardy, the novel requires a reader able partly to resist this mood, which is being mimicked rather than endorsed. At the same time, however, a claim is being made for the withdrawn sensibility of the writer, for whom the aesthetic representation is privileged over the Real.

This is a properly transitional postcolonial work, which is interrogative of ambivalent influences. 'Naipaul' is made representative of a particular migration within Empire, from India to Trinidad, that 'had given me the English language as my own, and a particular kind of education' (p. 52). The arrival of such a writer to chronicle the landscape of Stonehenge is enigmatic because it blurs easy perceptions of cultural difference: 'Naipaul' is disabused of his fantasy England, but by inhabiting the site of his projected identity, and writing through the ambiguous experience, a new form of post-pastoral (a topic examined more extensively in the following chapter) is glimpsed, where 'post' implies a 'continuation of' as well as 'coming after'.

This is the enigma of transitional postcolonial expression, which here betokens Naipaul's own arrival as a writer in the evolving canon of English literature. It is not an explosive, or iconoclastic gesture, because that is not the experience of the writing self. The canon is extended by Naipaul's wishing to join it, much as the English landscape, always in flux in any case, is altered by his integration within it. What appears to be a kind of capitulation is really a subtly radical challenge to codes of Englishness that can seem impregnable. The question that Naipaul's novel poses is how far this challenge is limited, the product of a dying tradition. The painting by de Chirico that gives Naipaul his title, inspires in the narrator an allegory of his own situation. From the painting he extrapolates the story of a traveller arriving in an ancient Mediterranean port, to a scene of mystery and desolation. The traveller loses the sense of his mission, and seeks in panic to flee. Eventually finding his way back to the quay, he sees that the ship that brought him has gone: 'the traveller has lived out his life' (pp. 91–2).

For Naipaul's narrator, the mission is less Kafkaesque, more productive; but there is still the sense of a life being lived to discharge a cultural mission that is beyond the traveller's control. Again, Naipaul is challenging glib assumptions, in this case the notion that migrant identity is paradoxically redefined, brought into sharper relief, by the shock of being uprooted. There is an interest, here, in a global cultural lack of belonging, and a shared dissolution. The (autobiographical) solution offered by *The Enigma of Arrival*, however, is both geographically and culturally specific. It is a mythologized account of how the writer inscribes himself in the English landscape, and, simultaneously, inserts himself into the canon of English literature.

A comic (and ultimately less celebratory) treatment of pastoral, and the cultural self-division it can entail, is Howard Jacobson's *Peeping Tom* (1984). Jacobson's novel stages the clash between the values of English literary pastoral (exemplified in the version of Thomas Hardy as 'rural novelist'), and the rootless (and urban) nature of British-Jewishness. Hardy becomes the 'other' for protagonist Barney Fugleman, embodying all that he is not, but representing a culture that has begun to take hold of him, but without admitting him, or bestowing upon him a sense of ownership.

This kind of attempt to reinterpret English ruralism remains unusual, however, and Naipaul's post-pastoral focus is quite different to that of most multicultural fiction. In a key passage he does indicate that the generally acknowledged locus of migrant attention is the city, particularly London, which conforms to the post-war pattern by which major national cities become 'cities of the world' (p. 130).

## Rushdie's Broken Mirror

A writer who stands in marked contrast to this mode of postcolonial writing is Salman Rushdie. Rushdie does not participate in the attempt to reclaim a particular geographical place, whether urban or rural, and to rethink national identity in relation to it. Rushdie, rather, is the chronicler of the unfettered migrant sensibility, that version of postcolonialism that unhooks historical tradition from place, and that creates new, self-conscious kinds of identity from a fragmentary vision. Rushdie's suggestion is that the displaced, fragmented vision, 'the broken mirror', is 'as valuable as the one which is supposedly unflawed'.[31]

Rushdie's view that the imagination 'is one of the keys to our humanity' supplies one of the keys, also to his approach to fiction.[32] History and the actual are vital to his method, but his own brand of magic realism is defined by the imaginative transformation of 'fact', in the process of reimagining history. This is a claim that is often made on behalf of significant postcolonial fiction, the assertion that it creates the freedom to rewrite 'official' colonial history: Rushdie's method, with its global significance, can be seen to epitomize this phase of literary history.

The novel that most clearly demonstrates Rushdie's inventiveness, but also his shortcomings, is *The Satanic Verses* (1988), a novel dense with sacred, literary, and cultural references, in which apparently conflicting modes – political satire and religious fable; realism and fantasy – are combined. The novel ranges historically from the seventh century to the twentieth century, and geographically from London and Bombay to the mythical 'Jahilia', a version of Mecca. It is a rich and complex work in which different narratives inform one another, so that at one point the character Gibreel can be said to be 'moving through several stories at once' (p. 457). The complexity can seem contrived, however, making it difficult to forget the grand design whilst reading the book.

The fantastic elements of the novel usually reveal pointed observations. In the opening scene, the protagonists Saladin Chamcha and Gibreel Farishta are in free-fall in the skies above the English Channel, descending from the wreckage of a jumbo jet that has been blown apart by hijackers. Both survive the fall that should be fatal, and begin a process by which their identity is given over to the broader forces of postcolonial change. Saladin, for instance, acquires horns, which, along whith other demonic features, attract the attention of the immigration authorities. Another designated illegal immigrant, appearing in the form of a manticore, explains that 'they have the power of description, and we succumb to the pictures they construct' (p. 168). Rushdie's fantastic mode supplies a succinct demonstration of how racist responses to immigration serve to distort the migrant's sense of self.

It is possible for the secular reader to locate the novel's true object of ridicule through its political satire, rather than through its religious allusiveness. The fundamentalism that is Rushdie's main concern then appears to have its root in Thatcher's Britain. Of particular purport is Rushdie's perception of institutionalized racial discrimination. His treatment of this topic can be put in the context of the riots of 1981 (especially in Brixton), insofar as these were a response to Thatcher's British Nationality Bill.[33] An important scene occurs towards the end of *The Satanic Verses* when the death of a black activist at the hands of the police prompts a riot. Before his death the unfortunate Uhuru Simba makes a speech in court (reported in the novel by his mother) that encapsulates the social basis of Rushdie's ideal multiculturalism, where migrants from different continents acknowledge that they 'have been made again' in England, and that they 'will also be the ones to remake this society, to shape it from the bottom to the top' (p. 414).

Rushdie was particularly outraged by the British Nationality Act of 1981, which, building on earlier legislation, sought further to erode the automatic right of British citizenship for people of the former British colonies: to be British one had to prove one's descent from an ancestor born in Britain (being born in Britain oneself was now insufficient). This attempt to shore up a national identity (for this was really about Englishness) on the basis of biology flew in the face of the migrant hybridity that the end of Empire brought with it. This radical Act also abolished, as Rushdie angrily observed in 1982, 'the *ius soli*, or right of the soil . . . the birthright of every one of us, black and white'.[34] On the face of it, there is something contradictory in Rushdie's fury at the loss of the *ius soli* since the migrancy he celebrates seems to hinge on being ungrounded, on flying by the nets of tradition and place. But what he is really identifying is the denial of the new, since if national identity is now located somewhere in the past, the arena in which multicultural life can expand has been removed.

*The Satanic Verses* is partly a challenge to this circumscribed nationalism, a challenge issued through the attempt to answer the question: 'how does newness come into the world?' (p. 8). The social necessity of the question is clearly signalled in Rushdie's concern at the government's attempt to turn away from its inevitable postcolonial future through legislative attempts to buttress a fictive version of the past.

Confronted with such a crisis, the novelist's solution is to yoke linguistic creativity to the goals of self-expression, as Rushdie symbolically does in *Midnight's Children* (1981), when the midnight child in the womb is said to grow from something no bigger than a full stop, until it grows into 'a book' or 'even a whole language' (p. 100). In *The Satanic Verses* the creative use of language is pointedly connected to political freedom when one character considers 'the real language problem: how to bend it shape it, how to let it be our freedom, how to repossess its poisoned wells, how to master the river of words of time of blood' (p. 281), and in doing so appropriates and inverts the 'rivers of blood' image used by Enoch Powell in predicting the racial conflict that unchecked immigration would cause. This is the kind of historically specific reference that gives substance to Rushdie's own claim that his novel 'celebrates hybridity, impurity, intermingling' and 'rejoices in mongrelizations' whilst it 'fears the absolutism of the Pure'.[35] But Rushdie is not insensitive to the contradictions inherent in postcolonial migrant experience, which can also issue in a refusal of cultural mingling. Thus, the Anglophile Saladin seeks to efface his own Indian background, whilst Gibreel seeks to remain 'joined to and arising from' *his* past (p. 427). There is something of a resolution of these alternatives in Saladin's eventual return to India, and his reconciliation with his dying father. Migrant self-identity finally emerges as a matter of appropriate sensitivity to the cultural multiplicity of one's own background. This is the locus of Rushdie's seriousness, and the essence of his own sacred subtext. Indeed, Baucom points out that in the novel's scheme blasphemy is defined as 'cultural': it is cultural blasphemy to deny one's past.[36]

If, however, Rushdie's attack on fundamentalism is directed at Thatcherism as well as at Islam, it does contain elements that are exceedingly provoking to Muslims. The prophet Mohammed is called by the derogatory title Mahound, implying false god, or even devil. In depicting the historical moment of the founding of Islam, Rushdie suggests an element of political investment in a human-authored religion. Still more provoking is the depiction of a brothel in which the prostitutes take on the names of the prophet's wives. Rushdie's target, of course, is absolutism, as demonstrated in his depiction of the Ayatollah Khomeni, the Imam of the novel, who appears in Gibreel's dreams resolutely opposed to historical development (p. 214).

In all of this there is sufficient provocation to ensure that the book's constructive message about migrant identity failed to reach many of those Asian-British migrants to whom it might have spoken most eloquently.[37]

*The Satanic Verses* thus opens up an unfortunate cultural divide, with Rushdie appearing to his detractors to have sold out to the relativism of Western intellectualism, and, in a sense, this is true. The author's motivation and intellectual sympathies are outlined in the 1990 lecture 'Is Nothing Sacred?' where Rushdie pins his colours to the postmodernist mast. He cites Lyotard and the 'rejection of totalized explanations' in identifying the new focus for the novel, the fact that 'reality and morality are not givens but imperfect human constructs'.[38] (Jameson's critique of postmodernism as the culture of pastiche is alluded to in the text [p. 261].)

From this intellectual perspective, Rushdie suggests that 'the row over *The Satanic Verses* was at bottom an argument about who should have power over the grand narrative, the story of Islam'.[39] This is revealing of his own self-conscious postmodernism and its limits. As events sadly demonstrated, the textual 'freeing up' of this master narrative provoked its emphatic reclamation in the real world, with more than twenty deaths as a consequence of riots or acts of terror.[40] Ultimately, there is no fruitful way beyond this opposition, since to Islam certain sacred things are unimpeachable or even (like the prophet Mohammed) unrepresentable, whilst to postmodernist practitioners everything is both questionable and available for any mode of representation.

## Towards Post-Nationalism

Much migrant writing in Britain, chary of identifying with unaccommodating England, seeks, ostensibly, to enlarge perceptions of 'Britishness' in pursuit of propitious hybrids (Black-British, Jewish-British, and so on). It is often the case, however, that it is 'Englishness' that is really at issue in the new formulations, for it is England, the original colonial mother country – found wanting in its historical obligations – that must be seen as the focus of critical migrant revisionism.

Bhabha's concern with 'the cultural construction of nationness as a form of social and textual affiliation' indicates the extent to which this process of refashioning Englishness is a necessary, but as yet incipient, project. Bhabha describes a complex tension between two contradictory (but interacting) forces: the 'pedagogic' tendency to assert an authoritative national identity based on 'pre-given or constituted historical origin or event', and the 'performative' process of reconstruction, an ongoing 'living principle' that 'must erase any prior or originary presence of the nation-people'. The two pulls act on the people, ensuring that they are doubly inscribed 'as pedagogical objects and performative subjects'. What emerges from this double inscription is not oppositional or confrontational. Indeed, it is cast as something that is at once more productive and inevitable. The process Bhabha describes is one by which the discourse of the minority challenges the 'powerful master-discourse', but obliquely, 'initially withholding its objective', thus 'insinuating itself' into the terminology of the dominant discourse, which is supplemented by the procedure. The tendency of that which is supplementary to *question* is conceived as 'a meditation on the disposition of space and time from which the narrative of the nation must *begin*'. Consequently, this supplementarity, rather than a negation, inspires 'the renegotiation of those times, terms, and traditions through which we turn our uncertain, passing contemporaneity into the signs of history'.[41]

All of this gives 'cultural difference' a very particular edge. In Bhabha's terms, 'cultural difference ... addresses the jarring of meanings and values generated in-between the variety and diversity associated with cultural plenitude' – no bland multiculturalism, this – and so 'it represents the process of cultural interpretation formed ... in the disjunctive, liminal space of national society'. That term 'liminal', it is worth noting, is well suited to Bhabha's purpose, since its two meanings – 'inhabiting a borderland', as well as 'incipient' or 'just emerging' – are simultaneously implied. Bhabha's process of 'dissemiNation' is one by which 'the radical alterity of the national culture will create new forms of living and writing', and will do so by rearticulating 'meaning, time, peoples, cultural boundaries and historical traditions'.[42]

A book that might be said to enact this principle of supplementation is Zadie Smith's *White Teeth* (2000), a novel – part celebration, part cautionary tale – that is an apt summation of the triumphs and the limits of English multiculturalism at the end of the century. The book's anchor is the relationship between Samad Iqbal, a Bengali Muslim, and Englishman Archie Jones, whose lifelong bond stems from serving together in the Second World War. This pre-given, and resonant national history supplies the 'pedagogic' pole (in Bhabha's terms) against which the 'performative' reinscription of the national culture takes its meaning. There is a crucial moment in the war episode when Samad and Archie capture a French scientist who is believed to have worked on the Nazi sterilization programme. Since they have not been involved in direct action, Samad feels they must seize this opportunity to play a part in the destruction of the 'great evil' that they have hitherto 'failed to fight'. At this 'moral crossroads', decides Samad, Archie must kill the scientist, to identify himself with England's future (p. 102–3). Archie takes the prisoner off, and returns, limping, after a shot is heard (p. 105). Samad assumes the deed has been done, but a mystery is installed at the outset of the novel that links its principal themes: the complexity of national identity and ethnicity, and the moral problems that complicate the active assertion – or, worse still, the attempted control – of ethnicity.

The novel questions the extent to which the attitudes of Samad and Archie amount to a reliable understanding of first-generation immigration and its reception. Smith is also careful to embed the representativeness of her characters more deeply, both historically and culturally. Samad's identity is fashioned from his pride in his great-grandfather Mangal Pande whose actions are said to have triggered the Indian Mutiny of 1857. Archie's sense of self, on the other hand, is rooted in the transformative experience of being saved from suicide (by a halal butcher): a personal revelation results, and within hours, in a new state of euphoria, he meets his future wife Clara whose Jamaican mother was sired by a colonial Englishman.

Samad's twin sons Magid and Millat epitomize the competing claims operating on the second-generation migrant. Horrified at Magid's willingness to absorb English culture, Samad has him sent 'home' to Bangladesh to be educated in 'the old ways' (p. 185). When he returns, however, he is the quintessential Anglo-Indian, having embraced the advice of an esteemed Indian writer that 'we must be more like the English' (p. 248). His willingness to defend genetic engineering – established somewhat archly as the millennial symbol of Western culture – locates him within a four-square secular Englishness, and brings him into direct conflict with his brother Millat, whose adolescent fascination with clans, especially 'clans at war' (p. 378), draws him into a militant Islamic group, with an 'acronym problem': Keepers of the Eternal and Victorious Islamic Nation (KEVIN) (p. 255). One of the four guiding principles of KEVIN is the need 'to purge oneself of the taint of the West' (p. 380); but since Millat's identity is fashioned by the unshakeable influence of Hollywood, and specifically by the gangster movie, his affiliation is hypocritical. But, Smith is suggesting, the incoherence has its source in the very idea of such militant religious youth groups, which, in Britain, thrive partly on account of the very cultural values they seek to exterminate.

It is in the satirical portrayal of Islamic militants that Smith projects an intention most explicitly. This is apparent, for example, in a brief treatment of the Rushdie Affair when Millat's 'Crew' take a trip to Bradford to participate in the ritual book burning. (Their cultivated lilting walk, a kind of 'funky limp', makes them appear to be 'slouching towards Bradford' in the manner of Yeats's 'rough millennial beast' in 'The Second Coming'.) They whip up their outrage, to ensure that it survives the impediment presented by their ignorance of the book's contents: 'you don't have to read shit to know that it's blasphemous', insists Millat (p. 202). When he gets home, his mother has made a bonfire of 'all his secular stuff' – records, trainers, posters, videos, books, his guitar – in order to teach him the lesson, which Smith seems partly to endorse, that 'either everything is sacred or nothing is' (p. 205). Yet Smith is also anxious to demonstrate how the ugliness that is dismissed as 'fundamentalism' is produced by an exclusive English ethnicity. Millat may not have been able to identify Rushdie if he saw him,

> but he knew other things. He knew that he, Millat, was a Paki no matter where he came from; that he smelt of curry; had no sexual identity; took other people's jobs . . . that no one who looked like Millat, or spoke like Millat, or felt like Millat, was ever on the news unless they had recently been murdered. In short, he knew he had no face in this country, no voice in the country, until the week before last when suddenly people like Millat were on every channel and every radio and every newspaper and they were angry, and Millat recognized the anger, thought it recognized him, and grabbed it with both hands. (p. 202)

The internalized 'knowledge' of racist interpellation and ethnic suppression generates a groundswell of justified rebelliousness waiting to be unleashed. The emerging Rushdie Affair supplies the required cause, and the means of translating that anger into a fleeting episode of ethnic visibility, or self-realization. Millat's 'misrecognition' has a generalized character: Rushdie becomes the convenient scapegoat for the society's systematic cultural insult.

The pattern of misrecognition does not, however, become an oppositional force in the novel. Rather, it becomes a pervasive source of cultural confusion. This serio-comedic aspect is particularly evident in the admirably orchestrated conclusion, where several important strands are interwoven. The final episode involves the launch of a high-profile genetic experiment, the 'FutureMouse©', a mouse engineered to live for exactly seven years, and to suffer predetermined genetic defects, including susceptibility to carcinomas, at set intervals (pp. 369–70). FutureMouse© is the work of Marcus Chalfen, and the Chalfens are a central target of Smith's social satire. These apparently well-adjusted middle-class rationalists are defined in terms of a normative model of genetic health and stability; but, having no friends, they interact only with their extended family, 'the *good genes*'.

The boredom that results from this enclosed perfection, with the family members seeming 'like clones of each other', leads the Chalfens to reach out, and to interfere in the lives of Magid and Millat, and in that of Irie, daughter of Archie and Clara (p. 271). Thus a mild but debilitating form of eugenics-in-practice is redeemed through its interaction with various migrant bodies. This necessary 'grafting on' is misperceived by the Chalfens, however, and is figured, condescendingly, as a channel for their own beneficent patronage. The stereotypical middle-class Englishness of the Chalfens, with its notion of biological 'purity', is eventually exploded when it is revealed that the Chalfens are 'immigrants too (third generation, by way of Germany and Poland)' (p. 283).

Josh Chalfen, disillusioned by his parents, joins an Animal Rights group to whom he is a prized member, as the son of a notorious geneticist, and in the concluding episode the various campaigning organizations converge on the launch of FutureMouse© with their separate plans of disruption. Millat and the Islamic militants, for whom genetic engineering is blasphemous interference in the work of Allah, are there; so, too, is Josh, together with the Animal Rights activists, for whom the concept of justice should be extended to all living creatures; also present are the Jehovah's Witnesses, whose simple choice between salvation and damnation is articulated with unswerving conviction by Clara's ageing mother Hortense.

When Millat pulls a gun with the intention of shooting at the scientists on the stage, Archie (for all the principal characters are here assembled) leaps to intercept the bullet heading for the ageing geneticist and mentor whom Marcus Chalfen has been publicly crediting with the groundwork for FutureMouse©. Of course, this is none other than the Nazi collaborator Perret, freed rather than executed by Archie, it is now revealed, but who had shot him in the leg when the opportunity arose: Archie is shot in the leg once more, in the process of saving the man for a second time (p. 461).

A number of things are accomplished in this ending. First, the genetic experimentation of Marcus Chalfen is linked overtly to Nazi eugenics. But this is overshadowed by Archie's instinctive act of saving the dubious Perret once more, a gesture of belief in a common humanity. From Smith's perspective we are all hybrid postcolonials, biologically as well as culturally, and the pursuit of pure ethnic origins presents an artificial barrier to the hybridity that is inevitable. In *White Teeth* this hybridity is a contradictory and haphazard phenomenon, not constitutive of a facile 'Happy Multicultural Land' (p. 398). It is closer to Irie's wish, based on her desire for a benign environment for her unborn child, which could be Magid's or Millat's:

> In a vision, Irie has seen a time, a time not far from now, when roots won't matter any more because they can't because they mustn't because they're too long and they're too tortuous and they're just buried too damn deep. She looks forward to it. (p. 450)

At the end, we are told, the twins Magid and Millat are so seriously confused in the testimony of eyewitnesses that a reduced punishment for the attempted attack (community service in a millennial garden) is shared by both of them. The two extreme responses of the migrant self – the willing assimilation of Magid and the repudiation of Millat – are thus both corrected and channelled into a communal project.

In the final scene, Archie and Samad recognize Perret at the same time. Samad initially feels betrayed by the deceit, the pretence of killing Perret, that Archie has sustained for fifty years. Then he has a moment of gleeful anagnorisis: '*this incident alone will keep us two old boys going for the next forty years. It is the story to end all stories. It is the gift that keeps on giving*' (p. 455). What Samad is anticipating is another shared refashioning of the past, the narrative lifeblood of all postcolonial futures, ensuring the characters' double inscription as pedagogical objects and performative subjects.

*White Teeth* is a celebration of the contingent and chaotic stuff of social life, an enactment of haphazard but vibrant multiculturalism. (This is the 'helpless heterogeneity' of which Caryl Phillips speaks in his review.)[43] It offers an end-of-millennium vision that self-consciously promotes a utopian hybridity. In this, Smith's novel corresponds with the aspiration of sociologist Paul Gilroy as laid out in *Between Camps* (also 2000). Gilroy, too, pursues a transcendence of the category 'race' in his 'transitional yearning' for a new kind of shared future, partly urged by the memory of the war against Nazism. The desire to 'liberate humankind from race-thinking' is intended also as a liberation from '"encamped" national cultures'. It is a projection of a world beyond identity politics and nationalism, which posits a single human race. Rather than a simplification of existing distinctions, this is an extension of them, an anticipation of the logic of hybridity very much in the spirit of Zadie Smith. Gilroy envisions a world in which humanity comes to recognize that given principles of differentiation have become outmoded, and so comes to embrace what he terms 'planetary humanism' instead.[44] But this new kind of humanism is only imaginable as a consequence of the postcolonial migrant experience, and the complex stages of renegotiating identities and national boundaries. As Zadie Smith well understands, the interim stage of interregnum is the one that still applies to the English, and broader British context.

## Chapter 6

# Country and Suburbia

The opening episode of John Fowles's *Daniel Martin* (1977) involves a Devon harvest scene during the Second World War. Traditional farming methods are in evidence, most notably the use of a horse-drawn reaper-binder for harvesting the wheat. As the horse pulls the machine, a team of labourers gathers the bound sheaves, building them into 'stooks' (p. 8). For the young Daniel Martin, this defining image of 'his Devon and England' is forever shattered by the rude intrusion of modernity in the form of a German bomber, an enormous Heinkel, flying just two hundred feet above the field, filling Martin with foreboding, and the sense that 'he is about to die' (p. 11).

The episode marks a symbolic death, and the demise of something within the character, too. Fowles is interested in the way of life that is brought to an end after the war. The 1951 Festival of Britain is identified, not as 'the herald of a new age, but the death-knell of the old one'; by this, narrator Martin (speaking for Fowles) means the loss of a collective principle of social organization, after which 'we then broke up into tribes and classes, finally into private selves' (p. 179). The novel is not straightforwardly nostalgic for the rural idyll that witnesses the co-operation of different social classes in the harvest ritual; yet the trope of an Edenic moment remains one aspect of Martin's quest for authenticity in the post-war world. But this authenticity is not to be found in taken-for-granted social relations, or in the (shattered) Devon pastoral of his youth. The quest takes Martin to California, Egypt, and Syria, and, crucially, involves an acceptance of the self-awareness that the twentieth century brings, and an associated determination to see contemporary individualism as a positive force (p. 555).

Daniel Martin's journey of self-discovery, in short, unveils a mode of living that has progressed far beyond the insular wartime Devon harvest. The 'rural', conceived as geographically bounded, and socially stable, is here made to stand for a world that no longer exists (however strong its nostalgic attractions), and that cannot supply the necessary model for social progress. *Daniel Martin*, in its ultimate rejection of a rural nostalgia to which it is also susceptible, is entirely representative of the treatment of rural themes in the

188

post-war novel, where contemporary analysis frequently does battle with a hankering for the past.

## The Death of the Nature Novel

The analysis that prompts Fowles to confine his traditional harvest scene to the past – as, in effect, a remnant of the nineteenth century – suggests a general difficulty of representation: depictions of the rural are invariably felt to be anachronistic. There is a perception, in fact, that the 'Nature novel' in Britain has run its course, and that serious fiction about rural life cannot hope to speak to a predominantly urban readership with sophisticated tastes. In such a view, the burning social questions are located where the power is and the people are: in the cities; or, increasingly, in suburbia. The focused opposition of country and city, with its instructive contradictions and interdependencies, thus gives way to a hazier, and less fertile distinction. As a crisis in farming deepens, with specific needs obscured by the European Common Agricultural Policy, so, too, does suburban expansion continue to redefine our perceptions of urban space.[1] The 'rural' and the 'urban' are both in flux, making the relationship between the two intensely problematic.

By a straightforward reckoning, the demise of the Nature novel might seem an established fact of literary history. Hardy, and then Lawrence, wrote complex versions of pastoral, making a naive mode of bucolic expression unthinkable. This problematizing of pastoral is sometimes seen (especially in Hardy) as sounding an elegiac note for a past rural existence. But Hardy and Lawrence were also playing their part in the ongoing re-evaluation of pastoral, infusing it with a modern social perspective. For both writers landscape is the arena of pressing historical change, rather than a scenic backdrop, or a poetic and contemplative retreat. Whether we think of Ursula Brangwen's vision of the rainbow above the colliers' houses of Beldover (*The Rainbow*), or of Eustacia Vye atop Rainbarrow (*The Return of the Native*), or Tess entering the vale of the Great Dairies like a fly on a billiard table (*Tess of the d'Urbervilles*), we are confronted with superficially 'natural' images in which questions of social history are inscribed in the landscape.

The question to address is whether or not the social challenge to the Nature novel sounds its death-knell, or its revival. In an excellent study, Glen Cavaliero makes the case for a continuing tradition in the earlier part of the century to 1939. He shows how pre-war rural novelists, both the contemporaries of Lawrence and his successors, were capable of producing something more than pastoral escapism. Cavaliero's selection includes Henry Williamson, Constance Holme, and T. F. Powys, but he tempers the claim for the writers he studies, acknowledging their sometimes limited geographical and psychological concerns. Despite this, he is still willing to assign a significant place in literary history to a rural tradition in which 'a love of landscape' combines with 'an awareness of the potential in human experience arising from it'. This 'potential' embraces human agency, conveying 'a sense of the significance of human beings as a vital and vitalising part of their surroundings'. This literature that traces the human interaction with environment is significant because it stands in contrast to 'the psychological, essentially solitary terms of so much modern [especially modernist] fiction'. The rural tradition thus 'provides a bridge between the introspective, subjective novelists [such as Woolf] and naturalistic writers like Maugham and Arnold Bennett'.[2]

It is difficult to make the same kind of claim for a post-war rural tradition, either for its place in literary history, or for its optimistic sense of human agency. Rapid social change appears to render the pre-war focus obsolete. The changing class structure, for instance, assists the process of displacing the rural. After the Edwardians, Cavaliero claims, one had to look to the rural tradition for thorough fictional treatments of working-class life. The claim is slightly dubious – what of Robert Tressell, or Walter Greenwood? – but Cavaliero's implicit point is that such a claim becomes untenable in the wake of Barstow and Sillitoe, and the post-war identification of working-class experience with the industrial north of England.

Other social changes already examined in this book have an impact on the credibility of the pastoral vision. The celebration of landscape as the source of national identity in the present becomes increasingly less tenable as the society, already predominantly urban, becomes increasingly suburban. The Wordsworthian notion of finding a home in the landscape, a place of belonging, is more and more unconvincing in the post-Romantic era. Since 1950, the break-up of Empire makes that connection between identity and place still more problematic: England (in particular) becomes the site for postcolonial contestation, as new identities are negotiated, and new grounds of 'belonging' are tentatively forged. The idea of pastoral for post-war writers, it seems, is stretched to breaking point.

## The Re-evaluation of Pastoral

It is, of course, inevitable that each generation will interrogate the relevance of pastoral writing, and in this dynamic of continuous critique it may be impossible to locate some earlier literary moment in which an Edenic version of pastoral achieves dominance. As human needs change, so does the function of pastoral evolve. In this light, the anxious post-war treatments of rural experience may represent a degree of continuity with earlier periods, even if the effort of re-evaluating pastoral may seem a more delicate and complicated operation than it had in the past.

A novel that yields a helpful overview of the post-war period is Isabel Colegate's *Winter Journey* (1995), in which a retrospective view of some significant social changes is offered, filtered through the lens of the English landscape. This account of late middle age, and the process of self-evaluation, centres on Edith's visit to her brother Alfred, in their childhood home in the Mendips. Edith, formerly an MP, and founder member of an 'Independent Citizens Party' (a mould-breaking initiative in British politics that 'set[s] the pattern' for the SDP [p. 52]), learns to accept her limitations, to temper her arrogance, and to fashion a purposive future role.[3] At the heart of this adjustment lies a belated understanding that her political attempts to promote multiculturalism had been clumsy, a misplaced 'acting for' that misread race tensions. A lost election and the end of her parliamentary career are the results of this insensitivity. Alfred observes that his sister would 'have made a fine colonial governor' (p. 158), and the lesson for Edith (and, through her, Middle England generally) is to find a more responsive way of engaging with ethnic difference. As she ponders a late career as a Euro-MP, Edith seems to have made the necessary adjustment (p. 197).

This reassertion of identity is made possible by the retreat to the Mendips, and the rural idyll that puts Edith back in touch with her cognitive origins. The decisive scene sees Edith contemplating a tall chestnut tree, and by association, bringing to mind key memories and the significant people in her life. Beneath the tree, Edith produces the memory of bouncing in her pram on the same spot nearly sixty years before, oblivious to danger, in possession of 'the crystal clarity of perfect bliss'. For Edith, the rediscovery of this essential kernel of Being is epiphanic, a self-defining bliss that is part of her physical being (p. 111).

Edith's revelation is unlocked by the chestnut tree, but this does not insist that her inner vitality is necessarily linked with, or bestowed by the natural landscape, although this is a hovering possibility. The case of Alfred is more complex, however. Like Edith, Alfred is a representative figure, an entrepreneur of swinging sixties London, turned photographer. The suicide of his wife Lydia, a celebrity model, reaffirms his tendency to emotional withdrawal, and leads to a semi-reclusive existence. For Alfred, consolation is produced by consorting with the natural world (pp. 166–7). He is determined in his resolution to preserve the family home and its environs, specifically by resisting a scheme for off-road motor sport, much as he had previously resisted plans for a dry ski-slope. This obstruction of the spread of town leisure pursuits is inspired by a desire to keep the environment as it is for his niece and her children. This involves reclaiming the house, which has degenerated into a bachelor dwelling, as a family space.

Alfred's impulse of reclamation is essentially conservative, a regressive retreat to the house and its setting, and the embracing of a nostalgic English ruralism. His father, a composer associated like Vaughan Williams with the evocation of Englishness, is linked with Alfred's new resolution. When he feels 'some kind of benediction' at the sight of a hare, creature of English myth and folklore, running along the roadside (p. 189), we are put in mind of his father's 'King Arthur' suite, a more elaborate attempt at patriotism, inspired by a different mythical icon of Englishness (pp. 136, 176). But the hare is an attribute of place, actual, unmediated. Like his father before him, Alfred is dissatisfied with his art, his landscape photography, and seeks to dispense with the mediation, to get back to the thing itself. A tension thus emerges between the social convictions of Edith, who has come to admire her brother's photography (p. 197), and the emotional directness of his own identification with place. The book embraces both perspectives – the desire for meaningful dwelling as well as the urge to participate in social change – and produces a representation of the English landscape that accords with that synthesis. Initially emulating Alfred's pictures of the Mendips in winter, frozen and grey, the book finishes as a thaw begins, heralding Edith's reinvigorated return to London (p. 195), and Alfred's conviction that he must look critically at the house, and think about its future as well as its past (pp. 199–200).

The conservative pull of a more traditional pastoral impulse is gently loosened in Colegate's novel, though similar effects are observable in surprising quarters. The Larkin novels of H. E. Bates, for example, seem to rely on an escapist fantasy of the rural good life, though in fact more interesting tensions are also at play in Bates's vision. The Larkin family sequence begins with *The Darling Buds of May* (1958), a comic pastoral entertainment in which the 'perfick' scene of natural abundance (in Pop Larkin's idiom) chimes with human happiness. The felicitous ending, with the announcement of an impending wedding, and a new baby on the way for Pop and Ma Larkin, is a fitting expression of 'full, high summer' after 'the buds of May had gone' (p. 158).

The broad conformity with the conventions of comic pastoral suggests an easy town/country opposition. Indeed, the unorthodox lifestyle of the Larkins is defined by their flouting of social convention. Ma and Pop Larkin have several children, but are unmarried; they resist centralized social organization and do not pay tax. Their hedonistic, non-judgemental enjoyment of life seems to put them in touch with the rhythms of the countryside. However, a less innocent rural economy is at work. At the outset, the beautiful daughter Mariette believes herself to be pregnant (mistakenly), and sets about the seduction of the tax inspector, Mr Charlton, who conveniently arrives on the scene on an impossible mission to secure a tax return from

Pop. Pop and Ma connive with Mariette's designs on Mr Charlton, a possible husband, and a solution to Mariette's problem. This concession to social decency, and the attempt to buy it with sex, obviously undermines the impression of sexual freedom and openness. As if to underscore the irony, Bates has a TV discussion of prostitution playing in the background as the seduction of Charlton, or 'Charley' as the Larkins dub him, is under way (p. 33). Notionally, Charley is seduced by the Larkins' way of life; but the motif of sexual bargaining throws this into doubt. Pop Larkin, with his love of cars and evident expertise in the black market economy, is a benevolent social outlaw, a champion of individual freedom, rather than a bucolic hero. *The Darling Buds of May* is not, in fact, the pastoral fantasy it seems to be, but rather – with the memories of post-war rationing still alive – a projection of contemporary sentiment against state interference on to the good life.

If the celebration of rural life can be used to project specific social moods, as in both *Winter Journey* at the end of the period, and in *The Darling Buds of May* at the beginning, how is the idea of 'pastoral' being deployed? A look at this literary term suggests there has been a significant extension of it, a continuation of the work most obviously associated in the modern novel with Hardy and Lawrence. In an authoritative account, Terry Gifford discerns three main uses of 'pastoral'. The first usage denotes that specific literary form, with its roots in Greek and Roman poetry, in which the countryside is represented in an idealized manner. Here, the dynamic of retreat serves the purpose of reflecting back on the situation of an urban audience. In the second, less precise usage, 'pastoral' denotes content, merely, a focus on the natural world or a rural setting. The third use is pejorative, indicating that the pastoral vision is limited or incomplete, perhaps failing to address the harsh reality of rural existence.[4] These tendencies often overlap in literary works, as Gifford observes in seeking to establish a nuanced understanding of pastoral, responsive to a well-established anti-pastoral tradition, and that benefits from contemporary insights in ecocriticism.

This posited vein of 'post-pastoral' writing allows for a coincidence between creative and critical perspectives, both emerging from a context in which traditional pastoral is not only contested, but is also seen as deeply suspect.[5] There are six aspects to Gifford's post-pastoral: first, an awe in response to the natural world; second, the recognition that creative and destructive forces coexist in nature; third, the realization that inner human nature is illuminated by its relationship to external nature; fourth, a simultaneous awareness of the cultural constructions of nature, and of nature as culture; fifth, a conviction that human consciousness should produce environmental conscience; and, sixth, the realization that environmental exploitation is generated by the same mind-set that results in social exploitation.[6]

This post-pastoral, which for Gifford is exemplified in the poetry of Ted Hughes, represents a challenge to contemporary alienation from the non-human world, as well as an enlightened engagement with the Real. In this respect, as a mode of critical understanding, post-pastoral implies the need to redeem the textual emphasis of post-structuralist criticism by finding 'a language that can convey an instinctive unity that is at once both prior to language and expressed by a language that is distinctively human'. (In *Winter Journey*, Edith's retrieval and articulation of her pre-linguistic moment of *joie de vivre* beneath the chestnut tree dramatizes this very principle.) All six elements of Gifford's definition will be present together only rarely in a single text; and, as this extended definition of post-pastoral was originally conceived in a discussion of contemporary poetry, its applicability to fiction remains to be tested. It is also important to note that Gifford does not imply a simple chronological progression from pastoral, to anti-pastoral, through to post-pastoral. On the contrary, he detects post-pastoral elements in Blake and Wordsworth, as well as Heaney and Hughes.[7] However, for the novel there does seem to be an *intensification* of post-pastoral concerns as post-war writers have grappled with ever more complex and self-conscious techniques in confronting the march of a progressively urbanized culture. In the face of a gathering millennial *Angst*, the post-pastoral novel becomes increasingly fraught, haunted by the sense of its own impossibility.

## The Post-Pastoral Novel

It is possible to see something of the self-conscious ethical and linguistic manoeuvring that must underpin the post-pastoral in several post-war novelistic engagements with the rural tradition; but it should be acknowledged that the specific features do not always find a suitable home in the novel. In particular, the cultivation of 'awe' in the face of the natural would seem to represent an embarrassment to the procedures of fiction (in contrast to the capacity of poetic diction). The illumination of human nature by its relationship with external nature, however, is a particular novelistic strength, especially where the cultural constructions of nature are also laid bare.

A fine example of post-pastoral is Bruce Chatwin's *On the Black Hill* (1982), which conveys a reverence for place combined with that 'anti-pastoral' awareness of the hardships, psychological as well as economic, that a rural existence can entail. The novel is set in the Black Mountains on the border of England and Wales, a place of particular importance to Chatwin, who felt that everyone needed 'a base', a place to identify with, that need be neither the place of birth, nor even the locale in which one is raised. This need for identification with a chosen place, with 'a sort of magic circle to which you belong', was satisfied for Chatwin by the Black Mountains.[8] The human focus of *On the Black Hill* is the relationship of Lewis and Benjamin Jones, hill farmers and identical twins, whose farm, named 'The Vision', is their lifelong home. Neither brother marries, and homosexual Benjamin's intense and jealous love for his brother is a key factor in their enduring insular bond. This bond is emphasized in the ability of Lewis to take on Benjamin's pain vicariously (pp. 42, 102, 109), an attribute that is reversed when Lewis dies (p. 247).[9] The situation of the twins is simultaneously productive and destructive on account of their self-containment as a unit: they are effective farmers, in control of an expanding holding, yet become increasingly out of touch with a century with which they are superficially in tandem (pp. 36–41). (They are born in the year of the Relief of Mafeking [1900].)

Chatwin's novel of successive generations experiencing the impact of social change is squarely in the tradition of Hardy and Lawrence; and, like both of these authors, he employs nature imagery in ambivalent fashion to register change. Late in the novel, as the twins' eightieth birthday approaches, the 'warm westerly breeze', together with the 'skylarks hover[ing] over their heads', and the 'creamy clouds ... floating out of Wales' are aspects of a reassuringly familiar landscape, its focus 'the whitewashed farmhouses where their Welsh forbears had lived and died'. This faith in continuity for the brothers is proof against the 'pair of jet fighters' that 'screamed low over the Wye, reminding them of a destructive world beyond' (p. 233). England, to the east, is the immediate source of this destructive world that is already unsettling the twins' domain. Lewis has a lifelong 'yearning for far-off places', even though neither twin ventures further than Hereford, aside from one seaside holiday in 1910 (p. 13); but an important aspect of Chatwin's novel is to resist the pull of nostalgia. Speaking of the people who inspired his rural characters, he said: 'I don't see these people as strange. I wanted to take these people as the centre of a circle and see the rest of our century as somehow abnormal.'[10] The positive element of Chatwin's ruralism is thus the attempt to offer a defamiliarizing, revisionist perspective on the early 1980s.

There are also global connotations to this contemporary world-view. The character Theo, a disaffected migrant from South Africa, represents the positive postcolonial energies that are beyond the understanding of the Lewises. Theo is a benign transnational presence who, having flirted with Buddhism in the Welsh hills, goes off 'to climb in the Himalayas' (pp. 228, 249). There is much in the novel to suggest that the comparative unworldliness of the Lewis twins renders them innocent and benighted at the same time. But Chatwin remains centrally interested in the motif of withdrawal, and the ambivalence it denotes. In this connection, it is Meg, left to manage the neighbouring farm alone on the death of the farmer, who emerges as the novel's significant figure. She is a symbol of endurance, and the vehicle of an uncluttered ethical mode of habitation based on harmony with the non-human world: 'Let all God's creatures live!' is her creed (p. 211). Writing of the real-life model for 'Meg the Rock', Chatwin described a woman who, despite suffering 'any kind of indignity', had managed to establish 'a basic standard of behaviour'. Consequently, she was, for him, 'a heroine of our time'.[11]

Given the novel's ambivalence, it is remarkable that Chatwin manages to include a harvest festival scene without embarrassment, as a celebratory ritual of fulfilment that, in the reading from Ecclesiastes ('A time to be born, and a time to die'), anticipates the imminent death of Lewis as a fitting sign of completion (pp. 243–6). Central to the integrity of this scene is the appearance in church of Meg, fresh from hospital, who has not previously left her farm in thirty years, accompanied by 'the giant South African' Theo (p. 244). Rather than a ritual celebrating a repetitive cycle of natural renewal, this is a celebration of *social* renewal, the community redeemed by the reassertion of its internal ethics that also reach outwards. The involvement of Theo, the migrant from apartheid South Africa, enlarges the significance of the desired regeneration.

A significant contrast to this, and a novel that helps define the limits of the post-pastoral, is Christopher Hart's *The Harvest* (1999). A much bleaker harvest is the concern of Hart's novel, which embraces a host of urgent social and environmental issues pertaining to the nature of a rural community and the relationship between town and country. Where Chatwin presents the hopeful spectacle of an enclosed community reaching outwards, Hart depicts the catastrophic consequences for rural life where no genuine external regeneration is made available. Lewis Pike, the chief focalizer, is a solitary teenager in a village in 'the Wessex downlands' overrun by wealthy city weekenders, and where economic survival for the indigenous village population depends upon the heritage industry. Confused ideas of rural life abound, most notably when the 'incomers' to the village want to resuscitate the harvest tradition of a life-size corn doll, 'sacrificed' on the church altar. Ultimately it is Lewis who fulfils the ritual: he merges this idea of sacrifice with fantasies of himself as a Christ-figure (pp. 204, 227–8), before killing himself in the church with his crossbow (p. 234).

The ambivalence about the moral 'ownership' of the country centres on Lewis Pike, who is the epitome of a new rural schizophrenia, an individual responsive to the natural world, yet whose confused bloodlust tips him over into excessive misanthropy and paranoid delusion. The scene in which Lewis kills a deer is especially poignant, and is representative of the agonized mood of this new ruralism. The episode reproduces Lewis's keen sensitivity to the sights and sounds of this woodland scene. Alive to the 'promise in the air', Lewis successfully tracks and kills a deer, sending a crossbow bolt into its brain. Fulfilling his adopted hunter's role, he butchers the deer on the spot, but as he disembowels the animal, he discovers the foetus of a fawn, and recoils in horror, vomiting. He curses himself, and reflects that 'it isn't the animals we should be killing' (pp. 182–5). This 'elemental' engagement with the environment is quite as groundless as the unwitting resurrection of pagan village tradition, or the scene that brings town and country folk together to witness a hellish dog-fight (p. 200). A governing framework for the human distortion of the natural is supplied by the freak hot weather that has brought on this harvest all too soon. Gerald, the dilettante incomer and poet, has published a collection entitled 'Lacunae' (p. 111), a title that signals Hart's own discovery of the absences at the heart of rural existence.

*The Harvest* is a powerful anti-pastoral that emphasizes the difficulty, at the end of the century, of finding positive instances of human activity illuminated in a non-human context. The book does imply the need for such a link, but its depiction of how lifestyle culture generates a false mode of engagement with rural existence is profoundly pessimistic. Hart's book also demonstrates a broader difficulty for the novel, since it illustrates those characteristic features of the form – the focus on personal development, on social rather than environmental concerns, and on time rather than space – that can contribute to an impression of alienation from the natural world.

Laurence Buell's checklist of the ingredients of 'an environmentally oriented work' reveals the anthropocentric bias of the dominant literary forms, particularly the novel, and serves to install non-fictional Nature writing as the mode that best suits Buell's projected 'aesthetic of relinquishment', the process by which environment might be privileged over 'intersocial events'. The first and most stringent of Buell's qualifying requirements is that '*the nonhuman environment is present not merely as a framing device but as a presence that begins to suggest that human history is implicated in natural history*'.[12] This is a difficult principle to sustain in novelistic discourse, although some attempts to make this kind of imaginative shift have been made. Raymond Williams's projected trilogy, *People of the Black Mountains* (left unfinished at his death) is a major experiment that has some connection with the kind of ecocentric principle Buell was subsequently to define.

In the same setting as Chatwin's *On the Black Hill*, *People of the Black Mountains* was conceived as a trilogy, spanning the period from 23,000 BC to the twentieth century (and the present day, in its frame of linking passages).[13] Williams's radical gesture in this work is to flout the novel's usual reliance on human continuity: with a few exceptions, each story is set at a much later time than its predecessor, and involves a fresh set of characters. This is particularly marked in the first book, *The Beginning*, where thousands of years may separate the stories. Narrative continuity is thus supplied by place rather than by character, an unusual privileging of environment that requires a significant adjustment in the reader's expectations. The experimental impetus of *People of the Black Mountains* might seem to chime with the ecocritical principle of recentring the non-human environment, though it requires a modification of this idea, too, as I shall suggest.

If Williams's refusal of immediate human continuity (in the form of a conventional deployment of character) suggests a downplaying of intersocial events, this is because he is attempting a panoramic social history of place. This is especially clear in the first book with its stress on the development of agricultural and social practices, often (though not always) in a history of human advancement, from hand-to-mouth hunting to settled communities. Folklore, in which the endeavours of 'deceased' characters survive, supplies another means of human connectivity. Williams made use of the available historical and archaeological sources (II, 326–30), but this is a historical novel that also questions its own historical premises, or at least signals that they are speculations, 'possible construction[s]', merely (I, 237). This kind of self-conscious disavowal only partly unsettles the reader's identification with particular episodes, which are sometimes powerfully evoked. The self-consciousness does denote a duality in the project overall, however, a desire simultaneously to engage and withdraw, to empathize and to analyse. The reader is being asked to embrace contradiction, to remain critical about the arbitrary element of historical construction, and yet to invest personally in the speculation about human continuity.

Another way in which *People of the Black Mountains* complicates its status as a historical novel is by consciously imposing a contemporary agenda on to the episodes of the past. This is most marked in the stories of prehistory, as when that contemporary demon, the abusive foster-father haunts a story set seventeen hundred years BC (I, 192–209). Williams's intellectual purpose in making this kind of extravagant anachronistic connection is revealed in one of the best stories, 'The Coming of the Measurer' (I, 151–87), set four thousand years ago. Here the 'measurer' Mered, from a 'Company of Measurers' on Salisbury Plain, embodies a peculiarly contemporary dilemma. The measurers, whose measurements of year and tides facilitate agricultural practices, represent an early instance of the division of labour: the 'people of the plain' bring food to the measurers in return for their knowledge (I, 177–8). It is this division of labour, however, that has produced Mered's personal crisis, which is the crisis of the professional intellectual living at one remove from practical matters of subsistence: how do you justify your existence when the pursuit of knowledge, 'the wonder of measuring' (I, 178), has become an end in itself? Mered tells the story of how the measurers used an eclipse of the sun (which they were able to 'predict' as a sign) to frighten the local people who had refused them food (p. 179). This early scientific rationality becomes disconnected from the society it serves, and introduces the hegemony of knowledge as power.

The novel's frame connects directly to this early instance of corruption through professionalization. The linking stories that comprise the frame follow Glyn Parry walking out in the Black Mountains in search of his grandfather Elis, who has failed to return from a walk. As Glyn traverses the landscape, aware of presences around him, he unleashes the various 'rising visions of the past' (I, 358). Glyn's absent father epitomizes the social catastrophe of the professional: a 'brilliant young man', he emigrates to Pittsburgh 'trailing his first book' and finds 'another job' and 'another woman', before dying in a plane crash (I, 9). The grandfather Elis supplies the 'real fatherly relationship' for Glyn. Pointedly, Elis's 'intense local interests', combining history and geography, contrast with the self-destructive root-lessness of Glyn's father (I, 8–9). The critique is made explicit in the reported convictions of Elis, who acknowledges the importance of the 'textual, comparative, theoretical' bent of 'professional scrutiny', whilst understanding the weaknesses of 'a number of disciplines':

> Pushing away, often coldly, the enthusiasms of the amateur, they would reduce what they were studying to an internal procedure; in the worst cases to material for an enclosed career. If lives and places were being seriously sought, a powerful attachment to lives and to places was entirely demanded . . . Only the breath of the place, its winds and its mouths, stirred the models into life. (I, 10)

Models, of course, remain necessary. Elis has himself constructed a polystyrene relief model of the mountains, which reveals the desire to reconstruct and simulate (I, 10). The literature of place, of course, is another kind of representation; but the point is that theories, models, and simulations must remain secondary, merely facilitating access. The place itself must remain the primary focus, as the cautionary parable of the measurer indicates.

A comparable attempt to supply surface narrative continuity through place rather than character is Adam Thorpe's *Ulverton* (1992), which spans over three hundred years (1650–1988), in twelve separate sections comprising a chronological sequence of different episodes in the life of a village in South-West England. Each section is written in a different style, and this gives the novel a rich and varied texture: there are letters, diary entries, a sermon, bar-room tales, a Molly Bloom-style soliloquy by a farm labourer, and, in the final section, the 'Post Production Script' for a television documentary, incorporating camera shots and sound directions.

Thorpe skilfully employs these different modes to convey the essence of characters in a brief appearance. Indeed, *Ulverton* is centrally concerned with the human drama, but Thorpe ensures that the personal is integrated within a broader historical dynamic. Thus, in the first section (1650), a soldier returns from Cromwell's Irish campaigns, clearly haunted by the part he has played in the massacres at Wexford and Drogheda. Yet the focus is his personal emotional situation, returning with red ribbons (now torn and faded) to fulfil a dream of his wife's. Presuming him dead, however, she has since remarried the mean-spirited Thomas Walters. The returning husband disappears, and the silence of the only witness to the probable murder – the shepherd who narrates the section – is bought by sexual favours from the inconstant wife.

Thorpe's real achievement is to make such moments of private drama, which are powerful stories in themselves, part of a larger fabric that builds into a poetic social history of place. In the final section the soldier's demise comes back to haunt a descendant of his usurper. Here the crass property developer Clive Walters has his building work in Ulverton halted by the discovery of the remains of a Cromwellian soldier, clutching a ribbon, killed by a blow to the head (pp. 358–9). The author 'Adam Thorpe' has assisted in uncovering the local legend of the soldier's cuckolding and untimely end (the first section now appears to be the work of this 'Adam Thorpe', published in a local journal).

The appearance of the author as character is quite distinct from the way this device is deployed in more overtly metafictional experiments (the 'Martin Amis' of *Money*, say). Thorpe seems to want to affiliate himself unequivocally at this point with rural tradition, by having himself appear as the enemy of the irresponsible developer. This is partly an argument against urbanization, but also against the empty rhetoric of progress, which cloaks the pursuit of personal gain. There is a nice irony in the fact that the discovered legend engenders a distrust of the developers, inspired by a contemporary superstition. This revives the 'Curse of Five Elms Farm' (p. 374), and the humility prompted by a fear of the unknown, which has characterized the denizens of Ulverton through the ages.

Another aspect of the novel's richness is its simultaneous celebration and distrust of local history. A case in point is the misfortune of the eighteenth-century wainwright Webb, who fears for his professional reputation when a man dies because of a split wheel. Webb is reassured by the farmer who is really to blame: he had left the offending wagon out in winter storms. Of course, the story of how Jepthah Webb was to blame for the poor craftsmanship that killed a man persists into the next century, and affects subsequent generations of Webbs, all carpenters (p. 116). Misunderstandings and misrepresentations abound as the sedimented layers of history obscure the past. Thorpe's powerful image for this is a series of mid-nineteenth-century photographic plates of the village, used by an old labourer as cloches for his cabbages: a generation later, the action of the sun has dissolved the impressions of past villagers (p. 200).

Of course, much of the impetus of Thorpe's narrative is to make his reimagined images indelible, to offer a resonant sense of significant or poignant or transforming private actions in the face of depersonalizing historical forces. The heroic resistance of under-gardener Percy Cullurne in the face of the enlistment drive of 1914 is the novel's most powerful scene: 'I'd rather bide at home', he tells the Squire, scandalizing the assembled village (p. 233).

Like Hardy, Thorpe is sensitive to the adverse social consequences of such things as the advent of the threshing machine, and there is a kind of nostalgic ruralism that pervades much of the novel, and that culminates in that concluding condemnation of the loss of rural land to housing estates, light industry, and golf courses (pp. 343, 364). In this connection, the use of 'Adam Thorpe' as a character enlisted in the fight to preserve the village, is a redeeming feature. Where this kind of metafictional conceit might more usually highlight the author's own agenda, the effect of this is to reduce the significance of the partisan 'Adam Thorpe', his function restricted to that of a campaigning dissenter in one section. The author's nostaligic ruralism is thus contained by his representative within a single section: it is an ambivalent, but self-deprecating gesture which preserves the complexity of the overall design.

Both *People of the Black Mountains* and *Ulverton* strive to make new kinds of connection for the novel between people and place. At the same time, the most affecting elements of both works are produced by the social struggle with particular contextual forces. This may involve the anachronistic embedding of contemporary concerns (as in Williams's reading of an episode of 2000 BC through the lens of modern professionalism), or the dependence on key historical markers (the resistance of enlistment in the 1914 episode of *Ulverton*, for example). This kind of emphasis indicates that these experimental works do *not*, in the final analysis, partake of a broader spatial turn in cultural thought, according to which time and history are ousted by place. Instead a different kind of interaction between history and place enables human history to be rendered poignantly on a broader and impersonal temporal canvas. In both works the attempt to generate a more compelling portrait of the social in its spatial context utilizes time as the central element.

The elaborate technique of both *People of the Black Mountains* and *Ulverton* emphasizes the necessary connection between place and human history, where that history is conceived as a dialogue between present frames of understanding and an imperfect reconstruction of the past. If an agreed and verifiable history of place is unavailable, there can be no authoritative version of regional belonging; but there can be an imaginative attempt to construct a version of regional inhabitation. This involves historical sensitivity towards one's region, and with one's ancestors, but with an awareness that the effort of reconstruction is piecemeal.

The failure to announce the fictional nature of this empathic 'reading back' brings with it the risk of seeking particular, exclusive social origins. This is Thorpe's concern in *Pieces of Light* (1998), a return to Ulverton in which a pointed ambivalence about the celebration of place emerges. Hugh Arkwright, Thorpe's protagonist, lodges with his aunt and uncle in their large Ulverton house 'Ilythia'. A debate about an elemental or 'primal' England stems from the significance of the old wood in the grounds of the house. Hugh's Uncle Edward believes this to be a remnant of the original forest that once covered England, and he hopes that this 'wildwood' will reassert itself, reclaiming the land. Edward's interest in pagan fertility rites and mythology is cast into doubt by his association with the Thule society: he deplores their nationalism, but is inevitably tainted by these Nazi sympathizers. Still more alarming is the possibility that he may have been storing nerve gas, perhaps one day to assist the primeval forest in its efforts to win back the land. The emphasis, here, is on the dangers implicit in a static perception of place and identity.

*Ulverton* begins on a hilltop defined by a barrow or burial mound, a detail that introduces the novel's preoccupation with the physical presence of human history. The archaeological motif is Hardyesque: in *The Return of the Native*, for example, the barrow represents collective human action in history, and offers a counterpoint (often ironic) to contemporary human activity on Egdon Heath. But if Rainbarrow casts a shadow of insignificance over ephemeral human endeavour, it is also a monument to human civilization which has withstood the ravages of time.

A similar process of ambivalent counterpoint structures Peter Ackroyd's *First Light* (1989), in which the twinned activities of archaeology and astronomy order a quest for origins. This interrogation of the connection between identity and place is, simultaneously, an investigation of the referential capacities of literature. The quest motif, in fact, marks a significant stage in Ackroyd's intellectual development, a partial progression beyond the partisan position he had taken in *Notes for a New Culture* (1976), in which he writes in favour of French 'postmodern', or poststructuralist thought, using this intellectual position to expose the moribund nature of English literary culture.[14] The pursuit of origins, of course, is the *bête noire* of much poststructuralist thinking, where it is presented as a central flaw in Western humanism, and *First Light* develops Ackroyd's engagement with this debate.

The novel's action links an observatory and an archaeological dig, in which various discoveries suggest a late-Neolithic knowledge and worship of the constellations. The actual pursuit of scientific knowledge, however, is unproductive since the astronomer Damian Fall is reduced to mental instability by his pursuit of the moment of ultimate origin, and his belief that the expansion of the universe from the big bang is going into reverse (p. 296). For archaeologist Mark Clare, the scientific pursuit of evidence is finally disrupted by the pressures of the present. The dig progresses away from the burial mound when a network of tunnels is discovered leading to another burial chamber beneath an adjacent stone circle. This chamber contains the remains of someone claimed as an ancestor by the local Mint family: down the centuries they have had access to the tunnels, and have incorporated this ancient ancestor into their own rites and rituals. When the archaeologists get too close, the Mints bear off the coffin of their ancestor, concealing it in a garden shed. A farcical tussle over the coffin is resolved when it is set on fire. The ancestor – or prized archaeological find – is thus 'returned to the frame of origin' (p. 326), in a mystical gesture that touches each of the characters present, who feel a 'moment of communion' that unites them with their dead loved ones.

The 'frame of origin', of course, is quite other than a moment of origin. Rather, the novel is projecting a Whitmanesque order of cosmic communion in which all matter is conjoined in a process of continual recycling. In this sense the reflections of the recuperating Damian Fall, which conclude the book, carry a summative authority: 'why is it that we think of a circular motion as the most perfect? Is it because it has no beginning and no end?' he wonders (p. 328). The succour that this cosmic philosophy is shown to offer does not entirely overshadow a sense of personal history. It is partly in tune with the evocation of the past as a determining feature of the present, and with the suggestion of a kind of constructed 'race memory' as a framework for continuity.

Overall, however, the novel is far less stable in its effects than this summary implies. It mixes its modes in an extravagant, dissonant fashion, switching from the portentous seriousness of its central theme, to moments of broad (and disturbing) comedy. This vacillation from one mode to another, with the uncertainty of tone that results, is a recurring characteristic of Ackroyd's novels, though it is nowhere more pronounced than in *First Light*. There is a deliberate policy of unsettling the reading experience underlying these procedures, and this gives a particular edge to the manner in which the novel places itself in the rural tradition of the English novel. This Dorset novel, with its reflections on place and history, makes many overt allusions to Hardy. It is a richly allusive work, but there is a sense of concentration in its references to a particular novel, *Two on a Tower* (1882), which is the locus of Ackroyd's ambivalent 'writing back' to tradition.[15] Hardy's tower is an eighteenth-century structure on a man-made hill. It is a place of solitary escape for the novel's heroine, and a site for the withdrawn star-gazing of the astronomer-hero: it is a place of asocial reflection. Human history is rendered inaccessible by such pursuits, and yet social pressures and obligations cut across the abstract philosophizing of the astronomer, and it is this incompatibility between social life and philosophical reflection to which Ackroyd particularly responds.

Many of Ackroyd's characters are grotesques, their attributes more disturbing than funny, as they have become constant, beyond the modifying influence of social intercourse. In this manner Ackroyd intensifies and updates the tensions of Hardy's fictional world, in which a definition of the 'natural' is subject to a constant renegotiation. Ackroyd, by contrast, does not indicate the grounds for such a redefinition. *First Light* collects an assemblage of grotesques and obsessives, all of whom are at odds with their environment in one way or another, and offers the notion of cosmic communion as the most likely source of collective feeling. Ultimately this serves to reinforce both the sense of displacement and the difficulty of writing in the rural tradition in the post-war era.

If the pursuit of origins implies a dubious, and reactionary motivation, does this not make the celebration of a particular place as a source of human continuity reactionary by definition? And, if so, does this make a stance of postmodern relativity a required feature in the treatment of place and identity, a necessary check on more insidious desires? A brilliant novel that is centred on this very tension between the construction of identity, and the identification with one particular landscape is Graham Swift's *Waterland* (1983). Swift's novel generates its effects by cultivating a sense of crisis about different kinds of narrative. The principal opposition is that between History and storytelling, but the combination of different narratives is complex. The book embraces both public, national histories, and private, 'dynastic' histories, with a focus on the human interaction with the environment. Other important strands include superstition and the supernatural, and, prominently, the natural history of the eel.

For the narrator, history teacher Tom Crick, the personal quest to make sense of the past involves combining these various elements, and also subjecting his own discipline to critical scrutiny. History is under threat at his school, not least because of his own unorthodox approach: feeling the limitations of textbook history, he has recourse to his own story to fill his lessons. He has concluded that the History he formerly sought, 'the Grand Narrative . . . the dispeller of fears in the dark' is no more than 'a yarn' (p. 53). This, apparently, sounds a note of postmodernist relativity, confirmed by the eclecticism in the combination of discourses, and seems to set up an opposition certain to aggravate the historian. Accordingly, in an article in *History Today*, John Brewer and Stella Tillyard express their annoyance that history in *Waterland* is 'a sign of man's enslavement', whilst 'nature' and 'fiction' supply 'the means by which he can be free'. These assumptions, indicative for Brewer and Tillyard of 'the rather extravagant claims of much modern literature', merely offer an empty postmodern vision of 'the positivist world turned upside down' in their view. Yet, revealingly, these historians confess that their enjoyment of the novel is unmarred, a fact 'attributable to the subtlety and skill with which Swift elaborates his themes'.[16] If the novel remains unmarred by the supposedly erroneous treatment of its central theme, perhaps we need to seek other critical terms to explain its achievement. Indeed, it is the subtlety and skill of the elaboration – which makes the extraction of a single theme problematic – that is the key. *Waterland*, in fact, may be seen to justify the 'extravagant claims' of modern literature, by offering the historian an alternative mode of thinking.

The novel does, it is true, offer a bleak account of English history, particularly in its association of imperialism and industrial exploitation. In reaction to this, Tom Crick has recourse to an unorthodox 'humble model for progress' in which 'the reclamation of land', a process of 'repeatedly, never-endingly retrieving what is lost', is analogous to the subjective and selective shoring-up process of telling stories about oneself (p. 291). Swift gets beyond the play of textuality, however. The real and the metaphorical are yoked together in the image of siltation, an 'equivocal operation' in its natural manifestation: silt 'drives back the sea', but also 'impedes the flow of rivers' making the new land susceptible to flooding. The human intervention, land reclamation, or 'human siltation', continues this natural process, and is similarly equivocal, an 'interminable and ambiguous process' (p. 8). Of course, there is a sense that Crick's conception of storytelling is the cultural equivalent of this struggle, and is similarly incomplete. But the metaphorical connection – and this is the crucial point – is not necessarily transferable: it works specifically, in the British context, for the Fens. The setting is vital, and supplies something more than the chance metaphor for the writer's textual games. Part of Swift's self-consciousness is to make use of a number of fictional genres identified with English fiction in the nineteenth century: the dynastic saga, the gothic novel, the detective story, and, most important, the provincial novel in which character is closely linked with environment. Rather than parodying these genres, Swift reinvigorates them; and it is the refashioned provincial novel that underpins the book's operation, since the separate themes are conjoined by the particular evocation of place.

The configuration of the novel's different strands involves a process of 'siltation' in Crick's quest to shore-up his shaken sense of self. The quest is conducted through the uncovering of layers of personal guilt – guilt by historical association as well as the guilt rooted in personal actions. The motif of siltation, over and above its thematic connotations, thus has a bearing on the structure, the emplotment, as well as supplying a bridge to an actual terrain. In this way, 'siltation' insists on certain connections in the construction of human identity: the necessary coexistence of private feeling and public event, but also the interdependence of time, place, and politics. If the discovery of human siltation brings the past vitally into the present, it does so by insisting on Being in an environment. This has to do not simply with matters of subsistence, but also with environment as a limit to consciousness: there are repeated references to how the flat Fenland landscape may have an adverse affect on the psyche, for example.

The perceived negativity of the novel, centred on the guilty, defeated Tom Crick, is circumvented by the way in which Swift hands the interpretive effort over to the reader, and forces our analytical hand. With increasing suspense, the plot winds towards its inevitable dramatic centre; and, at the point in the past when Dick – Tom's brain-damaged half-brother – discovers his personal history, the novel's tragic denouement unfolds. He is the product of an incestuous relationship between his mother and his unbalanced grandfather, who has hailed Dick as 'Saviour of the World'. However, the apparent irony of this designation is dissipated by Dick's suicide: he dives off the dredger on which he works (controlling the silt) and is imagined by Tom swimming out to sea like the eel, the mystical creature with which he is closely associated. The dive installs Dick as a scapegoat figure, sacrificed in expiation of a society's sins. He is the product of a multitude of sins by blood or association: industrial exploitation; imperialism; sexual jealousy; incest; murder; and a lost political vision. Dick swims back to his mythic origins, symbolically confirming the neglect of the natural, but, conversely, putting the society back in touch with the natural cycle through the ritualistic idea of atonement. Subtly, the focus on Tom Crick is displaced by this ending, which recentres the sense of tragedy on Dick.

The personal guilt of Tom Crick, however, has the same kind of components as the collective guilt projected on to Dick as scapegoat for a society's sins. By this correspondence the sense of personal time and personal history becomes necessarily linked to collective goals, which emerge from the realization that a disastrous banishing of the natural is the product of modern social and industrial history. Yet this more general implication is inevitably tempered by the novel's studious regionalism, and the memory that the ambivalence of human endeavour in the form of land reclamation merely extends the equivocations of a natural process. The hardship of subsistence, and the harshness of nature are the keynotes of this regionalism, an informed, self-conscious post-pastoral vision.

One of the main ecocritical objections to the novel as a form is its perceived stress on human history, and its denigration of natural history. The fundamental premise of *Waterland* is the *connection* between human and natural history, but it is clearly human-centred in its tragic momentum. It may seem curious that this degree of anthropocentrism should be objected to, since such a stance is surely an inevitable feature of human cultural endeavour. However, it is worth reflecting on the ecocritical calls for a mode of writing back which gives 'voice' to the non-human environment.[17] In *Man or Mango? A Lament* (1998), Lucy Ellmann includes a playful treatment of the voicing of nature in a novel that serves, in practice if not by design, to test the limits of this, and other ecocentric perspectives. Significantly, Ellmann puts her inquiry in the context of modern human history, and specifically in the context of a question that has haunted post-war literature and criticism: how can one justify imaginative writing after Auschwitz; or, more exactly, how can aesthetic or literary effects be brought out of that shadow of triviality cast by the Holocaust?[18]

The book sidesteps this issue in the event, and through the significant process of undertaking a more generalized deliberation on inhumanity and cruelty, as set against a celebration of nature. In a sense, Ellmann's purpose is to conjoin all our holocausts, thus making human failing irrefutable and unanswerable. Yet the novel also delights in a contradictory shuttling between its general philosophical concerns, and the particular theme of gender relations. Part One of the novel concludes with the deliberations of a female creative writing student on the issue of 'MANGO *vs.* MAN'. Here mangoes are deemed preferable to men because of such qualities as not monopolizing the conversation at dinner, or obliging one to wear lipstick and high heels in order to spend an evening with them (p. 129). Man, of course, *means* man in this comparison, which humorously undercuts the novel's broader philosophical pretensions and hones in on the question of sexual politics.

In its more serious application, Ellmann's style serves to underscore the importance of context to human understanding. A case in point is the poignant use of list-making, so that, for example, the meagre list of possessions in a Donegal parish in 1845 (recorded as the Irish famine is about to strike) offers a telling counterpoint to the list of valuables handed over to the Nazis in 1943 (pp. 12, 147). Yet Ellmann's use of collage, of which the deployment of lists is one aspect, can displace the human, and take the significance of her novel, and the generation of meaning, away from her various narrators' control. By combining different narrative elements she is able to switch perspective with great fluidity. Towards the end of the book there are sections narrated from the perspective of the Earth, which thus assumes the role of a character. This is a felicitous consequence of Ellmann's method: in a novel haunted by the prospect of environmental degradation, the fluidity of the narrative perspective mitigates the (inevitable) human-centredness of narrative fiction, and gestures towards something ecocentric.

Ultimately, of course, 'voicing' the Earth is not a fully realizable project. Ellmann is content to unsettle the anthropocentrism that usually dominates the processes of novel reading, and to create a consciously unstable mode of collage that generates her free-floating tragicomic effects. The novel engages fully with the inevitability of contradiction in human affairs, and forges a form appropriate to this task. Particular disapproval is directed against human control or cruelty, yet Ellmann, in an exaggerated gesture of authorial control, chooses to kill off her central character in an extravagant natural disaster. (This is also an external manifestation of that character's desires, since she wishes the world to end at the moment of her greatest happiness.) This illustrates the anthropomorphic double-bind: the dismissive manner in which the love interest is concluded makes it seem more trivial than the environmental issue; but it takes an extreme gesture of authorial control to make the point. By allowing Eloïse to conjure up a natural disaster in accordance with her wishes, Ellmann saves the novel from a trite resolution (p. 219).

Yet this crucial turning point in the plot also enacts that which is seen as the worst human failing: to dream of apocalypse. The form of the novel as a whole insists on this kind of contradiction between the claims of the environment and human desires. In a sense, Ellmann's work of collage is a qualified celebration, and one that enshrines the unavoidable principle that a degree of anthropocentrism underpins all that we do, and that there will be both discomfort and enjoyment in uncovering the contradictions that follow from this.

## The Country in the City

The proper process of re-evaluating the pastoral mode ought to be underpinned by a recognition of the economic and social interdependence of the urban and the rural – that interconnection of the country and the city that some versions of pastoral are apt to obscure. This interdependence is the focus of Raymond Williams's masterpiece of ecocriticism *The Country and the City* for example.[19] However, post-war Britain has experienced some rapid changes in the designation and articulation of space, so that stable definitions of the urban and the rural have become impossible. The interaction of the two then becomes intensely problematic. To choose a representative conundrum, one might question whether or not a farmer who turns land over for use as a golf course is still engaged in the rural economy.

Our understanding of the countryside is also affected by the dramatic spread of suburbia, most acutely when we revisit the fields of our youth to discover housing estates built over them. The competing, and often contradictory projections of human need involved in the new designations of place have made the post-pastoral an increasingly complex mode. Concerns about the rural, in fact, are apt to surface in novels ostensibly treating urban themes. A particular development of the post-pastoral, then, is the attempt to situate rural fantasies (or nightmares) in the context of city experience; and often, this imaginative resiting of the rural speaks directly to a mood of millennial uncertainty.

Jim Crace's *Arcadia* (1992) is unusual in that it attempts to reinscribe pastoral images and moods within an *idealized* cityscape. Crace's novel discovers the dystopia within the urban utopia, but also conveys the appeal of city life, its vibrancy and poetry, in such a way as to suggest that the celebration of the city is the new pastoral. It is this design that explains the style of a book that is otherwise difficult to classify: the vagueness of the setting suggests an allegorical or fabulistic impulse, and there are, indeed, moments that aspire to modern fables of the city. But this city, although portrayed in shorthand, with a simplified perception of the economic ties between the rural and the urban, is meant to be a representative late twentieth-century city, transforming itself into a postmodern space of glass and steel, detaching itself from the memories of a simpler existence held by the oldest inhabitants.

Those memories, however, may be false, a point encapsulated in the urban planning sponsored by Victor, wealthy patriarch of the city's fruit market, who at the age of eighty decides on an extravagant project of urban regeneration that will see the traditional fruit market, the nexus of country and city, incorporated within a domed mall with a controlled environment to sustain tropical birds and plants. This commercial absorption of the natural, which is realized in the book's final section, is called 'Arcadia', a projected 'rustic paradise', as well as a shopping arcade (p. 218). Arcadia denotes, of course, the ideal object of original pastoral; and Crace's awareness that this was always a cultural construction is implied in his narrative of a newly built urban Arcadia.

The ambivalence of the name emphasizes the continuing interdependence of country and city, but also implies a new phase, a failure of disconnection. The uncertainty has its source in Victor's personal confusion. He is originally brought to the town from the country by his penniless mother, who has been reduced to begging. Victor is thus confirmed as 'a townie almost through and through' (p. 75), taught to survive by selling produce, an opportunity bestowed by the town, in contrast to the harshness of the country from which his mother is forced to flee (p. 76). Despite this background, Victor has developed a hankering for the rural, and has created for himself a haven at the top of his twenty-seven-storey building with a rooftop greenhouse. Victor's false pastoral is pervasive: the lights in his skyscraper 'Big Vic' form the shape of a fir tree at night (p. 69); its atrium contains plastic foliage (p. 45); and his own rustic fantasy is compared to 'a theme park marketed as Rural Bliss' (p. 122).

Victor's entrepreneurial ambitions are also encapsulated in false organic metaphors. For example, he compares the fruit market to a plant, needing to grow and flourish in the manner that his Arcadia project will allow (p. 255). This conviction is merely vacuous, concealing the real economic relations. A provoked riot, interpreted as a protest at Arcadia, unleashes an elite police unit, illustrating the propensity of the city to suppress dissent (p. 293). The alliance of fiscal interest and the physical control of space characterizes the realized Arcadia too, which, like all malls, maintains 'policed doors' in 'its creed of Safety from the Streets' (p. 343).

Yet, in spite of the negative associations of Victor's false pastoral, the novel also embodies a qualified celebration of the city market, and the benediction latent within it. Much of this is implied in the sense of possibility bound up with the city, and the commendation of its variety and interest, a mood exemplified in the local images of market produce: 'no gallery of modern art could match the colours there, the tones, the shapes, the harmonies and conflicts on the stalls' (p. 17). The market, in short, is the locus of the city's culture.

In giving shape to this opened possibility, Crace echoes Lawrence's *The Rainbow*, which ends with the extravagant symbol of the rainbow as a hopeful sign of social renewal. The rainbow that appears at the end of *Arcadia* is more muted. It appears to connect 'the old town and the new', but the symbol is discarded as an effect of light, not an omen. Even so, the rainbow is accepted as a sign of passing rain, an indication 'that it is safe to walk onto the streets again' (p. 345). By reuniting the narrator with the streets, 'the blessing of the multitude' (p. 345), the rainbow does indeed serve its symbolic function of directing us to urban renewal, and the human possibility of a city that retains its pastoral symbolism.

The narrator supplies the bite to this paradoxical lyricism, too fuzzy, perhaps, for the clarity of conventional allegory. Such a mode is denied, in effect, by the function of the narrator, a journalist who formerly wrote a byline as 'The Burgher', and who is revealed as having been retained to write Victor's life (p. 330). This detail of verisimilitude partially justifies the narrator's omniscience, and establishes a realistic frame of sorts for this ambiguous city-pastoral. The novel's effects are concentrated in the image of Victor's mother as a beggar suckling the infant Victor in a show of poverty, an image celebrated in the bronze statue outside Arcadia (pp. 88, 339–40). The representation of 'Motherhood' (p. 88) records the interaction of country and city, the poverty that urban demands inflict on rural life, as well as the magnetic pull of opportunity that the city exerts. But, rather than simply illustrating an enduring human essence tested by economic hardship, the image also recalls the drama of the original begging episode, where breast-feeding becomes a performance, intended as either 'respectable' (p. 88) or titillating (by Victor's aunt) (p. 113), depending on which is the more lucrative. The image is both solemn and opportunistic, suggesting the balance of dignity and survival that the city demands.

*Arcadia* is a remarkable post-war novel in its simultaneous critique and celebration of the country in the city, the urbanization of a rural image. More common, however, is the evocation of ecological crisis, and the destruction of the country by the city. This sense of desecration, of building over, is conveyed in the title of Amis's *London Fields* (1989). Here Amis captures the *zeitgeist*, a mood of millennial *Angst* that is bound up with the novel's arresting metafictional gestures. Amis's vision comprises an apocalyptic association of ecological disaster, nuclear devastation, and social malaise. The anticipated moment of apocalypse, at the end of the millennium, is figured as simultaneously an astronomical and a human-authored event: at the time of a total eclipse of the sun over London, two nuclear explosions are rumoured to be planned, one over London, the other over Warsaw (p. 394). Reports of unusual or devastating meteorological phenomena punctuate the narrative, which projects the weather as 'superatmospheric' or 'supermeteorological' in raising the question of whether or not it can still be called 'weather' (p. 14).

This subtext is crucial to the book's style and its metafictional implications, because Amis's formal games, like the weather, stress the element of artificiality, but without detaching the book from its social and historical anchor. The 'end of weather' is a telling analogy for the writer's experiment since the more 'unnatural' the weather becomes, the more it forces us to confront the Real, the material fact of human frailty. Amis makes studied use of this analogy to lend *gravitas* to his implicit deliberations on the role of the narrator, and the moral function of fiction.

Samson Young comes to London on an apartment swap with the English writer Mark Asprey, whose initials (MA) signal Amis's background presence, and his use of Young as a proxy narrator. As he does in *Money* (1984), Amis is acknowledging the limits of omniscience, and the fragility of the contract between reader and author. To justify the narrator's insights, much is made of his involvement as a character in the action, with privileged access to the other characters' lives, even though this is actually gestural, since his point of view approximates old-style omniscience. Indeed, he becomes instrumental in 'composing' the story, despite his claims to being a passive recorder of reality (pp. 3, 39). Amis flags up his technical compromise, announcing it as a make-do solution. Young is ultimately dispensable: he is dying from a mysterious disease apparently contracted at the time his father was working on 'High Explosives Research' (p. 161).

The novel is driven by the search of Nicola Six, the 'murderee', for her murderer, in an echo of Muriel Spark's *The Driver's Seat* (1970). When, unexpectedly, the murderer turns out to be Young himself, perhaps set up by Mark Asprey/Martin Amis (p. 468), his functional role is clearly foregrounded. Having killed Nicola, Young takes a suicide pill (p. 466), and this death of the narrator is part of an elaborate procedure that preserves the function of the novel (and the novelist, whose controlling hand is made apparent) whilst also implying that their respective 'deaths' may have been deferred, merely.

The depiction of Nicola Six, who self-consciously cultivates her role as a 'male fantasy figure' (p. 260), seems wilfully to court the accusations of misogyny that were duly levelled at Amis. However, the intention is clearly to make the character 'a symbol of her age rather than a sign of her gender', and, again, it is the ecological theme that supplies the broader context.[20] Nicola's murder is scheduled to take place on her thirty-fifth birthday (p. 18), the day after the predicted apocalypse, so that when the world crisis is averted and the murder can take place, this becomes the true apocalypse. In this, the death-wish of Nicola Six is absorbed into the ecological theme, and, by virtue of the correspondence, becomes redolent of ecocide. Amis is here extravagantly subverting 'mother earth' imagery to stress his satirical point. Nicola's status as male fantasy figure is thus indicative that the planet is in terminal decline, since the destructive subversion and manipulation of woman/planet is identified as the disastrous impulse of self-destruction.

To be sure, Amis's novel partakes of the seedy and amoral universe it describes; but this collapse of distance is part of Amis's satirical purpose, a demonstration of his apocalyptic theme. The loss of vantage point stresses the difficulty of reading the present, and the sense of living 'inside history . . . on its leading edge, with the wind ripping past our ears' (p. 197). In this sense, the crisis for Amis's exaggerated characters/caricatures is shared by the author. Keith Talent signifies a world alienated from itself by the power of representation. For him, sex on video supplants the real thing, whilst his appreciation of a soccer match is complicated by the clichés of sports reporting, a discourse that conditions what he is able to see (p. 98). But Amis also acknowledges, implicitly, his own crisis of representation, the difficulty of finding a credible post-pastoral discourse. Frederick Holmes, for instance, detects at one point a 'close parody' of the opening of Lawrence's *The Rainbow*, in which the lives of the Brangwen men are absorbed by the rhythms of nature. In Amis's subversion of this, the pulsing rhythms describe the sordid and exploitative city adventures of Keith Talent (p. 114).[21]

The example demonstrates an arresting collapse of the pastoral ideal, and the difficulty of establishing any kind of normative purchase, since the parody seems to ridicule Lawrence as well as Talent.

## Trouble in Suburbia

Without question suburbia is the most difficult social space to describe adequately. The cliché that everyone comes from suburbia, and no one wants to go back, reveals one of the most telling quandaries of post-war social life, in the collective denial of common origins.[22] The problem is ideological: 'suburbia is a dirty word' writes Arthur Edwards, at the outset of his environmental history; and it is true that, for many people, the adjective 'suburban' defines a state of mind characterized by narrow middle-class aspirations.[23] This is a legacy of the rise of the Victorian suburb, where rapid speculative development often swamped the aristocratic pretensions of the new bourgeoisie.[24] Perceived as embodying a world-view, the 'suburban state of mind' can be ridiculed, consigned to the intellectual margins, just as its actual physical space notionally occupies the urban margins. In the popular imagination, then, suburbia is Middle England; it is preoccupied with shopping and cars; it breeds narrow attitudes, and wears naff styles; and it is mystified by artistic endeavour.

If the attitudes associated with suburbia are familiar, its actual geographical location is hard to pin down. The reason, of course, is that suburbia constantly relocates itself. Each wave of development corresponds to particular social aspirations, and may be dismissed (unreasonably) by those whose ambitions have already been fulfilled, and whose personal 'suburbia' has, perhaps, evolved into something more chic.

Novelists have played their part in establishing suburbia as an object of ridicule. In the provincial novel of the 1950s and 1960s suburbia figures as the index of a deadening culture that threatens to absorb more vital energies. This is true of Stan Barstow's *A Kind of Loving* (1960) and Alan Sillitoe's *Saturday Night and Sunday Morning* (1958), for example, even though Sillitoe's Arthur Seaton and Barstow's Vic Brown both collude, in different ways, with the emerging culture they would reject, through their pursuit of self-interest. 'The Movement' of the 1950s, ostensibly rooted in a challenge to the metropolitan centre of cultural authority, propagated a similar contradiction. The Movement novelists, Kingsley Amis and John Wain, seem to have set the tone for the undermining of provincial culture, since the protagonists of *Lucky Jim* (1954) and *Hurry on Down* (1953) are lauded for their distrust of London types, yet are both finally rewarded with jobs in London.

Such contradictions, and the general centripetal pull of post-war literary fashion, suggest that something is missing in the analysis, which betrays a failure to recognize the sociological importance of suburbia. This is troubling, given the rapid development of suburbia as a constant fact of recent human geography, and the tendency of commentators to assign it a central place in the explanation of twentieth-century experience.[25] Yet a more exacting description of suburbia is hard to establish. In trying to get beyond the perception of suburbia as a dirty word, Arthur Edwards establishes a broad definition that embraces the 'new build' of 'an estate-developer', whether city council, new-town corporation, builder, or farmer.[26] However, a sense of the difficulties of definition can be gleaned when this catch-all understanding is compared with David Harvey's remark about urban planning in post-war Britain: strict legislation was adopted, he suggests, the effect of which 'was to restrict suburbanization and to substitute planned new-town development or high-density infilling or renewal in its stead'.[27] 'Suburbanization' is here used to denote unchecked development on the peripheries of existing towns and cities, a trend that stands in *opposition*, not just to urban renewal, but also to the planning of New Towns. As they turned out, of course, British New Towns proved to be definitively suburban for the post-war era, comprising residential zones for car owners, loosely connected by new road systems, an aggregation with a focal point in the shopping centre. Milton Keynes is the prime example, a place that 'even at its core . . . remains stubbornly suburban'.[28]

This suggests a more satisfactory definition, in the realization that suburbia has come to represent the intersection of the domestic and the commercial. This is a crucial nexus, especially at the end of the century: 'the suburbs are where the people are, and the money is,' writes Paul Barker, in arguing that 'the mall is a magnet for development in the same way that cotton mills or docks once were'.[29] This locates the central difficulty in any new development, the problem of balancing those human and financial interests that may be in conflict. In theory, this ought to involve the resistance of external commercial concerns, whilst some conception of a living community is consolidated. Raymond Williams's novel *The Fight for Manod* (1979), concerning a planned new city in mid-Wales, is conceived as a dramatization of this complex dilemma. In its idealistic conception, the Manod development is an example of the post-war planning described by Harvey. Initially posited in the early 1960s, Manod represents an alternative to suburban infill and stands in contradistinction to the 'great sprawling and jammed conurbations' in which 'life is simply breaking down' (p. 12). Beyond this, Manod (which remains unbuilt) is extraordinarily ambitious, designed as a 'dispersed' city of 'hill towns', each divided by several miles of open farmland. A utopian future is glimpsed, where the investment will be social, rather than economic, for this, 'one of the first human settlements' conceived in 'post-industrial terms' (pp. 13, 77).

The green hue of Williams's ordinary culture also locates an *urban* ideal, and one that stands in opposition to actual post-war development. However, the novel finally suggests that a realized Manod would *conform* to this post-war experience, where fiscal questions crowd out the idealism, generating a principle of development that is less magisterial, more recognizably suburban. The local speculator John Dance has a narrow, opportunistic vision of 'modern houses' built 'six or eight to the acre' in 'one or two standard designs' (p. 122). Dance is skilled at producing personal inducements that tie the locals into his scheme. Significantly, he is also an agent for more than one international oil company. (He secures franchises for the conversion of wayside petrol stations [p. 113].) As the agent of external commercial interests, Dance seems set to preside over the devaluation of the Manod project, and the supplanting of genuine community-centred needs.

An earlier treatment of the New Town theme, by a writer usually deemed to be more closely wedded to the goals of realism, represents a rather different test of the novel's capacities. Angus Wilson's *Late Call* (1964) offers a satirical portrait of life in Carshall, a New Town in the Midlands, exposing the contradictions and inadequacies of the New Town philosophy. Sylvia Calvert and her deceitful, sponging husband come to live with their recently widowed son Harold and his family. The novel clinically undermines the 'social experiment' of Carshall (p. 120), particularly through the gradual collapse of Harold, a local headmaster, and Carshall's most stalwart proponent. An ideal of classlessness lies behind this advocacy, as he explains to his mother: 'Carshall must develop its own mixed society – status wise, I mean, nothing to do with class – or it must die of atrophy.' (p. 135) Harold's is a 'ranch-type house', one of those 'built to try to persuade our industrial executives to stay in the community' (p. 66). The point, of course, is that a community cannot be instantly produced, and especially not by seeking both to blur and sustain 'status' differentials. Neither, it seems, can inherited perceptions of class be expelled from the utopia: Harold's daughter Judy, much to his chagrin, is enchanted by the county set. Other social pressures and prejudices intrude. Harold's elder son, the homosexual Ray, feels himself to be hounded out by the scandal that drives his friend Wilf Corney to suicide. (Cosmopolitan London supplies the tolerance he finds lacking in the new suburbia [p. 287].) Only Mark, the younger son, is likely to make a life (in industry) in the New Town; but this is presented as a betrayal of his political ideals – a self-sacrificing response to his father's breakdown – and as a hollow parody of the embittered ambition of John Braine's Joe Lampton (p. 290).

The crucial episode, in the implicit debate about cultural forms, is Harold's production of *Look Back in Anger*, where Wilson makes a wry point about the limitations of the 'Anger' generation. At the same time, however (as with the allusion to John Braine), Wilson seems fascinated by the propensity of Carshall to nullify once challenging social texts, and reduce them, overnight, to clichéd period pieces. For Harold, Osborne's play is an attack on 'the sort of old-fashioned . . . Midland town that the New Towns are going to replace'. The production is thus self-congratulatory, utilitarian, and tendentious (p. 125).

Sylvia's untutored response to the play, however, is far more sensitive to the ambivalent anger of Jimmy Porter (portrayed by grandson Ray). This residual sensitivity is significant since Sylvia's identity in Carshall is swamped by the popular novels and 'tele' serials that fill her days. Margaret Drabble has astutely observed that the novel's 'subject matter is positively banal', and that 'the whole thing is like a parody of the soap operas to which Sylvia herself is addicted'.[30] This parodic impulse is manifest in the novel's conclusion. Following a breakdown, Sylvia is redeemed (in a rather false sequence) when she is shocked out of her self-absorption by the need to save a child in a lightning storm. This avowedly fictional solution nods at the easy resolution of popular narrative forms. But it is also an episode that confirms Sylvia's intrinsic antipathy to Carshall: her good work is chanced upon, whereas the Carshallites' acts of social conscience are a studied compensation for their narrow materialism. Even so, the 'redemptive' ending implies a stable kind of 'social manners' novel that is not there to be found, and this is what makes the novel challenging. Sylvia does not embody a set of values; rather, after her residual resistance is overcome, she is thrown a lifeline that is to haul her off the sinking ship, and effect her escape. (She has plans to move to 'somewhere near' the more human town centre [p. 303].) A vision of nullity is glimpsed at the heart of the New Town ideal, and Wilson, refusing to offset this analysis, chooses to mimic its effects.

The ability of suburbia to absorb and distort earnest literary projects has far-reaching implications for the suburban novelist. In making this capacity a theme, Wilson highlights the problem of purchase that *Late Call* is unable to solve, since it is partly colonized by the popular forms it seeks to parody. For the more overtly comic writer, this lack of purchase can be a source of humour in itself, where the pretensions of the suburbanite may be matched by the pretensions of the writer. In *The Wimbledon Poisoner* (1990), for example, Nigel Williams makes the ostentatious appreciation of literature part of the suburban identity he seeks to satirize, notably through 'poisoner' Henry Farr's attitude to his wife Elinor's friends, who sometimes sit in his front room, pontificating about foreign films and the situation in Nicaragua, or 'reading aloud from the work of a man called Ian McEwan, an author who, according to Elinor, had "a great deal to say" to Henry Farr' (pp. 6–7). Farr's unvoiced retort is that he 'had a great deal to say to Ian McEwan as well' (p. 7), an assertion of an undeveloped independence in the face of a nullifying conformity.

McEwan, of course, is noted for the revelation of psychological and emotional disturbances beneath an ordered social veneer, a challenge here rendered meaningless. In its place Williams produces a comic send-up of suburban mores that, in the final analysis, seems built on shifting ground. Would-be poisoner Henry Farr is the focusing eye for the novel's satirical portrait of Wimbledon types, such as 'Unpublished Magic Realist', and 'Jungian Analyst with Winebox', so that his focalization generates the humour. Finally, however, he is the principal butt, staunchest proponent of this, 'the most important suburb in the Western world', of which he is writing the 'Complete History' (pp. 55–6). The murderous hatred he hatches for his wife is the product of his own mid-life crisis and suburban malaise, a misogynistic 'phase' that jars with the appreciation Elinor elicits from everyone else. The reconciliation of Henry and Elinor, and the discovery that he is not the true poisoner, allows this comedy of suburban recognition to find some kind of balance. However, Farr has *intended* to commit murder, to destroy the cosy world he also documents and celebrates, and that defines him. In this sense the novel reveals its brutal subtext, the comedy, if comedy it is, of self-hatred and of a poisoned mind.

The philistinism of Henry Farr seems to underscore the antipathy between suburbia and socially coherent fiction, an antipathy that in *The Wimbledon Poisoner* results in the disruption of the writer's objective. Julian Barnes discovers a related impasse, albeit in richer terms, in *Metroland* (1980), where suburbia is articulated as the pressure to conformity felt, and resisted, by two intelligent schoolboys, narrator Christopher and his friend Toni. This sense of resistance stems from a familiar adolescent precocity, but is defined as the assertion of aesthetic sensibility, as in Christopher's condemnation of the orange sodium lighting that turns everything brown or orange in London's Metroland. 'They even fug up the spectrum', he complains, glossing 'they' as 'the unidentified legislators, moralists, social luminaries and parents of outer suburbia' (p. 14).

In an echo of Wilson, Barnes has Christopher worry about studying Osborne at school, and about the apparent institutionalization of 'the Anger generation' with which the two friends identify (p. 41). He also has them engage in a conversation about how parents 'fug you up', which paraphrases the first stanza of Philip Larkin's famous poem on this theme, 'This Be The Verse' (p. 39). This is a revealing moment, which is not the knowing ironic exchange of literary banter between schoolboys it appears to be. This section of the novel predates the Larkin poem in fact (1963 against 1971), so, assuming this is not a simple oversight, Barnes offers the allusion for the reader's recognition, implying that Larkin's observation is a truism that his characters can arrive at themselves, asserting a spark of creative independence.[31]

Yet, in the final section (set in 1977) Christopher, at the age of thirty, has been incorporated into Metroland: he is married with a child, a mortgage, and a good job in publishing. When inserted into this scene of domestic harmony, Toni is brash and resentful of his friend's capitulation. Toni has pursued a career as a minor writer, and has published a monograph on how all 'important books' are misinterpreted when they first appear (p. 170). Now more politically aware, Toni appears driven to understand why that vital art–life synthesis seems unattainable. Christopher, by contrast, has plans for a 'social history of travel around London', a project he conceals from Toni, and that he seems willing to advance by utilizing the 'Old Boy' network (p. 153). The final scene shows Christopher at home, unable to sleep, reflecting 'to no particular end' on how the orange light from the street turns all his pyjamas brown (p. 176). The reader recognizes that he has, indeed, become one of 'them', but this sense of a sell-out is mitigated by the air of calm and contentment that now pervades the narrative, a mood reflected in Christopher's outwardly calm acceptance of the news of his wife's past infidelity (p. 163). The novel thus ends with a simple choice between the embittered idealistic commitment to the literary life, and the suburban conformity that suffuses the final pages, like the streetlamps of Metroland itself. The major theme of *Metroland* – the impasse that suburbia represents for the writer – typifies the post-war perspective.

My examples thus far reproduce the familiar stereotype of post-war suburbia to a greater or lesser degree: the conviction that suburban life is deadening, unimaginative, representative of a low or restricted common denominator. There are two issues that are concealed in this dominant impression. First, the fact that there is actually something unplanned in the configuration of suburban living, unpredictable consequences of even the most rigorous (or cynical) social planning. The second concealment stems from the common experience of suburbia. A mode of living shared by so many people can surely only be seen as trivial if social life is trivial in general. And can such a common mode of living really be homogeneous to the core? Perhaps a more diverse culture is to be found beneath the surface uniformity. These two factors are necessarily linked since the centrality of suburbia hinges on the paradoxes and contradictions it generates and sustains. These are the fissures that make suburban life exemplary of contemporary experience, and make it more surprising than it appears.

Of course, the excavation of the truth beneath the surface is a familiar process in many representations of suburbia, a process that usually involves peeling away the veneer of civilized respectability to uncover the turmoil of repression or violence seething beneath. (In outline, the method is common to practitioners as diverse as David Lynch and Henrik Ibsen.) In post-war British fiction there have been some notable examples of this engagement with ideological contradiction, though the treatment has often been uncertain. One noteworthy book that utilizes the 'probing' method is Simon Mason's *Lives of the Dog-Stranglers* (1998), a book that is interesting because the discovered fragmentation of suburban lives becomes itself a structural principle. The inhabitants of Parkside, a Victorian suburb of a southern English city, are Mason's protagonists, whose disconnected and alienated lives are described in a short-story cycle. The chosen structure facilitates the use of a variety of voices, but this is done in such a way as to stress the isolation of self-absorbed individuals who fail to connect.

If Mason's book is formally interesting, then, it is no less bleak than the other works considered here. The exposed contradictions are unproductive since they corroborate the point of view of the horrified observer, revealing the fantastic freak-show embedded in the mundane. What kind of stance, then, might produce a more forgiving or insightful view of suburbia? Is it possible to inhabit this space genuinely and imaginatively, to live and write its contradictions whilst holding off the compelling motif of imprisonment, whether literal or psychological?

## Embracing the Suburban Experience

In a ground-clearing essay, Stefan Collini hints at such a stance. His aim is to define the historical perspective that would produce 'a story . . . "relevant" to the experience of living in contemporary Britain'.[32] He draws an implicit comparison between his own position and that of the eminent historian G. M. Trevelyan (1876–1962), best known for his *English Social History* (1944). Trevelyan's influence, suggests Collini, 'nourished and depended upon the widespread nostalgia' prevalent in Britain since the First World War. This dual relationship to nostalgia indicates a lack of historical responsiveness that leads Collini to summarize his writing in these terms: 'English history as told by Trevelyan was rather like a tour of a beautiful country house conducted by one of the last surviving members of the family.' Wallington Hall, the Trevelyan family home (a Northumbrian mansion, now owned by the National Trust) consequently seems an appropriate touchstone. Collini contrasts Wallington Hall with his own childhood home, a 'graceless 1950s bungalow on the edge of the Shirley Hills beyond Croydon'. This other location is much more representative, indicative of 'the second wave of suburban expansion, fed by car-ownership rather than the railway'. This suburbia expressed 'values of individualism, privacy, and ruralist nostalgia', a nostalgia partly inspired by writers like Trevelyan, as Collini wryly observes.[33]

Collini's purpose in making this 'symbolic contrast between the North-umbrian mansion and the suburban bungalow' is to suggest that the perspective available from the latter is less disabling than that afforded by the former. The historian from the suburbs, suspicious of the 'epic sweep' of a Trevelyan, has acquired a distancing self-consciousness that should make him or her alert to 'the contingency of so much that a well-connected Victorian gentleman took to be natural'. This new social historian, Collini implies, is 'formed by modern British culture', and is aware that 'there can be no one authoritative narrative of the national past'.[34] Collini's vantage point is meant to imply a position of self-effacing cultural authority, in which the overturning of traditional hierarchies is a cornerstone of the ethical point of view. It is the position from which a culture in transition can be best understood. In the post-war era, the novel that perhaps comes closest to enacting this stance of recentred authority is Hanif Kureishi's *The Buddha of Suburbia* (1990).

Ostensibly Kureishi's book is so structured as to stage a flight from suburbia. The personal development of protagonist and narrator Karim Amir is predicated on his progression from the suburbs of south London to the metropolitan centre. (He has formative experiences in New York as well as London.) In this dynamic of growth and advancement some of the familiar stereotypes of the suburban mind-set are evoked: the passive enjoyment of popular television programmes; the 'fanatical' approach to shopping; the passion for DIY; a philistine response to the arts. Karim's father Haroon, the Buddha of the novel's title, exposes the spiritual emptiness of the sub-urbanites on several occasions, as when he ridicules alcoholic Auntie Jean's insistence that her guests remove their shoes before walking on her carpet: 'What is this, Jean, a Hindu temple?' he asks, 'is it the shoeless meeting the legless?' (p. 41).

Karim's career might seem to demonstrate the need for the ambitious individual to exorcise the suburbanite from his or her soul. Part one of the novel, 'In the Suburbs', stresses the essential boredom of suburbia for young people, and the overwhelming desire to escape. 'Our suburbs were a leaving place, the start of a life', remarks the narrator as part one draws to a close, and life in the city is anticipated (p. 117). For Haroon and Eva also, self-realization seems to depend on this kind of repudiation.

There is, however, an undercurrent that runs counter to the theme of escape, and that implies the need for suburban roots to be recognized. For Karim there is no explicit repudiation *or* easy celebration of his inherited suburban outlook; rather, there is a calm interrogation of its value. It is worth remarking that the observations about suburbia continue throughout part two, 'In the City', so that the model of progression or rejection implied in the overall structure is subtly undermined by the narrator's continuing preoccupation with things suburban.

An important reflection occurs when Karim is in rehearsal with Pyke's theatre group, and his relationship with Eleanor is burgeoning. Feeling himself inferior, he defers to her 'sophisticated ideas' and her language which was 'the currency that bought you the best of what the world could offer'. Acknowledging the necessity of leaving his world, he resolves to lose his accent, to imitate Eleanor, even though he understands that for him, hers 'could only ever be a second language, consciously acquired'. Importantly, Eleanor is another character that Karim will grow beyond; but at this point, he ruminates ruefully on the nature of his own adventures, his own background: 'where I could have been telling Eleanor about the time I got fucked by Hairy Back's Great Dane, it was her stories that had primacy, her stories that connected to an entire established world' (p. 178). This is a crucial moment of self-reflexiveness that invites the reader's objection. For the memory that Karim denigrates – the episode in which Helen's racist father ('Hairy Back') tries to see Karim off his premises – is entirely representative of the novel's pointed comedy. Karim exposes Hairy Back's prejudice with innocent questions, whilst the intimidating dog proves amorous rather than aggressive (pp. 40–1). If this is the stuff of multicultural suburban identity, it is also the stuff of the narrative itself. Karim, besotted with Eleanor, acquires a false set of priorities, priorities that are opposed by the novel's own narrative procedures.

In this connection it may be significant that the most arresting episode of Eleanor's life is a story she finds too painful to tell, the story of her black boyfriend Gene, driven to suicide by the prejudice that blighted his acting career and his life (p. 201). But this is not 'her' story to tell. The purpose it serves is to locate the extreme effect of an ingrained racism that is directly challenged by the novel's own narrative energy. At the point where Karim decides to make a break with Eleanor, Gene's story, significantly, becomes part of his own:

> Sweet Gene, her black lover, London's best mime, who emptied bed-pans in hospital soaps, killed himself because every day, by a look, a remark, an attitude, the English told him they hated him; they never let him forget they thought him a nigger, a slave, a lower being. And we pursued English roses as we pursued England; by possessing these prizes, this kindness and beauty, we stared defiantly into the eye of the Empire and all its self-regard – into the eye of Hairy Back, into the eye of the Great Fucking Dane. We became part of England and yet proudly stood outside it.
> (p. 227)

Here the narrator explains how the novel should be read. The post-imperial challenge to Englishness, we are told, is both defiance and appropriation, an apposite formulation for the transitional nature of English postcolonial identity. The defining moments of Karim's formative years – exemplified by the episode with Hairy Back and the Great Dane – are explicitly shown to have this serious purport. These adventures in suburbia are the flipside of Gene's capitulation to the prejudice that poisoned his existence and eroded his sense of self; they are adventures, the narrator is telling us, that might have a place in that new construction of Englishness that is the novel's main concern. The kind of 'hybridity' personified by Karim Amir, born of an Indian father and an English mother, is thus a quality that has to be struggled for. This is, of course, unreasonable since it should be taken as a given, a fact of his situation.

Karim's quest for identity is also reflected in the novel's form. Steven Connor suggests that *Buddha* 'simultaneously summons and rebuffs the *Bildungsroman* with its typical equations between self and society'. For Connor there is also a tendency to 'signal and decline' an allegiance to 'the novel of class mobility and sexual discovery' as exemplified in writers such as Braine, Sillitoe, and Drabble. Such ambivalence produces a contradictory work, in Connor's reading, with Kureishi unable 'to resist the effects of typification' in the presentation of 'Indian Britons'. The problem of 'how to celebrate hybridity without regularizing it as a form' remains unresolved.[35]

It is possible to view these problems in a more positive light, however, especially if one reads the novel as an 'initiation' story tracing the first steps of an adolescent protagonist towards maturity. Rather than establishing an uneasy, semi-parodic relationship with the *Bildungsroman*, the book can be seen adequately to have delivered an initiation story with more limited goals, and goals more suitable to its essentially transitional world-view. Kureishi's ambivalent affinity with that roll-call of English novelists thus needs to be refocused. The treatment of class mobility in (especially) Braine and Sillitoe is fraught with contradiction, so Kureishi seems actually to have updated the difficulties the post-war novel has had in this area, and with a more purposive exploitation of that distinctive ambivalence.

It is the English comic novel, however, with which Kureishi has the greatest affinity, and this is something that he has acknowledged himself. In interview, he has given this account of his literary heritage: 'Looking back on the novel – though I might not like to admit it – I was influenced more by books like *Lucky Jim* and early Evelyn Waugh than I was by *On the Road*. You know funny books about boys growing up and getting into scrapes.'[36] The male initiation narrative, in a mode of comic realism, supplies the primary inspiration for the creation of Karim Amir, and in this light the worry about the restrictive effects of typification seems misplaced. Kureishi, in any case, alerts his readers to the danger of seeking to perceive a 'type' in the reception of a character: the censorship of Karim's portrayal of Anwar, whilst in rehearsal with Pyke, makes this point very effectively (pp. 180–1). There is also a convention in comic novels of this kind that the central protagonist is the richest and most fully (sometimes the only) developed character.

Yet despite the common ground between *Buddha* and a comic novel like *Lucky Jim*, one needs to take cognizance of the huge advance in this genre that Kureishi's novel represents. Where Jim Dixon's farcical predicaments are partly self-authored, Karim Amir's years of maturation are fashioned, unequivocally, by broader cultural forces; and where Dixon, the progenitor of the post-war provincial hero, happily turns his back on the provinces and heads for London, Amir's metropolitan experiences stage an enriching conflict between urban and suburban influences. When he lands the part of the 'rebellious student son of an Indian shopkeeper' in a new television soap opera intended to 'tangle with the latest contemporary issues' we see Kureishi's topical and formal concerns converge. Amir begins to succeed in the profession that had excluded the talented Gene; and in incorporating this 'new breed' of Englishman (p. 3), popular suburban culture (which is epitomized in the soap opera) is seen to adapt itself, to engage with issues of ethnicity and opportunity.

Kureishi, of course, has performed the same task for the English comic novel. Where Dixon's personal success, his luck, is fortuitous, unmotivated, the story of Karim Amir works resolutely through its attendant social and cultural forces, its productive contradictions. The new type of character that emerges is a fresh serio-comic figure, the embodiment of suburban multicultural identity. As a figure of enlightened literary revisionism, and as a character becoming in tune with his state of social being, it is Karim, and not his father, who emerges as the true Buddha of suburbia.

## Chapter 7

# Beyond 2000

In anticipating the topics that might preoccupy novelists and critics in the twenty-first century, it is helpful to reflect briefly on the half-century leading up to the millennium. If the novel is buoyant in 2000, this was by no means the case at the beginning of the period. In the late 1940s the novel in Britain was widely held to be in a state of crisis, principally because the evolving post-war society began to divest itself of its erstwhile principles of cohesion. The self-proclaimed values of the British at war – the tenacity, independence, and moral rectitude of an island people combating an evil dictator – had to be reconsidered in the face of burgeoning change. The certitudes of racial and national identity, gender roles, class, and the integrity of the countryside were all coming under pressure. In the second half of the twentieth century each of these benchmarks had to be recalibrated entirely; for the novelist, this presented all manner of opportunities for imaginative intervention in vertiginous social change, so that the perceived social disintegration that had made the novel seem moribund in the 1940s, seems, with hindsight, to have heralded the arrival of a revitalized culture and society as the century progressed. The novel of society in Britain can be said to have enjoyed a period of renaissance, even a period of unparalleled creativity, in the years 1950–2000. This renaissance, however, has not always been characterized by dramatic innovation. The key developments in this period of literary history have been made in the spirit of supplementing, rather than rejecting, given forms.

## Realism and Experimentalism

Creative literary movements have not necessarily depended upon extravagant or iconoclastic innovations for their productive energy. A more gradual process of evolution, as is certainly the case with post-war British fiction, can be equally significant. At the beginning of the period, there was a principle of reaction against modernism in the emerging dominant style. James Gindin's early account of the resurgent vitality of 1950s writing – particularly in the novels of Sillitoe, Amis, Wain, and Murdoch – detects, in contrast to the interiorizing impulse of the modernists, an 'interest in man's exterior relationships' underpinned by the deliberate attempt 'to re-establish older and more conventional prose techniques'.[1] Through the remainder of the century, a dependence on some version of social mimesis, and on some of these conventional prose techniques has been evident in the greater proportion of published serious fiction. If this can no longer be seen as a reaction against modernism, it should be understood as a marker of the topical expansion of the novel in Britain. The dramatic social changes that this book has described gave great scope for the reinvention and extension of existing forms, without the need for their radical overhaul. It is the very fact of social diversity that inspires the literary renaissance.

Debates about the novel, however, have sometimes failed to register this degree of vigour and vitality, rooted in diversity. Rather, concerns about the health of the novel have tended to concentrate on a simple division between realism and experimentalism, with individual practitioners choosing to come out in partisan support of one pole or the other. Thus C. P. Snow, Kingsley Amis, and Margaret Drabble stand on the side of realism, while B. S. Johnson and Christine Brooke-Rose are the most prominent and vociferous innovators. Andrzej Gąsiorek has observed that debates about the future of the novel have been ordered around the realist/experimental opposition throughout the post-war period, even whilst the practice of key novelists has often served to break the dichotomy down.[2] Novelists, then, have sometimes helped to perpetuate a clumsy and stark opposition that is insensitive to their more subtle achievements. Interesting and significant novels are rarely 'realist' or 'experimental' in any simple sense.

Literary criticism, too, has assisted in this process of over-simplification. This has become apparent at the end of the period, as post-structuralist criticism has found more responsive ways of interpreting texts. In its more youthful guise, however, the literary theory of the 1970s and 1980s contributed to the realist/experimental divide, mounting a rather brittle attack on realism, on the back of structuralist linguistics. The charge, put most forcefully in an influential book by Catherine Belsey, was that literary realism promotes a false claim to making the truth available, through a presumed correspondence between world and text. Partly, this was a critique of one literary critical account of nineteenth-century realism, a repudiation of the 'common-sense' assumptions of liberal humanist criticism, particularly the notion that valuable insights about human nature and society might inhere in a literary text, invulnerable to ideological interference in its composition, reception, and interpretation. But the stable and authoritative perspective, a false window on the world, is also an aspect of the classic realist text in Belsey's account; and this kind of complaint has coloured much subsequent thinking about realism.[3]

The critique of realism also implicitly favours a more playful postmodern style, especially where claims to authority are openly relinquished. Yet the repudiation of 'classic realism' is too systematic, projecting a technical uniformity on to a diverse body of works. When one sits down to think of a typical classic realist novel, a novel that might definitively illustrate the charges brought forward – the concealment of contradiction, the false claim of access to the social, and so on – one is hard pushed to find a straightforward example among the 'classic' authors. Eliot, Dickens, Hardy, Gaskell, the Brontës all turn out to be more complex, more self-conscious, and more divergent than these narrow charges allow.[4]

Gąsiorek shows how realism can be 'conceived in markedly different ways', that these multiple realisms can be linked with a variety of ideological perspectives, and also extended in the pursuit of divers creative projects, including 'experimental' ones. Thus the continual transformation of realism need not be taken as a sign of the collapse of the humanist vision, or as signalling the advance of a less tolerant and disintegrating society (as the defenders of humanism have sometimes feared): there is no necessary connection between a particular literary mode and any one ideological perspective. Gąsiorek demonstrates the possible compromise between realism and experimentalism in different types of post-war fiction: within a broad church he is able to distinguish 'postcolonialists' from 'socialists', and 'liberal humanists' from 'feminists', showing in the process how monolithic accounts of post-war fictional technique fail to account for the diversity of its concerns, and also that 'any simple distinction between experimental and traditional writing has long ceased to be pertinent'.[5]

Although some authors have fuelled the realism/experimentalism furore, the divisive spirit of this dispute is rarely reflected in the actual practice of writing. The process of influence and reaction can just as well be expressed in quite other terms. A good example of this is Angus Wilson's *The Middle Age of Mrs Eliot* (1958), a novel written in reaction to Virginia Woolf, but at the level of content rather than form. The persona of Mrs Eliot, a woman who takes pleasure in her husband's 'conventional masculinity' and in 'their relative positions' in the marriage, however 'archaic' it may seem (p. 23), is encapsulated in the party scene. Here she adopts a studiedly self-conscious role as society hostess, imagining herself 'playing Glencors Palliser, Oriane [de Guermantes], and Mrs Dalloway all at the same time' (p. 44). In a *Listener* article in 1950 Wilson, playing 'devil's advocate against the work of Mrs Woolf', offered a parody of Woolf's typical 'middle-aged, upper middle-class' female character. That he calls this type 'Mrs Green' gives the parody a literary-historical significance, for this is a deliberate echo of the 'Mrs Brown' Woolf had made central to her project: the quest for the inner life of Mrs Brown, the stranger in the train carriage travelling 'from one age of English Literature to the next', is emblematic of Woolf's innovation.[6]

The focus of Wilson's parody, however, is not form or technique. The main difficulty with 'Mrs Green', whether in the guise of Mrs Ramsay, Mrs Ambrose, or Mrs Dalloway, is the narrowness of her class affiliation, and it is this that Wilson levels as an unanswerable charge.[7] Wilson later came to admire Woolf very much, and in 1978 he dismissed his earlier parody as crude. He also pointed out that, a few years after his infamous attack on Woolf, he was composing *The Middle Age of Mrs Eliot*, a novel that 'owes everything in conception although nothing in form to *Mrs Dalloway*, so deep was the haunting presence of Virginia Woolf's work' that he had tried to ignore.[8] This celebratory essay does not quite efface the parodic impulse of Wilson's novel since the limitations of Mrs Eliot the society hostess are precisely those of Clarissa Dalloway parodied as Mrs Green; but, again, Wilson is not concerned with style, but with a content that is appropriate to the social context, and the class shake-up he prescribes for English fiction.

Wilson's evolving response to Woolf is representative of the blurring of tradition and innovation abroad in the literary culture. Indeed, the out-and-out experimental novel has never taken root in Britain. There is one writer, however, whose name is always mentioned in this connection – B. S. Johnson – and he stands out as an exceptional figure in the post-war years. Johnson enjoyed considerable fame in his short life, but is scarcely read today.[9] In critical discussions, however, Johnson figures as the central example of the 'experimental' novelist in the British post-war scene, so his short-lived popularity seems to embody a succinct judgement of experimental work in this tradition.

It should be noted that Johnson rejected that label 'experimental', though authors usually do resist the attempt to pigeonhole their work. He did not, in any case, reject the more productive implications of experimentation: he wished merely to distance himself from the association of 'experimental' with 'unsuccessful', implying that his published 'experiments' were successful solutions to the problems facing the novelist in the 1960s and 1970s.[10] In Johnson's view, film had supplanted the novel as the vehicle for storytelling, making the attempt to extend the achievements of nineteenth-century realism 'anachronistic, invalid, irrelevant, and perverse'. Instead, the novel must focus on its strengths, the 'exploitation of the technological fact of the book', and 'the explication of thought' through a development of Joycean interior monologue.[11] In effect Johnson produced a prescriptive manifesto (in a spirit of 'literary puritanism' according to Jonathan Coe), which was based on certain intractable principles, the foremost of which is that the novelist's business is to tell the truth based on personal experience.[12] It follows from this that the novel is not synonymous with 'fiction', but is, rather, opposed to it in Johnson's conception: 'I choose to write truth in the form of a novel', he stated.[13] Johnson's theory of the novel, as Coe observes, was ultimately reductive, 'a breathtaking insistence that all literature should reduce itself to the status of glorified memoir'.[14]

Johnson's importance can be judged from his most famous experimental book *The Unfortunates* (1969), his novel-in-a-box, published in twenty-seven unbound sections. Two sections are identified as 'First' and 'Last', but the remaining twenty-five can be read in any order. The novel is inspired by a trip Johnson made to Nottingham as a soccer correspondent for *The Observer*, a return to a city coloured by memories of a friend Tony Tillinghast, a cancer victim, who had died at the age of twenty-nine two years before.[15] Much of the novel consists of random memories relating to Tony and his death, so the random order of reading reproduces the non-chronological resurfacing of memories that Johnson experienced. The experience is a bleak one, especially if (as is possible) you read of Tony enjoying a drink after reading the accounts of his death and funeral. The pathos of such chance sequencing is to underscore the cruel selectivity of disease.

Johnson's purpose, his truth, is to reproduce the chaotic, random, and fluid nature of life, a goal that goes some way beyond modernist stream-of-consciousness writing since he also sought to produce a form that 'was itself a physical tangible metaphor for randomness and the nature of cancer'.[16] Patricia Waugh records that the box for the original 1969 publication was 'printed with luminously colourful images of inflated cancer cells', a detail that confirms the unflinching nature of Johnson's unappealing truth-seeking, but also its particular expedient in this instance.[17] Indeed, it is difficult to attach a more general technical significance to Johnson's grim elegy for a friend; it is not the flagship of a new avant-garde. The 'random' nature of the presentation reproduces the nature of the personal memories, a correspondence that could have been achieved, to a degree at least, in a conventionally bound volume. Johnson may have had a case when he objected to the 'stultifyingly philistine' nature of 'the general book culture in this country'; but his ambition to have picked up 'the baton of innovation' by generating usable models for the British novelist was to prove fanciful.[18] Coe's more sober assessment convincingly reclaims *The Unfortunates*, not as 'a quirky offshoot of sixties experimentalism', but as a contribution to the enduring tradition of confessional writing, which resurfaces in the 1990s.[19]

The idea of a novel-in-a-box, however, retains its unique status in British literary history, even if Johnson's experimentation did not have the far-reaching influence he might have wished.[20] The same judgement can be made of Johnson's debut, *Travelling People* (1963), in which the stylistic richness might seem an over-elaboration in what is in essence a conventional picaresque novel of self-discovery. The variety of styles includes a film script, letters, journal entries, interior monologue – a principle of diversity that extends to the typography: the advertisements seen on an escalator in the London Underground are presented in a descending diagonal sequence (p. 32), for instance, whilst the fatal heart-attack suffered by one character is marked, in the manner of Laurence Sterne, by two-and-a-half pages printed black (pp. 210–12). (An earlier attack, suffered in a swimming pool, is similarly marked, by grey wavy lines (pp. 197–9).) The stylistic self-consciousness is overshadowed, however, by the book's emotional centre, a celebration of human warmth in the social journey on which we are all fellow travellers (p. 278), and that has no obvious link with the formal playfulness.

If experimental writing has made only a minor appearance in post-war Britain, does this mean that postmodernism has bypassed British literary culture? A full answer to such a question would require a hefty book in itself; the short answer is that the conspicuous impact of postmodernism depends on how it is defined. Certainly, some postmodern attributes have had a considerable influence. The questioning of metanarrative, the decentring of cultural authority, and the ironic disruption of the self-contained fictional world have all figured prominently, making writers such as Peter Ackroyd, Salman Rushdie, Martin Amis, and Angela Carter sometimes seem representative postmodernists. But these are all writers whose works have also conveyed a conviction about the moral and emotional function of narrative fiction, and its ability to make readers re-engage with the world they know. In performing this role, the novel, in the hands of these writers, has depended on a reworking of the realist contract, involving the reader's willing acceptance that the text provides a bridge to reality. If postmodernist expression is conceived as a reworking of realism, rather than a rejection of it, and as a mode capable of generating an emotional response, beyond the distractions of self-conscious tricksiness, then it has a good deal of relevance to writers in Britain. This understanding of postmodernism, as a hybrid form of expression that renegotiates tradition, is the one that could make a case for 'British Postmodernism', and that could account for the work of important practitioners such as Margaret Drabble, Martin Amis, and Graham Swift.[21]

As an international phenomenon, however, postmodernism is often felt to foreground its artifice to such a degree that its self-conscious fictionality, rupturing all realist codes, becomes the dominant component. This degree of playfulness is self-deprecating in the sense that it has the effect of devaluing the role and function of 'literature'. No longer capable of high seriousness, the literary object colludes in its own debunking, participating in the cultural logic that blurs the distinction between 'high' and 'low' culture. The consequence of this is a culture of pastiche, with no vantage point from which value can be assigned with authority. The further consequence is a 'waning of affect', the production of a self-conscious culture in which powerful emotion can no longer be communicated without mediation, qualification, or reservation.[22] In literature, such an austere mode of writing is epitomized in the short fiction of American writer Donald Barthelme, whose work comprises a collage of contemporary discourses, a non-judgemental fusion of disparate sources. It is this kind of ludic postmodernism that has failed to gain a purchase in British literary culture.

A mode of postmodernist fiction that has fared better, and that is in the spirit of the reworking of realism outlined above, is that which Linda Hutcheon defines as 'historiographic metafiction', a mode in which the narrative status of history is subjected to scrutiny. Hutcheon offers Graham Swift's *Waterland* (1983) and *The White Hotel* (1981) by D. M. Thomas as examples of fictional treatments of history no longer concerned with the question, 'to which empirically real object in the past does the language of history refer'; rather, the question they pose is: 'to which discursive context could this language belong? To which prior textualizations must we refer?'[23] This greater degree of self-consciousness, with its emphasis on textuality, should not, however, conceal the manner in which the novels Hutcheon cites also seek to generate an intensity of feeling through their re-presentation of the past. In contrast to the more playful variety of postmodernism, with its waning of affect, a novel like *Waterland* asks searching questions about narrative authority, historical and fictional, but revivifies mimesis in the process.

Another branch of experimental writing that works in this way is the hybrid mode of magic realism, in which realistic codes are confounded yet still retained. A writer commonly identified with the magic realist attempt to offer a fresh perspective on a particular context, *through* the processes of innovation, is Jeanette Winterson. Winterson's style, in which realism is infused with fantasy, can seem pretentious or artificial; but at its best it can lend itself to the kind of social connection that it might seem devised to avoid. This becomes clear in *Art and Lies* (1994), a novel set in London in 2000, in which Winterson is explicitly critical of the desensitizing effects of a mass media implicated in a crisis of social disconnection. In response to a world where 'reportage is violence . . . to the spirit', packaged for consumption in such a way as to juxtapose the latest international catastrophe with a quiz show, Winterson seeks an alternative form of nourishment for people still longing 'to feel' (p. 14). The use of fantasy, incorporating an emotionally charged use of language, is Winterson's method for reinvigorating the channels of social connection.

Winterson's three principal characters in the London of 2000 are linked with the three historical artistic figures whose names they bear: Handel, Sappho, and Picasso. The method is an economical one for bringing historical artistic resonance into a contemporary context from which aesthetic value is felt to have been expelled. The use of fantasy in order to deliver a sharper perspective on the real tallies with a traditional conception of literature's function. Winterson underscores this by using a quote from A. C. Bradley, lecturing in 1901, as an epigraph. In the quoted section Bradley insists upon the separateness of the work of art, which must not be approached as 'a copy of the real world', but as an autonomous 'world in itself', the appreciation of which demands that the receiver 'enter that world' and 'conform to its laws'. Winterson is implying that her brand of magic realism, even in its more metafictional or frame-breaking moments, is not inconsistent with this enduring exhortation to respect the integrity of the artistic work; and, equally, she is arguing that such a critical approach need not be assumed to sever the connection between the literary text and its context. But this is also a particular expedient, where an extravagant departure from the real may be the best way to retrieve it, and, specifically, to combat the violence done to the spirit in the media age.

The work of Margaret Drabble supplies some of the most interesting examples of how a version of realism might respond to the implications of postmodernity whilst retaining its own integrity and identity. A central difficulty with Drabble is the extent to which her indecisiveness or ambivalence is an enforced formal problem, symptomatic of the era to which she responds. Certainly Drabble incorporates dissonant features in her narratives of the 1980s and beyond, but it might be helpful to see this developing self-consciousness (glimpsed, in any case, in her first novel) as a deliberate formal strategy for capturing social disruption and uncertainty. The most obvious feature of this strategy is the use of an intrusive narrator who periodically interrupts the narrative line in Drabble's trilogy (*The Radiant Way* [1987], *A Natural Curiosity* [1989], and *The Gates of Ivory* [1991]), thus drawing attention to the artifice of the fictional world. This element of self-reflexiveness has, certainly, been sufficiently pronounced to encourage critical speculation on Drabble's 'postmodern turn'.[24] However, Drabble insistently anchors her fictional world through allusions to actual historical figures and events, making it quite distinct from the ludic exploration of possible worlds, and levels of being, that is often present in postmodernist fiction.[25]

Drabble's own comments on mimesis in the post-war British novel suggest a still more coherent strategy of reasserting control. She argues that the use of an intrusive authorial narrator can *reinforce* the contract between reader and text: the disruptions caused by these narratorial interjections usually involve an admission of blindness or bias (this is certainly so in Drabble's fiction), and so are tantamount to 'a double bluff' that could be 'designed to aid, not to hinder, the suspension of disbelief'.[26] This principle, which could only really apply in fiction like Drabble's that seeks so earnestly to understand the contemporary, justifies the 'bossy authorial intrusion' that James Wood, for one, has associated with her work.[27] She has, in short, continued to find ways of developing her realist heritage that do not essentially contradict her view from the 1960s, when she explicitly rejected the 'experimental novel', and identified with realism, even if it meant aligning herself with 'a dying tradition'.[28]

Drabble's trilogy concludes with *The Gates of Ivory* (1991), a good example of her technical sophistication. The title is glossed by the epigraph taken from Book XIX of Homer's *Odyssey*, in which Penelope distinguishes between the two gates of dreams: one of horn (truth), the other of ivory (falsehood). The title has various connotations, but at a metafictional level it appears to signal Drabble's ongoing attempt to resuscitate a traditional mode of narrative fiction, both a kind of falsehood and a kind of dreaming, that retains its moral force by suggesting that an alternative 'truth' might arise through its oblique operations. Drabble's own uncertainty, the feature that often makes the trilogy disorientating to the reader, forms the thematic core. The question implicitly posed is whether or not it is still possible to expose the falsehoods of the many gates of ivory with assurance, and to pursue a sustaining moral seriousness in an encounter with an atomized social reality.

The quest is to produce a form governed by such moral seriousness, and it is directly related in the novel to the search of Stephen Cox, celebrated but restless Booker-winning novelist, who has gone missing in Cambodia. His mission, born of political despair, is to gather material on Pol Pot in the search for a grand theme (p. 16), and perhaps, as another character speculates, to produce 'the novel to end all novels' (p. 448). He wants to know why the socialist dream fashioned a road to the Killing Fields. In Phnom Penn, the 'divinely mad' Akira, who speaks up for the Khmer Rouge, appears to mark a natural end to Stephen's mission:

> He knows that this is what he came to find. He came to find the last believer. A breath of hope stirs like a sweet corrupt poison in his entrails. It is as though Akira were telling him that God, after all, is not dead, and salvation is still on offer. History is reprieved, the dead did not die in vain, the dry bones will live. (p. 229)

The 'last believer' confirms what he denies: that state socialism has been exposed as morally bankrupt, and has been eclipsed by a new world economic order. This version of the End of History, according to which actually existing socialism is extinguished by international capitalism, is Stephen Cox's heart of darkness.[29] The episodes involving Stephen unfold in flashback, and his grim fate, dying after capture by the Khmer Rouge, is felt as an inevitability. The irony of the Conrad motif – in a novel whose characters have a tired and dismissive knowledge of Conrad, even if they have not read him – is that the journey into the Cambodian interior is redundant. Stephen's encounter with the extraordinary Miss Porntip has effectively summarized the End-of-History lesson for him in Bangkok, a lesson that, since they meet on the plane from France, begins before Stephen sets foot in the East. Miss Porntip is an ex-Miss World, who emerged from an impoverished life in rural Thailand to head her own business empire. This dramatic economic evolution (which has its roots in sex-tourism) is made representative of the triumph of the global capitalism that Miss Porntip so eagerly espouses. After his affair with her in Bangkok, Stephen eventually continues his journey, but he seems more purposeless than ever after this encounter with the dazzling 'New Woman of the East', whose emphatic presence trivializes his mission (p. 79).

In the stereotypical and semi-absurd Miss Porntip Drabble unleashes the kind of postmodern forces in caricature that threaten not only Stephen's social vision, but the author's fictional method itself. The strategy, however, is one of containment. Drabble supplies an alternative focus to the seductive, unfettered capitalism of Miss Porntip through the continuity provided by her three main characters, Liz, Esther, and Alix, still struggling to make sense of the social turmoil. These characters, like the social matrices that define them, are more complex, and so more substantial, than the unswerving Miss Porntip. Alix, for example, enjoys a return to those socialist roots that she was losing sight of in *The Radiant Way* (p. 111); her convictions, however, are thrown into uncertain perspective, we feel, by her visions of the dead (p. 287), by her reading in chaos theory (p. 440), and by the appeal of religion in the face of mortality (p. 439). This is recognizable Drabble, a method by which characters are embedded in the competing intellectual claims of their day. The texture that results enables the book to out-manoeuvre its own two-dimensional creations, and to enshrine in its form Drabble's aversion to political extremes. *The Gates of Ivory* continues a process in the trilogy that sees the author driven to elaborate procedures to preserve the core traditionalism of her method. It is a novel, then, that enacts Drabble's political sensibility at the level of form. This intensely serious working through of technical problems is very much a response to a context in which a socialist vision is difficult to sustain. If *The Gates of Ivory* extends the trilogy's more parochial concern with English politics, bringing it into contact with the capitalist global village, it still takes the felt crisis in the English political scene as its foundation. In this, Drabble is representative of a resistance to the forces of globalization in serious British fiction.

## Technology and the New Science

The dominant transnational forces of globalization are promoted through developments in science and technology, and this has become an area of human experience that is especially difficult for the novel to register. To engage with rapid technological change, an instantaneous response is demanded, and this is beyond the capabilities of a literary form that is, rather, cumulative in its procedures of reflection and commentary. This sense of relative disengagement, however, can yield an autonomous and longer-term perspective on changes that are inadequately examined in more immediate forms of cultural response. This withdrawn, or philosophical point of view has often led novelists towards an adverse judgement on the implications or applications of technology.

In Winterson's *Art and Lies*, for example, the technological world in general is an alienated world, where a faith in scientific progress is misplaced: 'the latest laser scan refuses to diagnose' an enduring 'nagging pain in the heart' (p. 8). 'Health' is here conceived as a spiritual dimension, requiring the nourishment of art; technology is the distraction, offering an illusory salvation.

A still more disturbing meditation on technology is found in J. G. Ballard's *Crash* (1973), a novel that takes the car manufacturer's favourite advertising ploy, the presentation of the car as a commodity imbued with sexuality, to its logical conclusion. A nightmare fantasy of violence and sexual fetishism – and eventual psychological collapse – is the result of this logic. The narrator, one 'Ballard', implicates the author in this ambivalent excursus that focuses on how 'Ballard' is seduced by the jaundiced eroticism of Robert Vaughan, a TV scientist turned 'nightmare angel of the expressways' (p. 84). Vaughan's ultimate goal is to die in a head-on collision with Elizabeth Taylor, as the final expression of the sexualized violence he associates with car crashes and their victims. 'Ballard' and his wife Catherine find themselves bedazzled by 'the excitements of a new violence', in which genital wounds become an erotic focus, and where the various other scars of crash victims are reconceived as new 'sexual apertures' (p. 179).

'Ballard' is uncertain in his response to the brand of sexuality that is revealed to him: he considers the technology that generates it by turns 'perverse' or 'benevolent', 'deviant' or 'benign'. But he is aware that the way in which the car crash is equated with a sexual response means that such a response is devoid of a conventional emotional charge: both crash and sex 'were conceptualized acts abstracted from all feeling, carrying any ideas or emotions with which we cared to freight them' (p. 129). The novel thus uncovers the psychological distortion of a commodity culture in which human response is displaced by the machine, a 'technological landscape' where 'the human inhabitants . . . no longer provided its sharpest pointers, its keys to the borderzones of identity' (pp. 48–9). The sense of a 'coming autogeddon' is the focus of this psychological dislocation.

If there is a cautionary note in *Crash*, however, it also reproduces the extreme it seeks to anatomize. In the enthusiasm of 'Ballard' for 'the new zodiac of our minds' (p. 224), fantasies of sexual violence, conjoining semen, blood, and oil, become depressingly frequent. This makes the book an unpleasant read, but there may be a sense of exorcism in the writing in this connection, where the excesses of unfettered sexuality, emptied of all emotional content, are emptied of all sense of *frisson*, too: 'Ballard', by the end of the novel, seems to fantasize as a kind of automaton.

A more fertile point of contact between science and the novel has emerged in the more philosophical investigations of the physical universe, promoted in the popular discourse of the new science, especially in the form mediated for general consumption by Stephen Hawking and others. The most arresting instance of a direct influence from the new physics occurs in Ian McEwan's *The Child in Time* (1987), where children's author Stephen Lewis, whose own daughter has been snatched in a supermarket and never found, apparently slips into the past to see his mother, carrying the unborn Stephen, but contemplating an abortion, through a pub window (p. 59). Later, Stephen's mother corroborates the episode, explaining that the appearance at the window of her unborn child had convinced her to keep the baby (pp. 175–6). McEwan here employs the post-Einsteinian conception of the plasticity of time and space to allow his protagonist to intervene in the past and secure his own future. Such a fluid perception of time suits McEwan's purpose admirably in a novel about the child within us all, and the need to foster strong personal, and inter-generational bonds as a necessary component of the healthy body politic.

But there is an intriguing impulse to push beyond this essentially metaphorical connection between the social theme and the scientific speculation. Thelma Darke's 'lecture' to Stephen on the need to reconcile and transcend relativity and quantum theory, in order to prove why the 'common-sense' version of time as 'linear, regular, absolute' is 'either nonsense or a tiny fraction of the truth', envisages a 'mathematical and physical' explanation for Stephen's personal time-slip (pp. 117–19). McEwan insists on the possibility of a literal explanation for the fantastic experience. Partly, this is a strategy to distance this political novel from the less tangible operations of magic realism; at the same time, McEwan's novel serves to undermine scientific pretensions to the discovery of absolute truth. If the discussion of 'a higher order of theory' (p. 118) in the field of physics stands, ultimately, as a metaphor for McEwan's social theme, so too does McEwan remind us that all science must have recourse to metaphor, in seeking to explain phenomena for which there are no pre-existing terms. The new science, in *The Child in Time*, might be said simply to reinforce the novel's unique capacity to unite past, present, and future in the depiction of personal time.

If the novel has generated some poetic correspondences with science, the element of distrust has remained predominant: science, to the novelist, more often supplies the material for a cautionary tale. Zadie Smith's *White Teeth* (2000) is an effective instance of how such suspicions can become a sustained compositional principle. Smith's dismantling of the grounds for racism corresponds, interestingly, with the *implications* (at least) of contemporary work in genetics. I am thinking of the manner in which the genome project generates knowledge that implies 'a particular kind of totality, or species being, as well as a specific kind of individuality'.[30]

Despite the common conclusions that can be drawn, however, *White Teeth* remains sharply critical of genetics in its contemporary guise, and in this respect Smith's millennial world-view is in conflict with the cultural perspective typified by the influential Donna Haraway. Smith's FutureMouse© is based on the actual OncoMouse™, an engineered type of laboratory animal bred for research, with a cancer-inducing bit of DNA. Haraway is alert to the moral and ethical difficulties that are concentrated on the 'first patented animal in the world' (OncoMouse™ was patented in 1988, and licensed to Du Pont), a manifestation of that 'transnational enterprise culture' that Haraway calls the 'New World Order, Inc.'; even so, she is still enthused by the transgressive implications of 'transgenic creatures' like OncoMouse™, the very existence of which dramatizes the kind of 'border-crossing' that 'pollutes lineages': for a transgenic organism, of course, it is 'the lineage of nature itself' that is crossed, thus 'transforming nature into its binary opposite, culture'. 'Culture', here, is employed loosely to denote anything resulting from human activity; and it is made to carry a particularly heavy load of credulity in relation to a manufactured breed of mouse, available in several genetically defective varieties.

Rather curiously, Haraway aligns this transgressive potential with a challenge to racism, since in the criticism of biotechnology she detects a mystification of natural purity that is 'akin to the doctrines of white racial hegemony' in the US. Such uncomfortable associations, as in a blood-and-soil Green fascism, are certainly possible; but in hearing 'the dangers of racism in the *opposition* to genetic engineering and especially transgenics', Haraway makes the enemy of technoscience by default also the opponent of the 'mess[y]', 'dangerous', 'thick', and 'satisfying' multiculturalism she seeks to promote.[31]

In direct contrast, Zadie Smith's novel stands as testimony that such a rich and heterogeneous multiculturalism can be realized textually by the writer positioned broadly in opposition to technoscience. Whether her acquaintance with Haraway is first- or second-hand, Smith's vision offers an alternative route to the dismantling of racial culture.[32] It is a vision premised on the particular postcolonial history of Britain, but that is nostalgic insofar as it insists on a refusal of that transnational alliance of scientific and economic enterprise that postmodernity entails. Indeed, such futuristic global trends are necessarily at odds with the messy, but particular history that is Smith's cultural material. Thus, Smith's method serves to 'funnel' attention inwards towards a specific historical and geographical present, which is diverse and secular. Haraway's rhetorical structuring, by contrast, 'funnels' outwards to a global, post-Christian scientific utopia of the future, a kind of mysticism that is explicitly rejected at the end of *White Teeth*; when the wounded Archie Jones sees FutureMouse© scurrying off down an air vent in the mayhem at the close: '*go on, my son!*', he thinks, on Zadie Smith's behalf (p. 462). Smith puts her faith in 'the liminality of the people' (in Homi Bhabha's phrase) and the ways in which identity is *culturally* engineered.[33]

Perhaps the crucial technological issue in this period is the technology of the printed book itself, which has flourished despite perceived threats from film, television, and, more recently, the electronic media available via the Internet. The notion that the computer age might change the nature of the book has been an enduring speculation, but one that has proved insubstantial in relation to the novel. However, there are now signs (I am writing at the end of 2000) that the electronic book – the 'ebook' – might begin to take off, after several false dawns. The increasing popularity of the palmtop computer, which will eventually be incorporated in the ubiquitous mobile phone, suggests a wider audience, since these machines are now equipped to read 'ebooks' in the form of electronic files. This has clear implications for the printed book, but for the novel this may not imply a dramatic change of form or structure. The new technology for the 'ebook' seeks to imitate the 'interface' of the printed book, rather than to replace it by exploiting the 'Hypertext' potentialities of the electronic form.[34]

If there are currently no signs that this technology is going to have an immediate influence on the manner in which novels are written, one can predict that the broader electronic revolution will bring with it significant cultural changes. One might expect, for example, a mutation of the language following the introduction of an electronic form of pidgin English through email and text messaging. Eventually this will have some effect on the language of the novel. More significantly, perhaps, the instantaneous nature of electronic communication may alter the individual's perception of self, and so necessitate a reorientation of the novel in treating personal identity. These are merely speculations, however; and at the end of the century there has been no demonstrable impact on novelistic form or manner.

This is not to say that the computer age has not been mined by novelists for inspiration. Jeanette Winterson's *The.Powerbook* (2000) is an example of a novel that deliberates on the psychological effect of electronic communication, but without allowing its form to be radically altered. Given the admonitory attitude to new technology that Winterson expresses in *Art and Lies*, it is surprising to see her conversion to the creative possibilities of the computer. In the round of interviews to publish *The.Powerbook*, Winterson claimed to 'love email' on account of its swiftness: 'I love the thought that there are no obvious barriers between us, and I like the pretence of it.'[35] To the extent that the immediacy of email opens up new possibilities for human relationships, Winterson has found an aspect of the new technology that reinforces her previous fictional concerns; there is no real sense of a changed sensibility. In its original publication the book is square, in the manner of some computer user manuals, and some of its section titles employ computer terms that supply obvious puns: 'VIEW AS ICON', 'EMPTY TRASH', and so on. The use of this terminology is cosmetic, however, and the novel is reminiscent of earlier Winterson novels such as *Written on the Body* and *Art and Lies* in its attempt to mount a lyrical exploration of erotic love. When Winterson implicitly compares email to a story, described as 'a tightrope between two worlds' (p. 119), she produces the kind of image that is applicable to much of her writing, with its effort to bridge imagination and reality. Neither the attempt to import the discourse of Information Technology, nor the investigation of its effects, results in noteworthy changes of form in *The.Powerbook*.

Winterson's somewhat mannered engagement with the computer age is representative of how mainstream British fiction has remained impervious to its effects. If the novel has thus far staved off the threat posed to its identity by the computer, there is one technological advance that has drastically affected its fortunes: the rise of film. A common view of film is that it has supplanted the novel as the dominant narrative form in an increasingly visual culture, where the visual is prioritized over the narrative element. In such a view there is a dubious technological determinism; that is, the questionable assumption that because technology has been developed in a particular way, that usage is inherent in the technology itself. But of course 'film' is not to blame for the Hollywood blockbuster, fostering a taste for sophisticated special effects, and a distaste for historical verity. Visual media, to pursue the example, could just as well be used to strengthen the public grasp of complex narrative, and in a way that would supplement rather than overshadow its written forms.

A more temperate treatment of film is found in David Lodge's first novel *The Picturegoers* (1960). The novel seems to stage a simple confrontation between the religious and the secular, specifically through the conflict of Catholic piety, and the licentiousness of Hollywood. Yet Lodge is really interested in the culture that bonds the 'picturegoers' of Brickley, a London suburb based on Brockley and New Cross where Lodge grew up.[36] Lodge has indicated the 'sociological and cultural' emphasis of his treatment, and also the novel's indebtedness to Richard Hoggart's analysis of popular culture and its effect on its consumers.[37] The novel ponders the possibility that 'the cinema, or the whole system of processed mass-entertainment for which it stood, had already become an acceptable substitute for religion'. Beyond this is the fear 'that in time it might become an acceptable substitute for living' (p. 107). Here the familiar concern that visual communication will supplant the novel, especially in the guise of 'processed mass-entertainment', is held up for analysis; and, finally, *The Picturegoers* implies something much more positive about popular culture. The screening of *Rock Around the Clock* (originally released in 1956) has the picturegoers of Brickley dancing in the aisles, producing a genuine sense of community. The actual film provoked 'serious riots in several countries', and Lodge is alluding in an enlightened way to the challenge and power of these combined cultural forms, cinema and music;[38] there is a bonding power in the Bacchanalian scene that the movie inspires, sufficient even to redeem Harry, the would-be rapist, who is coaxed out of his vicious misogyny by the warmth and inclusiveness of 'Rock and Roll' (pp. 228–30). What resonates is the sense that apparently 'valueless' popular cultural forms have the power to 'awaken . . . many deadened souls to some kind of life', a suggestive and forward-looking perspective for the time of publication (p. 228).

The suspicious regard of new media, however, has been the more common attitude amongst novelists, revealing the concern that the novel might soon be eclipsed by other cultural forms. Predictions about the death of the novel have been current at every stage of its history, of course, so one should view these with caution; yet the rapid rise to prominence of film, and especially television, as carriers of popular forms of fictional narrative in the post-war years, has placed a particular squeeze on the novel. A comparison with painting is instructive here. The development of photography can be seen to have freed painters from the obligation to produce an imitation of the real, thus enabling them to develop new, and more specifically painterly codes in those genres – portraiture, landscape, and so on – where photography could be relied upon for a more accurate record. There is a comparable sense that the novel has concentrated its efforts in those technical areas that remain unique to it. This has principally to do with the contrasting angle of vision identified with written and filmic narrative respectively. The camera may not provide a reliable 'all-seeing' eye, but it has the capacity to imply either the grand vista, or the partial view, and to switch easily between these alternatives. The filmic mode of documentary realism may sometimes conceal a partisan view; but it is the impression of authoritative social coverage in this genre (or in allusions to it) that requires novelists to rethink what kind of claim to social coverage is viable in fiction. The capacity of the camera, then, displaces the convention of third-person omniscience in the novel, and the mode of fictional realism associated with it, so that the reworking of socially engaged fiction has depended upon the avowedly incomplete or partial perspective that a first-person narrator can supply.

The technical adjustment of narrative fiction from the 1960s through to the end of the century, with its stress on the role of the first-person narrator, has been systematic and intelligent. And the consequences of this redefinition – a greater degree of relativity, and an emphasis on the personal voice – need not be viewed as a negative development. As the novel (with some notable exceptions) has tended to distance itself from the grand social vista, so has it paid scrupulous attention to technical consistency.

## Towards the New Confessional

*The French Lieutenant's Woman* (1969) by John Fowles is a landmark work that crystallizes the gathering mistrust of authorial omniscience. In a novel that emulates (whilst parodying) the achievements of Victorian realism, Fowles seeks also to extend those achievements by adding into the compositional equation a measure of self-consciousness appropriate to the twentieth century. The direct authorial address of chapter thirteen acknowledges that the author is 'still a god' in that he or she creates the fictional world, but indicates that different cultural conditions demand a higher degree of self-consciousness: 'what has changed is that we are no longer the gods of the Victorian image, omniscient and decreeing; but in the new theological image, with freedom our first principle, not authority' (p. 86). The 'new theological image', in Fowles's ironic designation, is that of a secular age in which a character's apparent freedom to act must outweigh the impression of authorial decree. The foregrounding of narrative artifice thus becomes a way of relinquishing a degree of authorial control, and incorporating a greater sense of contingency into a novel's pattern. Accordingly, Fowles supplies alternative endings in the final two chapters of *The French Lieutenant's Woman* (there are three possible endings if the earlier imagined outcome related in chapter forty-four is counted), and these alternatives enrich the sense of complexity in the drawing of character and narrative situation.

Another writer who has raised some challenging questions in connection with narrative voice is Christine Brooke-Rose. Influenced by poststructuralist theory, Brooke-Rose's novels mark her as 'defiantly and terminally "experimental"', in Lorna Sage's phrase;[39] 'terminally' because the overt theoretical self-consciousness of her later novels has proved too dry and academic for the tastes of English readers. This marginalization has tended to apply to the critical reception, too, as Brooke-Rose has herself observed.[40] The uncertain attempts to classify her work indicate the continuing lack of purchase achieved by experimental fiction in the English tradition, as well as the demanding challenge that Brooke-Rose embodies.

One of Brooke-Rose's books puts her metafictional deliberations clearly in the context of debates about the future of the novel. This is *Textermination* (1991), the title of which denotes its dual interest in internal fictional codes and limits (the termination of the text), as well as a concern at the dwindling readership for serious fiction, and the 'extermination' of the novel this might herald. The investigation of fictional limits concentrates on the ontological status of character, and the fact that a literary character depends upon the reader to give him or her 'life'. *Textermination* presents a literary convention held in San Francisco where the delegates are characters from fictional works (especially 'classic' novels): Emma Bovary, Emma Woodhouse, Casaubon, Dorothea Brooke, and Gibreel Farishta (from *The Satanic Verses*) are among the more prominent delegates. The sessions available at the convention include assemblies of 'prayer for being', offered by the characters to 'Our Creator, Our Implied Reader', the reader hailed as the divinity who might 'deliver' the character from 'the unjust and the ignorant man' (pp. 24, 26, 27). Like the convention, the novel is 'not about events but about characters and their discourse' (p. 148). Much discursive play results from the interaction of characters from different novels. At times this produces a mingling of discourses, and a consequent challenge to the ontological limits seen to operate on the category of 'character';[41] at other times, however, the humour is generated by the opposing sense that the characters are confined by the fictional worlds that contain them. The episode of the 'assembly of prayer for being' for those characters of 'the Judeo-Graeco-Christian culture' is disrupted by Islamic militants (looking for Rushdie's Gibreel Farishta). They are promptly beheaded, and Emma responds to the ensuing chaos according to the codes of her own limited world: 'Emma is profoundly vexed. How dreadfully mortifying etc. Such manners' (p. 31).

The novel thus enacts opposing tendencies: the power of the reader to reimagine and fashion character, and the alternative sense that the framework of a text establishes the parameters for understanding character. In effect, such metafictional deliberations dramatize the competing claims of different critical emphases, from authorial intent, to a narrow focus on the text itself, to a consideration of reader-response. When an 'I-narrator' intrudes into the text, it is to give an account of how literary critics have 'passed imperceptibly from phrases such as "the author's intention here is clearly" to "the text clearly says", and then to "the reader clearly infers"'. This narrator continues: 'But behind this lip-service to fads, what the author intends, what the text says, what the reader infers, is in every case what the one critic interprets. He too is Reader, he too is God' (p. 107). To the extent that *Textermination* celebrates the plurality of meaning in fiction, and the role of the reader in giving 'life' to the novel, it serves, gesturally, to 'exterminate' the finite critical reading. The Rushdie theme is related to this idea, since Brooke-Rose's novel implicitly criticizes the fundamentalists' failure to read *The Satanic Verses* as an indeterminate fiction.

Brooke-Rose's key technical project is the pursuit of a 'narratorless present tense', in an intended development of Alain Robbe-Grillet's *nouveau roman* and its interrogation of narrative subjectivity. This development, which is also a rejection of the logical inconsistencies of much modern fiction, results in a narrative technique she calls a 'restraint', a method that concentrates on 'the constant impact of outside phenomena on an active, but not always reflective consciousness', and that represents an austere formal extreme in English fiction.[42]

Brooke-Rose's worry about the 'narrator' does have something in common with the broader loss of faith in the third-person narrator with pretensions to omniscience; but the issue here is a precise, technical one. In Brooke-Rose's argument, logic demands that the term 'narrator' be reserved for the character-narrator created by the author, and involved in the action. In contrast, the technique of reported thought and speech in third-person narrative always reveals the author's controlling hand, since such reportage produces a kind of sentence construction that is peculiar to narrative fiction, and that could not be spoken in everyday speech.[43] A question to ask is: what drives this desire for technical purity? Novel readers, in fact, become very adept at the silent reading and assimilation of the 'unspeakable sentence', a convention that may become part of the pleasurable 'contract' between author and reader. The element of narrative 'inconsistency' may, indeed, form a conscious part of the pleasure of reading fiction. It can also provide thematic structure for a writer. For example, the interplay between author and narrating persona, and the attendant vacillation between first- and third-person narrative, supplies the means by which John Fowles advances his principal theme of authenticity in *Daniel Martin* (1977).

A novel that relies on a similar investigation of narrative inconsistency or tension, though without the extended use of narration in the third person, is *Money* (1984) by Martin Amis. It is the blurred distinction between author and character that inspires Amis, enabling him to find a formal solution to the apparently intractable problem that has repeatedly confronted the post-war novelist: how to write a work with a coherent moral or ethical vision, but that does not rely on a shared sense of the social totality, or an unquestioned omniscient vantage point. Amis's narrator John Self embodies the 1980s world of greed and self-indulgence that is the book's satirical target, so that Amis's problem also requires him to unsettle or get behind the narrative voice in some way. The solution is the strategic deployment of an 'intrusive author', which is more subtle in the case of *Money* than it appears at first.[44]

The obvious manifestation of this intrusion is the appearance of a character called 'Martin Amis' who conveniently puts across several of the author's dicta about the state of fiction. There are two significant convictions. The first of these is that conventional motivation in the portrayal of character is no longer appropriate in a world that is unpredictable, and without obvious codes of social co-operation. 'As a controlling force in human affairs', says the fictional 'Martin Amis', 'motivation is pretty well shagged out by now' (p. 359). As a demonstration of this hugely significant loss, the yardstick by which human action is conventionally explained, the novel incorporates a confidence trick (in which Self inadvertently squanders his own money) that seems entirely unmotivated. The representation of confidence trickster Fielding Goodney involves another perception of 'confidence'. As Amis has explained, Goodney 'embodies confidence', a quality that is 'identified as a psychopathic state', a 'wildly inappropriate response to present-day life'. In accordance with this distrust of the sure action, Amis wished Goodney's confidence trick to be 'absolutely unexplained'.[45]

The second conviction stems from the felt loss of motivation, and concerns the popular quest for 'form', the individual's desire to give 'artistic shape' to his or her life, even if that shape is likely to be mediated by the multiple models of identity offered by film and television. The presence of 'Martin Amis' expounding the nature of fiction supplies some important signposts for the reader. 'Is there a moral philosophy of fiction?' he asks, pondering specifically the author's moral accountability to his characters (p. 260). The novel's answer lies in an ever-closer affinity between Amis and Self, a deliberate strategy in a novel that forces us 'to examine the extent to which the novel's various voices both are and are not claiming to be aspects of a single consciousness'.[46]

This double-voiced device produces paradoxical results. On the one hand, Self's 'sins' are made to seem venial, since the author's sensibility tempers his unpleasantness, producing an engaging self-irony in the character, and, at one point, even the desire to 'burst out of the world of money' and into 'the world of thought and fascination' (p. 123). But this also emphasizes the author as ventriloquist, controlling his dummy in a way that might be seen as morally dubious (p. 260). Yet Amis's 'moral philosophy of fiction' depends upon the overt admission of authorial control, the flagging up of that which is constructed. The sense of authorial duty has then to do with discovering the extent of 'the realism problem', the lack of motivation or moral pattern in a world where all values are fiscal, and all behaviour conditioned or mediated by film and television. Amis's great achievement in *Money* is to have refused the outmoded devices of narrative fiction where these imply assumptions about the social order that (Amis feels) no longer apply; and yet at the same time, to have created a vital monster of a protagonist who 'lives' in the enigmatic space between author and text. The metafictional aspect of the novel, its deliberation about the uncertain relationship between author and character, supplies the means by which the 'Real' is opened up.

These overt deliberations about the narrator and the authorial voice are the more dramatic instances of a prevailing attitude in serious post-war fiction, characterized by a massive turning away from the use of a third-person narrator. This shunning of a tradition that reached its height in the nineteenth century has its roots in an anxiety, not so much about what can be spoken, but rather about what can reasonably be known by a narrator. The majority of the novels examined in this survey, in fact, are narrated in the first person by a character involved in the action (though there are important exceptions to this). Sometimes such a narrator seems to stand for the author, so the risk of 'authorial intrusion' is minimized, though such a technique might be said to represent the continuation of third-person narrative by other means. In general, however, novelists have become extremely circumspect in restricting the angle of vision, and limiting the narrator's knowledge. The consequence of this, and the dominance of the first-person character-narrator, is to place stress on internal reflections as a standard form. Leaving aside the technical virtuosity of an Amis or a Fowles, this new standardization might seem to imply a restriction on technical innovation, and to represent a different momentum to that established by the psychological novel pioneered by the modernists, when the representation of internal moods was still felt to be challenging and new.

If the post-war era is dominated by a new kind of confessional mode in the novel, there have still been some interesting attempts to stretch the limits of first-person writing. In Tibor Fischer's *The Collector Collector* (1997), for example, the narrator is an ancient antique bowl, so old that it claims to have acquired the knowledge of five thousand languages in its various experiences. Initially, this seems to be a way of justifying a quasi-omniscient vantage point, as is implied when the bowl asserts that 'things are done in front of me that wouldn't be done in front of pets' (p. 19). Fischer includes a large measure of the fantastic, however, making this appeal to plausibility merely one aspect of his interrogation of novelistic limits. Through its vast experience, the bowl has acquired the habit of describing human attributes and behaviour through an elaborate system of classification. Detecting a duplicitous character the bowl records: 'this is number fifty-nine of the two hundred and ten ways of lying, the technique I like to call the wild strawberry' (p. 13). The humour of this device soon palls; but what it highlights is an assumption about fiction in which the unrestricted knowledge of a narrator demonstrably breaks the expected limits of the narrative range, producing, in this case, knowledge that can have no relationship to a reader's experience.

In *Scepticism Inc.* (1998) Bo Fowler also creates a non-human narrator – his is a supermarket trolley with a belief in God – but makes the conceit part of an elaborate fusion of fictional modes. Science Fiction provides the stimulus for the shopping trolley fitted with an 'Infinity Chip', which boasts consciousness and artificial intelligence (p. 24), and which has been programmed with a belief in God (p. 29). Set mainly in the 2020s, the book is essentially a satire on organized religion; the novel has an elaborate plot in which the trolley becomes agnostic, through the influence of Edgar Malroy, a philanthropist who establishes the vast empire of 'Scepticism Inc.' with profits from a global chain of metaphysical betting shops. The agnostic Malroy goads believers of all faiths and creeds to place bets on metaphysical (and so unprovable assertions), thereby accruing huge wealth, which is redirected to ambitious philanthropic projects embracing world peace, Third World regeneration, and the ending of world hunger. In pursuing his moral – 'people matter more than The Truth' (p. 248) – Fowler progresses far beyond a restricted mode of internal reflection, and produces a hybrid fable: explicit, humorous, fantastic, yet rooted in a considered analysis of global human organization. However, a consequence of this kind of hybrid, with an emphasis on a complex and fast-moving plot, is that the style can seem mechanistic, bereft of description or poetic resonance.

## The Fallacy of the New

In his review, Andy Beckett felt its Spartan style made *Scepticism Inc.* representative of 'a kind of modern writing' in which 'the spareness is playful, a mocking of literary craft'.[47] Perhaps, in constructing a moral fable with global implications, Fowler is justifiably impatient with the finer points of literary expression; but does his ethical motivation reveal a writer in pursuit of an entirely new literary sensibility? Beckett observes that the ultimate failure of the humanitarian project in *Scepticism Inc.* is rendered through a mood of sadness, and this encourages him to make an interesting link: 'like Damien Hirst's better work, the melancholy makes all the tricks worth bearing'.[48] Is there, then, a connection between the challenge of modern British art, with its visceral emphasis on biological decay, and its (apparently) vigorous reconceptualization of the art object, and a new mood in contemporary British fiction, similarly reconceiving the novel, and seeking to make more immediate connections with an ethics in which the consciousness of human mortality is paramount? Here a degree of critical scepticism is called for, however: there are grounds for questioning whether or not the sense of newness or 'sensation' that is sometimes claimed for contemporary British art is much more than a marketing ploy.[49] For the literary culture, assessed over a fifty-year period – a relatively short time-span in literary history – one can discern the appearance of many dynamic new writers and important trends; but such trends do not emerge overnight.

An instructive example of how newness can be overstated is embodied in a collection of short stories written by fifteen celebrated young writers (including Bo Fowler), entitled *All Hail the New Puritans* (Nicholas Blincoe and Matt Thorne, eds. [London: Fourth Estate, 2000]). The contributions of the assembled new literati are required to conform to an austere set of commandments, an ambiguous gesture that is 'partly playful, but equally serious'. The strictures that form 'The New Puritan Manifesto' privilege storytelling over the self-conscious technical experiments of the likes of B. S. Johnson or Italo Calvino, an emphasis that involves the shunning of 'poetry and poetic licence in all its forms' and the adherence to 'temporal linearity'. The favoured principle of 'textual simplicity' necessitates a 'vow to avoid all devices of voice: rhetoric, authorial asides', whilst an emphasis 'on the present day' with its actual 'products, places, artists and objects' is a direct challenge to the perceived dominance of the historical novel, and the 'heritage theme park' version of literature it implies. The stress on 'the here and now' is presented as the antidote to the loss of faith in literature, a redressing of the balance that is conceived as an ethical responsibility, the obligation for the writer 'to create entirely new ways for people to relate to each other'.[50] Fowler's *Scepticism Inc.* might be said to work in the spirit of these injunctions, if they are interpreted broadly.

'The New Puritan Manifesto' introduces an exercise in short-story writing, but is really an intervention in the state of the novel. It is remarkable, however, for retreading very familiar ground, and reasserting an enduring tradition of affiliation to the prosaic, the tried and tested, in post-war literature. In this respect, a line of continuity can be drawn between the Movement writers of the 1950s, and the stated intention of these not-so-new puritans, whose manifesto is scarcely the radical challenge it purports to be. Neither has there been a paucity of writing about the 'here and now', as the current survey, with its stress on the social and historical dimension of the post-war novel, shows. But it is also the technical and perspectival diversity that signals the value of post-war British fiction, rather than its conformity to the narrow 'English ideology' that resurfaces here, with its distrust of experimental excess.[51] In fact, the collection features some interesting writers whose careers can scarcely be said to conform to the straitjacket of the puritan manifesto.

Geoff Dyer's *The Colour of Memory* (1989), for instance, flouts most of the rules. Dyer's debut conveys the uncertain mood of a lost generation of would-be artists and intellectuals in 1980s London, struggling to find meaning in a context where money is all-significant, and where politics seems pointless. For the narrator, agreeing to be a respondent in telephone market research seems 'a more effective form of political involvement than voting' (p. 150). Dyer steeps his novel in the mood of a Bohemian Brixton in which friendship and the pursuit of personal pleasure ameliorate the deadening effects of an increasingly materialistic and violent city, and in this there is a powerful evocation of the 'here and now'. Even so, Dyer's main preoccupation is with the sensibility of his lost generation, and in evoking this he eschews a plot-driven narrative, and writes an impressionistic set of episodes in which the favoured technique is the self-conscious search for poetic effects. The kind of patterning the reader is encouraged to recognize is indicated in the novel's title, with its Proustian suggestion of the sensory labelling of a particular moment, creating a pattern of mnemonics that operates beyond the level of the simple narrative.

Many of the episodes end with archly poetic effects. Thus the sound of Mahler and the reading of Nietzsche on a Brixton rooftop combine to emphasize the need to live for the moment (pp. 82–3); a hazy mist surrounding Big Ben and the Houses of Parliament makes the seat of power seem momentarily insubstantial (p. 119); a conversation is coloured by the perception that the pattern on a door evokes 'the mast of a sinking ship' (p. 105). The book overall is so structured as to deny temporal linearity: the episodes are numbered in reverse, producing a countdown to zero that corresponds with the electronic countdown to the year 2000 outside the Pompidou Centre in Paris. The narrator recalls this as denoting 'a new kind of time' that is 'both awe-inspiring and, at the same time, absolutely pointless: pure anticipation' (p. 207). It is this empty march of time, in an England 'getting very close to being uninhabitable' (p. 109), that the novel reproduces in its own apocalyptic countdown, whilst offering resistance, simultaneously, through its arresting poetic images.

Candida Clark is another 'new puritan' with false credentials. *The Last Look* (1998) avoids a simple temporal linearity, and deploys a style of high lyrical sensuality, a mode that is often (and rather dubiously) seen as a peculiarly feminine phenomenon, where 'feminine' denotes a primary interest in the relationship between sexuality and internal feelings, rather than in social and historical context. (In *Sleepwalking* [1994] Julie Myerson shows herself a prime exponent of this type of writing.) A first glance at Clark's *The Last Look* suggests a self-enclosed rendering of intense but destructive private passion, where love and ruin are two sides of a single coin (p. 35). But a more sustained look might detect the hint of an allegory about (and a repudiation of) that enduring post-war concern that the English novel is overshadowed by the achievements of American fiction. This is obvious enough in the lifelong passion of an English writer for an American author known only briefly; yet the English writer emerges as the sole survivor of the (reciprocated) passion, and in this there is a suggestion of defiant independence, a quality that can also be ascribed to Clark's writing. In this novel Clark takes the notionally enclosed 'feminine' style into a metafictional territory with which it is not usually associated.

These examples illustrate the general principle that interesting and significant novels do not adhere to a programmatic manner of composition; the edifying model is one of evolution, rather than revolution. Literary history enjoins us to appreciate innovation as a gradual process; it also exposes the false claims of literary fashion. A case in point is the rise, in the 1990s, of so-called 'Lad Lit' and 'Chick Lit' novels that concern themselves with the tribulations of urban twenty- and thirty-somethings faced with changing heterosexual mores and the pursuit of a desired lifestyle. This is a prime example of a phenomenon that reveals its significance in an evolving paradigm of novelistic change, but that surrenders its import once refashioned as a new vogue. Nick Hornby might be hailed as the originator of 'Lad Lit', whilst its counterpart might be said to originate with Helen Fielding. This has certainly been the view of broadsheet articles on the phenomenon, of which the following is representative: 'The Chick-Lit novel (twenty-something-girl-shares-flat-has-crap-job-and-life-full-of-petty-annoyances-which-can-only-be-alleviated-by-finding-the-right-guy) is a relatively new genre, dating no further back than Bridget Jones.'[52] It is worth remembering, lest critical amnesia might be said to replicate the self-congratulatory narrowness of these genres, that this kind of genre fiction has actually been a more enduring feature of the post-war literary scene. In 1970 Bernard Bergonzi lamented the repetitive types into which new fiction frequently fell, one of which he summarized in this manner: 'Fey, mixed-up Joanna, in Earl's Court bedsitter, has trouble with boy – and girl – friends.' Another recognizable type comprised the 'lightly written tale of nice young adman with scruples. He overcomes them, sleeps with the boss's wife, but marries the girl from back home.' These types, emphasizing the sexual and professional anxieties of the urban young, anticipate 'Lad' and 'Chick Lit' very closely.

The crucial difference is that, for Bergonzi, the repetitiveness found in contemporary fiction a generation ago was 'unconsciously generic', partly on account of 'the narrowness of the experience which the authors can put into it', but also because of the formulaic nature of the modern novel, which these writers had internalized.[53] By contrast, 'Lad' and 'Chick Lit' is *consciously* generic, and aggressively marketed on this basis. The formulae dictated by the generic type might appear to enforce a disastrous delimitation; yet the principal novels of Nick Hornby and Helen Fielding reveal something more interesting about the social function of the novel than the generic straitjacket was soon to allow.[54] With the false claims of newness put in perspective, both writers can be seen to have afforded a revealing insight into the social moment.

Fielding's *Bridget Jones's Diary* (1996) is based on a column written for *The Independent*, so it might seem inappropriate to project the criteria for a serious novel on to a book that started life as a series of humorous newspaper sketches. The finished novel, however, is well-crafted, taking Austen's *Pride and Prejudice* as its ironic blueprint. Moreover, *Bridget Jones's Diary* has proved hugely influential in the resurgence of lifestyle fiction, and precisely because it is felt to have accurately recorded the *zeitgeist* of the 1990s. As the *TLS* reviewer put it, the book 'rings with the unmistakable tone of something that is true to the marrow; it defines what it describes. I know for certain that if I were a young, single, urban woman, I would finish this book crying, "Bridget Jones, c'est moi." '[55]

Bridget Jones, a thirty-something with a junior post in publishing, embodies the anxieties of the single woman in a society that makes her feel the desperate urgency of finding Mr Right; or, as Bridget's new year resolution puts it, the need to 'form functional relationship with responsible adult' (p. 3). Her diary entries begin with a ready reckoning of, for instance, how many calories, cigarettes, and alcohol units she has consumed, the occasional self-congratulation for abstemiousness punctured by the cumulative impression that personal desire and the need for solace run counter to faddish restraints. Insofar as Fielding's humour deflates Bridget's idealized self-image, the vanity and self-regard of this social world becomes a focus of satire, as when Bridget reflects that a close friend could have been suicidal, unbeknown to friends, who are 'all so selfish and busy in London' (p. 261). The structure of the book, meanwhile, colludes with Bridget's romantic projection, tracing her misguided affair with her sexually incontinent boss, an 'emotional fuckwit' in the parlance of Bridget's circle of female friends, through to the satisfactory romantic conclusion of her sexual union with the high-profile barrister Mark Darcy. Bridget's response to this Darcy, who is explicitly compared with Austen's (p. 244), mimics the slowly dawning awareness of Elizabeth Bennet: Bridget, too, must overcome a misperception of her Darcy's haughtiness, to allow her love, rooted in admiration for his dynamic masculine moral rectitude, to flourish. The parallel is ironic, of course, though it does supply Fielding's narrative structure.

In a retrospective review of *Bridget Jones's Diary* Zoë Heller places the novel in a new tradition of confessional feminine first-person narrative (or FFPN) in which the aim 'to replicate the easy, jokey, demotic tone of girl talk', involves a 'candid admission of female silliness and vanity'. Heller sees this as an aspect of 1990s post-feminism, the 'subversion of the expectations created by all those Virago paperbacks'. Bergonzi's identification of the earlier generic type – 'fey, mixed-up Joanna, in Earl's Court bedsitter' – shows that the situation of a Bridget Jones has a longer provenance. The shift towards the confessional style is also part of a more gradual change. Yet the new emphasis of FFPN explicitly challenges the 'feminist postures' of the intervening period (that is, since 1970), which are characterized by 'self-sufficiency and sisterhood'. FFPN is thus reinvigorating in Heller's account, offering 'resoundingly incorrect' elements of female experience (such as the desire 'to be sexually objectified'), making women's writing 'surprising again' before hardening into a 'new literary orthodoxy'.[56] This is well observed, and it may be Fielding's novel alone that will emerge as the significant example of this fleeting moment of genuine post-feminist surprise.

In many ways Nick Hornby's *High Fidelity* (1995), set in north London, is the masculine precursor to Fielding's portrait of female insecurity in the 1990s. Hornby's first book, the confessional memoir *Fever Pitch* (1992), introduced the kind of soft-hearted, but honest analysis of the confused male identity that Hornby develops in *High Fidelity*, his first novel. As with the treatment of Bridget Jones, the gender-specific foibles and shortcomings of Rob Fleming, the confessional narrator, are exposed in such a way as to insist on the ordinariness of his plight. This is the essence of the broad appeal of both works: each one relies on the comedy of recognition in its depiction of social and (especially) sexual inadequacy in a 'smart' singles culture where weakness is deemed to be unappealing. Both Bridget Jones and Rob Fleming resist the lifestyle that superficially circumscribes them, and both seek solace in the comforts of popular culture, as significant protagonists in post-war fiction, from Jim Dixon onwards, invariably have. And where the quest of Bridget Jones is for that 'functional relationship with responsible adult', Rob Fleming's tacit goal is to become 'a fully-functioning human being' (p. 153).

It is in the structure of the personal quest, however, that *High Fidelity* reveals greater pretensions to seriousness than are found in *Bridget Jones's Diary*. In delivering an idealized romantic conclusion, albeit with an element of irony, Fielding's book effectively refashions its heroine as the deserving recipient of the modern-day Darcy's attentions: the comic structure undermines the critical self-analysis. Rob Fleming, however, goes through a more protracted process of self-evaluation that forces him to confront the source of his emotional immaturity. In this sense the novel is one of moral growth in which the protagonist begins to realize his potential 'as a human being' (p. 210), by finding a new language, and a new way of relating to women.

As the owner of a small record shop, Fleming has retained the musical snobbishness of the teenage male, together with a simplistic way of classifying experience. Rob's partner Laura has left him at the beginning of the book, and the narrative focus is on the terms of their eventual reunion, after Rob's misguided 'what-does-it-all-mean' (p. 161) attempt to make contact with the women listed in his 'top five most memorable split-ups' (p. 9), and his brief affair with an American folk/country singer-songwriter.[57] Hornby brazenly uses the psychoanalytic 'truism' that it is a fear of mortality that makes men resist monogamy and domestic stability, but pushes this further to suggest that a direct confrontation with death might also have the reverse effect. The death of Laura's father is the *deus ex machina* that brings them back together, and that eventually elicits from him a fumbling, unromantic proposal, which is appreciated, but not accepted (pp. 249–50).

The relationship had started with Rob making a compilation tape for Laura of his favourite music; it ends with his epiphanic realization that it would be better to compile a tape that's 'full of stuff she's heard of, and full of stuff she'd play' (p. 253). This represents a surprisingly moving conclusion, because it condenses the sense of ordinary, masculine impercipience that pervades the novel. It is a simple enough recognition of the need to privilege the needs of another, but one that profoundly contests the surrounding lifestyle culture. Both *High Fidelity* and *Bridget Jones's Diary* advance the democratization of narrative fiction – one of the keynote developments in the post-war novel – in which the distinction between high- and low-brow expression is satisfactorily blurred.[58] It is ironic that works that exhibit a degree of contempt for the cult of materialistic self-definition should have spawned the generic lifestyle fiction of their 'Lad' and 'Chick Lit' imitators.

## A Broken Truth: Murdoch and Morality

The thread that links many of the works discussed in this survey is the pursuit of a viable ethical stance or vision. The implicit claim I am making is that the social novel, in the post-war years, has consolidated its claim to being the privileged form of moral discourse in a secular world. The novel, with its imaginative range, and its freedom from 'factual' codes, becomes an important focus for the society's alternative, redemptive, and connective thought. In the light of this assertion, it seems appropriate to conclude this survey with a consideration of the writer most closely associated with the moral philosophy of fiction: Iris Murdoch. In tracing, briefly, some of Murdoch's philosophical ideas, particularly those that have a bearing on novelistic form, I have in mind their more general relevance to the literary culture, and especially to the formal problems that surface in the work of writers such as Angus Wilson, Margaret Drabble, Graham Swift, Kazuo Ishiguro, Martin Amis, and Ian McEwan.

Iris Murdoch's fiction is underpinned by a moral philosophy, though it could be claimed that her novels approach a kind of moral philosophy itself, in practice. The distinction is between writing that is influenced by philosophical ideas, and writing that approximates philosophical expression.[59] The grounds for making the more extravagant claim – for Murdoch as the author of 'philosophical novels' – is suggested in her 'polemical sketch' theorizing about the role of fiction, called 'Against Dryness' (1961). Here Murdoch seeks to identify two opposing views of individual motivation and behaviour. On the one hand, there is 'the Humian and post-Humian side' that stresses the significance of public language and concepts to the realization of the 'inner life', concepts that can only be established 'on the basis of overt behaviour'. The alternative tradition is derived from Kant, and (for Murdoch) is epitomized in the work of Sartre, where the individual is deemed to be solitary and 'totally free'. Yes, there are 'psychological desires and social habits and prejudices', but these are distinct from the will. What Murdoch is after is a synthesis of these opposing philosophical views, a theory that perceives the individual to be free and separate, but at the same time involved with the social world as 'a moral being'.[60]

Murdoch goes on to characterize two types of twentieth-century novel, both of which are unable to resolve the perceived philosophical dichotomy. First, there is the 'crystalline' or 'quasi-allegorical' novel that fails to produce characters in the manner of the nineteenth-century novel; second, there is the 'journalistic' or 'quasi-documentary' novel, defined as a 'degenerate descendant' of the achievements of the previous century. Acknowledging that the better novels are those written in the 'crystalline' mode, Murdoch then reveals its real danger: the tendency to console us with myths or stories, but without seeking to grapple with 'reality'. The solution to this formal problem involves the recuperation of a moral world with a structure more complex than that defined by liberal democratic society. This is the heart of Murdoch's polemic, in which freedom hinges upon a more complex form of attention than that encouraged by a welfare state. Significantly, Murdoch places literature at the centre of this project, arguing that it has taken over some of philosophy's own tasks. She is after a form of fiction that will make us realize that 'reality is not a given whole'. Such a realization involves 'a respect for the contingent', and privileges 'imagination' over 'fantasy'. The failure conceived as a consequence of an impoverished world-view is here reconfigured as a problem of literary form, in which the desire for consolation can be overcome by a broader concept of form that embraces contingency, and does so, particularly, through the naturalistic deployment of character.[61]

This is really a manifesto for the kind of novel that will foster a complex moral and social identity. Such a formulation, however, might seem to overstate the political role of the novel, which is minimal, by any tangible measure; but Murdoch's theory seeks to establish the *capacity* of the novel, from which its social *function* – at the level of ideas – might be assumed to follow. There is also a sense of *duty* about this that makes novelistic composition itself a moral process: it is the form of the novel that might now carry the ideas formerly treated in philosophy. This actually puts a different complexion on the distinction between a fully fledged 'philosophical novel', and one that is merely influenced by philosophical ideas. According to Murdoch's understanding one might call a novel philosophical by virtue of its overall formal properties, even if the prose itself does not attempt the intellectual rigour of philosophical discourse. Equally, however, if prose fiction has usurped the social function of philosophy, then the term 'philosophical novel' would seem limiting, even redundant: all successful novels will, by definition, address the philosophical problems Murdoch identifies, in some measure, and will have a recognizable social character.

Murdoch's first novel *Under the Net* (1954) anticipates the kind of novel she appears to have in mind in her polemical sketch. The novel is so structured as to frame a lesson for its narrator Jake Donaghue, who progresses from a solipsistic hater of contingency (p. 24), to someone who stands on the brink of celebrating his place in a broader social network. He stands also on the point of beginning a career as a creative writer, as he perceives the shortcomings of his juvenilia, as well as the possibility of doing better. Jake, it seems, will put aside his translation work, and become a novelist in the Murdoch mould (pp. 250–1).

The net of language, however, is shown to present an obstruction to the attainment of objective truth; and, in this there is a warning against the consoling falsity of stories, indicating the difficulty the artist faces: 'only the greatest men can speak and still be truthful. Any artist knows this obscurely' (p. 81). This identifies the paradox that the novel treats discursively. The potential failure of words, and the moral deficiency this implies, is amply illustrated in the befuddled career of Jake Donaghue. In this sense, the novel appears as a ground-clearing exercise, demonstrating the falsity of language through the purblindness of its protagonist. This might seem merely to bring the character to the brink of a new kind of moral seriousness that the novel itself lacks. Murdoch contrives through emplotment to realize that all-important social and moral matrix; but there is an unresolved conflict in *Under the Net* between order and chaos, so the novel is an enactment of the problem rather than an approximate solution to it. The 'solution', which Murdoch worries away at throughout her career, appears, in the end, to involve a more rigorous manner of embracing that tension between order and chaos.

A further key to understanding Murdoch's fiction is contained in her substantial work of philosophy, *Metaphysics as a Guide to Morals* (1992). Here Murdoch sets out to confront that persisting paradox, in which the attempt to theorize in abstract terms – to impose some kind of shape or order on human experience – seems not to chime with the chaotic and contingent nature of individual lives. The approach Murdoch seeks is one that can embrace the two contrary pulls, the systematic and the particular. In a lucid essay Maria Antonaccio shows how this two-way movement is central to her theory of art as well as to her moral thought: for Murdoch 'a truthful apprehension of individuals' requires unifying thought, the imposition of 'artful shape' on 'fragmentary lives', in combination with 'a particularizing kind of thinking, which resists the impulse to order or classify and instead individuates phenomena'. This paradox is paralleled in Murdoch's theory of the novel, in the necessary tension between form and contingency, the need for a 'unified aesthetic whole' set against the requirement to evoke the 'disunity and randomness' of 'ordinary life'.[62]

It is a difficult balance to achieve, especially as the need for formal unity can easily tip the balance towards the kind of gratification or consolation that serves to conceal truth. Aesthetic form is thus ambivalent, in itself presenting a moral dilemma for the artist.[63] Antonaccio summarizes this theory succinctly: 'the truth captured by art remains a broken truth; the novel remains a provisional art form, aware of its own consolations'.[64]

What makes this theory of the novel distinct from similar theories – a Structuralist-Marxist account of formal dissonance, for example – is the philosophical understanding of human consciousness that underpins it. Again, Antonaccio accounts lucidly for the way in which, for Murdoch, 'the structure of consciousness' is also 'the mode of moral being'. Murdoch identifies two constitutive features of consciousness, the first of which is the need to make unity and order out of randomness, an aspect that is 'correlative to . . . the metaphysical attempt to impose unity or order on our moral existence'. The second feature of consciousness is the pursuit of truth, and the associated tendency to make value judgements on the basis of truth and falsity. Thus human consciousness is usually structured to pursue truth or goodness by enacting the same kind of tussle that issues in the tension between form and contingency found in the novel.[65]

If this seems an idealistic perception of humanity, its formal implications are intriguing, since, in Murdoch's view, the novel is *necessarily* constituted as a moral investigation, staging the conflict, and seeking the combination of, the two distinctive tendencies of moral inquiry. This lends an underlying seriousness to certain characteristics of her novels that might otherwise seem trite or insignificant. Take, for example, the neat conclusion of *The Nice and the Good* (1968) in which the goodness of John Ducane enables him to preside over the series of felicitous romantic attachments that, in the manner of Shakespearean comedy, resolves the various love conflicts and disappointments. It is a tidy ending that renders insignificant the novel's burdensome evils, such as McGrath's inclination to blackmail, Radeechy's black magic, and even Willy Kost's burden of guilt from the Holocaust. Yet this consoling triumph of formal resolution does not go unremarked: at the very end the twins Henrietta and Edward are seen observing the flying saucer that had previously seemed a product of their childish imagination (pp. 361–2). They imagine the craft to contain 'good people', thus extending the pattern of unity and beneficence to the extra-terrestrial realm. Murdoch, clearly, is sending up her own comedy, undermining its neatness in the process.

The novel that enacts Murdoch's theory of the novel most explicitly is *The Black Prince* (1973), where even the suggestive title resists a unified reading. The Black Prince evokes the fourteenth-century historical figure, son of Edward III, as well as the devil, referred to as 'The Black Prince' in *All's Well That Ends Well* (IV.v.42). The dominance of *Hamlet* as a leitmotif, however, especially in key scenes, makes a parallel between Hamlet and narrator Bradley Pearson unavoidable. Pearson is also associated with Apollo or Loxias, the Greek god with several powers pertinent to Pearson's various predicaments, and to his function in the novel's implicit investigation of the artist's role. Apollo is a paradox, a sun god who inspired the arts, was a healer and a prophet, yet who is also associated with death and destruction. Pearson's initials (BP) signal, of course, that he is the ambivalent Black Prince, an identity central to the novel's argument about art.

Pearson considers himself a writer, and has retired from his work as a tax inspector to devote himself to writing. His reputation rests, however, on just three 'slim volumes': two novels and a book of '*pensées*' (p. 13). By contrast, his friend and arch rival Arnold Baffin is a prolific and popular novelist, a 'one-book-a-year man' (p. 23) who represents the opposing pole in the debate about writing.[66] Murdoch, of course, is the prime example of an author who can combine the seriousness of a Bradley Pearson with the work-rate of an Arnold Baffin, and the novel makes an implicit case for this kind of intellectual middle-ground. Pearson has, initially, a precious and pompous attitude to novel writing, epitomized in the review he has drafted of Baffin's latest novel, which he describes as 'a thriller' (not merely 'like a thriller', as its blurb implies), and, therefore, not 'a work of art'. *The Black Prince*, of course, is both a thriller and an accomplished piece of serious writing.

For Pearson, the turning point comes when he experiences a mad passion for Baffin's daughter, Julian, a girl thirty-eight years his junior, who has always admired him. There is a very funny sequence in which the infatuated Pearson feels at one with the world; but the more significant aspect of this new harmony is his understanding that his erstwhile attitude to writing may have been wrong. 'Even great art is jumble in the end' (p. 240), he acknowledges, in a major concession to the impact of contingency, and in this mood he wonders if he has been unfair to Baffin, and resolves to read 'the whole of his work' (p. 216). It is not, however, a permanent change of heart: as the love affair begins to fail, principally as a result of Baffin's interference, Pearson writes carpingly to him that 'some part of you has always envied me because I have kept my gift pure and you have not' (p. 352).

The various love complications result in catastrophic violence. Arnold Baffin is killed by his wife Rachel, who has discovered his attachment to Pearson's ex-wife. Rachel also contrives to frame Pearson for the murder, and the 'thriller' aspect leads to this drama. The novel's frame establishes that the narrative 'Bradley Pearson's Story', perhaps his great work, is a recollection written from prison, and edited by a fellow inmate 'P. A. Loxias'. The conceit is that Loxias (whose surname is another name for Apollo) has invited some of the 'dramatis personae' to read and comment on the manuscript. Pearson's story is duly followed by several self-justifying postscripts, including contributions from his ex-wife Rachel Baffin and Julian herself. A postscript by Loxias concludes the novel, in which the death of Pearson is revealed. Loxias also points out the contradictions in the other postscripts, and this serves to privilege the perspective of Pearson.

It is Julian's postscript that is the most uncomfortable. She has become a writer, and articulates her response in the form of disinterested theorizing. It is just possible to read this cruel response as a kind of self-protection; but one is more inclined to see in Julian the development of the worst kind of artist (for Murdoch), the abstract thinker who denies the contingent muddle of life, and for whom 'true art is very very cold' (p. 410). Julian does, however (though somewhat dismissively), reveal that her love for Pearson had been genuine, and this is crucial. For her, it was 'a love which words cannot describe' (p. 411).

By contrast, Pearson subtitles his story 'A celebration of Love', indicating that, for all his uncertainty and vacillation about the business of writing, his own major effort engages primarily with the messy business of articulating his own grand passion. If this seems too egotistical for Murdoch's views on the selflessness of proper novelistic intervention, the danger is countered by the revelation of Pearson's death. The killing off of her Black Prince is, of course, a characteristic double-move by Murdoch, serving both to heighten our sense of his tragedy, and to move us through and beyond the excessive engagement with one particular self; but it is a discomfiting book, which offers no overt consolation to the reader.

The process of self-advancement for characters such as Jake Donaghue and Bradley Pearson depends upon the acceptance of contingency and a concomitant flight from egoism. But, seen in terms of these opposing worldviews, the moral dilemma in unresolved. The element that requires further elaboration is causality, another Murdochian preoccupation surrounded by ambivalence. For Jake Donaghue, the defeat of egoism involves the recognition that other people had not been affected by him in the way that he had imagined, and this might seem to suggest that, in a contingent world, the outcomes of an individual's actions cannot be predicted or known. But, of course, Murdoch is very much concerned with the broader social network that surrounds the individual, and the responsibility taken for actions. In a contingent world causality is fraught with difficulty.

This concern is prominent in *The Sea, The Sea* (1978), the first of a group of longer, later novels in which Murdoch's investigation of goodness engages more overtly with mystical and religious questions. This is not to imply a lack of clarity, for the dilemma of narrator Charles Arrowby is sharply drawn. Arrowby, a famous man of the theatre (actor, playwright, and director), buys a house at the sea's edge, and plans to retire to a life of solitude from which a memoir will emerge. (The memoir/diary he starts to write forms the novel.) The irony is that he is hardly alone at all before his past comes to haunt him, in the form of various associates and ex-lovers.

Towards the end, Arrowby begins to realize his own complicity in the chain of causality that stems from his interference in the lives of others (p. 459). His extreme actions, prompted by his obsessive desires, are redeemed by the benign influence of his cousin James, whose Buddhist philosophy has a direct bearing on the topic of causality. The teaching of Buddhism, of course, places great stress on the consequences of actions and on individual responsibility – until one is liberated from the wheel of life. (James, who wills his own death having assisted in the resolution of Arrowby's muddle as far as he can, appears to achieve liberation.) At a formal level, Murdoch demonstrates that, ultimately, the novel cannot approach this kind of transcendence. The episode at the sea ends in a mood of serenity, with Arrowby finally encountering the seals he had previously longed to see. He feels the blessing of these beneficent beings (p. 476), which supplant the image of the sea-monster that had haunted him before. The novel proper ends at this point, but rather than conclude with this state of grace, Murdoch writes a postscript that sees Arrowby back in London, and apparently on the verge of recommencing his monstrous old life. Just as Buddhism cannot contain the devastating effects of worldly human passion, neither does Murdoch leave the redemptive conclusion of Arrowby's seaside sojourn undisturbed: the postscript is presented in a studiously piecemeal and inconclusive fashion.[67]

Murdoch's art is a fitting subject with which to conclude a survey that has sought to uncover the element of continuity in the evolving trends of post-war British fiction, for Murdoch's theory of the novel furnishes us with an intellectual bridge in two ways. First, she helps us discern a point of continuity between different critical perspectives. Her moral philosophy has something in common with the best elements of the liberal humanism that dominated the literary criticism of the 1950s and 1960s; yet the importance of contingency to her moral thought suggests a progression beyond this old-style humanism with its foundational roots, and in a way that anticipates the 'postmodern ethics' of the 1980s and 1990s. As John Sturrock rightly claims, 'the highest of moral values' for Murdoch is 'a total attentiveness to what is other than oneself'.[68] Murdoch seems to have fashioned a philosophy for the novel that is precisely in tune with the ethical project of Emanuel Levinas – the principal intellectual inspiration for most postmodern ethics – and his preoccupation with 'the responsibility for the Other, for another freedom'.[69] In the new critical elaboration of ethics, one finds a Murdochian stress on imagination, understood as a power of 'speculation and adumbration'.[70] In this conception, 'ethics' combines the desire for convergence with a studied irresolution, and is very much in the spirit of what Murdoch means by 'morals'.[71]

The second, and most important, chain of association that Murdoch provides is in linking the different novelists at work throughout the period. Her scrupulous thinking about the role of the novel and the novelist in the advancement of an ethical world-view, suggests a fruitful way in which the vision of many novelists can be appreciated in their struggle with form. One thinks instantly of Margaret Drabble or Ian McEwan, Martin Amis or Graham Swift, in this connection.

In the case of writers like McEwan or Amis, the ethical content is often embedded in disturbing fictions, in which a narrator may take up a position that is dubious or depraved. The sense of complicity with the corrupt late twentieth century is part of the writing strategy in the work of these writers, since both seek to convey the seductive appeal of contemporary addictions and appetites, in order to make them fully understood. The recurring trope of innocence in McEwan and Amis, as Kiernan Ryan has shown, reminds us that complicity is 'not innate but acquired', thus supplying one way out of the circle of violence and ugliness.[72] What makes Murdoch's own moral philosophy unique is her conviction that human consciousness works in such a way as to stage repeated moral dilemmas, in a perpetual effort to balance the claims of unity and discrimination. McEwan and Amis represent a more tortuous ethical effort that implies that the writer needs to be unhampered by 'conscious educative intent and political decorum' in order to 'push back the frontiers of moral understanding'.[73] There is no certainty about innate human goodness in this, but a determination to use fiction to exorcise our collective complicity in the worst excesses of the contemporary.

The persistence of moral or ethical inquiry in successive generations of novelists underscores the link between the novel and society, concerning especially our perception of public life, our understanding of cultural forms, and the construction of our personal identities. And I have tried to borrow from this ethical orientation: the mission of this survey overall has been to explore the diverse strands of the post-war novel that treats of contemporary social themes, but without seeking to discover monolithic formal rules. I have chanced upon different brands of formal hybridity, where 'innovation' can embrace tradition, and where the reworking of realism can be just as insightful as its rejection. Each of the novels discussed, whether apparently 'realist' or 'experimental', makes its discursive intervention in such a way as to reinforce connections between text and context. (As Paul Ricoeur's theory of mimesis implies, the self-conscious text can emphasize the mimetic effect — conceived as 'representation' rather than 'imitation' — especially well.[74])

As the viability of the realist/experimental dichotomy has broken down, so have critical efforts to retain its terminology been strained to their limits.[75] It may be, however, that the critical attempt to establish schools or categories, an imperfect, but necessary process of explication, needs to be explicitly understood as a *provisional* process. In making this case, I am advocating a critical practice that resists the logic of academic professionalization, as well as the normative approach taken by most novel reviewers, who, when finding fault with a novel, usually do so on the grounds that it does not conform to some hidden template. What is required is a properly ethical criticism, sensitive to its object as other, and that is willing to withhold its own frameworks of understanding in the critical encounter (as far as this is possible). Such a criticism would resist the temptation to prioritize a system of interpretation, complete in itself; it would privilege, instead, the text's own individual attributes, allowing these to modify the critical language. (The critical-creative cross-fertilization this implies would seem to be especially important in the difficult process of interpreting contemporary writing, without the advantage of historical hindsight.) This method — of, essentially, allowing the accumulating body of evidence to fashion the critical judgement — is one that I have tried to pursue, however imperfectly, in the writing of this survey. Looking back at the diversity of my findings, I can at least claim that the approach has revealed a variety of impressive formal solutions to the perennial problem of reinventing the social novel. And this permits me the luxury of a concluding (but suitably open) critical judgement: the novel of post-war history and society in Britain has been phenomenally rich and inventive, a genre in a state of creative expansion, and as far removed from terminal decline as it is possible to imagine.

# Notes

## Introduction

1. Steven Connor, *The English Novel in History, 1950–1995* (London: Routledge, 1996), p. 1.
2. Andrzej Gąsiorek, *Post-War British Fiction: Realism and After* (London: Edward Arnold, 1995).
3. See, for example, Meredith Veldman, *Fantasy, the Bomb, and the Greening of Britain: Romantic Protest, 1945–1980* (Cambridge University Press, 1994).
4. Homi Bhabha, 'DissemiNation: Time, Narrative, and the Margins of the Modern Nation', in Bhabha, ed., *Nation and Narration*, (London: Routledge, 1990), pp. 291–322.
5. James Gindin, *Postwar British Fiction: New Accents and Attitudes* (Berkeley: University of California Press, 1963), p. 12.
6. *Ibid.*, pp. 105–6.
7. For an account of the significant developments in publishing and the evolving readership see Connor, *The English Novel in History*, pp. 13–27.
8. D. J. Taylor, *A Vain Conceit: British Fiction in the 1980s* (London: Bloomsbury, 1989), p. 14.
9. Arthur Marwick, *British Society Since 1945*, third edn (Harmondsworth: Penguin, 1996), pp. 97, 76.
10. David Lodge, 'The Novelist at the Crossroads' (1969), abridged version printed in Malcolm Bradbury ed., *The Novel Today: Contemporary Writers on Modern Fiction*, new edn (London: Fontana, 1990), pp. 87–114.
11. Bernard Bergonzi, *The Situation of the Novel* (1970; Harmondsworth: Penguin, 1972), pp. 67, 68.
12. In his subsequent criticism Bergonzi saw in the English novel grounds for greater optimism. See, for example, his celebration of J. G. Farrell in 'Fictions of History', in Malcolm Bradbury and David Palmer eds., *The Contemporary English Novel* (London: Edward Arnold, 1979), pp. 42–65. Interviewed in 1990, Bergonzi looked back on the late 1960s and early 1970s, recalling the 'literary critical myth' that 'English fiction was domestic and dull and commonplace and small-scale, whereas the Americans were going for the biggie'. In 1990, Bergonzi saw 'much less of a clear distinction' between English

and American fiction. Martin Amis's *Money* betokened a productive cross-fertilization, 'a most brilliant novel which has a great deal of American writing in it – Mailer, Burroughs and so on – but which is also a painfully sharply observed work of English social comedy'. From an interview with Nicolas Tredell, extract reprinted in Tredell, ed., *The Fiction of Martin Amis: A Reader's Guide to Essential Criticism* (Cambridge: Icon, 2000), pp. 60–1.

13. Taylor, *A Vain Conceit*, pp. 131, 132.

14. See, for example, Bradbury's summary of three strong generations of writers, from the 1950s through to the 1990s, in *The Modern British Novel* (London: Secker and Warburg, 1993), p. 455.

15. In 1970 Bergonzi contrasted the attitude of young American writers, who thought 'that novels must be *written*', with young English writers who seemed 'merely to exude them'. Bergonzi declared himself to be 'on the side of the Americans' with their enthusiasm for the school of creative writing, at that time 'often sneered at from this side of the Atlantic'. Bergonzi, *The Situation of the Novel*, pp. 81, 83.

16. The recent rise of courses in creative writing in British universities puts a new complexion on the debate about the professionalization of writing: Robert Eaglestone counts more than forty courses in creative writing in 2000 (as opposed to two in the 1970s). See 'Undoing English', *CCUE News*, 13 (Summer, 2000), 6–8 (8).

17. I include Irish writing that pertains to the Irish migrant experience in Britain; there is also a section on the Troubles in Northern Ireland. For an authoritative overview of post-war Irish literature in context, see Ray Ryan, ed., *Writing in the Irish Republic: Literature, Culture, Politics 1949–1999* (Basingstoke: Macmillan, 2000).

18. For an introduction to British Studies see Nick Wadham-Smith, ed., *British Studies Now*, 1–5 (anthology issue) (British Council, 1995).

19. Ian Baucom, *Out of Place: Englishness, Empire, and the Locations of Identity* (Princeton University Press, 1999), p. 6.

20. Paul Gilroy, *Between Camps: Race, Identity and Nationalism at the End of the Colour Line* (London: Allen Lane, 2000), p. 2.

21. See Paul Ricoeur, *Time and Narrative*, trans. Kathleen McLaughlin and David Pellauer, 3 vols. (Chicago University Press, 1984–8).

22. I am borrowing here from Laurence Buell. See *The Environmental Imagination: Thoreau, Nature Writing, and the Formation of American Culture* (Cambridge (Mass.): Harvard University Press, 1995), p. 97.

# 1. The State and the Novel

1. Malcolm Bradbury, 'Introduction' to *Animal Farm: A Fairy Story* (1945; Harmondsworth: Penguin, 2000), pp. v–xvi (p. v).

2. Orwell returned from Spain 'bitterly hostile towards Moscow-led communism', as Ben Pimlott observes. See 'Introduction' to *Nineteen Eighty-Four* (1949; Harmondsworth: Penguin, 2000), pp. v–vxii (p. xiv).

3. Peter Clarke, *Hope and Glory: Britain 1900–1990* (1996; Harmondsworth: Penguin, 1997), pp. 213–14.

4. Dennis Kavanagh, *Thatcherism and British Politics: The End of Consensus?*, third edn (Oxford University Press, 1990), p. 34.

5. For an overview of this period see Clarke, *Hope and Glory*, pp. 216–31. Clarke puts the cost at '28 per cent of the country's wealth' (p. 27).

6. The use of 'Britain' and 'England' as interchangeable terms, which is troubling in 2000, seems to have been less problematic to a 1950s audience, perhaps because the Scots, Welsh and English had the recent memory of fighting together within the British forces.

7. See Alan Sinfield, *Literature, Politics and Culture in Postwar Britain*, second edn (London: Athlone, 1997), p. 52.

8. Malcolm Bradbury, 'William Cooper and the 1950s: *Scenes From Provincial Life*', reprinted in *Possibilities: Essays on the State of the Novel* (Oxford University Press, 1973), pp. 192–200 (pp. 192, 194).

9. Bradbury, *Possibilities*, p. 194.

10. See Gąsiorek, *Post-War British Fiction*, pp. 2–3. Gąsiorek's book properly shows how this opposition has been overstated.

11. Bradbury, *Possibilities*, p. 199.

12. Peter Conradi, *Angus Wilson* (Plymouth: Northcote House, 1997), p. 14.

13. Patrick Swinden offers a lucid discussion of this. See *The English Novel of History and Society, 1940–80* (London: Macmillan, 1984), pp. 150–1.

14. Bergonzi, *The Situation of the Novel*, p. 179.

15. *Ibid.*

16. On this point, see Gąsiorek, *Post-War British Fiction*, p. 101.

17. Middleton is either 64 (p. 13), or 62 (p. 32) at the start of the novel: the text is inconsistent.

18. Bergonzi, *The Situation of the Novel*, p. 145.

19. For example, comparing the surveys of 1948 and 1984 cited by Arthur Marwick, one finds a significant decline in those designating themselves as 'upper class': 2 per cent in 1948 against 0.2 per cent in 1984. See Marwick, *British Society Since 1945*, pp. 44, 329.

20. Neil McEwan, *Anthony Powell* (Basingstoke: Macmillan, 1991), p. 125.

21. Marwick, *British Society Since 1945*, p. 123.

22. Ian Hamilton, 'Bohemian Rhapsodist' (profile of Mackay), *The Guardian*, Saturday 10 July 1999, 'Saturday Review', pp. 6–7 (p. 6).

23. Blake Morrison, 'Introduction' to *A Clockwork Orange* (Harmondsworth: Penguin, 1996), pp. vii–xxiv (p. xvi).

24. In the original American edition of the novel, as in Stanley Kubrick's notorious film version, this final section is omitted. On the implications of this for the

novel see John Cullinan, 'Anthony Burgess' *A Clockwork Orange*: Two Versions', *English Language Notes*, 9 (1972), 287–92.

25. Morrison observes that the title is taken from a Cockney expression, 'as queer as a clockwork orange' which means 'very queer indeed', with or without a sexual implication. 'Introduction', p. viii.

26. In 1944, Burgess's first wife was raped in London by a gang of GI deserters; the attack on the writer's wife in the novel is based on this terrible experience. See Morrison, 'Introduction', p. xiv.

27. Arthur Marwick, *The Sixties: Cultural Revolution in Britain, France, Italy, and the United States, c. 1958 – c.1974* (Oxford University Press, 1998), pp. 7, 77.

28. Marwick, for instance, observes that the faith in LSD was 'totally misguided'. See *The Sixties*, p. 482.

29. *Ibid.*, p. 18.

30. For an important development of Althusser's notion of the relatively autonomous role of art in the superstructure see Fredric Jameson, *The Political Unconscious: Narrative as a Socially Symbolic Act* (1981; London: Methuen, 1986).

31. See Kavanagh, *Thatcherism and British Politics*, pp. 16–17.

32. See Marwick, *British Society Since 1945*, pp. 273–4.

33. D. J. Taylor, *After the War: The Novel and England Since 1945* (1993; London: Flamingo, 1994), p. 286.

34. *Ibid.*

35. Drabble acknowledges that Wilson was a great influence on her work in her biography, *Angus Wilson* (1995; London: Minerva, 1996), p. xviii.

36. Another theory is that Hilda Murrell was falsely targeted by the Intelligence Services on account of her nephew Robert Green's naval connections. Green had access to the secret information concerning the decision to sink the Argentine battleship *General Belgrano* during the Falklands conflict; and so when confidential information about the *Belgrano* was leaked, Murrell may have come under suspicion as a possible source. See Judith Cook, *Unlawful Killing: The Murder of Hilda Murrell* (London: Bloomsbury, 1994).

37. Maggie Gee, 'Clinging to the Coat-Tails of Fact', *Times Literary Supplement*, 4928, 12 September 1997, 10.

38. Thatcher coined this negative definition of consensus in 1981, in response to the criticism of Edward Heath, her predecessor as leader of the Conservative Party, that she was abandoning consensus politics. See Kavanagh, *Thatcherism and British Politics*, p. 7.

39. HMSO is the abbreviation for 'Her (or His) Majesty's Stationery Office', which publishes official government documents and legislation.

40. Sheila Rowbotham, *A Century of Women: The History of Women in Britain and the United States* (1997; Harmondsworth: Penguin, 1999), p. 505.

41. Sheila Rowbotham quotes an example of Thatcher as the 'forthright defender of working mothers' in 1954. See *A Century of Women*, pp. 293–4.

42. See Charles Webster, *The National Health Service: A Political History* (Oxford University Press, 1998), p. 126.

43. *Ibid.*, p. 159.

44. Jane Campbell, '"Both a Joke and a Victory": Humor as Narrative Strategy in Margaret Drabble's Fiction', *Contemporary Literature*, 32 (1991), 1, 75–99 (78).

45. Ian Haywood, *Working-Class Fiction: From Chartism to 'Trainspotting'* (Plymouth: Northcote House, 1997), p. 158.

46. Sinfield, *Literature Politics and Culture in Postwar Britain*, p. xxviii.

47. The author had made a similar joke-pact with a psychiatrist friend, which inspired this theme (and the novel's title): 'Amsterdam!' then became a grimly jocular rebuke for absent-mindedness, between the two. See 'Flashes of Inspiration', interview with Robert Hanks, *The Independent*, 12 September 1998, 'Weekend Review', p. 14.

## 2. Class and Social Change

1. See Clarke, *Hope and Glory: Britain 1900–1990*, p. 207.

2. Marwick, *British Society Since 1945*, p. 38.

3. David Cannadine, *Class in Britain* (London: Yale University Press, 1998), p. 7.

4. Marwick, *British Society Since 1945*, pp. 44, 154, 208, 329.

5. For an extensive discussion, see Blake Morrison, *The Movement: English Poetry and Fiction of the 1950s* (Oxford University Press, 1980).

6. Morrison, *The Movement*, pp. 4, 9. Amis, Wain and Braine were all dismissive of the 'Angry' label. For some representative remarks by these writers on this topic see Dale Salwak, *Interviews With Britain's Angry Young Men* (San Bernardino: Borgo Press, 1984).

7. Rubin Rabinovitz offers a useful survey of Amis's criticism of the 1950s, in which his stance is established. See *The Reaction Against Experiment in the English Novel, 1950–1960* (New York: Columbia University Press, 1967), ch. two.

8. Richard Bradford, *Kingsley Amis* (Plymouth: Northcote House, 1998), p. 2.

9. See Morrison, *The Movement*, p. 57.

10. See *ibid.*, pp. 58–9.

11. John Wain, 'Introduction' (1977) to the Penguin reprint of 1979, pp. 1–5.

12. Commenting on Jim Dixon in 1958, Amis presents him as an archetypal scholarship boy, suspicious of 'the conventional Oxford-Cambridge academic type'. In 1986 a more irascible Amis wrote, 'on *Jim* and related matters', that he 'had no social (class etc.) intentions at all'. See *The Letters of Kingsley Amis*, ed. Zachary Leader (London: HarperCollins, 2000), pp. 522, 1028.

13. Morrison, *The Movement*, pp. 57, 68, 69, 73, 77.

14. See, for example, John Rodden, '"The Rope That Connects Me Directly with You": John Wain and the Movement Writers' Orwell', *Albion*, 20 (1988), 1, 59–76.

15. A useful source of information on working-class fiction in Britain is M. Keith Booker's *The Modern British Novel of the Left: A Research Guide* (London: Greenwood Press, 1998).

16. The novel begins in September 1946 (since Joe is 25, and was born in January 1921) (pp. 7, 97, 148). However, at one point Joe seems to miscalculate the years (he reckons December 1946 to be 'six years after' the death of his parents in August 1941 [pp. 91, 95]).

17. Stuart Laing's very good essay on the novel traces its relationship to the changing social and class structure, embracing the poverty of the 1930s, the austerity of the 1940s, and the affluence of the 1950s: '*Room at the Top*: The Morality of Affluence', in Christopher Pawling, ed. *Popular Fiction and Social Change*, (London: Macmillan, 1984), pp. 157–84.

18. Mary Eagleton and David Pierce, *Attitudes to Class in the English Novel* (London: Thames and Hudson, 1979), p. 139; Haywood, *Working-Class Fiction*, p. 96.

19. Bergonzi's description of the book as a work of 'four square realism' is representative. See *Wartime and Aftermath: English Literature and its Background 1939–1960* (Oxford University Press, 1993), p. 208. On the biographical detail, see Malcolm Pittock, 'Revaluing the Sixties: *This Sporting Life* Revisited', *Forum for Modern Language Studies*, 26 (1990), 2, 97–108 (102, 107).

20. Bradbury, *The Modern British Novel*, p. 325.

21. On this point see Ingrid von Rosenberg, 'Militancy, Anger and Resignation: Alternative Moods in the Working-Class Novel of the 1950s and Early 1960s', in H. Gustav Klaus, ed., *The Socialist Novel in Britain: Towards the Recovery of a Tradition* (Brighton: Harvester, 1982), pp. 145–65 (p. 162).

22. Booker, *The Modern British Novel of the Left*, p. 302.

23. Andrew Adonis and Stephen Pollard show how the social scientists' seven-class schema also divides 'occupations into classes along a broad manual/ non-manual spectrum'. See *A Class Act: The Myth of Britain's Classless Society* (London: Hamish Hamilton, 1997), p. 6.

24. This overview of the post-war working-class novel has achieved consensus: see, for example, Taylor, *After the War*; Haywood, *Working-Class Fiction*; Eagleton and Pierce, *Attitudes to Class in the English Novel*.

25. See Clarke, *Hope and Glory: Britain 1900–1990*. Clarke gives the eleven-plus pass statistic for the period 'after the Second' World War, in comparison with a pre-First World War figure of a one-in-a-hundred chance of secondary education for children of unskilled manual workers (p. 284).

26. Eagleton and Pierce present class betrayal as a central issue. See *Attitudes to Class in the English Novel*, pp. 130–47.

27. Sinfield, *Literature, Politics and Culture in Postwar Britain*, p. 266.

28. Richard Hoggart, *The Uses of Literacy* (1957; Harmondsworth: Penguin, 1992), pp. 292–3.

29. Williams, 'The Social Significance of 1926', reprinted in Robin Gable, ed., *Resources of Hope: Culture, Democracy, Socialism* (London: Verso, 1989), pp. 105–10 (pp. 106, 105).

30. *Ibid.*, p. 106.
31. Williams, 'The Importance of Community', reprinted in Gable, ed., *Resources of Hope*, pp. 111–19 (p. 115).
32. Raymond Williams, *Politics and Letters: Interviews with 'New Left Review'* (London: New Left Books, 1979), pp. 272–3.
33. *Ibid.*, p. 275.
34. Williams, *The English Novel From Dickens to Lawrence* (1970; London: Hogarth Press, 1987), pp. 14, 12.
35. *Ibid.*, pp. 178, 183–4.
36. Williams, 'The Importance of Community', *Resources of Hope*, p. 114.
37. *Ibid.*, p. 117.
38. Williams, 'The Social Significance of 1926', *Resources of Hope*, p. 108.
39. Jan Gorak, *The Alien Mind of Raymond Williams* (Columbia: University of Missouri Press, 1988), p. 106.
40. Pittock, 'Revaluing the Sixties', pp. 103, 104.
41. Haywood, *Working-Class Fiction*, p. 109.
42. Carmen Callil and Colm Tóibín, *The Modern Library: The Two Hundred Best Novels in English Since 1950* (London: Picador, 1999), p. 160.
43. Cairns Craig, 'Resisting Arrest: James Kelman', in Gavin Wallace and Randall Stevenson, eds., *The Scottish Novel Since the Seventies* (Edinburgh University Press, 1993), pp. 99–114 (p. 101).
44. Williams, 'The Social Significance of 1926', p. 109.
45. Working-class support for labour, determined by the voting habits of manual workers, ranged from 62–69 per cent in the 1960s, but fell from 57 per cent in 1974 to 50 per cent in 1979 and then to 38 per cent in 1983. See Dennis Kavanagh, *Thatcherism and British Politics: The End of Consensus?*, pp. 168–9.
46. Cannadine, *Class in Britain*, pp. 19–20.
47. Hoggart, *The Uses of Literacy*, p. 24.
48. Ian Haywood wonders whether or not the brutality of Billy's mother and brother 'could be read as confirmation of Richard Hoggart's fear that the working class was being dehumanized by consumerism and mass society'. See *Working-Class Fiction*, p. 132.
49. Clarke, *Hope and Glory*, pp. 293–4.
50. Cannadine, *Class in Britain*, p. 4.
51. See *ibid.*, pp. 178, 181.
52. Adonis and Pollard, *A Class Act*, pp. 12–13.
53. The title story of one of Wilson's early volumes, *Such Darling Dodos* (London: Secker and Warburg, 1950), designates a familiar Wilsonian type, the character bypassed by social change.
54. Michael Cotsell, *Barbara Pym* (Basingstoke: Macmillan, 1989), p. 76.
55. For a useful overview of Pym's career see *ibid.*, pp. 1–8.
56. See 'The Novelist in the Field: 1964–74', the brief memoir by Hazel Holt (Pym's literary executor, and her assistant at the institute), in Dale Salwak, ed., *The Life and Work of Barbara Pym* (Basingstoke: Macmillan, 1987), pp. 22–33.

57. Muriel Schulz, 'The Novelist as Anthropologist', in Salwak, ed., *The Life and Work of Barbara Pym*, pp. 101–19 (p. 113).
58. Penelope Lively, 'The World of Barbara Pym', in *ibid.*, pp. 45–9 (pp. 46, 48).
59. Alev Adil, 'Middle England' (review of *Beyond the Blue Mountains*), *TLS*, 4915, 13 June 1997, 24.
60. See Arran Gare, *Postmodernism and the Environmental Crisis* (London: Routledge, 1995), pp. 6–8, 10.
61. *Ibid.*, p. 9.
62. Raymond Williams, *Towards 2000* (London: Chatto and Windus, 1983), p. 89.
63. There is a marked contrast here with Williams's first novel which went through seven drafts between 1947 and publication in 1960. See *Politics and Letters*, p. 271.
64. *Ibid.*, pp. 300, 298, 299.

## 3. Gender and Sexual Identity

1. Germaine Greer distinguished the revolutionary impetus of the second feminist wave, from the clamour for reform associated with the suffragettes, and the first wave. See *The Female Eunuch* (1970; London: Flamingo, 1999), pp. 13–14.
2. As Sheila Rowbotham shows, the consumer boom had important gender and party-political implications: 'the Conservative consumer wife came to be associated with freedom of choice and abundance', while Labour was 'stuck with the 1940s' image of austerity'. See *A Century of Women*, p. 288.
3. It is interesting to note that popular women's writing of the 1950s may have been more responsive, showing, it is claimed, 'a marked continuity with women's experiences and aspirations during the war years', thus contributing to a negotiated 'new model of femininity'. See Deborah Philips and Ian Haywood, *Brave New Causes: Women in British Postwar Fictions* (London: Leicester University Press, 1998), p. 3.
4. I am drawing here on Hans-Peter Wagner's intriguing essay, 'Learning to Read the Female Body: On the function of Manet's *Olympia* in John Braine's *Room at the Top*', *Zeitschrift für Anglistik und Amerikanistik*, 42 (1994), 1, 38–53.
5. Rowbotham, *A Century of Women*, pp. 306, 342, 360.
6. Ellen Cronan Rose, *The Novels of Margaret Drabble: Equivocal Figures* (London: Macmillan, 1980), pp. 1–2. Rose argues that in *A Summer Bird-Cage* the character Simone – a figure idealized by Drabble's heroine, but who never appears – is 'a kind of cartoon representation of Simone de Beauvoir' (p. 5).
7. On this feature of *Lucky Jim* see Richard Bradford, *Kingsley Amis*, pp. 11–16.
8. Joanne Creighton reports that, in an unpublished interview, Drabble insists this interruption was not 'a conscious decision'. See *Margaret Drabble* (London: Methuen, 1985), p. 116.
9. Ellen Cronan Rose, though dissenting from this view, reports that it is one shared by 'most critics' as well as 'most women readers I have talked to'. See *The Novels of Margaret Drabble*, p. 21.

10. Tess Cosslett, 'Childbirth on the National Health: Issues of Class, Race, and Gender Identity in Two Post-War British Novels', *Women's Studies*, 19 (1991), 99–119.

11. *Ibid.*, p. 108.

12. Margaret Drabble offers a useful contextual overview in her introduction to the Virago edition of *Poor Cow* (London: Virago, 1988), pp. xi–xviii.

13. Drabble, 'Introduction', p. xii.

14. *Ibid.*, p. xviii.

15. Williams applies his term to Robert Tressell's *The Ragged-Trousered Philanthropists* in an essay with a tangential relation to my discussion. Williams's objective, however, is to locate the broader class challenge of Tressell's book, to offset the suggestion of an absorbed middle-class prejudice. See 'The Ragged-Arsed Philanthropists', in Williams, *Writing in Society* (1983; London: Verso, 1985), pp. 239–56 (pp. 254–6).

16. Rowbotham, *A Century of Women*, p. 339.

17. *Ibid.*, pp. 361, 364.

18. Rosalind Coward, *Sacred Cows: Is Feminism Relevant to the New Millennium?* (London: HarperCollins, 1999), p. 23.

19. For a brief overview of the Situationists see Marwick, *The Sixties*, p. 32.

20. *Ibid.*, p. 559.

21. Fay Weldon, 'Preface' to Jill Neville, *The Love Germ* (1969; London: Verso, 1998), pp. vii–ix (p. viii).

22. Looking back on the 1960s, there is one book in particular that now seems ahead of its time: Doris Lessing's *The Golden Notebook* (1962). The book discovers a formal correlative for the break-up of Western gender patterns, in the process anticipating the social, economic and psychological transformations in women's identity that were to become visible in the following decade. *The Golden Notebook* is partly inspired by Lessing's African experiences, however, and so is beyond the remit of this survey with its focus on the British context.

23. On this issue, see Linden Peach, *Angela Carter* (Basingstoke: Macmillan, 1998), pp. 73–4.

24. On the 'interdiction' and its violation as key functions in the Russian folk and fairy tale, see Vladimir Propp's *Morphology of the Folktale*, trans. Laurence Scott (Austin: University of Texas Press, 1968), pp. 26–7.

25. Coward, *Sacred Cows*, p. 4.

26. Rowbotham, *A Century of Women*, pp. 402, 404–5, 407. For an account of the ways in which equality legislation was evaded in the 1970s see pp. 413–14.

27. Weldon, 'Preface' to Jill Neville, *The Love Germ*, p. viii.

28. Weldon herself worked as an advertising copywriter, writing television advertisements. She is credited, for example, with the famous slogan of the 1960s, 'Go to Work on an Egg'. See Jenny Newman, ' "See Me as Sisyphus, But Having a Good Time": The Fiction of Fay Weldon', in Robert E. Hosmer, ed., *Contemporary British Women Writers* (Basingstoke: Macmillan, 1993), pp. 188–211 (p. 189).

29. Newman, 'See Me As Sisyphus', p. 188.
30. In Lorna Sage's inventive reading, this sense of a short-circuited feminist text is rendered less central. The novel, Sage argues, 'stages a confrontation between two genres – Gothic versus romantic fiction, hate story versus love story – and thus makes novelistic conventions themselves the protagonists'. In this sense, the self-imprisonment of Ruth as Mary Fisher's double serves the purpose of 'the most mutilating kind of satire' in which neither Gothic nor romantic forms seem propitious: 'Ruth is caged in the patterns of reversion, her anger bottled up to render it the more explosive.' To my mind this compounds the claustrophobic sense of an embattled feminism, finding an appropriate outlet neither in the represented social structures, nor the available fictional forms. See Lorna Sage, *Women in the House of Fiction: Post-War Women Novelists* (Basingstoke: Macmillan, 1992), pp. 158–9.
31. In the dynamic of 'return' there is a complex rewriting of traditional stories of maturation, which works to overturn the usual element of competition between mother and daughter (in fairy tales, for example). On this, and on Winterson's biblical sources, see Laurel Bollinger, 'Models for Female Loyalty: The Biblical Ruth in Jeanette Winterson's *Oranges Are Not the Only Fruit*', *Tulsa Studies in Women's Literature*, 13 (1994), 2, 363–80.
32. Rowbotham, *A Century of Women*, pp. 431, 407.
33. *Ibid.*, pp. 432–3, 471–2, 480–1.
34. On this point see Linden Peach's summary of critical opinion, in *Angela Carter*, pp. 142–4.
35. Compare *The Merchant of Venice*, II, ii, 73: 'it is a wise father that knows his own child'.
36. Natasha Walter, 'A World Elsewhere', review of *Altered States*, by Anita Brookner, *The Guardian*, section 2, 14 June 1996, p. 8.
37. Kate Fullbrook, 'Anita Brookner: On Reaching for the Sun', in Abby H. P. Werlock, ed., *British Women Writing Fiction* (Tuscaloosa: University of Alabama Press, 2000), pp. 90–106 (p. 91).
38. Rowbotham, *A Century of Women*, p. 512.
39. Coward, *Sacred Cows*, pp. 7, 16.
40. *Ibid.*, pp. 45, 47.
41. The details indicate a 'real time' gap between the two books, published in 1967 and 1996, respectively: Joy has her twenty-second birthday at the beginning of *Poor Cow* (p. 5); in *My Silver Shoes* we discover that she left her husband twenty years ago on her thirtieth birthday (p. 49). The later novel thus picks up Joy's life twenty-eight years on.
42. See Natasha Walter, *The New Feminism* (1998; London: Virago, 1999), p. 175. The alternative view, quoted as a riposte, is from Coward, *Sacred Cows*, p. 8.
43. See Maureen Freely, 'Sugar and Spite', *The Observer*, 18 January 1998, 'Review', p. 4.
44. Weldon quoted by Freely, 'Sugar and Spite', p. 4. It is the wider significance that is Weldon's focus. She does not, in any case, write with the kind of precision

required for a *roman-à-clef*, though the involvement of Callil is intriguing: *Big Women* was also a TV mini-series, purportedly from an original idea by Callil, and scripted by Weldon before the novel was written. ('Sugar and Spite', p. 4.).

45. The underground magazine *Oz* was founded by Richard Neville in 1967. For an overview of the underground press see Arthur Marwick, *The Sixties*, pp. 490–1. Virago was founded in 1973.

46. Weldon in interview with Miranda Sawyer, in 'Telling Tales', *The Observer* 25 January 1998, 'Life', pp. 4–8 (p. 7).

47. Coward, *Sacred Cows*, p. 219.

48. Germaine Greer, *The Whole Woman* (London: Doubleday, 1999), p. 325.

49. *Ibid.*, pp. 321, 330.

50. Mackay's career is also indicative of the changing role of women in the post-war era, as well as the particular difficulties the female writer must negotiate. She began publishing in 1964, and was fêted not just as an original stylist, but also as 'the youngest and prettiest girl-novelist in town'. A career break between 1971 and 1983 – during which Mackay raised her three daughters and was preoccupied with domestic concerns – left her approaching her forties, without a publisher, and needing to relaunch her career. This she duly did, with the assistance of endorsements from Brigid Brophy and Iris Murdoch. See Ian Hamilton, 'Bohemian Rhapsodist' (profile of Shena Mackay), *The Guardian*, 'Saturday Review', 10 July 1999, pp. 6–7.

51. There is a personal resonance in this obvious satirical signpost: when she was little, Mackay's family moved to Hampstead, and lived next door to the Saatchis for a time, and 'little Charles', according to Mackay, 'would now and then come crawling through their hedge'. See Ian Hamilton, 'Bohemian Rhapsodist', pp. 6–7 (p. 6).

52. Rowbotham, *A Century of Women*, p. 568.

53. Sinfield, *Literature, Politics and Culture in Postwar Britain*, p. 76.

54. This surprise is inevitable in the twenty-first century reader; but I am also projecting it backwards as a necessary response for readers in the 1950s, given Wilson's technique.

55. Mars-Jones has been critical of that treatment of AIDS which assumes it has 'nothing in common with anything else in the world'. See 'Survivor Art', in *Blind Bitter Happiness* (London: Chatto and Windus, 1997), pp. 80–4 (p. 80).

## 4. National Identity

1. Eric Hobsbawm, *Nations and Nationalism Since 1780: Programme, Myth, Reality* (Cambridge University Press, 1991), p. 12.

2. Declan Kiberd suggests that the number of recognized nation-states has risen from about fifty in 1945 to 'something more like two hundred' at the end

of the century. See 'Reinventing England', *Key Words: A Journal of Cultural Materialism*, 2 (1999), 47–57 (47).

3. Neil Lazarus, *Nationalism and Cultural Practice in the Postcolonial World* (Cambridge University Press, 1999), p. 76.

4. For Chris Harman, such economic collaboration is best described as 'trans-state' capitalism, rather than 'multinational' or 'transnational' capitalism, since the prosecution of the multinationals' interests depends upon the willingness of individual states to accommodate them, and on the links that are forged between states in advancing such interests. See 'The State and Capitalism Today', *International Socialism*, 51 (1991), 3–54 (33–4). Neil Lazarus demonstrates the relevance of Harman's views to the problem of nationalism in *Nationalism and Cultural Practice*, pp. 72–3.

5. See the 1964 essay 'On Being English But Not British', reprinted in John Relf, ed., *Wormholes: Essays and Occasional Writings* (London: Jonathan Cape, 1998), pp. 79–88 (p. 85).

6. As Ian Sansom points out, the conceit of Barnes's novel is borrowed. The architect Clough-Williams, who founded Portmeirion (Gwynedd, Wales), imagined (in a book about The National Trust) all of the National Trust buildings and lands reassembled on an island with a compass smaller than the Isle of Wight. See 'Half-Timbering, Homosexuality and Whingeing', review of *England, England*, in *London Review of Books*, 20:19, 1 October 1998, 31–2 (31).

7. See (anonymous) interview with Julian Barnes, *The Observer*, 30 August 1998, 'The Review', p. 15.

8. Benedict Anderson, *Imagined Communities*, second edn (London: Verso, 1991), pp. 6–7.

9. *Ibid.*, pp. 24–6.

10. *Ibid.*, pp. 6, 35, 36.

11. Antony Easthope, *Englishness and National Culture* (London: Routledge, 1999), p. 10.

12. *Ibid.*, p. 208.

13. Jeremy Paxman, *The English: A Portrait of a People* (London: Michael Joseph, 1998), p. 23.

14. Broadcast on the BBC Home Service, 25 February 1943; quoted in Paxman, *The English*, p. 151.

15. Paxman, *The English*, pp. 22–3.

16. Baucom, *Out of Place*, pp. 6, 7.

17. See Baucom, 'Introduction' to *ibid.*

18. Margaret Scanlan, *Traces of Another Time: History and Politics in Postwar British Fiction* (Princeton University Press, 1990), p. 155.

19. Richard Todd, *Consuming Fictions: The Booker Prize and Fiction in Britain Today* (London: Bloomsbury, 1996), p. 82.

20. Bergonzi, 'Fictions of History', pp. 56–7.

21. Lavinia Greacen's account of Farrell's research trip to India is illuminating. See *J. G. Farrell: The Making of a Writer* (London: Bloomsbury, 1999).

22. Ralph Crane and Jennifer Livett indicate that Farrell has in mind Thomas Jones Barker's painting 'The Relief of Lucknow': *Troubled Pleasures: The Fiction of J. G. Farrell* (Dublin: Four Courts Press, 1997), p. 87.

23. Greacen, *J. G. Farrell*, p. 255.

24. Crane and Livett, *Troubled Pleasures*, pp. 85, 84.

25. James Vinson, ed., *Contemporary Novelists* (London: St James Press, 1970), pp. 399–400. Lavinia Greacen reports that Farrell superstitiously 'wondered if he had somehow evoked the current troubles'. *J. G. Farrell*, p. 255.

26. Reported in *ibid.*, p. 277.

27. Some critics have complained about this narrative procedure, which serves to marginalize the oppressed group in the novel. Margaret Scanlan, for example, protests that the 'restricted narrative point of view shuts out the Catholic Irish and, thereby, becomes complicit in their dehumanization by the British'. See *Traces of Another Time*, p. 61. As I indicate, Farrell's formal strategy indicates a different intention.

28. Richard Kirkland, *Literature and Culture in Northern Ireland Since 1965: Moments of Danger* (London: Longman, 1996), p. 46.

29. Eve Patten, 'Fiction in Conflict: Northern Ireland's Prodigal Novelists', in Ian A. Bell, ed., *Peripheral Visions: Images of Nationhood in Contemporary British Fiction* (Cardiff: University of Wales Press, 1995), pp. 128–48 (p. 129).

30. *Ibid.*, p. 132.

31. Gerry Smyth, *The Novel and the Nation* (London: Pluto, 1997), p. 42.

32. Patten, 'Fiction in Conflict', p. 132.

33. The thriller format has proved amenable to the treatment of the Troubles, though often in a formulaic manner. Bill Rolston argues that the stereotypes emerging in Troubles thrillers, especially in the presentation of women, are to be found also in 'literary' novels. See 'Mothers, Whores and Villains: Images of Women in Novels of the Northern Ireland Conflict', *Race and Class*, 31 (1989), 41–57 (41). A slightly more interesting case than the norm is Brian Moore's *Lies of Silence* (1990). The novel belongs to the genre of the 'Troubles thriller', and, although this is not his most respected novel, its subtext of personal duplicity reveals something interesting which lifts it beyond the type.

34. Patten, 'Fiction in Conflict', pp. 129–30.

35. Kiberd, 'Reinventing England', p. 56.

36. Eamonn Hughes, ' "Lancelot's Position": The Fiction of Irish-Britain', in Lee, ed., *Other Britain, Other British*, pp. 142–60 (p. 143).

37. *Ibid.*, pp. 143, 150.

38. Katie Gramich observes, as one would expect, that surveys bear this out. See 'Cymru or Wales?: Explorations in a Divided Sensibility', in Susan Bassnett, ed., *Studying British Cultures: An Introduction* (London: Routledge, 1997), pp. 97–112 (p. 97).

39. On this see Katie Gramich, 'Cymru or Wales?', pp. 98–100.
40. See Tony Bianchi, 'Aztecs in Troedrhiwgwair: Recent Fictions in Wales' in Bell, ed., *Peripheral Visions*, pp. 44–76 (p. 48); and Raymond Williams, 'The Welsh Industrial Novel', in *Problems in Materialism and Culture* (London: Verso, 1980), pp. 213–29 (p. 227).
41. Williams, 'The Welsh Industrial Novel', p. 227.
42. See Tracy McVeigh, 'How Phoney Was My Valley', *The Observer*, 5 December 1999, p. 3.
43. Llywelyn ap Gruffud (1246–82), the 'last' Prince of Wales, came close to establishing an independent Welsh principality.
44. Emyr Humphreys, *The Taliesin Tradition* (1983; Bridgend: Seren, 2000), p. 1.
45. Bianchi, 'Aztecs in Troedrhiwgwair', p. 65.
46. Humphreys, 'Preface' to *Outside The House of Baal* (1965; Bridgend: Seren, 1996), pp. 7–13 (pp. 11, 8).
47. Humphreys, *Taliesin Tradition*, p. 4.
48. Cairns Craig, *The Modern Scottish Novel: Narrative and the National Imagination* (Edinburgh University Press, 1999), pp. 14, 20, 31, 33.
49. Alison Lee, *Realism and Power: British Postmodern Fiction* (London: Routledge, 1990), pp. 100–1.
50. Craig, *The Modern Scottish Novel*, p. 181.
51. It is prudent to remember that critical enthusiasms can generate 'movements' which might not otherwise have existed, at least not in the form they are given by a critical consensus which has established a head of steam. For a cautionary note on the 'renaissance' of Scottish writing in the 1980s, see Dorothy McMillan, 'Constructed Out of Bewilderment: Stories of Scotland', in Bell, ed., *Peripheral Visions*, pp. 80–99.
52. Ian Rankin, 'The Deliberate Cunning of Muriel Spark', in Wallace and Stevenson, eds., *The Scottish Novel Since the Seventies* (1993; Edinburgh University Press, 1994), pp. 41–53 (pp. 51, 52).
53. Judy Little, 'Muriel Spark's Grammars of Assent', in James Acheson, ed., *The British and Irish Novel Since 1960* (Basingstoke: Macmillan, 1991), pp. 1–16 (p. 15).
54. Joseph Hynes, 'Muriel Spark and the Oxymoronic Vision', in Hosmer, ed., *Contemporary British Women Writers: Texts and Strategies* (Basingstoke: Macmillan, 1993), pp. 161–87 (p. 161).
55. *Ibid.*, p. 170.
56. A. L. Kennedy, 'Not Changing the World', in Bell, ed., *Peripheral Visions: Images of Nationhood in Contemporary Britain* (Cardiff: University of Wales Press, 1995), pp. 100–2.
57. Anderson, *Imagined Communities*, p. 7.
58. Craig, *The Modern Scottish Novel*, p. 237. (Craig here is following Tom Nairn.)

## 5. Multicultural Personae

1. I am drawing on Helen Tiffin's formulation in 'Post-Colonial Literatures and Counter-Discourse', *Kunapipi*, 9 (1987), 3, 17–34.
2. In relation to the second novel, *An Artist of the Floating World*, Bruce King shows how the narrative method stems from a discursive mode with its roots in Japanese culture, an 'indirect polite circling round a subject' so that its significance only gradually becomes clear. See 'The New Internationalism: Shiva Naipaul, Salman Rushdie, Buchi Emecheta, Timothy Mo and Kazuo Ishiguro', in Acheson, ed., *The British and Irish Novel Since 1960* (Basingstoke: Macmillan, 1991), pp. 192–211 (p. 208).
3. In his ambitious fourth novel, *The Unconsoled* (1995), Ishiguro's concern with global forces is extended, though the challenge is partially thwarted. This enigmatic and at times Kafkaesque novel, narrated by an anonymous protagonist, and set in a nameless European country, combines comedy, nostalgia and sadness, within a governing mood of persisting mystery. The book performs, through its narrative mood, the triumph of the inexplicable sometimes associated with postmodernity, as well as the sense that the only available response to this stifling moment is the cultivation of a culturally indistinct nostalgia.
4. Bryan Cheyette, 'Preface' and 'Introduction' to Cheyette, ed., *Contemporary Jewish Writing in Britain and Ireland: An Anthology* (London: Peter Halban, 1998), pp. xi–lxxi (pp. xi, xiii).
5. Cheyette, 'Introduction', pp. xxvi, xxxv.
6. Michael Woolf, 'Negotiating the Self: Jewish Fiction in Britain Since 1945', in Lee, ed., *Other Britain, Other British*, pp. 124–42 (p. 125).
7. Salman Rushdie, 'The New Empire Within Britain', in *Imaginary Homelands: Essays and Criticism 1981–91* (1991; London: Granta Books, 1992), pp. 129–38 (p. 130).
8. *Ibid.*, pp. 129, 137.
9. A. Robert Lee, 'Introduction', Lee, ed., *Other Britain, Other British: Contemporary Multicultural Fiction* (London: Pluto Press, 1995), pp. 1–3 (p. 2).
10. Homi Bhabha, 'DissemiNation: Time, Narrative, and the Margins of the Modern Nation', in Bhabha, ed., *Nation and Narration* (London: Routledge, 1990, pp. 291–322 (p. 318).
11. Rushdie, *Imaginary Homelands*, p. 132.
12. For a useful summary of the legislation, see Dennis Kavanagh, *British Politics: Continuities and Change*, third edn (Oxford University Press, 1996), pp. 32–4.
13. I do not favour the term 'multiracial', since it is implicitly divisive in its tacit denial of a common humanity.
14. Peter Clarke observes that the national census of 1951 recorded 100,000 born in the New Commonwealth, a figure that had quadrupled in ten years. See *Hope and Glory*, p. 325.
15. Mark Looker, *Atlantic Passages: History, Community, and Language in the Fiction of Sam Selvon* (New York: Peter Lang, 1996), p. 2.

16. On the question of Selvon's style, see *ibid.*, p. 74.
17. See Susheila Nasta, 'Setting Up Home in a City of Words: Sam Selvon's London Novels', in Lee, ed., *Other Britain, Other British*, pp. 48–68 (p. 57).
18. Nasta, 'Setting Up Home in a City of Words', p. 57.
19. Kenneth Ramchand, 'Introduction', Selvon, *The Lonely Londoners* (1956; London: Longman, 1998), pp. 3–21 (p. 20).
20. A representative sample of Powell's views, in the form of an extract from *Still to Decide* (1972), is included in Onyekachi Wambu, ed., *Empire Windrush: Fifty Years of Writing About Black Britain* (London: Victor Gollancz, 1998), pp. 139–45.
21. Clarke, *Hope and Glory*, p. 326.
22. See Marwick, *British Society Since 1945*, p. 458.
23. See Kavanagh, *Thatcherism and British Politics*, p. 32.
24. Katherine Fishburn, *Reading Buchi Emecheta: Cross-Cultural Conversations* (London: Greenwood Press, 1995), p. 53.
25. See Buchi Emecheta, *Head Above Water: An Autobiography* (1986; Oxford: Heinemann, 1994), p. 39.
26. Helpful in this connection is C. L. Innes's essay, 'Wintering: Making a Home in Britain' in Lee, ed., *Other Britain, Other British*, pp. 21–34. Responding to Phillips's grim treatment of this issue, Innes suggests that *The Final Passage* is a transitional work, located 'between the novels of displacement and the novels of settlement' (pp. 22–3).
27. Bhabha, 'DissemiNation', p. 306.
28. Baucom, *Out of Place*, p. 176.
29. Maya Jaggi, review of *Disappearance* by David Dabydeen, *TLS*, 4693, 12 March 1993, 20.
30. Baucom, *Out of Place*, pp. 177–8.
31. Rushdie, *Imaginary Homelands*, p. 11.
32. *Ibid.*, p. 143.
33. On this issue, see Baucom, *Out of Place*, pp. 190–218.
34. Rushdie, *Imaginary Homelands*, p. 136.
35. *Ibid.*, p. 394.
36. Baucom, *Out of Place*, p. 207.
37. On this issue, see Michael Hanne, *The Power of the Story: Fiction and Political Change* (Oxford: Berghahn Books, 1996), p. 212. Hanne's balanced overview is an excellent place to start in the bewilderingly large literature on the events surrounding the publication and reception of Rushdie's novel.
38. Rushdie, *Imaginary Homelands*, p. 422.
39. *Ibid.*, p. 432.
40. For a brief summary of the sequence of events see Damian Grant, *Salman Rushdie* (Plymouth: Northcote House, 1999), pp. 88–93.
41. Bhabha, 'DissemiNation', pp. 292, 297, 302, 306.
42. *Ibid.*, pp. 312, 317.

43. Caryl Phillips, 'Mixed and Matched', review of *White Teeth, The Observer*, 'Review', 9 January 2000, p. 11.
44. Gilroy, *Between Camps*, pp. 2, 12, 18, 328.

## 6. Country and Suburbia

1. In *The Killing of the Countryside* (1997; London: Vintage, 1998), Graham Harvey shows how EU subsidies and quotas have unhooked the imperatives of production from actual needs.
2. Glen Cavaliero, *The Rural Tradition in the English Novel, 1900–1939* (Basingstoke: Macmillan, 1977), pp. ix, 205.
3. The Social Democratic Party (SDP) was formed in 1981, as a centre-left alternative to the Labour Party, which had responded to its election defeat of 1979 by moving further leftwards. The SDP is often used by novelists to symbolize a concerned liberal stance. The SDP was a short-lived political phenomenon, however, being absorbed in an alliance with the Liberals in 1988. For a brief account of these developments see Bill Coxall and Lynton Robins, *British Politics Since the War* (Basingstoke: Macmillan, 1998), pp. 130, 184, 190–1.
4. Terry Gifford, *Pastoral* (London: Routledge, 1999), pp. 1–2.
5. *Ibid.*, pp. 146, 147.
6. *Ibid.*, pp. 152–65.
7. *Ibid.*, pp. 8, 150, 169. See also Gifford's *Green Voices: Understanding Contemporary Nature Poetry* (Manchester University Press, 1995).
8. Nicholas Shakespeare, *Bruce Chatwin* (1999; London: Vintage, 2000), pp. 375–6.
9. This kind of 'telepathic' empathy has sometimes been recorded in identical twins, and Chatwin's diligent research into the phenomenon of twins implies a factual, rather than a fantastic impulse in this connection. See Shakespeare, *Bruce Chatwin*, pp. 382–4.
10. From Chatwin's interview with Melvyn Bragg on *The South Bank Show* (1982), quoted in Shakespeare, *Bruce Chatwin*, p. 387.
11. *Ibid.*, p. 387.
12. Buell, *The Environmental Imagination*, pp. 7–8, 168. Buell expresses some noteworthy ecocritical concerns about the dynamic of fiction: see pp. 83–114.
13. Williams died leaving the project uncompleted – the second volume ends in AD1415 – though his widow Joy adds a postscript detailing the plans for the unwritten book. See *People of the Black Mountains, II: The Eggs of the Eagle* (London: Chatto and Windus, 1990), pp. 318–23.
14. Peter Ackroyd, *Notes for a New Culture: An Essay on Modernism* (London: Vision, 1976).
15. I am aware of John Peck's warning against the pursuit of connections between the two novels: 'it would be hard to think of anything more unhelpful than showing off one's familiarity with *Two on a Tower* as a way of establishing

central control over *First Light*, he writes. ('The Novels of Peter Ackroyd', *English Studies* 5 (1994), 442–52 (448).) This seems a curious argument to me, since Ackroyd embeds the allusion for the reader's attention. Pursuing it need not misrepresent the novel's distrust of tradition, or the playfulness of the allusion.

16. John Brewer and Stella Tillyard, 'History and Telling Stories: Graham Swift's *Waterland*', *History Today*, 35 (1985), January, 49–51 (51).

17. Patrick D. Murphy has made a systematic attempt to theorize the literary 'voicing' of nature in *Literature, Nature, and Other: Ecofeminist Critiques* (SUNY Press, 1995).

18. For some famous reflections on this see George Steiner, *Language and Silence: Essays 1958–1966* (1967; London: Faber and Faber, 1985).

19. Raymond Williams, *The Country and the City* (1973; London: Hogarth Press, 1985).

20. Penny Smith, 'Hell Innit: The Millennium in Alasdair Gray's *Lanark*, Martin Amis's *London Fields*, and Shena Mackay's *Dunedin*', extract printed in Tredell, ed., *The Fiction of Martin Amis: A Reader's Guide to Essential Criticism* (Cambridge: Icon Books, 2000), pp. 100–3 (p. 101). The section of this Guide devoted to *London Fields* supplies a useful overview of the book's perceived misogyny, and the possibility that this explains its omission from the 1989 Booker prize shortlist.

21. See Richard Holmes, 'The Death of the Author as Cultural Critique in *London Fields*', extracts in Tredell, ed., *The Fiction of Martin Amis*, pp. 110–18 (p. 115).

22. The social stigma this implies may be a predominantly English phenomenon. In her investigation of suburbia as 'a manner of living', Miranda Sawyer finds no identification with suburbia amongst the Irish or Welsh, but some recognition amongst Scottish interviewees. See Miranda Sawyer, *Park and Ride: Adventures in Suburbia* (London: Little Brown, 1999), pp. 9, 10.

23. Arthur Edwards, *The Design of Suburbia* (London: Pembridge Press, 1981), p. 1.

24. Roger Silverstone, 'Introduction' in Roger Silverstone, ed., *Visions of Suburbia*, (London: Routledge, 1997), p. 3.

25. It is this perceived 'centrality of suburbia for an understanding of modernity and of the twentieth century' that links the divers essays in *Visions of Suburbia*. See Silverstone, 'Introduction', p. 14.

26. Edwards, *The Design of Suburbia*, p. 1.

27. Harvey, *The Condition of Postmodernity*, p. 69.

28. Tim Mars, 'The Life in New Towns', in Anthony Barnett and Roger Scruton, eds., *Town and Country* (London: Jonathan Cape, 1998), pp. 267–78 (p. 272).

29. Paul Barker, 'Edge City', in Barnett and Scruton, eds., *Town and Country*, pp. 206–216 (p. 210).

30. Margaret Drabble, '"No Idle Rentier": Angus Wilson and the Nourished Literary Imagination', reprinted in Jay L. Halio, ed., *Critical Essays on Angus Wilson* (Boston, Mass.: G. K. Hall, 1985), pp. 182–92 (p. 187).

31. Anthony Thwaite gives a completion date of April 1971 for Larkin's 'This Be The Verse', with no periodical publication prior to its inclusion in *High Windows* (1974). See Philip Larkin, *Collected Poems*, ed. Anthony Thwaite (London: Faber and Faber, 1988), p. 180.

32. Stefan Collini, *English Pasts: Essays in History and Culture* (Oxford University Press, 1999), p. 19.

33. *Ibid.*, pp. 23–5.

34. *Ibid.*, pp. 25–8.

35. Connor, *The English Novel in History, 1950–1995*, pp. 94–5, 98.

36. Interview quoted in Kenneth C. Kaleta, *Hanif Kureishi: Postcolonial Storyteller* (Austin: University of Texas Press, 1998), p. 77.

## 7. Beyond 2000

1. Gindin, *Postwar British Fiction*, p. 11.

2. Gąsiorek, *Post-War British Fiction*, ch. 1.

3. See Catherine Belsey, *Critical Practice* (London: Methuen, 1980).

4. In *James Joyce and the Revolution of the Word* (1979; Basingstoke: Macmillan, 1983) Colin McCabe makes the bold, but perhaps misguided, attempt to establish George Eliot as the exemplar of classic realism, understood as a mode which places its faith in the transparency of language in the process of depicting reality.

5. Gąsiorek, *Post-War British Fiction*, pp. 5, 8, 18–19.

6. Virginia Woolf, *Collected Essays*, ed. Leonard Woolf, 4 vols. (London: Hogarth Press, 1966–7); vol. I (1966), p. 330.

7. Angus Wilson, *Diversity and Depth in Fiction: Selected Critical Writings of Angus Wilson*, ed. Kerry McSweeney (New York: Viking Press, 1983), pp. 121–2.

8. *Ibid.*, p. 175.

9. Johnson committed suicide in 1973 at the age of 40. Jonathan Coe records his fame and notoriety (he made regular television appearances, for example) in the 'Introduction' to the reissue of Johnson's *The Unfortunates* (London: Picador, 1999), pp. v–xv (pp. v–vi).

10. B. S. Johnson, 'Introduction' to *Aren't You Rather Young to be Writing Your Memoirs?*, printed in Malcolm Bradbury, ed., *The Novel Today: Contemporary Writers on Modern Fiction*, new edn (London: Fontana, 1990), pp. 165–83 (p. 172).

11. Johnson, 'Introduction', pp. 165, 166, 167.

12. Coe, 'Introduction', p. vii.

13. Johnson, 'Introduction', p. 168.

14. Coe, 'Introduction', p. viii.

15. For the background see Johnson, 'Introduction', pp. 177–9. The identity of 'Tony' in the novel is supplied by Coe, 'Introduction', p. viii.

16. Johnson, 'Introduction', pp. 168, 178.

17. Patricia Waugh, *Harvest of the Sixties: English Literature and its Background 1960–1990* (Oxford University Press, 1995), p. 132.
18. Johnson, 'Introduction', p. 182.
19. Coe, 'Introduction', pp. xiv–xv.
20. There is another unbound novel, presented for the reader to rearrange, entitled *Numéro Un*, by the French novelist Marc Saporta. (See Bergonzi, *The Situation of The Novel*, p. 37. Coe records the English title of this work as *Composition 1*, 'Introduction', p. x.)
21. Some of the essays in Theo D'haen and Hans Bertens, eds., *British Postmodern Fiction* (Amsterdam: Rodopi, 1993) rely on such a compromise. Alison Lee, however, pits postmodernism against a 'Realism' which is tied to the ideology of liberal humanism. See *Realism and Power: Postmodern British Fiction* (London: Routledge, 1990).
22. I am, of course, drawing on Fredric Jameson's work in this discussion of post-modern pastiche, and the 'waning of affect'. See, especially, *Postmodernism, or, the Cultural Logic of Late Capitalism* (London: Verso, 1991).
23. Linda Hutcheon, *A Poetics of Postmodernism: History, Theory, Fiction* (1988; London: Routledge, 1995), p. 119.
24. See, for example, Roberta Rubenstein, 'Fragmented Bodies/Selves/Narratives: Margaret Drabble's Postmodern Turn', *Contemporary Literature*, 35 (1994), 1, 136–55.
25. On this see, especially, Brian McHale's account of postmodernism's 'ontological dominant' in *Postmodernist Fiction* (1987; rep. London: Routledge, 1991).
26. Margaret Drabble, 'Mimesis: The Representation of Reality in the Post-War British Novel', *Mosaic*, 20 (1987), 1, 1–14 (13).
27. James Wood, *The Broken Estate: Essays on Literature and Belief* (London: Jonathan Cape, 1999), p. 175.
28. From a 1967 radio interview, quoted by Bernard Bergonzi in *The Situation of the Novel*, p. 78.
29. See Francis Fukuyama's, *The End of History and the Last Man* (Harmondsworth: Penguin, 1992). (The book develops the theme of an earlier, and widely dis-cussed essay.)
30. See Donna J. Haraway, *Modest_Witness@Second_Millennium.FemaleMan©_Meets_OncoMouse*™ (London: Routledge, 1997) p. 247.
31. *Ibid.* Specific reference is made to pp. 253, 80, 58, 56, 60, 80, 61, 62, 264.
32. In her research, Smith admits to having 'read one "incredibly boring" book about onco-mice and cancer genes in mice', and to consulting with informed friends. 'A Willesden Ring of Confidence', interview with Christina Patterson, *The Independent*, 'The Weekend Review', 22 January 2000, p. 9.
33. Bhabha, 'DissemiNation', p. 302.
34. See Richard McPartland, 'Death of Paper?', *Personal Computer World*, December 2000, 146–50.
35. Libby Brooks, 'Power Surge', interview with and profile of Winterson, *The Guardian*, 'Weekend', 2 September 2000, 10–16 (10).

36. See Lodge's 'Introduction' to the Penguin reissue of the novel (Harmondsworth: Penguin, 1993), p. xii.
37. *Ibid.*, pp. x–xi. Lodge indicates that he read *The Uses of Literacy* 'shortly after it was published in 1957', and that it was a direct influence on the novel (p. xi).
38. The riots are noted in *Halliwell's Film and Video Guide*, ed. John Walker, twelfth edn (London: HarperCollins, 1996), p. 637.
39. Lorna Sage, 'A Place for Displacement', review of *Christine Brooke-Rose and Contemporary Fiction*, by Sarah Birch, *TLS*, 4767, 12 August 1994, 21.
40. See Christine Brooke-Rose, *Stories, Theories and Things* (Cambridge University Press, 1991), p. 4.
41. Sarah Birch makes this claim in *Christine Brooke-Rose and Contemporary Fiction* (Oxford University Press, 1994), pp. 138–9.
42. Christine Brooke-Rose, 'Narrating Without a Narrator', *TLS*, 5048, 31 December 1999, 12–13 (13).
43. *Ibid.*, 12. Brooke-Rose is commenting on Ann Banfield's book, *Unspeakable Sentences: Narration and Representation in the Language of Fiction* (London: Routledge and Kegan Paul, 1982).
44. See Richard Todd, 'The Intrusive Author in British Postmodernist Fiction: The Cases of Alasdair Gray and Martin Amis', in Matei Calinescu and Douwe Fokkema, eds, *Exploring Postmodernism* (Amsterdam: John Benjamins, 1990), pp. 123–37.
45. Interview with John Haffenden, excerpted in Tredell, ed., *The Fiction of Martin Amis*, pp. 61–6 (p. 62).
46. Todd, 'The Intrusive Author', p. 133.
47. Andy Beckett, 'Perishability', *London Review of Books*, vol. 22 no. 17, 3 September 1998, 27.
48. *Ibid.*, 27.
49. 'Sensation' was the title of a Royal Academy exhibition in 1997, which displayed part of Charles Saatchi's collection of modern British art, and asserted the claim to sensational newness. David Hopkins, however, suggests that the most arresting manifestations of British art in the 1990s were actually 'reprocessing 1960s ideas'. See David Hopkins, *After Modern Art: 1945–2000* (Oxford University Press, 2000), pp. 238–9.
50. Nicholas Blincoe and Matt Thorne, 'Introduction: The Pledge' to Blincoe and Thorne, eds., *All Hail the New Puritans* (London: Fourth Estate, 2000), pp. vii–xvii.
51. On the 'English Ideology' see Bergonzi, *The Situation of the Novel*, pp. 67–94.
52. Brandon Robshaw, 'Shaking Hands Across the Great Divide', *The Independent*, 'The Weekend Review', 17 June 2000, 10. Bridget Jones is in her thirties, in fact: the imitators of Hornby and Fielding have tended to create younger protagonists, presumably in the pursuit of a younger readership.
53. Bergonzi, *The Situation of the Novel*, pp. 30–1.
54. D. J. Taylor, in a piece on 'moribund genres' offers a parodic summary of the typical 'Girl-about-town' and 'Boy-about-town' novels, in which each is the

mirror image of the other. See ' "Lee Fredge: My Story". Er, No Thanks…',
*The Independent*, 'Weekend Review', 18 December 1999, 10.

55. Nicola Shulman, 'Some Consolations of the Single State', review of *Bridget Jones's Diary* by Helen Fielding, *TLS*, 4883, 1 November 1996, 26.
56. Zoë Heller, 'Dumped', review of *Animal Husbandry* by Laura Zigman, *Bridget Jones's Diary* by Helen Fielding, and *Does My Bum Look Big in This?* by Arabella Weir, *London Review of Books*, vol. 20, no. 4, 19 February 1998, 24.
57. The description of Marie LaSalle (p. 57) suggests the folk/country singer Mary Chapin Carpenter as a possible model. The 'Steve' referred to (p. 110) suggests Steve Earle, broadly in the same musical category.
58. One can find the same kind of duality is less obviously populist modes of writing. For instance, A. S. Byatt's Booker winner, *Possession: A Romance* (1990), has been accurately hailed as a novel with 'an appeal to a popular readership that does not compromise intellectual standards or aspiration'. (See Richard Todd, *A. S. Byatt* (Plymouth: Northcote House, 1997), pp. 1–2.)
59. Hilda Spear suggests this distinction needs constantly to be kept in view when assessing Murdoch's novels; she concludes that Murdoch is 'a novelist of ideas, a philosopher who dares to introduce philosophic discussion into her novels'. Hilda D. Spear, *Iris Murdoch* (London: Macmillan, 1995), pp. 7, 121.
60. Iris Murdoch, 'Against Dryness: A Polemical Sketch', in Bradbury, ed., *The Novel Today*, pp. 16, 17, 19.
61. *Ibid.*, pp. 20, 21, 22, 23.
62. Maria Antonaccio, 'Form and Contingency in Iris Murdoch's Ethics', in Maria Antonaccio and William Schweiker, eds., *Iris Murdoch and the Search for Human Goodness*, (Chicago: University of Chicago Press, 1996), pp. 110–37 (p. 112–13). See Iris Murdoch, *Metaphysics as a Guide to Morals* (1992; Harmondsworth, Penguin, 1993), p. 93.
63. Antonaccio, 'Form and Contingency in Iris Murdoch's Ethics', p. 121.
64. *Ibid.*, p. 124.
65. *Ibid.*, pp. 129–30.
66. A similar theme of literary rivalry is at the heart of Martin Amis's *The Information* (1995).
67. For a more detailed account of Arrowby's career in relation to Buddhist philosophy, see Lindsay Tucker, 'Released From Bands: Iris Murdoch's Two Prosperos in *The Sea, The Sea*', *Contemporary Literature*, 27 (1986), 3, 378–95.
68. John Sturrock, 'Reading Iris Murdoch', *Salmagundi*, 80 (1988), 144–60 (158).
69. Emanuel Levinas, *Otherwise than Being, or Beyond Essence*, trans. Alphonso Lingus (1974; Pittsburgh: Dusquesne University Press, 1998), p. 11.
70. Andrew Gibson, *Postmodernity, Ethics and the Novel: From Leavis to Levinas* (London: Routledge, 1999), p. 16.
71. *Ibid.*, p. 16. In Gibson's definition, 'ethics' is 'dis-interested', but is also 'bound everywhere' by particular 'moral' choices, codes and conventions (p. 15) Ethics, here, subsumes particular moral systems. These terms are variously defined, however: in Zygmunt Bauman's *Postmodern Ethics* (1993; Oxford:

Blackwell, 1998), for example, ethics is the more particular, rule-bound term, while moral responsibility is the 'first reality of the self, a starting point rather than a product of society' (p. 13).

72. Kiernan Ryan, 'Sex, Violence and Complicity: Martin Amis and Ian McEwan', in Rod Mengham, ed., *An Introduction to Contemporary Fiction* (Cambridge: Polity Press, 1999), pp. 203–18 (p. 215).

73. *Ibid.*, p. 206.

74. See the 'Introduction' above for an account of the importance of Ricoeur's theory of mimesis, as expounded in *Time and Narrative*.

75. Intriguingly, one critic coins the term 'British Postmodern Realism' in an attempt to account for hybrid forms that refuse to conform to the given categories. See Amy J. Elias, 'Meta-*mimesis*? The Problem of British Postmodern Realism', in Theo D'haen and Hans Bertens, eds., *British Postmodern Fiction* (Amsterdam: Rodopi, 1993), pp. 9–31.

# Bibliography

## 1. Post-War Fiction in Britain

(Date of original publication given first, where a later edition is used.)

Ackroyd, Peter, *First Light* (1989; Harmondsworth: Penguin, 1993)

Amis, Kingsley, *Lucky Jim* (1954; Harmondsworth: Penguin, 1992)

Amis, Martin, *Money* (1984; Harmondsworth: Penguin, 1985)

    *Einstein's Monsters* (London: Jonathan Cape, 1987)

    *London Fields* (London: Jonathan Cape, 1989)

    *The Information* (London: HarperCollins, 1995)

Bainbridge, Beryl, *The Bottle Factory Outing* (London: Duckworth, 1974)

    *A Quiet Life* (1976; Glasgow: Collins, 1979)

    *Every Man for Himself* (1996; London: Abacus, 1997)

    *Master Georgie* (London: Duckworth, 1998)

Ballard, J. G., *Crash* (1973; London: Vintage, 1995)

Banks, Lynne Reid, *The L-Shaped Room* (1960; London: The Reprint Society, 1961)

Barker, Pat, *Union Street* (1982; London: Virago, 1997)

    *Liza's England* (originally published as *The Century's Daughter*) (1986; London: Virago, 1997)

    *The Regeneration Trilogy* (London: Viking, 1996) (comprising: *Regeneration* [1991; Harmondsworth: Penguin, 1992]; *The Eye in the Door* [1993; Harmondsworth: Penguin, 1994]; *The Ghost Road* [1995; Harmondsworth: Penguin, 1996])

Barnes, Julian, *Metroland* (1980; London: Picador, 1990)

    *England, England* (London: Jonathan Cape, 1998)

Barstow, Stan, *A Kind of Loving* (1960; Harmondsworth: Penguin, 1962)

Bates, H. E., *The Darling Buds of May* (1958; London: Michael Joseph, 1979)

Beckett, Mary, *Give Them Stones* (1987; London: Bloomsbury, 1988)

Birch, Carol, *Life in the Palace* (1988; London: Virago, 2000)

Blincoe, Nicholas, and Matt Thorne, eds., *All Hail the New Puritans* (London: Fourth Estate, 2000)

Bradbury, Malcolm, *Stepping Westward* (1965; London: Arena, 1986)

    *The History Man* (1975; London: Arrow, 1982)

Braine, John, *Room at the Top* (1957; London: Mandarin, 1996)

Brooke-Rose, Christine, *Textermination* (1991; Manchester: Carcanet, 1997)

Brookner, Anita, *Hotel du Lac* (London: Jonathan Cape, 1984)
    *Altered States* (London: Jonathan Cape, 1996)
Burgess, Anthony, *A Clockwork Orange* (1962; Harmondsworth: Penguin, 1996)
Byatt, A. S., *Possession: A Romance* (1990; London: Vintage, 1991)
Carter, Angela, *The Magic Toyshop* (1967; London: Virago, 1994)
    *Nights at the Circus* (1984; London: Vintage, 1994)
    *Wise Children* (1991; London: Vintage, 1992)
Chaplin, Sid, *The Day of the Sardine* (1961; Essex: Scorpion, 1989)
Chatwin, Bruce, *On the Black Hill* (1982; London: Picador, 1983)
Cheyette, Bryan, ed., *Contemporary Jewish Writing in Britain and Ireland:
    An Anthology* (London: Peter Halban, 1998)
Clark, Candida, *The Last Look* (1998; London: Vintage, 1999)
Coe, Jonathan, *The Accidental Woman* (1987; London: Sceptre, 1989)
    *A Touch of Love* (1989; London: Sceptre, 1990)
    *What a Carve Up!* (1994; Harmondsworth: Penguin, 1995)
    *The House of Sleep* (London: Viking, 1997)
Colegate, Isabel, *Winter Journey* (1995; Harmondsworth: Penguin, 1996)
Cooper, William, *Scenes From Provincial Life* (1950; Harmondsworth:
    Penguin, 1961)
Cordell, Alexander, *Rape of the Fair Country* (1959; London: Sphere, 1991)
Cowan, Andrew, *Pig* (1994: Harmondsworh: Penguin, 1995)
Crace, Jim, *Arcadia* (London: Jonathan Cape, 1992)
Dabydeen, David, *Disappearance* (London: Secker and Warburg, 1993)
Dennis, Nigel, *Cards of Identity* (1955; Harmondsworth: Penguin, 1999)
Doyle, Roddy, *Paddy Clarke Ha Ha Ha* (1993; London: Minerva, 1997)
Drabble, Margaret, *A Summer Bird-Cage* (1963; Harmondsworth:
    Penguin, 1967)
    *The Millstone* (1965; Harmondsworth: Penguin, 1968)
    *The Radiant Way* (1987; Harmondsworth: Penguin, 1988)
    *A Natural Curiosity* (1989; Harmondsworth: Penguin, 1990)
    *The Gates of Ivory* (1991; Harmondsworth: Penguin, 1992)
    *The Peppered Moth* (Harmondsworth: Viking, 2000)
Dunn, Nell, *Up the Junction* (1963; London: Pan, 1966)
    *Poor Cow* (1967; London: Virago, 1996)
    *My Silver Shoes* (1996; London: Bloomsbury, 1997)
Durrell, Lawrence, *The Alexandria Quartet* (London: Faber and Faber, 2001)
    (comprising: *Justine* [1957]; *Balthazar* [1958]; *Mountolive* [1958];
    *Clea* [1960])
Dyer, Geoff, *The Colour of Memory* (1989; London: Abacus, 1997)
Ellmann, Lucy, *Man or Mango? A Lament* (London: Headline Review, 1998)
Emecheta, Buchi, *In the Ditch* (1972; Oxford: Heinemann, 1994)
    *Second-Class Citizen* (1974; Oxford: Heinemann, 1994)
Farrell, J. G., *Troubles* (1970; London: Phoenix, 1993)
    *The Siege of Krishnapur* (London: Weidenfeld and Nicolson, 1973)
Feinstein, Elaine, *Loving Brecht* (1992; Sevenoaks: Sceptre, 1993)

Fielding, Helen, *Bridget Jones's Diary* (1996; London: Picador, 1997)
Fischer, Tibor, *The Collector Collector* (1997; London: Vintage, 1998)
Fowler, Bo, *Scepticism Inc.* (1998; London: Vintage, 1999)
Fowles, John, *The French Lieutenant's Woman* (1969; London: Pan, 1987)
    *Daniel Martin* (1977; London: Picador, 1989)
Freud, Esther, *Hideous Kinky* (1992; Harmondsworth: Penguin, 1993)
Galloway, Janice, *The Trick is to Keep Breathing* (1989; London: Minerva, 1991)
Gee, Maggie, *Grace* (1988; London: Abacus, 1989)
Golding, William, *Lord of the Flies* (1954; London: Faber and Faber, 1971)
Gray, Alasdair, *Lanark: A Life in 4 Books* (1981; London: Picador, 1994)
Greene, Graham, *The End of the Affair* (1951; Harmondsworth: Penguin, 1975)
Hart, Christopher, *The Harvest* (London: Faber, 1999)
Healy, Dermot, *A Goat's Song* (1994; London: Harvill, 1997)
Hensher, Philip, *Kitchen Venom* (1996; Harmondsworth: Penguin, 1997)
Hines, Barry, *A Kestrel for a Knave* (1968; Harmondsworth: Penguin, 1986)
Hollinghurst, Alan, *The Swimming-Pool Library* (1988; London: Vintage, 1998)
Hornby, Nick, *High Fidelity: A Novel* (London: Victor Gollanncz, 1995)
Humphreys, Emyr, *Outside the House of Baal* (1965; Bridgend: Seren, 1996)
Ishiguro, Kazuo, *A Pale View of Hills* (1982; London: Faber and Faber, 1991)
    *An Artist of the Floating World* (1986; London: Faber and Faber, 1987)
    *The Remains of the Day* (London: Faber and Faber, 1989)
    *The Unconsoled* (London: Faber and Faber, 1995)
Jacobson, Howard, *Peeping Tom* (1984; London: Vintage, 1999)
Johnson, B. S., *Travelling People* (1963; London: Panther, 1967)
    *The Unfortunates* (1969; London: Picador, 1999)
Johnson, Pamela Hansford, *The Humbler Creation* (1959; Harmondsworth:
    Penguin, 1961)
Johnston, Jennifer, *Shadows on Our Skin* (1977; Harmondsworth:
    Penguin, 1991)
    *The Railway Station Man* (1984; London: Headline Review, 1998)
Jones, Mary, *Resistance* (Belfast: Blackstaff Press, 1985)
Kelman, James, *How Late it Was, How Late* (1994; London: Minerva, 1995)
Kennedy, A. L., *Looking for the Possible Dance* (1993; London: Vintage, 1998)
Kureishi, Hanif, *The Buddha of Suburbia* (London: Faber, 1990)
Lamming, George, *The Emigrants* (London: Michael Joseph, 1954)
Lessing, Doris, *The Golden Notebook* (1962; London: Grafton, 1989)
Lively, Penelope, *Spiderweb* (1998; Harmondsworth: Penguin, 1999)
Llewellyn, Richard, *How Green Was My Valley* (1939: Harmondsworth:
    Penguin, 1991)
Lodge, David, *The Picturegoers* (1960; Harmondsworth: Penguin, 1993)
    *Nice Work* (1988; Harmondsworth: Penguin, 1989)
Lowry, Malcolm, *Under the Volcano* (1947; Harmondsworth: Penguin, 1985)
McCabe, Patrick, *The Butcher Boy* (1992; London: Picador, 1993)
    *The Dead School* (1995; London: Picador, 1996)
    *Breakfast on Pluto* (London: Picador, 1998)

Macaulay, Rose, *The World My Wilderness* (London: Collins, 1950)
McEwan, Ian, *The Child in Time* (London: Jonathan Cape, 1987)
    *Amsterdam* (London: Jonathan Cape, 1998)
MacInnes, Colin, *City of Spades* (1957; London: Allison and Busby, 1993)
    *Absolute Beginners* (1959: London: Allison and Busby, 1985)
Mackay, Shena, *The Artist's Widow* (1998; London: Vintage, 1999)
MacLaverty, Bernard, *Cal* (1983; London: Vintage, 1998)
Madden, Deirdre, *Hidden Symptoms* (1986; London: Faber, 1988)
Manning, Olivia, *The Balkan Trilogy* (London: Mandarin, 1990) (comprising: *The Great Fortune* [1960]; *The Spoilt City* [1962]; *Friends and Heroes* [1965])
Mantel, Hilary, *Every Day is Mother's Day* (1985; Harmondsworth: Penguin, 1986)
    *Vacant Possession* (1986; Harmondsworth: Penguin, 1987)
Mars-Jones, Adam, *The Waters of Thirst* (London: Faber and Faber, 1993)
Mason, Simon, *Lives of the Dog-Stranglers* (London: Jonathan Cape, 1998)
Michael, Livi, *Under a Thin Moon* (1992; London: Minerva, 1994)
    *All the Dark Air* (1996; London: Vintage, 1997)
Mo, Timothy, *Sour Sweet* (1982; London: Vintage, 1992)
Moore, Brian, *Lies of Silence* (1990; London: Arrow, 1991)
Murdoch, Iris, *Under the Net* (1954; Harmondsworth: Penguin, 1982)
    *The Nice and the Good* (1968; Harmondsworth: Penguin, 1986)
    *The Black Prince* (1973; Harmondsworth: Penguin, 1975)
    *The Sea, The Sea* (1978; Harmondsworth: Penguin, 1980)
Myerson, Julie, *Sleepwalking* (1994; London: Picador, 1995)
Naipaul, V. S., *The Enigma of Arrival* (1987; Harmondsworth: Penguin, 1988)
Naughton, Bill, *Alfie* (1966; London: Allison & Busby, 1993)
Neville, Jill, *The Love Germ* (1969; London: Verso, 1998)
O'Riordan, Kate, *Involved* (London: Flamingo, 1995)
Orwell, George, *Animal Farm: A Fairy Story* (1945; Harmondsworth: Penguin, 2000)
    *Nineteen Eighty-Four* (1949; Harmondsworth: Penguin, 2000)
Patterson, Glenn, *Burning Your Own* (1988; London: Minerva, 1993)
Pears, Tim, *A Revolution of the Sun* (London: Doubleday, 2000)
Phillips, Caryl, *The Final Passage* (1985; London: Picador, 1995)
Powell, Anthony, *A Question of Upbringing* (1951; London: Flamingo, 1986)
    *The Military Philosophers* (1968; London: Flamingo, 1987)
    *Temporary Kings* (1973; London: Flamingo, 1983)
    *Hearing Secret Harmonies* (1975; London: Flamingo, 1983)
Pym, Barbara, *Excellent Women* (1952; Harmondsworth: Penguin, 1986)
    *A Glass of Blessings* (1958; Harmondsworth: Penguin, 1985)
    *Quartet in Autumn* (1977; London: Granada, 1982)
Read, Piers Paul, *A Married Man* (1979; London: Phoenix, 1996)
Roberts, Michèle, *The Visitation* (1983; London: The Women's Press, 1994)
Rubens, Bernice, *The Elected Member* (1969; London: Abacus, 1995)

Rushdie, Salman, *Midnight's Children* (1981; London: Picador, 1982)
    *The Satanic Verses* (1988; London: Vintage, 1998)
Ryan, James, *Home From England* (1995; London: Phoenix, 1996)
Scott, Paul, *The Raj Quartet* (1966–75) (comprising: *The Jewel in the Crown*
    [1966; London: Arrow, 1995]; *The Day of the Scorpion* [1968;
    London: Mandarin, 1995]; *The Towers of Silence* [1971; London:
    Mandarin, 1995]; *A Division of the Spoils* [1975; London:
    Mandarin, 1995])
    *Staying On* (1977; London: Arrow, 1997)
Selvon, Sam, *The Lonely Londoners* (1956; Harlow: Longman, 1998)
    *Moses Ascending* (1975; Oxford: Heinemann, 1984)
    *Moses Migrating* (London: Hutchinson, 1983)
Sillitoe, Alan, *Saturday Night and Sunday Morning* (1958; London:
    Flamingo, 1994)
    *The Loneliness of the Long-Distance Runner* (1959; London:
    Flamingo, 1994)
Sinclair, Clive, *Blood Libels* (London: Allison and Busby, 1985)
Smith, Zadie, *White Teeth* (London: Hamish Hamilton, 2000)
Spark, Muriel, *The Prime of Miss Jean Brodie* (1961; Harmondsworth:
    Penguin, 1985)
    *The Driver's Seat* (1970; Harmondsworth: Penguin, 1974)
Storey, David, *This Sporting Life* (London: Longmans, 1960)
    *Flight into Camden* (1960; Harmondsworth: Penguin, 1979)
    *Pasmore* (1972; Harmondsworth: Penguin, 1980)
    *Saville* (1976; Harmondsworth: Penguin, 1978)
    *A Serious Man* (1998; London: Vintage, 1999)
Swift, Graham, *Waterland* (1983; London: Picador, 1984)
Syal, Meera, *Anita and Me* (1996; London: Flamingo, 1997)
Thomas, D. M., *The White Hotel* (London: Victor Gollancz, 1981)
Thorpe, Adam, *Ulverton* (1992; London: Minerva, 1993)
    *Pieces of Light* (London: Jonathan Cape, 1998)
Tolkien, J. R. R., *The Lord of the Rings* (London: HarperCollins, 1991)
    (comprising: *The Fellowship of the Ring* [1954]; *The Two Towers*
    [1954]; *The Return of the King* [1955])
Trocchi, Alexander, *Cain's Book* (1963; London: John Calder, 1998)
Wain, John, *Hurry on Down* (1953; Harmondsworth: Penguin, 1979)
Warner, Alan, *Morvern Callar* (1995; London: Vintage, 1996)
    *These Demented Lands* (London: Jonathan Cape, 1997)
Waterhouse, Keith, *Billy Liar* (1959; London: Penguin, 1962)
Waugh, Evelyn, *The Sword of Honour Trilogy* (Harmondsworth: Penguin, 1984)
    (comprising: *Men at Arms* [1952]; *Officers and Gentlemen* [1955];
    *Unconditional Surrender* [1961])
Weldon, Fay, *Praxis* (1978; London: Coronet, 1985)
    *The Life and Loves of a She-Devil* (1983; London: Sceptre, 1984)
    *Big Women* (1997; London: Flamingo, 1998)

Welsh, Irvine, *Trainspotting* (1993; London: Minerva, 1994)
    *Marabou Stork Nightmares* (London: Jonathan Cape, 1995)
    *Filth* (London: Jonathan Cape, 1998)
Williams, Nigel, *The Wimbledon Poisoner* (1990; London: Faber, 1994)
Williams, Raymond, *Border Country* (1960; London: Hogarth Press, 1988)
    *Second Generation* (1964; London: Hogarth Press, 1988)
    *The Fight for Manod* (1979; London: Hogarth Press, 1988)
    *The Volunteers* (1978; London: Hogarth Press, 1985)
    *People of the Black Mountains, I: The Beginning* (London: Chatto and
        Windus, 1989)
    *People of the Black Mountains, II: The Eggs of the Eagle* (London: Chatto and
        Windus, 1990)
Wilson, Angus, *Such Darling Dodos* (London: Secker and Warburg, 1950)
    *Hemlock and After* (1952; London: Penguin, 1992)
    *Anglo-Saxon Attitudes* (1956; London: Penguin, 1992)
    *The Middle Age of Mrs Eliot* (1958; London, Penguin, 1992)
    *The Old Men at the Zoo* (1961; London: Penguin, 1992)
    *Late Call* (1964; London: Penguin, 1968)
Wilson, Robert McLiam, *Ripley Bogle* (1989; London: Minerva, 1997)
    *Eureka Street* (1996; London: Minerva, 1997)
Winterson, Jeanette, *Oranges Are Not the Only Fruit* (1985; London: Vintage, 1996)
    *Sexing the Cherry* (1989; London: Vintage, 1990)
    *Written on the Body* (1992; London: Vintage, 1996)
    *Art and Lies* (1994; London: Vintage, 1995)
    *The.Powerbook* (London: Jonathan Cape, 2000)

## 2. Other Works Cited

Acheson, James, ed., *The British and Irish Novel Since 1960* (Basingstoke:
        Macmillan, 1991)
Ackroyd, Peter, *Notes for a New Culture: An Essay on Modernism* (London:
        Vision, 1976)
Adil, Alev, 'Middle England' (review of *Beyond the Blue Mountains*), *TLS*, 4915,
        13 June 1997, 24
Adonis, Andrew, and Stephen Pollard, *A Class Act: The Myth of Britain's Classless
        Society* (London: Hamish Hamilton, 1997)
Amis, Kingsley, *The Letters of Kingsley Amis*, ed. Zachary Leader (London:
        HarperCollins, 2000)
Anderson, Benedict, *Imagined Communities*, second edn (London: Verso, 1991),
        pp. 6–7
Antonaccio, Maria, 'Form and Contingency in Iris Murdoch's Ethics', in Maria
        Antonaccio and William Schweiker, eds., *Iris Murdoch and the Search for
        Human Goodness* (Chicago: University of Chicago Press, 1996),
        pp. 110–37

Banfield, Ann, *Unspeakable Sentences: Narration and Representation in the Language of Fiction* (London: Routledge and Kegan Paul, 1982)

Barker, Paul, 'Edge City', in Anthony Barnett and Roger Scruton, eds. *Town and Country*

Barnes, Julian, anonymous interview with, *The Observer*, 30 August 1998, 'The Review', p. 15.

Barnett, Anthony, and Roger Scruton, eds., *Town and Country* (London: Jonathan Cape, 1998)

Bassnett, Susan, ed., *Studying British Cultures: An Introduction* (London: Routledge, 1997)

Baucom, Ian, *Out of Place: Englishness, Empire, and the Locations of Identity* (Princeton University Press, 1999)

Bauman, Zygmunt, *Postmodern Ethics* (1993; Oxford: Blackwell, 1998)

Beckett, Andy, 'Perishability', *London Review of Books*, vol. 22 no. 17, 3 September 1998, 27

Bell, Ian A., ed., *Peripheral Visions: Images of Nationhood in Contemporary British Fiction* (Cardiff: University of Wales Press, 1995)

Belsey, Catherine, *Critical Practice* (London: Methuen, 1980)

Bergonzi, Bernard, *The Situation of the Novel* (1970; Harmondsworth: Penguin, 1972)

'Fictions of History', in Malcolm Bradbury and David Palmer, eds., *The Contemporary English Novel*, pp. 42–65

*Wartime and Aftermath: English Literature and its Background 1939–1960* (Oxford University Press, 1993)

Beveridge, William, *Social Insurance and Allied Services* (London, 1942)

Bhabha, Homi, 'DissemiNation: Time, Narrative, and the Margins of the Modern Nation', in Bhabha, ed., *Nation and Narration* (London: Routledge, 1990), pp. 291–322

Bianchi, Tony, 'Aztecs in Troedrhiwgwair: Recent Fictions in Wales' in *Peripheral Visions*, ed. Ian A. Bell, pp. 44–76

Birch, Sarah, *Christine Brooke-Rose and Contemporary Fiction* (Oxford University Press, 1994)

Blincoe, Nicholas and Thorne, Matt, 'Introduction: The Pledge' in Blincoe and Thorne, eds., *All Hail the New Puritans* (London: Fourth Estate, 2000)

Bollinger, Laurel, 'Models for Female Loyalty: The Biblical Ruth in Jeanette Winterson's *Oranges Are Not the Only Fruit*', *Tulsa Studies in Women's Literature*, 13 (1994), 2, 363–80

Booker, M. Keith, *The Modern British Novel of the Left: A Research Guide* (London: Greenwood Press, 1998)

Bradbury, Malcolm, *Possibilities: Essays on the State of the Novel* (Oxford: Oxford University Press, 1973)

ed., with David Palmer, *The Contemporary English Novel* (London: Edward Arnold, 1979)

ed., *The Novel Today: Contemporary Writers on Modern Fiction*, new edn (London: Fontana, 1990)

*The Modern British Novel* (London: Secker and Warburg, 1993)

'Introduction' to *Animal Farm: A Fairy Story* (1945; Harmondsworth: Penguin, 2000), pp. v–xvi

Bradford, Richard, *Kingsley Amis* (Plymouth: Northcote House, 1998)

Brewer, John, and Stella Tillyard, 'History and Telling Stories: Graham Swift's *Waterland*', *History Today*, 35 (1985), January, 49–51

Brooke-Rose, Christine, *Stories, Theories and Things* (Cambridge University Press, 1991)

'Narrating Without a Narrator', *TLS*, 5048, 31 December 1999, 12–13

Brooks, Libby, 'Power Surge' (interview and profile of Jeanette Winterson), *The Guardian*, 'Weekend', 2 September 2000, 10–16

Buell, Laurence, *The Environmental Imagination: Thoreau, Nature Writing, and the Formation of American Culture* (Cambridge (Mass.): Harvard University Press, 1995)

Calinescu, Matei, and Douwe Fokkema, eds., *Exploring Postmodernism*, (Amsterdam: John Benjamins, 1990)

Callil, Carmen, and Colm Tóibín, *The Modern Library: The Two Hundred Best Novels in English Since 1950* (London: Picador, 1999)

Campbell, Jane, '"Both a Joke and a Victory": Humor as Narrative Strategy in Margaret Drabble's Fiction', *Contemporary Literature*, 32 (1991), 1, 75–99

Cannadine, David, *Class in Britain* (London: Yale University Press, 1998)

Cavaliero, Glen, *The Rural Tradition in the English Novel, 1900–1939* (Basingstoke: Macmillan, 1977)

Cheyette, Bryan, 'Preface' and 'Introduction' to Cheyette, ed., *Contemporary Jewish Writing in Britain and Ireland: An Anthology*, Cheyette (London: Peter Halban, 1998), pp. xi–lxxi

Clarke, Peter, *Hope and Glory: Britain 1900–1990* (1996; Harmondsworth: Penguin, 1997)

Coe, Jonathan, 'Introduction' to B. S. Johnson, *The Unfortunates* (1969; London: Picador, 1999), pp. v–xv

Collini, Stefan, *English Pasts: Essays in History and Culture* (Oxford University Press, 1999)

Connor, Steven, *The English Novel in History, 1950–1995* (London: Routledge, 1996)

Conradi, Peter, *Angus Wilson* (Plymouth: Northcote House, 1997)

Cook, Judith, *Unlawful Killing: The Murder of Hilda Murrell* (London: Bloomsbury, 1994)

Cosslett, Tess, 'Childbirth on the National Health: Issues of Class, Race, and Gender Identity in Two Post-War British Novels', *Women's Studies*, 19 (1991), 99–119

Cotsell, Michael, *Barbara Pym* (Basingstoke: Macmillan, 1989)

Coward, Rosalind, *Sacred Cows: Is Feminism Relevant to the New Millennium?* (London: HarperCollins, 1999)

Coxall, Bill, and Lynton Robins, *British Politics Since the War* (Basingstoke: Macmillan, 1998)

Craig, Cairns, 'Resisting Arrest: James Kelman', in Gavin Wallace and Randall
 Stevenson, eds., *The Scottish Novel Since the Seventies* (Edinburgh
 University Press, 1993), pp. 99–114
 *The Modern Scottish Novel: Narrative and the National Imagination* (Edinburgh
 University Press, 1999)
Crane, Ralph, and Jennifer Livett, *Troubled Pleasures: The Fiction of J. G. Farrell*
 (Dublin: Four Courts Press, 1997)
Creighton, Joanne, *Margaret Drabble* (London: Methuen, 1985)
Cullinan, John, 'Anthony Burgess' *A Clockwork Orange*: Two Versions', *English
 Language Notes*, 9 (1972), 287–92
D'haen, Theo, and Hans Bertens, eds., *British Postmodern Fiction*, (Amsterdam:
 Rodopi, 1993)
Drabble, Margaret, '"No Idle Rentier": Angus Wilson and the Nourished
 Literary Imagination', reprinted in Jay L. Halio, ed., *Critical Essays on
 Angus Wilson*, pp. 182–92
 'Mimesis: The Representation of Reality in the Post-War British Novel',
 *Mosaic*, 20 (1987), 1, 1–14
 'Introduction' to *Poor Cow* by Nell Dunn (1967; London: Virago, 1988),
 pp. xi–xviii
 *Angus Wilson* (1995; London: Minerva, 1996)
Eaglestone, Robert, 'Undoing English', *CCUE News*, 13 (Summer 2000), 6–8
Eagleton, Mary, and David Pierce, *Attitudes to Class in the English Novel* (London:
 Thames and Hudson, 1979)
Easthope, Antony, *Englishness and National Culture* (London: Routledge, 1999)
Edwards, Arthur, *The Design of Suburbia* (London: Pembridge Press, 1981)
Elias, Amy J., 'Meta-*mimesis*? The Problem of British Postmodern Realism', in
 Theo D'haen and Hans Bertens, eds., *British Postmodern Fiction*, pp. 9–31
Emecheta, Buchi, *Head Above Water: An Autobiography* (1986; Oxford:
 Heinemann, 1994)
Fishburn, Katherine, *Reading Buchi Emecheta: Cross-Cultural conversations* (London:
 Greenwood Press, 1995)
Fowles, John, *Wormholes: Essays and Occasional Writings*, ed. J. Relf (London:
 Jonathan Cape, 1998)
Freely, Maureen, 'Sugar and Spite', *The Observer*, 18 January 1998, 'Review', p. 4
Fukuyama, Francis, *The End of History and the Last Man* (Harmondsworth:
 Penguin, 1992)
Fullbrook, Kate, 'Anita Brookner: On Reaching for the Sun', in Abby H. P.
 Werlock, ed., *British Women Writing Fiction*, pp. 90–106
Gare, Arran, *Postmodernism and the Environmental Crisis* (London: Routledge, 1995)
Gąsiorek, Andrzej, *Post-War British Fiction: Realism and After* (London: Edward
 Arnold, 1995)
Gee, Maggie, 'Clinging to the Coat-Tails of Fact', *Times Literary Supplement*,
 4928, 12 September 1997, 10
Gibson, Andrew, *Postmodernity, Ethics and the Novel: From Leavis to Levinas*
 (London: Routledge, 1999)

Gifford, Terry, *Green Voices: Understanding Contemporary Nature Poetry* (Manchester University Press, 1995)
    *Pastoral* (London: Routledge, 1999)
Gilroy, Paul, *Between Camps: Race, Identity and Nationalism at the End of the Colour Line* (London: Allen Lane, 2000)
Gindin, James, *Postwar British Fiction: New Accents and Attitudes* (1962; Berkeley: University of California Press, 1963)
Gorak, Jan, *The Alien Mind of Raymond Williams* (Columbia: University of Missouri Press, 1988)
Gramich, Katie, 'Cymru or Wales?: Explorations in a Divided Sensibility', in Susan Bassnett, ed., *Studying British Cultures: An Introduction*, pp. 97–112
Grant, Damian, *Salman Rushdie* (Plymouth: Northcote House, 1999)
Greacen, Lavinia, *J. G. Farrell: The Making of a Writer* (London: Bloomsbury, 1999)
Greer, Germaine, *The Female Eunuch* (1970; London: Flamingo, 1999)
    *The Whole Woman* (London: Doubleday, 1999)
Halio, Jay L., ed., *Critical Essays on Angus Wilson* (Boston: G. K. Hall, 1985)
Hamilton, Ian, 'Bohemian Rhapsodist', profile of Shena Mackay, *The Guardian*, Saturday 10 July 1999, 'Saturday Review', pp. 6–7
Hanks, Robert, 'Flashes of Inspiration', interview with Ian McEwan, *The Independent*, 12 September 1998, 'Weekend Review', p. 14
Hanne, Michael, *The Power of the Story: Fiction and Political Change* (Oxford: Berghahn Books, 1996)
Haraway, Donna J., *Modest_Witness@Second_Millennium. FemaleMan©_Meets_OncoMouse*™ (London: Routledge, 1997)
Harman, Chris, 'The State and Capitalism Today', *International Socialism*, 51 (1991), 3–54
Harvey, David, *The Condition of Postmodernity* (1980; Oxford: Blackwell, 1990)
Harvey, Graham, *The Killing of the Countryside* (1997; London: Vintage, 1998)
Haywood, Ian, *Working-Class Fiction: From Chartism to 'Trainspotting'* (Plymouth: Northcote House, 1997)
Heller, Zoë, 'Dumped', review of *Animal Husbandry* by Laura Zigman, *Bridget Jones's Diary* by Helen Fielding, and *Does My Bum Look Big in This?* by Arabella Weir, *London Review of Books*, vol. 20, no. 4, 19 February 1998, 24
Hobsbawm, Eric, *Nations and Nationalism Since 1780: Programme, Myth, Reality* (Cambridge University Press, 1991)
Hoggart, Richard, *The Uses of Literacy* (1957; Harmondsworth: Penguin, 1992)
Holmes, Richard, 'The Death of the Author as Cultural Critique in *London Fields*', extracts in Nicolas Tredell, ed., *The Fiction of Martin Amis*, pp. 110–18
Holt, Hazel, 'The Novelist in the Field: 1964–74', in Dale Salwak, ed., *The Life and Work of Barbara Pym* (Basingstoke: Macmillan, 1987), pp. 22–33
Hopkins, David, *After Modern Art: 1945–2000* (Oxford University Press, 2000)
Hornby, Nick, *Fever Pitch: A Fan's Life* (London: Victor Gollancz, 1992)

Hosmer, Robert E., ed., *Contemporary British Women Writers: Texts and Strategies* (Basingstoke: Macmillan, 1993)

Hughes, Eamonn, '"Lancelot's Position": The Fiction of Irish-Britain', in A. Robert Lee, ed., *Other Britain, Other British*, pp. 142–60

Humphreys, Emyr, *The Taliesin Tradition* (1983; Bridgend: Seren, 2000)

Hutcheon, Linda, *A Poetics of Postmodernism: History, Theory, Fiction* (1988; London: Routledge, 1995)

Hynes, Joseph, 'Muriel Spark and the Oxymoronic Vision', in Robert E. Hosmer, ed., *Contemporary British Women Writers*, pp. 161–87

Innes, C. L., 'Wintering: Making a Home in Britain' in A. Robert Lee, ed., *Other Britain, Other British*, pp. 21–34

Jaggi, Maya, review of *Disappearance* by David Dabydeen, *TLS*, 4693, 12 March 1993, 20

Jameson. Fredric, *The Political Unconscious: Narrative as a Socially Symbolic Act* (1981; London: Methuen, 1986)

*Postmodernism, or, the Cultural Logic of Late Capitalism* (London: Verso, 1991)

Johnson, B. S., 'Introduction' to *Aren't You Rather Young to be Writing Your Memoirs?*, reprinted in Malcolm Bradbury, ed., *The Novel Today: Contemporary Writers on Modern Fiction*, pp. 165–83

Kaleta, Kenneth C., *Hanif Kureishi: Postcolonial Storyteller* (Austin: University of Texas Press, 1998)

Kavanagh, Dennis, *Thatcherism and British Politics: The End of Consensus?*, third edn (Oxford University Press, 1990)

*British Politics: Continuities and Change*, third edn (Oxford University Press, 1996)

Kearney, Hugh, *The British Isles: A History of Four Nations* (1989; Cambridge University Press, 1998)

Kennedy, A. L., 'Not Changing the World', in Ian A. Bell, ed., *Peripheral Visions*, pp. 100–2

Kiberd, Declan, 'Reinventing England', *Key Words: A Journal of Cultural Materialism*, 2 (1999), 47–57

King, Bruce, 'The New Internationalsim: Shiva Naipaul, Salman Rushdie, Buchi Emecheta, Timothy Mo and Kazuo Ishiguro', in James Acheson, ed., *The British and Irish Novel Since 1960*, pp. 192–211

Kirkland, Richard, *Literature and Culture in Northern Ireland Since 1965: Moments of Danger* (London: Longman, 1996)

Klaus, H. Gustav, ed., *The Socialist Novel in Britain: Towards the Recovery of a Tradition* (Brighton: Harvester, 1982)

Laing, Stuart, '*Room at the Top*: The Morality of Affluence', in Christopher Pawling, ed., *Popular Fiction and Social Change* (London: Macmillan, 1984), pp. 157–84

Larkin, Philip, Anthony Thwaite, ed., *Collected Poems* (London: Faber and Faber, 1988)

Lazarus, Neil, *Nationalism and Cultural Practice in the Postcolonial World* (Cambridge University Press, 1999)

Lee, A. Robert, ed., *Other Britain, Other British: Contemporary Multicultural Fiction* (London: Pluto Press, 1995)

Lee, Alison, *Realism and Power: British Postmodern Fiction* (London: Routledge, 1990)

Levinas, Emanuel, *Otherwise than Being, or Beyond Essence*, trans. Alphonso Lingus (1974; Pittsburgh: Dusquesne University Press, 1998)

Little, Judy, 'Muriel Spark's Grammars of Assent', in James Acheson, ed., *The British and Irish Novel Since 1960*, pp. 1–16

Lively, Penelope, 'The World of Barbara Pym', in Salwak, ed., *The Life and Work of Barbara Pym*, pp. 45–9

Lodge, David, 'The Novelist at the Crossroads' (1969), abridged version printed in Malcolm Bradbury, ed., *The Novel Today*, pp. 87–114

Looker, Mark, *Atlantic Passages: History, Community, and Language in the Fiction of Sam Selvon* (New York: Peter Lang, 1996)

McCabe, Colin, *James Joyce and the Revolution of the Word* (1979; Basingstoke: Macmillan, 1983)

McEwan, Neil, *Anthony Powell* (Basingstoke: Macmillan, 1991)

McHale, Brian, *Postmodernist Fiction* (1987; rep. London: Routledge, 1991)

McMillan, Dorothy, 'Constructed Out of Bewilderment: Stories of Scotland', in Ian A. Bell, ed., *Peripheral Visions*, pp. 80–99

McPartland, Richard, 'Death of Paper?', *Personal Computer World*, December 2000, 146–50

McVeigh, Tracy, 'How Phoney Was My Valley', *The Observer*, 5 December 1999, p. 3

Mars, Tim, 'The Life in New Towns', in Anthony Barnett and Roger Scruton, eds., *Town and Country*, pp. 267–78

Mars-Jones, Adam, *Blind Bitter Happiness* (London: Chatto and Windus, 1997)

Marwick, Arthur, *British Society Since 1945*, third edn (Harmondsworth: Penguin, 1996)

   *The Sixties: Cultural Revolution in Britain, France, Italy, and the United States, c.1958–c.1974* (Oxford University Press, 1998)

Mengham, Rod, ed., *An Introduction to Contemporary Fiction* (Cambridge: Polity Press, 1999)

Morrison, Blake, *The Movement: English Poetry and Fiction of the 1950s* (Oxford University Press, 1980)

   'Introduction' to *A Clockwork Orange* (Harmondsworth: Penguin, 1996), pp. vii–xxiv

Murdoch, Iris. 'Against Dryness: A Polemical Sketch' (1961), in Malcolm Bradbury, ed., *The Novel Today: Contemporary Writers on Modern Fiction*, pp. 15–24

   *Metaphysics as a Guide to Morals* (1992; London, Penguin, 1993)

Murphy, Patrick D., *Literature, Nature, and Other: Ecofeminist Critiques* (SUNY Press, 1995)

Nasta, Susheila, 'Setting Up Home in a City of Words: Sam Selvon's London Novels', in A. Robert Lee, ed., *Other Britain, Other British*, pp. 48–68

Newman, Jenny, ' "See Me as Sisyphus, But Having a Good Time": The Fiction of Fay Weldon', in Robert E. Hosmer, ed., *Contemporary British Women Writers*, pp. 188–211

Patten, Eve, 'Fiction in Conflict: Northern Ireland's Prodigal Novelists', in Ian A. Bell, ed., *Peripheral Visions: Images of Nationhood in Contemporary British Fiction*, pp. 128–48

Patterson, Christina, 'A Willesden Ring of Confidence', interview with Zadie Smith, *The Independent*, '*The Weekend Review*', 22 January 2000, p. 9

Pawling, Christopher, ed., *Popular Fiction and Social Change* (London: Macmillan, 1984)

Paxman, Jeremy, *The English: A Portrait of a People* (London: Michael Joseph, 1998), p. 23.

Peach, Linden, *Angela Carter* (Basingstoke: Macmillan, 1998)

Peck, John, 'The Novels of Peter Ackroyd', *English Studies* 5 (1994), 442–52

Philips, Deborah, and Ian Haywood, *Brave New Causes: Women in British Postwar Fictions* (London: Leicester University Press, 1998)

Phillips, Caryl, 'Mixed and Matched', review of *White Teeth* by Zadie Smith, *The Observer*, 'Review', 9 January 2000, p. 11

Pimlott, Ben, 'Introduction' to *Nineteen Eighty-Four* (1949; Harmondsworth: Penguin, 2000), pp. v–vxii

Pittock, Malcolm, 'Revaluing the Sixties: *This Sporting Life* Revisited', *Forum for Modern Language Studies*, 26 (1990) 2, pp. 97–108

Propp, Vladimir, *Morphology of the Folktale*, trans. Laurence Scott (Austin: University of Texas Press, 1968)

Rabinovitz, Rubin, *The Reaction Against Experiment in the English Novel, 1950–1960* (New York: Columbia University Press, 1967)

Ramchand, Kenneth, 'Introduction', Sam Selvon, *The Lonely Londoners* (1956; London: Longman, 1998), pp. 3–21

Rankin, Ian, 'The Deliberate Cunning of Muriel Spark', in Gavin Wallace and Randall Stevenson, eds., *The Scottish Novel Since the Seventies*, pp. 41–53

Ricoeur, Paul, *Time and Narrative*, trans. Kathleen McLaughlin and David Pellauer, 3 vols. (Chicago University Press, 1984–8)

Robshaw, Brandon, 'Shaking Hands Across the Great Divide', *The Independent*, 'The Weekend Review', 17 June 2000, 10

Rodden, John, ' "The Rope That Connects Me Directly with You": John Wain and the Movement Writers' Orwell', *Albion*, 20 (1988), 1, 59–76

Rolston, Bill, 'Mothers, Whores and Villains: Images of Women in Novels of the Northern Ireland Conflict', *Race and Class*, 31 (1989), 41–57

Rose, Ellen Cronan, *The Novels of Margaret Drabble: Equivocal Figures* (London: Macmillan, 1980)

Rosenberg, Ingrid von, 'Militancy, anger and resignation: alternative moods in the working-class novel of the 1950s and early 1960s', in H. Gustav Klaus, ed., *The Socialist Novel in Britain: Towards the Recovery of a Tradition* (Brighton: Harvester, 1982), pp. 145–65

Rowbotham, Sheila, *A Century of Women: The History of Women in Britain and the United States* (1997; Harmondsworth: Penguin, 1999)

Rubenstein, Roberta, 'Fragmented Bodies/Selves/Narratives: Margaret Drabble's Postmodern Turn', *Contemporary Literature*, 35 (1994), 1, 136–55

Rushdie, Salman, *Imaginary Homelands: Essays and Criticism 1981–91* (1991; London: Granta Books, 1992)

Ryan, Kiernan, 'Sex, Violence and Complicity: Martin Amis and Ian McEwan', in Rod Mengham, ed., *An Introduction to Contemporary Fiction*, pp. 203–18

Ryan, Ray, ed., *Writing in the Irish Republic: Literature, Culture, Politics 1949–1999* (Basingstoke: Macmillan, 2000)

Sage, Lorna, *Women in the House of Fiction: Post-War Women Novelists* (Basingstoke: Macmillan, 1992)

'A Place for Displacement', review of *Christine Brooke-Rose and Contemporary Fiction*, by Sarah Birch, *TLS*, 4767, 12 August 1994, 21

Salwak, Dale, *Interviews With Britain's Angry Young Men* (San Bernardino: Borgo Press, 1984)

ed., *The Life and Work of Barbara Pym* (Basingstoke: Macmillan, 1987)

Sansom, Ian, 'Half-Timbering, Homosexuality and Whingeing', review of *England, England*, by Julian Barnes, *London Review of Books*, 20:19, 1 October 1998, 31–2

Sawyer, Miranda, 'Telling Tales', interview with Fay Weldon, *The Observer* 25 January 1998, 'Life', pp. 4–8

*Park and Ride: Adventures in Suburbia* (London: Little Brown, 1999)

Scanlan, Margaret, *Traces of Another Time: History and Politics in Postwar British Fiction* (Princeton University Press, 1990)

Schulz, Muriel, 'The Novelist as Anthropologist', in Dale Salwak, ed., *The Life and Work of Barbara Pym*, pp. 101–19

Shakespeare, Nicholas, *Bruce Chatwin* (1999; London: Vintage, 2000)

Shulman, Nicola, 'Some Consolations of the Single State', review of *Bridget Jones's Diary* by Helen Fielding, *TLS*, 4883, 1 November 1996, 26

Silverstone, Roger, ed., *Visions of Suburbia* (London: Routledge, 1997)

Sinfield, Alan, *Literature, Politics and Culture in Postwar Britain*, second edn (London: Athlone, 1997)

Smith, Penny, 'Hell Innit: The Millennium in Alasdair Gray's *Lanark*, Martin Amis's *London Fields*, and Shena Mackay's *Dunedin*', extract printed in Nicholas Tredell, ed., *The Fiction of Martin Amis*, pp. 100–3

Smyth, Gerry, *The Novel and the Nation* (London: Pluto, 1997)

Spear, Hilda D., *Iris Murdoch* (London: Macmillan, 1995)

Steiner, George, *Language and Silence: Essays 1958–1966* (1967; Faber and Faber, 1985)

Sturrock, John, 'Reading Iris Murdoch', *Salmagundi*, 80 (1988), 144–60

Swinden, Patrick, *The English Novel of History and Society, 1940–80* (London: Macmillan, 1984)

Taylor, D. J., *A Vain Conceit: British Fiction in the 1980s* (London: Bloomsbury, 1989)

*After the War: The Novel and England Since 1945* (1993; London: Flamingo, 1994)

'"Lee Fredge: My Story". Er, No Thanks . . .', *The Independent*, 'Weekend Review', 18 December 1999, 10

Tiffin, Helen, 'Post-Colonial Literatures and Counter-Discourse', *Kunapipi*, 9 (1987), 3, 17–34

Todd, Richard, 'The Intrusive Author in British Postmodernist Fiction: The Cases of Alasdair Gray and Martin Amis', in Matei Calinescu and Douwe Fokkema, eds., *Exploring Postmodernism*, pp. 123–37

*Consuming Fictions: The Booker Prize and Fiction in Britain Today* (London: Bloomsbury, 1996)

*A. S. Byatt* (Plymouth: Northcote House, 1997)

Tredell, Nicolas, ed., *The Fiction of Martin Amis: A Reader's Guide to Essential Criticism* (Cambridge: Icon Books, 2000)

Tucker, Lindsay, 'Released From Bands: Iris Murdoch's Two Prosperos in *The Sea, The Sea*', *Contemporary Literature*, 27 (1986), 3, 378–95

Veldman, Meredith, *Fantasy, the Bomb, and the Greening of Britain: Romantic Protest, 1945–1980* (Cambridge University Press, 1994)

Vinson, James, ed., *Contemporary Novelists* (London: St James Press, 1970)

Wadham-Smith, Nicholas, ed., *British Studies Now*, 1–5 (anthology issue) (London: British Council, 1995)

Wagner, Hans-Peter, 'Learning to Read the Female Body: On the function of Manet's *Olympia* in John Braine's *Room at the Top*', *Zeitschrift für Anglistik und Amerikanistik*, 42 (1994), 1, 38–53

Wain, John, 'Introduction' to *Hurry on Down* (reprinted Harmondsworth: Penguin, 1979), pp. 1–5

Walker, John, ed., *Halliwell's Film and Video Guide*, twelfth edn (London: HarperCollins, 1996)

Wallace, Gavin, and Randall Stevenson, eds., *The Scottish Novel Since the Seventies*, (1993; Edinburgh University Press, 1994)

Walter, Natasha, 'A World Elsewhere', review of *Altered States*, by Anita Brookner, *The Guardian*, section 2, 14 June 1996, p. 8

*The New Feminism* (1998; London: Virago, 1999)

Wambu, Onyekachi, ed., *Empire Windrush: Fifty Years of Writing About Black Britain*, (London: Victor Gollancz, 1998)

Waugh, Patricia, *Harvest of the Sixties: English Literature and its Background 1960–1990* (Oxford University Press, 1995)

Webster, Charles, *The National Health Service: A Political History* (Oxford University Press, 1998)

Weldon, Fay, 'Preface' to Jill Neville, *The Love Germ* (1969; London: Verso, 1998), pp. vii–ix

Werlock, Abby H. P., ed., *British Women Writing Fiction* (Tuscaloosa: University of Alabama Press, 2000)

Williams, Raymond, *The English Novel From Dickens to Lawrence* (1970; London: Hogarth Press, 1987)

*The Country and the City* (1973; London: Hogarth Press, 1985)

*Politics and Letters: Interviews with 'New Left Review'* (London: New Left Books, 1979)

*Problems in Materialism and Culture* (London: Verso, 1980)

*Towards 2000* (London: Chatto and Windus, 1983)

*Writing in Society* (1983; London: Verso, 1985)

*Resources of Hope: Culture, Democracy, Socialism*, edited by Robin Gable (London: Verso, 1989)

Wilson, Angus, *Diversity and Depth in Fiction: Selected Critical Writings of Angus Wilson*, edited by Kerry McSweeney (New York: Viking Press, 1983)

Wood, James, *The Broken Estate: Essays on Literature and Belief* (London: Jonathan Cape, 1999)

Woolf, Michael, 'Negotiating the Self: Jewish Fiction in Britain Since 1945', in A. Robert Lee, ed., *Other Britain, Other British*, pp. 124–42

Woolf, Virginia, *Collected Essays*, ed. Leonard Woolf, 4 vols. (London: Hogarth Press, 1966–7)

# Index

abortion, 84, 86, 95
Achebe, Chinua, 168
  *Things Fall Apart*, 168
Ackroyd, Peter, 202–4, 229
  *First Light*, 202–4
  *Notes for a New Culture*, 202
Act of Union (1707), 149
AIDS, 116–17
Amis, Kingsley, 3, 4, 6, 50, 51–2,
  87, 213, 222–3, 224, 225, 250
  *Lucky Jim*, 3, 6, 50, 51–2, 87, 213,
  222–3, 250
Amis, Martin, 3, 5, 7, 30–31, 200,
  211–13, 229, 242–4, 251, 258
  *Einstein's Monsters*, 5
  *London Fields*, 211–13
  *Money*, 3, 30–31, 200, 211, 242–4
Anderson, Benedict, 121–2, 154–5
Angelou, Maya, 110
Anglo-Irish Agreement (1985), 132
'Angry Young Men', 7–8, 50, 52–7,
  84, 215–16
anthropology, 79–80
Antonaccio, Maria, 254
atomic bomb, 5, 15, 41
Attlee, Clement, 14
Atwood, Margaret, 110
Austen, Jane, 77, 249
  *Emma*, 77
  *Mansfield Park*, 77
  *Pride and Prejudice*, 249
austerity, 13, 53

Bainbridge, Beryl, 3, 162–3
  *The Bottle Factory Outing*, 3, 162–3

*Every Man for Himself*, 3
  *Master Georgie*, 3
  *A Quiet Life*, 3
Bakhtin, Mikhail, 3–4, 104–5
  carnival, 104–5
Ballard, J. G., 234–5
  *Crash*, 234–5
Banks, Lynne Reid, 85–6
  *The L-Shaped Room*, 85–6
Barker, Pat, 8, 40–41, 68, 162
  *Liza's England*, 40–41
  *Regeneration Trilogy*, 8
  *Union Street*, 68, 162
Barker, Paul, 214
Barnes, Julian, 120–21, 124, 217–18
  *England, England*, 120–21, 124
  *Metroland*, 217–18
Barstow, Stan, 55, 71–2, 190, 213
  *A Kind of Loving*, 55, 71–2, 213
Barthelme, Donald, 230
Bates, H. E., 192–3
  *The Darling Buds of May*, 192–3
Baucom, Ian, 124–5, 177, 181
BBC, 15
Beauvoir, Simone de, 86
  *The Second Sex*, 86
Beckett, Andy, 245
Beckett, Mary, 136–7
  *Give Them Stones*, 136–7
Beckett, Samuel, 139
Belsey, Catherine, 225
Bennett, Arnold, 190
Bergonzi, Bernard, 6–7, 20–21,
  45, 127, 248, 249
Betjeman, John, 123